MUSIC IN
SHAKESPEAREAN TRAGEDY

STUDIES IN THE HISTORY OF MUSIC

EDITED BY EGON WELLESZ
C.B.E., F.B.A., Hon. D. Mus. Oxon.
Fellow of Lincoln College

Uniform with this Volume

MUSIC IN MEDIEVAL BRITAIN
by Frank Ll. Harrison

THE FUGUE IN
BEETHOVEN'S PIANO MUSIC
by John V. Cockshoot

WILLIAM LAWES
by Murray Lefkowitz

MUSIC IN SHAKESPEAREAN TRAGEDY

by

F. W. STERNFELD

LONDON: Routledge and Kegan Paul

NEW YORK: Dover Publications

First published 1963
in Great Britain by
Routledge & Kegan Paul Limited
and in the U.S.A. by
Dover Publications, Inc.

Made and printed in Great Britain by
William Clowes and Sons, Limited

108999

FOR SOPHIA

CONTENTS

MUSIC EXAMPLES AND FACSIMILES

ILLUSTRATIONS

Between pages 138 *and* 139

ACKNOWLEDGEMENTS

The author wishes to thank the following institutions and private owners for permission to reproduce items in their possession: Col. R. G. W. Berkeley; Sir John Hanbury-Williams; Ledreborg Castle, Denmark; The Lord de l'Isle; The National Trust; The Trustees of the National Portrait Gallery; The Trustees of the British Museum; The Curators of the Bodleian Library.

PHOTOGRAPHIC ACKNOWLEDGEMENTS

Miss E. Auerbach (4); *The Connoisseur* (5); Munksgaard, Copenhagen (3); Bodleian Library (8b); British Museum (8a); National Portrait Gallery (1, 2, 6, 7).

ABBREVIATIONS

The plays of Shakespeare follow the abbreviations in C. T. Onions's *Shakespeare Glossary* and the *Oxford English Dictionary*. The First Folio of 1623 prints thirty-six plays, to which modern editors usually add two plays written, in part at least, by Shakespeare, namely *Pericles* and the *Two Noble Kinsmen*. Most of Onions's abbreviations are obvious references to the main noun, such as: *Ado, Caes, Kins, Per, Wiv*.

Other equally obvious abbreviations of Onions are:

All's W	*All's Well that Ends Well*
F_1, F_2	1st Folio of 1623 (*Mr. William Shakespeare's Comedies, Histories and Tragedies*), 2nd Folio of 1632, etc.
LLL	*Love's Labour's Lost*
3 H 6	*Henry VI, Part III*
Lr	*King Lear*
Mer V	*Merchant of Venice*
MND	*Midsummer Night's Dream*
Q_1, Q_2	1st, 2nd Quarto edition of a play
Tp	*Tempest*
Tw N	*Twelfth Night*

In quotations from the plays S.D. stands for Stage Direction.

(J)	Caulfield	*Collection of the Vocal Music in Shakespeare's Plays*, 2 vols., London, 1864
(EK)	Chambers	*Elizabethan Stage*, 4 vols., Oxford, 1923
	Chambers WS	*William Shakespeare*, 2 vols., Oxford, 1930
(W)	Chappell	*Popular Music of the Olden Time*, 2 vols., London, 1855–59
(CL)	Day and (EB)	Murrie *English Song Books 1651–1702*, London, 1940
	Fitzwilliam	*Fitzwilliam Virginal Book*, edd. J. A. Fuller-Maitland and W. Barclay Squire, 2 vols., London and Leipzig, 1894–99

(J)	Fletcher	*Works of Beaumont and Fletcher*, edd. A. Glover and A. R. Waller, 10 vols., Cambridge, 1905–12
(WW)	Greg	*Bibliography of Printed English Drama*, London, 1939 ff. Vol. I: 1939, Vol II: 1951, Vol. III: 1957, Vol. IV: 1959
	Greg FF	*Shakespeare First Folio*, Oxford, 1955
(A)	Harbage	*Annals of English Drama*, Philadelphia, 1940
(B)	Jonson	*Works of Benjamin Jonson*, edd. C. H. Herford and P. Simpson, 11 vols., Oxford, 1925–52
(GL)	Kittredge	*Complete Works of Shakespeare*, ed. G. L. Kittredge, Boston, 1936
	Kittredge SP	*Sixteen Plays of Shakespeare, with full explanatory notes*, Boston, 1946
(J)	Marston	*Works of John Marston*, ed. H. Harvey-Wood, 3 vols., Edinburgh, 1934–39
	NA	*New Arden Edition of Shakespeare's Works*, edd. U. Ellis Fermor and others, London, 1946 ff.
	NS	*New [Cambridge] Shakespeare Edition*, edd. J. D. Wilson and others, Cambridge, 1921 ff.
	NV	*New Variorum Edition of Shakespeare's Works*, edd. H. H. Furness and others, Philadelphia, 1871 ff.
(T)	Nashe	*Works of Thomas Nashe*, edd. R. B. McKerrow and F. P. Wilson, 5 vols., Oxford, 1958
(EW)	Naylor	*Shakespeare and Music*, 2nd ed., London, 1931
	Naylor PM	*Poets and Music*, London, 1928
	Naylor SM	*Shakespeare Music*, 2nd ed., London, 1928
(R)	Noble	*Shakespeare's Use of Song*, London, 1923
(CT)	Onions	*Shakespeare Glossary*, 2nd ed., Oxford, 1919, rev. 1953
	Onions SE	*Shakespeare's England*, edd. C. T. Onions, S. Lee, W. Raleigh and others, 2 vols., Oxford, 1916
(J)	Playford	*English Dancing Master, 1651*, facsimile reprint, ed. M. Dean-Smith, London, 1957
	Plutarch	*Plutarch's Lives of the Noble Grecians and Romans, Englished by Sir Thomas North, anno 1579*, intr. G. Wyndham (Tudor Translations, 1st Series, ed. W. Henley), 6 vols., London, 1895–96

(AW) Pollard STC (and G. R. Redgrave) *Short Title Catalogue . . . 1475–1640*, London, 1926

(J) Webster *Complete Works of John Webster*, ed. F. L. Lucas, 4 vols., London, 1928

(D) Wing STC *Short Title Catalogue . . . 1641–1700*, 3 vols., New York, 1945–51

(HE) Wooldridge *Old English Popular Music*, 2 vols., London, 1893 [a revision of Chappell], reprinted New York, 1961.

PREFACE

To offer yet another book on Shakespeare seems rash. Yet, the particular subject of music is none too well covered in an otherwise vast literature, and few would deny that the student eager to grasp Shakespeare's art as a whole cannot afford to ignore the playwright's use of music. To probe this subject calls for a combination of historical, literary and musical skills, and for one person to acquire all of these is difficult indeed. I can only hope that the usefulness of this monograph will outweigh its imperfections.

Most of us come to a prolonged study of Shakespeare by way of our experiences as schoolboys. In these early, impressionable years, we react to the plays as readers, listeners and even as amateur actors and producers. From the beginning I was fascinated by certain lyrics such as the grave-digger's song in *Hamlet* and Pandarus' air in *Troilus*, and realized how much of the pathetic effect of Ophelia hinges on her mad-songs. But, instinctively, one felt that the music usually heard in the commercial theatre was quite wrong and clashed with the 'tone' of the verse. To find the right tone and atmosphere, to unlock the treasury of Elizabethan music and provide Shakespearean producers and audiences with the fitting vocal and instrumental strains seemed an urgent duty. The books of Chappell, Naylor, Warlock and others were read with fascination and profit but, grateful as I have remained to these distinguished predecessors, I encountered more riddles than answers.

After the war a colleague, Professor H. B. Williams (Dartmouth College, U.S.A.), invited me to provide the music for several of his Shakespearean productions. Influenced by Poel, Craig and Granville-Barker, Williams stressed the continuity of the plays, respected the full text and used the acting area in a manner corresponding to the Elizabethan platform stage. In permitting me to use Elizabethan music while New York's Broadway and London's West End continued in the idiom of nineteenth-century romanticism, he offered me an audience that was much wider than the one restricted to students in the history of music. (One suspects that, in a more important way, Arnold Dolmetsch reached a larger circle of listeners before the First World War when he provided music for William Poel's presentations of Shakespeare.)

In the process of working with a producer I was bound to learn a good deal about timing in the live theatre, a necessary awareness to complement one's more bookish researches. But, most of all, in this practical experience I found my theories vindicated: what was the right music historically proved also to be the right music for the general public. Audiences, not in the least tainted by antiquarian tendencies, loved the old music, and, without false modesty, the musician could claim to have contributed towards a theatrical success. In a few instances it was possible to unearth the old songs. In other cases it was necessary to adapt some other music of the period. But the obvious aim was to find more of the original music and have fewer adaptations.

For one winter I resided at the Institute for Advanced Study in Princeton, relieved from teaching duties and privileged to discuss my work with Professor E. Panofsky, whose knowledge of Renaissance Art, including drama and poetics, is rivalled by few. At the same time, I began to compare notes with fellow-workers in the field, notably Mr. Sydney Beck of the New York Public Library, whose performing version of 'O mistress mine, where are you roaming?' appeared in *Renaissance News* in 1953. To our delight, Alfred Deller was quick to use this version, and it became popular in a gramophone recording. But, clearly, the perusal of the resources of American libraries, and the patient study of microfilms from Britain, could be no substitute for consulting printed and manuscript sources in the original. Between 1954 and 1956 work was pursued in the British Museum, and since 1956 research has been carried on at the Bodleian Library. As a result, I have not only had access to the treasures of that great institution, but also profited from the kindness and learning of my fellow-teachers and Bodleian's staff.

The original plan was to deal with all of Shakespeare's plays. But it quickly became evident that the cruxes and problems were considerable. On the 'Willow Song' alone it took years of work before the pieces began to fall into place. It seemed desirable, therefore, to present one's views and findings, for what they were worth, without further delay, and the result is this volume on the tragedies—with a further instalment on the comedies in the offing. Nevertheless, an endeavour has been made to have the present book as comprehensive as possible. The Index of Lyrics is a dictionary catalogue of the songs in all of Shakespeare's plays, listing even mere allusions to ballad titles. The retrospect of scholarship and the bibliography similarly deal with the entire Shakespearean *œuvre*, and, indeed, with the wider question of poetry-and-music in the Elizabethan and Jacobean ages. By way of the bibliographical Addenda, which have also been indexed, the aim has been to cover the sources known as recently as 1962.

A word should be said about the transcription of the old texts. All literary quotations of Shakespeare and his contemporaries are offered in modern spelling. The same is true of the titles of books, except in a few instances where the old form is sufficiently standard to make modernization awkward (*Schoole of Musicke, Cittharn Schoole*, etc.). Whenever there was doubt about modernization or emendation, the original spelling of Folio and/or Quarto is given in a footnote. Similarly, the musical transcriptions are offered in modern clefs with modern bar-lines. The purpose of this book is not only to serve students of the history of music, but also lovers and producers of Shakespeare. All songs have therefore been transposed for medium voice range, and the accompaniment can readily be performed by an amateur at the keyboard. The notes on transcription record both the original key and any emendations made. Facsimiles of eight of the original sources, supplemented by full bibliographical descriptions of all sources will offer the music historian all the relevant information. It is planned to publish the songs by themselves, for various voice ranges, and in lute tablature.

To present one's results between two covers naturally entails bringing research to a temporary halt. The subject of the Homerus Latinus, referred to in a brief footnote on page 90, could easily be expanded into a full-length article, and the subject of Senecan tragedy on which I have touched at various places deserves a monograph of its own. Since the completion of this volume I have written a paper on 'Music in Neo-Senecan Drama of the Elizabethan Period', dealing particularly with Chapman, and I now believe that Chapman's stage direction, referred to on page 19, belongs not to Tamyra and her maid but to a subsequent scene. (This paper is to appear in the Proceedings of a Seneca Congress, held in Paris in 1962, to be published by the Centre National de la Recherche Scientifique, under the editorship of J. Jacquot.)

Another piece of unfinished research is indicated by plates 8(a) and (b), that fascinating transformation of Saint Cecilia playing the organ into an English Lady playing the virginals. Dr. D. Rogers of the Bodleian and I are preparing an article on the subject, to appear in *The Library*; in the meantime, a chronological bibliography appears following this preface.

Finally, it remains my pleasant duty to acknowledge the many acts of kindness and assistance offered to me in the course of this study. In matters of palaeography I have received help on puzzling questions from Miss Margaret C. Crum, Mr. Ian Harwood and Mrs. Diana Poulton. On bibliographical problems I have had the aid of Dr. H. K. Andrews, Mr. Sydney Beck, Professor Thurston Dart and Mr. J. G. McManaway. On individual songs I was able to avail myself of suggestions and criticisms by Miss Helen L. Gardner and Dr. Frank Ll. Harrison. Several persons were kind enough to read parts of this book in typescript and offer critical comments on substance and detail, notably Mr. David J. Greer, Mrs. Jean Robertson-Bromley, Mr. Ernest Schanzer, Mr. Virgil Thomson and Dr. D. P. Walker. Finally, it was my good fortune to have Professor F. P. Wilson take time from his many duties to peruse the entire typescript and let me have the benefit of his criticisms. Needless to say, such imperfections as remain are my own.

In regard to the pictorial illustrations, Dr. Roy Strong of the National Portrait Gallery provided a list of Elizabethan portraits showing musical matters and made many helpful suggestions regarding permissions and photographic reproductions. Dr. E. J. Wellesz, editor of this series, gave me much needed advice from his rich fund of experience; and Mr. Colin Franklin, of the publishing house, listened sympathetically to my ideas, even when some of them, such as the placement of footnotes and facsimiles, were distinctly out of fashion.

Acknowledgements for the Illustrations are made following the List of Illustrations. For the Music Examples and Facsimilies, I am indebted to the governing bodies or librarians of the following institutions:

Aberystwyth, National Library of Wales; Arundel, Library of the Duke of Norfolk; Cambridge, University Library; Dublin, Trinity College Library; London, British Museum; New York, Public Library; Paris, Bibliothèque du Conservatoire; Washington, Folger Library.

The following editors have permitted me to reprint material previously published in the form of articles: A. S. Downer (*English Institute Essays*); J. Jacquot (*Fêtes de la Renaissance*); A. Nicoll (*Shakespeare Survey*); G. Thibault (*Annales Musicologiques*).

During the course of this work I have received research grants from the Institute for Advanced Study in Princeton and the American Philosophical Society. To all these persons and institutions I offer my sincere and humble gratitude. My greatest obligation is expressed in the dedication of this book.

F.W.S.

Faculty of Music
University of Oxford

PRELIMINARY BIBLIOGRAPHY
ON THE TITLE PAGE OF
PARTHENIA

1612/13   *Parthenia* [Pollard-Redgrave, *Short Title Catalogue*, nos. 4252, 11827], copy in Huntington Library.

c. 1613   *Parthenia* [not distinguished by *Short Title Catalogue*]. A second state which differs from the Huntington copy in two respects: First, the leaf bearing the dedication to Prince Frederick and Princess Elizabeth is omitted; secondly, there are several minor pages on the engraved title page, notably,

     (a) 'Dedicated to all the Maisters and Louers of Musick' has been added;

     (b) 'Dor: Euans' has been expanded to 'Dorethie Euans';

     (c) 'Are to be sould by G. Lowe print^r in Loathberry' has been changed to 'Printed at London by G: Lowe and are to be soulde at his howse in Loathberry'.

     Several copies of this second state survive, among them two in the British Museum and one in the Bodleian [Arch. A. c. 11]. The Bodleian copy was acquired by the Library prior to 1620, probably under the copyright agreement which had been concluded in 1610.

1803–21   A. Bartsch, *Le Peintre Graveur*, 21 vols., Vienne, III.197.

1952–55   A. M. Hind, *Engraving in England*, 2 vols., Cambridge, II.335–338.

1959   O. E. Deutsch, 'Cecilia and Parthenia', *Musical Times*, C.591–592.

1961   T. Dart, intr., *Parthenia In-Violata*, facsimile edn., New York, pp. 32 ff.

I

TRADITION OF VOCAL
AND INSTRUMENTAL MUSIC
IN TRAGEDY

Tragedy demanded less music than any other genre on the Elizabethan stage. The tradition of the theatre favoured an abundance of song in comedy but little or no lyric relief in tragedy. This custom pertained primarily to the companies of adult players such as the Lord Chamberlain's Men and the Lord Admiral's Men and, to a lesser extent, to the companies of juvenile players such as the Children of Paul's and the Children of the Chapel. The differences between a tragic drama performed by adults and one performed by boys will occupy us later. Shakespeare's plays were written exclusively for performance by the Chamberlain's Men (after 1603 the King's Men).

In endeavouring to explain the Elizabethan opposition to song in tragedy one might advance several reasons, among them the classical precedent of Senecan tragedy. But more vital to the tradition of the theatre was the very nature of the tragic experience. We are inclined to posit with Aristotle that one of the essential ingredients of the tragic genre is magnitude, provided it can still be grasped as a whole. To interrupt the drama by *divertissements* would destroy, or at least endanger, that magnitude. Only too often a song in spoken drama was nothing more than an ill-concealed diversion, rather than an element integrated into the dramatic structure. Perhaps there was some method behind the restraint of Shakespeare's contemporaries and his own procedure in the earlier plays.

When Englishmen wrote their first formal five-act tragedies and comedies in the sixteenth century, ancient dramas were among the most prominent models. It was in the light of the classical precedent that writers like Sir Philip Sidney evaluated the works of their contemporaries. Mention of the 'practice of the ancients' occurs so frequently in discussions of drama in the sixteenth and seventeenth centuries that the modern reader (whose knowledge of ancient tragedy is largely based on Sophocles and Euripides) finds himself confronted with some seeming contradictions. For one thing, the Elizabethans looked to the Romans rather than the Greeks for their classical models. Seneca was favoured for tragedy, Plautus and Terence for comedy. Moreover, the Greek notion of the use of song in tragedy was quite contrary to that of the Roman. Song was employed by the Greek tragic playwrights and approved by Aristotle, though he frowned on its use when it was not connected with the plot. Seneca's tragedies, on the other hand, are largely rhetorical; they abound in bloodshed, ghosts and moralizing, but certainly not in lyrics. The collection, *Seneca his ten tragedies translated into English*, was published in London in 1581, but individual translations had appeared earlier and, in any event, Seneca had provided material for study and performance in the schools.

Norton's and Sackville's *Gorboduc*, acted before Queen Elizabeth in 1562, was the first formal five-act tragedy in blank verse. It is heavily indebted to the Roman model, for there are no songs and the moralizing choruses at the end of the acts are verbal, not musical. Yet, there is a deviation in this early English tragedy from its classical model. A dumb-show precedes each one of the five acts, to the accompaniment of instrumental music. The stage directions designate specific instruments to provide music suitable to the action. (Marlowe, Shakespeare and Webster were not slow to profit from this example.) *Gorboduc* may be said to combine two traditions: the theory of the schoolmen that tragedy must be Senecan; and the practical custom of the theatre that drama must be enlivened by spectacle. The vitality of the Elizabethan playwright asserts itself here with the injection into the classical model of such elements as

2

dramatic exigence and the expectations of the audience might dictate. E. K. Chambers traces these spectacles, whether dumb-show or masque, to the Italian *intermedii* and observes that such inter-acts must have offered a welcome contrast to the body of Senecan tragedy with its over-riding rhetoric. In the few treatises dealing with the propriety of having music at the con-clusion of an act we find the view that these entertainments were inserted 'to the intent the people might be refreshed and kept occupied' and to offer 'relief . . . if the discourses have been long'.[1]

The courtly *intermedii*, popular jigs and other such additions were natural opportunities for music-making in a medium that was almost exclusively verbal. But in order that the spectacle should not overwhelm the drama, the early inter-act was gradually absorbed into the main fabric. The question remains, how closely or loosely these additions were tied to the main theme, and in this respect sensibilities vary a good deal. That one of Shakespeare's finely chiselled tragedies should be followed by a pantomime, a 'jig', with its admixture of clowning, dancing and improvisation, would seem to a fastidious critic quite out of order and more appropriate to comedy. Yet, Thomas Platter, a Swiss visitor to London, was not at all discomfited when, on 21 September 1599, at the Globe Playhouse, he attended 'the tragedy of the first emperor Julius . . . at the end they danced according to their custom with extreme elegance. Two in men's clothes and two in women's gave this performance, in wonderful combination with each other'. He continues: 'On another occa-sion, I also saw after dinner a comedy. . . . At the end they danced very elegantly both in English and in Irish fashion.' This suggests that the Elizabethan audience, like its Italian counterpart, expected music to be included in their dramatic diet. To satisfy this demand, some bit of comedy was inserted into the early tragedies or added at the end, and it seems a fair assumption that the musical accompaniment of these additions was an important part of the relief.

The custom which limited the use of song in tragedy did not

---

[1] Puttenham, *Art of English Poesy*, 1589 (G. G. Smith, ed., *Elizabethan Critical Essays*, II.38); Dryden, *Essay on Dramatic Poesy*, 1668 (*Works*, edd. W. Scott and G. Saintsbury, XV.332). Puttenham's discussion of ancient practice actually reveals the Elizabethan attitude.

apply to instrumental music. Wordless music has, through the ages, lent its assistance to the depiction of pathos, horror and mystery. In Elizabethan drama its use can be traced from the 1560s to the end of Shakespeare's career: from the dumb-shows with music in Thomas Norton's and Thomas Sackville's *Gorboduc* (acted 1562, printed 1565) and George Gascoigne's *Jocasta* (acted 1566, printed 1573) to the dead march in *Coriolanus* (1608). Dumb-shows, dead marches and masques account for the greater part of these instrumental passages apart from music which mysteriously accompanies scenes of divine prophecy (such as the oboes heard by the soldiers in *Antony and Cleopatra* before their leader's downfall).

In casting about for an explanation of the greater use of instrumental music as compared with vocal music in tragedy one can only surmise that its inclusion in the early tragedies at significant steps of the plot proved so successful that its presence was soon taken for granted. Because there is no text, instrumental music has a quick suggestiveness and poignancy that speaks eloquently to the emotions and the imagination. Modern manifestations of this phenomenon are found in the Grand Guignol and the horror films and 'tear-jerkers' of today's cinema. In the absence of modern lighting and staging, with its artful suggestiveness, Elizabethan productions could rely on instrumental music to be an auxiliary device of some importance. Particularly in passages where the declamation of blank verse came to a halt, for one reason or another, incidental instrumental passages were more likely than song to assist the action and less likely to be irrelevant. For the decisive issue, once again, lay in the size and wholeness of the tragedy. Aristotle speaks of the 'interlude' when he praises the lyrics of Sophocles over those of Agathon and Euripides. And, indeed, the concept of 'interlude' or *divertissement* is a legitimate touchstone for the propriety of instrumental music. If it be the business of tragedy, as Aristotle has it, to arouse pity and fear, or—as some Renaissance authors have varied the phrase—wonder and pity, what better means of assisting these emotions than in the sounding of miraculous and pathetic strains? Thus administered, these passages become integral parts of the drama. The 'sound' to which the ghost of Helen is conjured up in Marlowe's *Doctor Faustus* (1588–92), and the dead march in Kyd's *Spanish Tragedy* (1585–

1590), lead to the instrumental passages in Shakespeare's later plays: the strains to which the old Lear is cured; the protagonist buried in *Coriolanus*; and the statue brought to life in the *Winter's Tale*.

The total absence of any musical relief, whether instrumental or vocal, was a marked characteristic of Seneca's closet dramas, that is to say, of plays to be read, not performed. Their non-musical austerity was counterbalanced, however, by the lusty comedies of Plautus, which abound in song, and the tragedies of the Elizabethan theatre were to profit from the leavening effect of music in comedy. Terence, whom the schoolmasters favoured, was too refined for the robust atmosphere of the Elizabethan playhouses. True, the Terentian five-act dramas were of import-ance for their formal structure, but it was Plautine comedy that furnished a Shakespeare and a Molière with prototypes and dramatic technique.

The first regular English comedy to be modelled after the ancients was Nicholas Udall's *Roister Doister* (*ca.* 1553). The ribaldry of Plautus, his stock types such as the braggard soldier, and his abundant lyrics (*cantica*) were among the main elements of Udall's comedy. Indeed, the first printed copy of *Roister Doister* (undated, *ca.* 1567) resembles the sixteenth-century printings of Plautus, for a rapid glance shows that Udall's songs are set off typographically in the same manner as the *cantica* of Plautus, and occur with comparable frequency. In some other instances the printed text of *Roister Doister* merely gives a stage remark, as 'cantet' or 'Here they sing' without printing the lyric. (At the end of the book four lyrics are given to fill in the gaps.)

Between such early prototypes as *Roister Doister* and the comedies of Shakespeare there intervenes a variety of models, among them the court dramas of John Lyly whose plots were often punctuated by song at points of dramatic propriety and plausibility. Clearly, an Elizabethan tradition of several decades lies behind the profusion of songs in *As You Like It* and *Twelfth Night*. But in the hands of lesser playwrights the songs were apt to be irrelevant diversions, alien to the plot, and their broad humour was likely, at times, to descend to mere smut. (The fourth stanza of Feste's 'For the rain it raineth every day' has been criticized as dramatically pointless, in poor taste, and, for

5

those reasons, not by Shakespeare.) Elizabethan writers on the drama put tragedy on the higher plane: 'The stately tragedy scorneth the trifling comedy'; and the question of stylistic propriety was always in the foreground, hence, mixing Seneca and Plautus was considered improper. Thomas More insisted that 'such a tragical comedy or galli-maufry must be avoided'.[1] About seventy years later Philip Sidney, in condemning Shakespeare's predecessors, felt moved to write:

I know the ancients have one or two examples of tragi-comedies as Plautus hath Amphitrio. But if we mark them well, we shall find that they never, or *very daintily*, match horn-pipes and funerals. [italics added]

Sidney's qualification absolves him from the pedantry of those moralists who attacked comedy and song simultaneously. He was convinced, nevertheless, that 'plays be neither right tragedies nor right comedies; mingling kings and clowns'. Who would 'make a clown companion with a king' and 'in their grave counsels . . . allow the advice of fools' also came in for the ready censure of George Whetstone, in the dedication of his play *Promos and Cassandra* (1578). Certainly, the difficulties of stylistic integration were great when song was introduced in tragedy. The mature Shakespeare could and did weld together an assortment of elements which lesser authors were incapable of doing. But as long as the ideal tragedy, in the minds of educated and serious Elizabethans, concerned itself with affairs of state and presented these affairs through the actions of royalty or nobility, it was logical that the inclusion of the clown would be considered incongruous.

Nor were the neo-classic authors of the seventeenth century less severely opposed to such a mixture of styles. In a poem addressed to John Fletcher and printed in 1647 the playwright William Cartwright reasons:

> Shakespeare to thee was dull whose best jest lies
> I' the ladies' questions, and the fool's replies;
> Old-fashioned wit, which walk'd from town to town,
> In turn'd hose, which our fathers call'd the clown,
> Whose wit our nice times would obsceneness call . . .

[1] *Utopia: written in Latin by Sir Thomas More . . . and translated into English by Raphe Robinson . . . London . . . 1551*, ed. J. H. Lupton, Oxford, 1895, p. 99.

After the Restoration Dryden defended this interfusion of the tragic and comic in his *Essay on Dramatic Poesy* of 1668:

A scene of mirth, mixed with tragedy, has the same effect upon us which our music has betwixt the acts; and that we find a relief to us from the best plots and language of the stage, if the discourses have been long. I must therefore have stronger arguments, ere I am convinced that compassion and mirth in the same subject destroy each other; and in the meantime, cannot but conclude, to the honour of our nation, that we have invented, increased, and perfected a more pleasant way of writing for the stage, than was ever known to the ancients or moderns of any nation, which is tragi-comedy.

But this liberal view of the stage was disallowed by Thomas Rymer who published two books, in 1678 and 1693, in which he contrasted the 'Practice of the Ancients'[1] with the tragi-comedies of Shakespeare and of Beaumont and Fletcher, the better to extol the virtues of the neo-classic Jonson, 'honest Ben'. In Rymer's view Shakespeare's stylistic incongruities show a lack of distinction between high and low art. In a phrase reminiscent of Bottom's preference for the 'tongs and bones' Rymer objects to comic scenes in tragedy and their musical concomitants. He feels that comic characters in the tragedies of Shakespeare and of Beaumont and Fletcher are

thrust into the principal places, when we should give our full attention to what is tragedy. When we would listen to a lute, our ears are rapt with the tintamarre [i.e. hubbub] and twangs of the tongs ...

In the main, the opposition to the clown was, of course, based on his function as the purveyor of humour. But he was also the chief musician of the adult companies, the one actor who could be relied upon to sing as well as speak. The Senecan tradition was slow to give way, however, and for a century to come after *Gorboduc* the clown and his music were still considered vulgar and out of place, which makes the more remarkable the song of the grave-digger in *Hamlet*.

The star performers of the adult companies did not sing. 'Dick' Burbage and 'Ned' Alleyn illuminated the pathos of

---

[1] *Tragedies of the Last Age, Considered and Examined by the Practice of the Ancients*, London, 1678, pp. 140 ff.; *Short View of Tragedy . . . with Some Reflections on Shakespeare*, 1693, p. 9.

Hamlet or Faustus through the poet's verse. On the distaff side, Ophelia and Desdemona are notable exceptions even in the Shakespeare canon, for no other of Shakespeare's great heroines sings: Juliet, Calpurnia, Cordelia, Lady Macbeth, Cleopatra. In the rare instances where song does occur in a tragedy, the part is most often given to a boy attendant or to a clown or court-fool. In *Julius Caesar* the boy Lucius sings to Brutus, and an anonymous boy-servant sings for the three world rulers in *Antony and Cleopatra*. King Lear's fool is 'full of songs' and the grave-digger-clown in *Hamlet* performs his task to the rhythm of 'In youth when I did love'; whilst Peter, the serving-man-clown in *Romeo and Juliet* sings the first stanza of 'When griping grief the heart doth wound'. Pandarus in *Troilus and Cressida* (*ca.* 1602), like his counterpart Balurdo in John Marston's *Antonio and Mellida* (1599), has a unique role in that he is nominally a member of the nobility. But these characters debase their ranks when they solicit laughter and applause rather than admiration and pity.

Shakespeare dared to mingle the banter of clowns with the cares and anxieties of kings and in so doing exposed himself to the intense disapproval of fastidious critics, in particular his contemporary Ben Jonson. Jonson is a prominent link in a tradition that extends from the humanists of the sixteenth century to the time of the Restoration, from Thomas More and Philip Sidney to John Dryden and Thomas Rymer. Indeed, Voltaire and Dr. Johnson in the eighteenth century still conceived of tragedy in terms of the Latin classical heritage, that is to say, they disavowed the comical and lyrical relief which the clown's songs could provide.

Shakespeare employed two different techniques by means of which he wove songs into his tragedies: tragic song was employed to supplement tragic speech; and comic song was made to participate in the tragic whole. The Willow Song in *Othello* (discussed in Chapter II) is a supreme example of the tragic lyric, an exceptional device of Shakespeare's own creation. Comic song as a strand in the tragic fabric is less rare in Elizabethan drama. In its use Shakespeare's distinction lies both in the numerical incidence of his songs and in the degree of their integration into the tragedy as a whole. Both the grave-digger's song in *Hamlet* and Pandarus's song in *Troilus and Cressida* are treated in a manner which deprives them of their wholly comic character and makes them part of the general artistic design. This compounding of the tragic and comic genres is one aspect which critics of Shakespeare's tragedies have found most difficult to accept. The role of the serving-man Peter with his song in *Romeo and Juliet* was offensive even to Goethe, just as the porter-scene in *Macbeth* exceeded Coleridge's tolerance.

Adult Companies

In a garrulous, but useful and much-quoted book, the *Palladis Tamia: Wits Treasury*, 1598, Francis Meres deals, among many topics, with drama:

As Plautus and Seneca are accounted the best for comedy and tragedy among the Latins: so Shakespeare among the English is the most excellent in both kinds . . .

He goes on to enumerate those whom he considers the most eminent tragic playwrights, including in his list Sackville, Marlowe, Peele, Kyd, Shakespeare, Chapman and Jonson, whose works come under our consideration. (Chapman will be discussed in the section devoted to the juvenile companies.) Thomas Kyd's *Spanish Tragedy* was one of the most popular plays of the age. First performed *ca.* 1585–90, it had ten printings between 1592 and 1633, and it is even possible that there were additional printings of which no extant copies are known. This popularity cannot be accounted for by its Senecan flavour and structure, its ghost and revenge plot. True, it shares with the Elizabethan translations of Seneca the lack of songs. But it adds to Senecan rhetoric a stageworthiness that is alien to the Latin model. Among these additions we may single out two devices, both of which re-appear in *Hamlet*: the play within the play, and the burial at the end. The 'show' which Hieronymo presents to re-enact the murder of Horatio undoubtedly had its musical trappings, though unfortunately no stage direction calling for music survives in the printed copies. (Shakespeare's corresponding stage direction in the third act of *Hamlet* calls for trumpets in the good Quarto of 1604 and for oboes in the Folio of 1623. Kyd, too, must have intended some musical 'noise' to set off the inserted playlet from the drama proper.) The burial

9

scene at the end of the *Spanish Tragedy* again introduces instrumental music. The stage direction reads:

The trumpets sound a dead march; the King of Spain mourning after his brother's body, and the King of Portugal bearing the body of his son.

It is worth noting that at the conclusion of *Hamlet*, after Fortinbras has called for 'the soldiers' music', there is a corresponding stage direction, upon which the drama ends. In Kyd, however, there follow nearly fifty lines of verse spoken by the figures of 'Ghost' and 'Revenge', the effect of which tends to be an anticlimax. Still, the effectiveness of the *Spanish Tragedy* as a model for *Hamlet* in musical as well as other matters cannot be denied.

Music as a means to enhance and underline a tragic plot—this lesson Shakespeare learned from Marlowe. Marlowe's blank verse rises above the pioneering attempts of Sackville and the impressive ranting of Kyd to such poetic beauty that it has justly been called musical. Songs as such do not cut across these sonorous lines, but the dumb-shows which punctuate Marlowe's dramas depend on instrumental music to gain their full effect. When

Music sounds and Helen passeth over the stage

the instrumental strains assist in creating the dream of the beautiful image that appears before Faustus. The authorship of this scene, and of other blank verse passages dealing with music, has never been in doubt. But there remains the enigma of the comic prose scenes which contain several musical cues. *Doctor Faustus* was first performed 1588–92, but the earliest extant printed edition dates from 1604, eleven years after Marlowe's death. It is generally agreed that the comic interludes were not written by Marlowe. Even so, the author, whoever he may have been, was obviously aware of the wishes of the audiences and gave them 'what you will' within the stately frame-work of tragedy. These interspersed scenes of devils chasing a clown or friars chanting a dirge provide lyric relief in allowing an opportunity for music in addition to the clowning. Furthermore, they support the charges of irrelevancy and inappropriate clowning so often aired in discussions of mixing Plautus and Seneca. (An evaluation of the musical effects in Marlowe's *Tamburlaine* is to be found in Chapter VIII.)

Whereas the majority of Elizabethan tragedies deal with royalty and nobility, whether of ancient or of later European history, there are a few exceptions to this custom. Among them we may note the anonymous *Arden of Feversham* (printed 1592), a domestic tragedy with no music. There is also George Peele's *David and Bethsabe* (1594 or earlier), a biblical tragedy which, in addition to its singular subject, contains a song. The lyric of the lovely Bethsabe is remarkable in the annals of Elizabethan drama for several reasons: for the fact that singing does occur in this early play and that it is performed by a main character rather than an attendant.[1] Finally, the surrounding dialogue makes specific reference to the lyric. At the play's opening Bethsabe sings, unaware that she is being observed by King David,

> Hot sun, cool fire, temper'd with sweet air,
> Black shade, fair nurse, shadow my white hair . . .
>   Let not my beauty's fire
>   Inflame unstaid desire . . .

Her lyric prompts the king to comment

> What tunes, what words, what looks, what wonders pierce
> My soul, incensed with a sudden fire?

Ashley Thorndyke has said of Peele's play that

It does not give us reality or wisdom or truth; it carries us into a world of verbal felicity, of music and fancy—a world that the Elizabethans loved, where the author of *Romeo and Juliet* was king.

This is an apt gloss, in general as well as in particular regard to the scene. Peele's poetry is pleasing, and he has a knack of echoing words, such as sun, fire, air and black shade, that explain his fame as a verbal craftsman, a *primus verborum artifex*. Yet, dramatically, the lyric is inapposite and untrue. In the context it would make sense for the king, not Bethsabe, to sing of the flame of unstaid desire which her beauty has kindled; or the scene might have received comment from the traditional chorus of tragedy. But Peele's heroine reveals nothing of herself

---

[1] Peele's allocation of song to a principal character may be connected with his experience as the writer of the Lord Mayor's pageants, 1585–95, I owe this suggestion to Jean Robertson-Bromley, co-editor of *Dramatic Records . . . of the Livery Companies of London* (Malone Society Collections III), London, 1954. Cf. pp. xxxi, xxxiv & 54.

except, perhaps, her vanity. By contrast, Shakespeare's heroines articulate their innermost thoughts through their lyrics, and what they sing about is not a projection of the feelings of other characters.

Ben Jonson's tragedy of *Sejanus* was acted at the Globe Playhouse in 1603 with Shakespeare in the cast. Comparisons between the two playwrights continue to this day. They were provoked by the learned and proud Ben himself, who charged Shakespeare with 'small Latin and less Greek'. His barbed thrusts at those who 'beget tales, tempests and such drolleries...' did not spare Shakespeare's apt use of the clown. In his comedies Jonson used song with telling effect, as one would expect from a poet and playwright of his stature, though even here he is more economical and less fantastic than Shakespeare. But in the tragedies Jonson rigorously and carefully avoided song, and preferred to make his effects solely by verbal means. This is true both of *Sejanus* and of the later *Catiline* (1611). Jonson's concern with the practice of the ancients is exemplified in the address 'To the Readers' of *Sejanus*. He apologizes for the want of a proper chorus, for the lack of the old splendour, and refers to his commentary of Horace's *Ars poetica*. But he hopes that

in truth of argument, dignity of persons, gravity and height of elocution, fulness and frequency of sentence, I have discharged the other offices of a tragic writer.

Jonson's taut construction is clearly much closer to Seneca than to *Hamlet*; and it is easy to see why—three-quarters of a century later—the neo-classical Rymer would prefer the art of 'honest Ben' to that of Shakespeare or Beaumont and Fletcher. Yet, success on the stage rested with the latter, and music played an increasing part in the tragedies written after *Hamlet* and *Sejanus*. Of such works, written for the adult companies, we may consider the following tragedies by Shakespeare's contemporaries as both successful and representative:

? Tourneur	*Revenger's Tragedy*	King's Men, 1607
Beaumont & Fletcher	*Maid's Tragedy*	King's Men, 1610
John Webster	*White Devil*	Queen's Men, 1612
John Webster	*Duchess of Malfi*	King's Men, 1613

The Revenger's Tragedy depends for its music on instrumental interludes only—there are no songs. The stage directions of the final scene call for a 'dumb-show' which is followed shortly by a masque. Both the concept of the dumb-show and even the use of the term decrease in importance during the Jacobean period, though as late as 1613 the stage direction 'dumb-show' appears in the *Duchess of Malfi* (III.iv).

On the other hand, the masque gained steadily as a device of dramatic construction and was frequently inserted into spoken plays. It was, after all, one of the chief forms of entertainment at the court of King James, graced by the poetic talents of Campion and Jonson and the designs of Inigo Jones. In the *Revenger's Tragedy* the masque which succeeds the dumb-show is integrated with the plot in that it provides the revengers with the opportunity to execute their murders. Here we have a new development in dramatic technique: the revenge, which is the essence of Senecan tragedy in English drama, now takes place to the accompaniment of music and dance—a Jacobean development which is not without its Italianate tinge. In the more virile climate of 1600–01 dumb-shows and the play within the play had served to provide Hamlet with the proof of his suspicions; the deaths of the protagonists, however, take place later on in the play in a less operatic setting. The absence of song in the *Revenger's Tragedy* conformed to the prevalent Elizabethan tradition, whilst the instrumental music and the dance of the masquers, which had become accepted practice, offered relief from verbal monotony.

By 1610 the successes of *Hamlet* and *Othello* were established, and echoes of Shakespeare's methods may be observed in the work of Webster, and Beaumont and Fletcher. The latter's *Maid's Tragedy* has no character comparable to Ophelia or Desdemona, but there are five songs: three form part of a masque entertainment in Act I and the remaining two are sung in Act II while Evadne is preparing for her wedding night. Aspatia's song, which treats of willow branches and imminent death, has an obvious affinity with Desdemona's lyric. Although Aspatia and her song do not command the same weight or eloquence, the role has more significance than was usually allotted to boy singers. But the poignant effect of the song is dulled, if not indeed spoiled, by the frivolous lyric of the attendant which follows hard upon it at Evadne's request. Moreover, if Aspatia's song was to be an anticipation of the tragic events to come, the intervention of three acts before the realization of the tragedy seems too great a lapse of time.

The *White Devil* contains several Shakespearean echoes beside 'the sad willow' (Act IV). Cornelia's mad scene in Act V and her references to the symbolic nature of rosemary and rue have an antecedent in Ophelia's lines, the more so as it is the first and only time that Webster introduces song in this play. The details are not too clear in the printed text: at Cornelia's entrance a stage direction calls for 'A song', and twenty-nine lines later Cornelia has a lyric beginning

Call for the robin red-breast and the wren.

There is a difference of opinion whether the lyric is to be spoken or sung. The lines do not have the ballad-like simplicity of Ophelia's ditty and if we assume that Cornelia, a minor character, actually sings, her song does not advance the action or intensify the emotion in any significant manner.

Webster's *Duchess of Malfi* was acted by the King's Men about 1613/14, at a time when Shakespeare was no longer active as a playwright. The tragedy contains three songs, the first of which, in Act III, is rather poor. Webster disclaims its authorship in the quarto of 1623—'as well he might', to quote F. L. Lucas, his editor. Two songs, both dramatically apposite and effective, occur in the Masque of Madmen in Act IV. But they are not sung by a major character.

Boys' Companies

The popularity of musical interludes played its part in the relationship between the Chamberlain's/King's Men (and other adult companies) and the rival children's companies of St. Paul's and the Chapel Royal. In the Induction to Marston's *Malcontent* (1604) Burbage explains that additions to the original Blackfriars play were necessary at the Globe Playhouse '. . . to abridge the not received custom of music in our theatre'.[1] This much-discussed passage is usually interpreted to mean that the children's companies offered more music before and after

---

[1] Marston I.xxiii, 143, 238; Webster III.303, 307; Chambers ES II.542.

the play, as well as between the acts. There is no reason why the term 'abridge' should not be extended to music and songs within the play as well. It goes without saying that the musically-trained choristers of the Paul's School or the Children of the Chapel Royal, who performed at the Blackfriars, could outdo the adult companies in musical offerings. Their training, both vocal and instrumental, was of a high order. As a result, the repertories of the boys' companies resembled the musical (or operetta) of today, whilst the adult companies offered plays with incidental music. In advancing his art Shakespeare would not have overlooked the methods of these rival organizations.

The character of the plays performed by the boys' companies was, of course, affected by many considerations in addition to those of casting and musical competence. The size of the private theatres (which offered better acoustics), the price of admission, the frequency of performance, were some of the determining agents. Over and above these, the sophisticated courtly audiences attending the productions of the boys' companies demanded a different sort of drama from that offered by the adult companies. Between the two kinds of repertory there were striking contrasts in ideas of morality, patriotism and kingship.[1]

If consideration of the contemporary boys' repertories be restricted to two playwrights, the tragedies of John Marston and George Chapman appear most worthy of examination. Marston's tragedy *Antonio and Mellida* was produced in 1599. True to custom it contains more music than would a comparable tragedy by an adult company. Of the play's eight songs three appear in the last act as part of a contest for 'music's prize' and, in addition, there is a funeral procession with instrumental music at the end, with an unexpected *coup de théâtre* when Antonio rises from his coffin. Vocal as well as instrumental resources of masque-like proportions are employed to wind up the play. It is interesting that all of the songs are sung by the clownish knight Balurdo and that none of the songs are as integrally related to the drama as are Shakespeare's songs in *Hamlet* and *Othello*. None are sung by a major character: neither Mellida, the heroine, nor Maria, the widow of Andrugio, sings. This is surprising in a company of boy-choristers. The famous stage

---

[1] Alfred Harbage, *Shakespeare and the Rival Traditions*, New York, 1952.

direction in the first quarto of *Hamlet*, 'Enter Ophelia, playing on a lute, and her hair down, singing' discloses that the Chamberlain's Men had found a boy-actor who could also sing. We are led to wonder, therefore, whether the dramatists writing for Paul's or the Blackfriars were aware of the potent effect of mingling song with blank verse, particularly in a major role.

It is also significant that the texts of the lyrics in *Antonio and Mellida* do not survive in the printed copy. The stage direction states briefly, 'Cantant', and there was consequently no assurance that the same songs would be sung as time passed, or that the dialogue and lyrics would have any relation to each other. Marston was not ignorant of music, nor was he averse to achieving an occasional effect by quoting from a well-known song. After singing an unnamed lyric Balurdo suggests in the course of some self-admiring banter, 'Do me right and dub me knight Balurdo' (V.i), an adaptation of an old drinking song which also appears in Shakespeare's *Henry IV, Part II* ('Do me right and dub me knight Samingo'). Earlier in his tragedy Marston combines the refrains of two of the songs which Ophelia sings, 'How should I your true love know' and 'Bonny sweet Robin' (Marston I.53). The stage directions indicate that full stanzas were sung but, contrary to the procedure in Shakespeare's plays, we are denied the texts or any reference to them in the dialogue.

Marston's sequel, *Antonio's Revenge*, written in the same year as *Antonio and Mellida*, follows the example of its predecessor in its application of music. There are allusions in the spoken dialogue and stage directions, such as 'Cantat', indicating that six songs were sung. None of them are assigned to a major character and there are no texts. The final act achieves its climax with the aid of three songs and a dance in the manner of the traditional masque. The dirge 'Mellida is dead' heightens the tragedy. This much may be said of Marston's early plays: his musical metaphors and puns are skillfully handled and his easy familiarity with the technical aspects of music is borne out by repeated references to such matters as breves and semi-quavers, descants and grounds. In addition, Marston's quips and sallies utilizing musical terms aptly complement the actual singing and playing.

With *Sophonisba* (1606) Marston set out deliberately to establish his reputation as a tragic poet. The reader is warned in the introductory address that the author had 'not laboured . . . to transcribe authors, quote authorities, and translate Latin prose orations into English blank verse'. This barb was aimed at Ben Jonson, but the differences between Jonson's *Sejanus*, performed by an adult company and *Sophonisba*, acted by the Children of Paul's, exceed the mere 'translation' of Latin sources. In Marston's drama there are, to be sure, echoes of the phraseology of Livy and of the plot as told by Appian. Of greater significance is Marston's attitude towards his models. Jonson's tragedy is neo-classical in the Senecan manner and throws into bold relief Marston's melodramatic style with its romantic drift. The abundance of music in *Sophonisba* and its absence in *Sejanus* are an aspect of this difference in spirit and attitude. In the same way Samuel Daniel's neo-Senecan *Cleopatra* (1594) with classical choruses but no music may be compared with Shakespeare's *Antony and Cleopatra*. Shakespeare differs from Daniel in utilizing both song and instrumental music, but he also differs from Marston by employing his musical resources more economically. The absence of this economy and, indeed, of any semblance of Senecan frigidity is so marked in *Sophonisba* that Marston felt obliged to add an epilogue in which he appeals to the reader 'not to tax me for the fashion of the entrances and music of this tragedy, for know it is printed only as it was presented by youths and after the fashion of the private stage'.[1] Indeed, Marston's stage directions, otherwise fairly detailed, are here uncommonly elaborate. As an example the direction for the song in Act III deserves to be quoted in full:

Cornets and Organs playing full music. Enters the solemnity of a sacrifice, which being entered whilst the attendants furnish the altar[,] Sopho[nisba's] song: which done she speaks

This is the first occurrence of a tragic heroine's singing aside from Peele's Bethsabe and Shakespeare's Desdemona and Ophelia. A similar procedure is to be observed a few years later in Chapman's *Revenge of Bussy D'Ambois*. Is it fanciful to suspect the successful model of Shakespeare behind these lyrics? In *Sophonisba* the most spectacular application of music takes place in Acts IV and V. Instrumental music accompanies the entrance of the enchantress Erictho in the guise of Sophonisba (IV) and

---

[1] In this instance the Blackfriars; Marston II.64.

the 'infernal' music sustains the sorcery as Syphax anticipates the realization of his desires, and there is a 'short song to soft music above'. Marlowe had used instrumental music similarly evocative in *Doctor Faustus*. It was to be expected, with the vocal resources of the children's companies, that a 'short song' would be added to the infernal music as the scene proceeds. But a musical climax of dramatic appositeness is reached in Act V when Marston symbolizes Rome's triumph and the downfall of Carthage by means of contrasting bands of instruments. Scipio, the conqueror, marches in to the blare of cornets while the 'mournful solemnity' of Masinissa presenting Sophonisba's dead body is carried out to the soft strains of 'organ and recorders'. Although the play continues for another few lines to the stage direction 'cornets a short flourish', to all intents the tragedy concludes with the traditional dead march. This convention must have appealed to Marston in view of the mock funeral march with which he ends *Antonio and Mellida* and the dirge 'Mellida is dead' in *Antonio's Revenge*.

Funereal strains were among the formalities to mark the end of a noble hero or heroine, both at the children's private theatres and at the public playhouses. In contemplating the fates of Mellida and Sophonisba the catharsis experienced by the audience is assisted by the sounding of the dead march. Shakespeare also accompanies the deaths of his noble heroes with appropriate music. But the ceremony of the dead march is withheld when a character is sullied by crime, a custom undoubtedly familiar to audiences. The absence of the dead march in Chapman's *Bussy* tragedies would seem to point in this direction.

In *Bussy D'Ambois* (ca. 1604) the adulterous and criminally ambitious hero falls by treachery. It is the most successful tragedy Chapman ever wrote. Dryden, who had 'indignation enough to burn a D'Ambois annually to the memory of Jonson' had to admit how effectively this drama of rant and cruelty wrought its spell. Chapman's contemporary subject matter contrasts with the traditional topics of the neo-classical tragedies of a Daniel or Jonson. The title page speaks of 'A Tragedy: as it hath been often presented at Paul's', but there is surprisingly little actual music in a play apparently written for a boys' company. Some scholars are inclined to think that *Bussy D'Ambois* was originally written for the Admiral's Men, that is to say, an adult company.[1] A stage direction calls for 'Music' in Act IV, scene ii, when Bussy's mistress, the Countess Tamyra, enters with her maid, but this can hardly be termed significant.

Chapman's sequel, *The Revenge of Bussy D'Ambois* (*ca.* 1610), is close to *Hamlet* both in subject matter and in method. In Act I Tamyra, bereft of her lover, sings to relieve her despondent spirit. Whereas the text of the song does not survive, the importance of Tamyra's role and the circumstances of her singing, as already noted, remind us of Ophelia. The third scene of Act V also recalls *Hamlet* when the ghost (umbra) of Bussy D'Ambois interrupts the argument between Tamyra, Renel and the Countess:

> Away, dispute no more; get up and see!
> Clermont must author this just tragedy.

No music accompanies the appearance of the ghost. Indeed, a musical accompaniment was not customary within the tragic convention in a scene where a solitary ghost appealed to the conscience of the revenger or the revengers. On the other hand, a macabre masque, performed by a number of spirits, was another matter, and the musical resources of his boys' company were not ignored by Chapman. When Bussy's ghost soliloquizes that

> The black soft-footed hour is now on wing,
> Which, for my just wreak, ghosts shall celebrate
> With dances dire and of infernal state

we know what to expect—a dance, that is to say, a masque. In their ability to perform these masques which succeeded the dumb-shows of the sixteenth century, the Blackfriars or Paul's boys held a distinct advantage over the adult companies. When Bussy has been revenged we have this stage direction, the fullest yet in the two tragedies:

Music, and the Ghost of Bussy enters, leading the Ghost of the Guise, Monsieur, Cardinal Guise, and Chatillon; they dance about the dead body, and Exeunt

[1] Cf. J. Jacquot, ed. *Chapman: Bussy D'Amboise*, Paris, 1960, pp. xvii f. This theory receives further support from the re-dating of Chapman's tragedy by E. Schwartz, who assigns *Bussy* to *ca.* 1597 and the *Revenge* to *ca.* 1602/03; cf. *Modern Philology*, LVII (1959–60), 80–82.

In addition to putting to work the talents of the company, this masque has a functional importance: it divulges to Clermont the news that the Guise whom he thinks 'yet living' has been slain. True, the events are later verified in the flesh but Jacobean playwrights favoured these miraculous and musical prophecies, which, moreover, provided them with an opportunity to delight their courtly audiences with a popular form of entertainment.

After the King's Men acquired the lease of the Blackfriars Theatre in 1608, along with some of its resources, these ballet-like performances began to appear in Shakespeare's plays. In *Cymbeline* (1609/10) the Leonati 'circle' about the sleeping Posthumus, and in *Henry VIII* (1613) in the vision of Catherine the appearances 'first congee unto her, then dance'. Each scene is a miraculous foretelling in the form of an enjoyable ballet, danced by spirits. In the circumstances one feels that Chapman's editor was unduly severe when he commented on the dance of the ghosts in the *Revenge of Bussy d'Ambois*:

The stage direction . . . probably represents an attempt on the part of the management of the Whitefriars theatre to add a little spectacular divertissement to what must have seemed to most of the audience an appallingly heavy play. The entrance and dance of the ghosts certainly serves no dramatic purpose.[1]

The dramatic motivation may, indeed, have been slight but by 1610 the masque had become a staple device in the tragedies, anticipated and enjoyed by the audience, regardless of the purpose it served.

A survey of the practices of Shakespeare's contemporaries inevitably raises certain questions as to the manner and justification of the poet's own procedure. Points of both contrast and similarity emerge from a comparison of Shakespeare's work with that of other Elizabethan and Jacobean playwrights. In regard to instrumental music, there are distinct resemblances in the treatment of dead marches and dumb-shows, as we have seen, as well as in the fashion in which the supernatural is introduced on the stage.

The ubiquitous presence of 'mood' music was not observed by the Elizabethan dramatists. A distinction was made between

1 *The Tragedies of Chapman*, ed. T. M. Parrott, London, 1910, p. 587.

the magic intervention of supernatural powers in the affairs of men and the solemn appearance of a departed spirit appealing to the conscience or intellectual judgment of one or more of the play's characters. Thus, Ariel's chastisement of Alonso in the *Tempest* is underlined by music. But neither in Shakespeare's *Hamlet* nor in Chapman's *Revenge of Bussy d'Ambois* does music accompany the appeal of the ghost. By contrast, our modern audiences take for granted a musical accompaniment whenever supernatural forces are at work, an attitude for which the 'ombra' scenes of Italian opera (of which *Don Giovanni* is a fine example) and the 'ghost' music of the modern cinema are responsible.

One obvious point of contrast between Shakespeare and his contemporaries is the treatment of boy-singers who represent heroines. With the exception of Bethsabe's lyric in Peele's biblical tragedy our survey reveals nothing, prior to 1604, to be compared to the lyrics of Ophelia or Desdemona. The exceptional fashion in which Shakespeare's tragic heroines are given songs to perform is discussed in the following two chapters.

Another contrast which has much impressed students is concerned with the presence or absence of the texts of songs in the extant copies of the tragedies. The best summary of the scholarly literature on this subject has been given by William Bowden[1] who employs the convenient term 'blank song' for lyrics which are indicated only by rubrics or context but are not preserved in the text. Two blank songs occur in Shakespeare's early work, the Welsh song in *Henry IV, Part I* (III.i) and the lute song in *Julius Caesar* (IV.iii). But, clearly, any Welsh melody will do for the history play and any sleepy tune for the Roman tragedy. In the mature tragedies, from *Hamlet* to *King Lear*, there are no blank songs, and when we compare the lyrics of Ophelia and of the grave-digger in *Hamlet* with the blank songs—and there are none other—in Marston's *Antonio's Revenge* or Chapman's *Revenge of Bussy*, the contrast is striking indeed. A similar situation pertains to the comedies where Chapman's *All Fools* (1604?) has blank songs only, whilst Shakespeare's *Twelfth Night* (1602) or Jonson's *Volpone* (1605/06) include the text. We are bound to search for some reason.

[1] *The English Dramatic Lyric, 1603/42*, New Haven (Conn.), 1951, pp. 87–94, 113–114

The frequent absence of the texts of the songs is probably connected with the difficulties of musical notation which is legible only to theatre musicians and a few actor-singers but is a mystery to most scribes and prompters. For this reason songs usually were, and are, rehearsed from a sheet of music containing text and tune, and such sheets are generally kept separate from the body of the play. When an old prompt-book had worn out and re-copying was in order, the songs were not necessarily included in the new book if, indeed, they had ever been in the old one. It must be remembered that a prompter is of little use during the performance of a song, so that the frequency with which blank songs occur in Elizabethan plays has a good practical basis. The prompt-book, of course, derives from the author's copy. We may assume that there were two kinds of authors' manuscripts, those where the text of a song was not given because any song would do and those where the playwright included the text of the song for the sake of dramatic wholeness. Presumably, then, the presence of texts of songs in the printed plays of Shakespeare and Jonson must have had its beginning in the author's manuscript.[1]

It cannot be argued that Shakespeare and Jonson considered the convenience of the singer, for musicians would still need the music for purposes of rehearsal, and the same considerations of convenience must have existed for other playwrights as well. Rather, one feels that it was the aim of literary excellency that motivated Shakespeare and Jonson. The echoes of verbal phrases from a lyric in the surrounding dialogue, the close integration of the lyric into the dramatic structure, demanded that the text of the song be determined by the dramatic poet and that improvisation on the part of the actor be avoided. Several instances are offered in the following chapters of the close integration between the text of the song and the text of the dialogue.

---

[1] That Jonson himself supervised the printing of his plays is indubitable. In the case of Shakespeare the printed text is probably based on manuscripts in the possession of the Chamberlain's/King's Men, derived in turn from the author's 'true original copies'. It is not feasible in this study to discuss the tangled question of the lyrics in Lyly's comedies. The comedies were written for a boys' company and are earlier in date than the works of Marston and Chapman. The authorship of these lyrics, their absence in the first printed edition and their appearance in the posthumous edition of 1632 is discussed in a monograph by George K. Hunter, London, 1962.

II

THE WILLOW SONG

THERE is a common note of pessimism, at times bordering on
cynicism, in the plays that appeared in Shakespeare's mature
period, immediately following the turn of the century: *Hamlet*
(*ca.* 1600); *Troilus and Cressida* (*ca.* 1602); *Othello* (*ca.* 1604);
King Lear (*ca.* 1605/06); *Macbeth* (*ca.* 1605/06); *Timon of Athens*
(*ca.* 1605/08); *Coriolanus* (*ca.* 1607/08).

As to the reasonableness of including *Troilus and Cressida* and
Timon of Athens in the same category with *Hamlet, Othello* and
King Lear, a number of considerations favour this grouping. The
sparseness of the music and the treatment of the vocal and
instrumental resources, as well as the presence of the stark note
of death at the end of each play are significant. The appearance
of *Timon of Athens* among the tragedies of the First Folio of 1623
in the space originally intended for *Troilus and Cressida*[1] is also
to be noted. The slaying of Hector and the death of Timon are
of a magnitude to dwarf the comic and satirical elements in the
plays, and there are moments when the satire is of such a bitterness and acerbity as to eclipse the comic. When Troilus dis-
covers Cressida and Diomedes, his apprehension calls to mind
Othello's revulsion on observing the supposedly adulterous
Cassio jesting with Iago about amorous affairs (IV.i). The
cynical comments in both plays on the faithlessness of woman-

---

[1] Cf. the NS editions of *Troilus and Cressida* (p. 122) and of *Timon of
Athens* (pp. ix and 87). *Troilus and Cressida* defies a neat classification; with
its mixture of the comic and tragic it is wholly *sui generis.*

hood have been aptly compared with Lear's remarks on adultery (IV.vi.114):

> The wren goes to't, and the small gilded fly
> Does lecher in my sight.
> Let copulation thrive, for Gloucester's bastard son
> Was kinder to his father than my daughters . . .
> Down from the waist they are centaurs,
> Though women all above.

The domestic tragedy which Shakespeare wove out of the passions of Othello was a favourite with audiences up to the time the Puritans closed the theatres. Performances were recorded at Whitehall (1604, 12, 13), the Globe (1610), Oxford (1610), Blackfriars (1635) and Hampton Court (1636). At Oxford Henry Jackson, a member of Corpus Christi, was moved to record his impressions, and it is noteworthy that he singles out the performance of Desdemona without bothering to mention other members of the cast:

At verò illa apud nos a marito occisa, quanquam optimè semper causam egit, interfecta tamen magis movebat; cum in lecto decumbens spectantium misericordiam ipso vultu imploraret.[1]

Othello shares with its predecessors, *Hamlet* and *Troilus*, Shakespeare's preoccupation with the frailties of the feminine sex, whereby the moral strength and weaknesses of Ophelia and Gertrude, Cressida and Helen, Desdemona and Emilia are precisely explored. Whether by chance or design, their problems and frustrations offered an opportunity for using music as a means to expose their characters; not to mention the certain effect its inclusion would have upon the audience. Desdemona's final scene is given added poignancy by her singing of the Willow Song; here Shakespeare offers a fine illustration of his skill in integrating music into the structure of his plot. In the later tragedies the notion of kingship and affairs of state supersede Shakespeare's concern with domestic intrigues. Antony's tragedy is that he loses the empire. The promiscuities of Goneril and Regan are a mark of their sullied characters, but the tragedy of *King Lear* as a whole is concerned with filial devotion and with

---

[1] She who was killed by her husband acted excellently throughout but was nevertheless more moving when dead; as she lay on the bed she appealed to the compassion of the spectators by the very expression of her face.

kingship, in contrast to the purely personal relationships and attitudes which Iago's intrigue succeeds in fomenting.

The singing of the Willow Song in Act IV is one of the means by which Shakespeare creates the pathos of the strangled heroine 'in lecto decumbens', for the notion of the dejected and melancholy lover by the side of a tree had great popular appeal and could be relied upon to arouse a sympathetic response. The lyric occurs in numerous versions in the sixteenth century, and its appearance among the Roxburghe Ballads and the Pepys Ballads confirms its perennial popularity. But the valid inclusion of the song in the text of the play has long been a tangled question, since it involves the acceptance of the Folio edition (F) of 1623 as a superior and more authentic source than the Quarto edition (Q) of 1622. Among modern editors a solitary argument in favour of Q is put forward by M. R. Ridley:[1]

IV.iii.31–52 and 54–56. I think probably a cut, because of the apparently consequential cut at V.ii.247. But it may be that all the passages were added because at some point in the stage history of the play a boy actor was available with a greater talent for singing than the one for whom Shakespeare first wrote the part.

On the other hand, A. Walker, summarizing the conclusions reached by Chambers, Hinman and Greg, as well as her own, has this to say:

That F. preserves the better text has never seriously been in doubt . . . Q (1622) was printed by Nicholas Okes for Thomas Walkley . . . On the evidence of Q's readings, Walkley's manuscript seems to have been a careless transcript of the play as cut for acting. Q is shorter than F by about 160 lines. Some of its lacunae were undoubtedly due to negligence in printing . . . The bulk of the omitted matter, however, fairly certainly represented cuts for performance, motivated, like those of the F *Lear* by practical rather than artistic considerations. Minor characters are relieved . . . Othello's Pontic Sea simile (3.3.455–62) seems to have been cut and, more lamentable still from a dramatic standpoint, Desdemona's 'Here I kneel . . .' (4.2.152–165) . . . The Willow song is omitted in 4.3. and Emilia's reference to it in 5.2. As Chambers argued, the integration of the Willow theme in the dialogue makes it unlikely that . . . Shakespeare would have introduced a song in the first instance for a boy actor who could not sing, it looks as if this cut at least was necessitated by a change in

[1] NA 201.

casting. . . . That the majority of the Q variants are perversions is evident from F, on balance the sounder text, and editors of literary discrimination have traditionally steered a steady course between Okes's Scylla and Jaggard's [Folio] Charybdis, giving the former the wider berth. Some indication of their comparative merits can be derived from the texts of the Old Cambridge editors, Craig (in his Oxford edition), Kittredge, Alexander and Sisson, who are unanimous in rejecting about 170 F readings against about 500 of Q . . .[1]

Greg's conclusion[2] that the collation of the Q text with the prompt book 'generally resulted . . . in a considerable improvement of the text' is corroborated by an analysis of other musical material in the play as well as the Willow Song. There are, for instance, different versions[3] in Q and F of Iago's drinking song, and a comparison of the two establishes the superiority of the F text. Since the Willow Song occurs only in F, no textual decisions are necessary, but it is important whether we regard Desdemona's performance in Act IV and Emilia's reference to it in Act V as part of Shakespeare's original design or whether we treat these passages as later insertions. To credit the first theory assumes a general agreement that the F text is superior to Q and that the hypotheses of Greg and Walker are tenable, namely, that the omission in Q represents a cut. The associations that the Willow Song evokes are essential to the characterization of Desdemona: her innocence, the fear of impending death, her revulsion at Othello's accusation of adultery, must first be established. Otherwise her question

> Wouldst thou do such a deed, for all the world?

which is not omitted in Q comes too abruptly to be convincing.

The following text (pages 27 and 28) has the customary modernizations of spelling and punctuation, and minor discrepancies between the two texts have been ignored. The longest cut in the Quarto occurs between the second half of line 31 and the first half of line 53. Following the form used in the Folio,

---

[1] NS 121–126.

[2] Greg FF 371; cf. also p. 358 to the effect that the omission of the song in the Quarto was presumably the result of a cut.

[3] Cf. Chapter V on Adult Song.

QUARTO

Othello, Act IV, scene iii.

My mother had a maid call'd *Barbary.*
She was in love; and he she lov'd prov'd mad
And did forsake her. She had **a song of Willow.**
An old thing t'was; but it expressed her fortune,
And she died singing it. That song to-night
Will not go from my mind;

FOLIO

DES
26 My mother had a maid call'd *Barbary.*
27 She was in love; and he she lov'd prov'd mad
28 And did forsake her. She had **a song of Willow.**
29 An old thing 'twas; but it expressed her fortune,
30 And she died singing it. That song to-night
31 Will not go from my mind; I have much to do
32 But to go hang my head all at one side
33 And sing it like poor *Barbary.* Prithee dispatch.
34 Shall I go fetch your night-gown?
                        No, unpin me here.

EMIL
DES
35 This Lodovico is a proper man.
EMIL 36 A very handsome man.
DES 37 He speaks well.
EMIL 38 I know a lady in Venice would have
39 walk'd barefoot to Palestine for a touch of his
40 nether lip.

DES
41 *The poor soul sat sighing by a sicamore tree,*
42 *Sing all a green willow;*
43 *Her hand on her bosom, her head on her knee,*
44 *Sing willow, willow, willow.*
45 *The fresh streams ran by her, and murmur'd her moans,*
46 *Sing Willow, etc.*
47 *Her salt tears fell from her, and soft'ned the stones,*

48 *Sing Willow, etc.* (Lay by these.)
49 *Willow, willow*
50 (Prithee, hie thee; he'll come anon.)
51 *Sing all a green willow must be my garland.*
52 *Let nobody blame him, his scorn I approve,*
53 (Nay, that's not next. Hark, who is't that knocks?
EMIL 54 It's the wind. [)]
DES 55 *I call'd my love false love; but what said he then?*
56 *Sing willow, etc.*
57 *If I court moe women, you'll couch with moe men*
58 So, get thee gone, good night; mine eyes do itch;
59 Doth that bode weeping?
EMIL   'Tis neither here nor there.
DES 60 I have heard it said so. O, these men, these men!
61 Dost thou in conscience think (tell me *Emilia*)
62 That there be women do abuse their husbands
63 In such gross kind?
EMIL   There be some such, no question.
DES 64 Wouldst thou do such a deed for all the world?
EMIL 65 Why would not you?
DES   No, by this heavenly light?
EMIL 66 Nor I neither, by this heavenly light;
67 I might do't as well i' th' dark.
DES 68 Wouldst thou do such a deed for all the world?
EMIL 69 The world's a huge thing . . .

Hark, who is't that knocks?

It's the wind.

So, get thee gone, good night; mine eyes do itch;
Doth that bode weeping?
'Tis neither here nor there.

Wouldst thou do such a deed for all the world?
Why would not you?
No, by this heavenly light
Nor I neither, by this heavenly light;
I might do't as well i' th' dark.
Wouldst thou do such a deed for all the world?
The world's a huge thing . . .

the italic type between lines 41 and 57 distinguishes the lines to be sung from those to be spoken.[1]

We learn from both texts that the song was old, so that it is fair to assume that it was known to the audience. Q and F agree also on Desdemona's expressions of anxiety and apprehension and Emilia's reassurances. The importance of line 64 is emphasized by its repetition in line 68. But the suddenness of Desdemona's reiterated question as it comes in the Quarto would be difficult to explain without the hypothesis of a cut. In the Folio, lines 55 and 57, introducing unfaithfulness and promiscuity, and 60–68, 'these men, these men', 'abuse their husbands' and 'gross kind', give point to the reiterated question. In particular, the topic of conjugal faithfulness, which also dominates *Hamlet* and *Troilus*, has not been touched upon earlier in the scene. That the melody is in Desdemona's head and that she feels inclined to sing it is shown in Folio lines 31–33: 'I have much to do/But to go hang my head all at one side/And sing it like poor *Barbary*.' The actual singing, then, at 41–57, comes as no surprise.

The stanza proper, without the refrain, consists of two long lines of four stresses each. The first unit is composed of lines 41 and 43; the second of lines 45 and 47. 'Let nobody blame him, his scorn I approve' at line 52 is, in fact, out of its order[2] and is rightly dismissed by Desdemona as a false start. Her final stanza is made up of 55 and 57.

The refrain, 'Sing all a green willow' or 'Sing willow, willow'

Ex. 1.

Sing all   a green wil - low

Sing all   a green wil - low
Sing wil - low wil-low wil - low

---

[1] In modern editions proper nouns and lyrics are usually given in ordinary Roman type, although, generally speaking, the italic type in F and Q is an important clue in determining where Shakespeare wished a lyric to be sung.

[2] See p. 33, stanza VII of London Book version.

is clearly intended to intervene after each line. The slight variations are of no account, as the two most likely melodic turns will accommodate either phrase. The false start is understandably left without a refrain, and with the odium of promiscuity at 57 the singing stops abruptly.

Desdemona's interruption of herself at line 52, 'No, that's not next' is almost certain proof that 'the song of Willow, an old thing' had many more stanzas than the play allows. Its antiquity and popularity are further affirmed by the fact that the refrain was a favourite in many poems of the sixteenth and seventeenth centuries.

The anapaestic rhythm is a marked characteristic of Desdemona's doleful knell.[1] The two unstressed syllables, intervening between the accents, give a distinctive lilt to texts that trip on the tongue like this:

John Heywood

[Heading] All a green willow willow willow willow

> Alas by what mean may I make ye to know
> The unkindness for kindness that to me doth grow . . .
> For all a green willow is my garland.[2]

Gorgeous Gallery of Gallant Inventions

> My love what misliking in me do you find,
>   Sing all a green willow:
> That on such a sudden you alter your mind,
>   Sing willow willow willow.

(Ed. Rollins, 1926, p. 83.)

---

[1] Six iambic willow songs, of which three have the burden 'willow, willow, willow' have been described in 'Shakespeare's Use of Popular Song', *Elizabethan and Jacobean Studies*, Oxford, 1959, pp. 154–156. To these should be added the song by Henry Lawes, 'A Willow Garland thou didst send' from Playford's *Select Musicall Ayres*, 1652, p. 35. A new iambic Willow Song has come to light in a fragment in the New York Public Library. It is discussed in Appendix IV to this chapter, p. 49.

[2] B.M. Add. MS 15233, f. 48, facsimile of first stanza in J. O. Halliwell Phillipps, ed., *The Moral Play of Wit and Science and early Poetical Miscellanies*, (Shakespeare Society Publications), London, 1848. Redford's play of *Wit and Science* and Heywood's verse have been variously edited since.

Howell's *Devises*, *1581*

[Heading] All of green Willow, Willow, Willow, Willow

> Embrace your bays sweetly that smile in love's sight . . .
> To me most unhappy, still spurned by despite,
> Is given writhed willows to express my state right.
> (Ed. Raleigh, 1906, p. 23.)

Howell's *Devises*, *1581*

[Heading] All of green laurel

> Look up to the laurel, and let willow go,
> And trust to the true friend, embrace not thy foe,
> Sing all of green laurel.
> (Ibid., ll. 9–14. The first half (ll. 1–8) is iambic.)

Gentle Craft, Part II, 1598 (?)

> When fancy first framed our likings in love,
> Sing all of green willow:
> And faithful affection such motions did move
> For willow, willow, willow.
> (*T. Deloney: Works*, ed. Mann, 1912, p. 165.)

British Museum, Add. MS 15117, f. 18

> The poor soul sat sighing by a sycamore tree,
> Sing willow, willow, willow,
> With his hand in his bosom and his head upon his knee,
> O willow willow willow willow.

Pelham Humfrey (1647–74)

> A young man sat sighing by a sycamore tree,
> Sing willow willow,
> With his hand in his bosom, his head on his knee,
> O willow willow, o willow willow.
> (Reprinted Stafford Smith's *Musica Antiqua*,
1812, p. 171.)

Playford's *Pleasant Musical Companion*, 1686

> A poor soul sat sighing near a gingerbread stall,
> O gingerbread, oh, oh, gingerbread, oh.
> (Third Part, no. 17, *The Second Book of the*
Pleasant . . ., Wing STC, S2261.)

Gilbert and Sullivan, *The Mikado*, 1885

> On a tree by a river a little tomtit
> Sang 'Willow, titwillow, titwillow'.

Popular lyrics of the Elizabethan age were commonly transcribed in purely instrumental versions, in books for the lute, the cittern or virginal. They were identified by a title or a marginal rubric, such as 'Greensleeves', or 'O Mistress mine'. In such sources we must seek, and hope to find, a likely tune to fit the verbal lyric which more often than not appears in a truncated version in one of the contemporary plays.[1] This adaptation of text to tune frequently necessitates the repetition of lines or half-lines of the verse in order to suit the music[2] and there is abundant evidence that Shakespeare and his contemporaries varied text and tune as occasion might require. In the case of the Willow Song we have three contemporary musical versions from which an adaptation of Desdemona's lyric may be made. They are contained in the following manuscripts:

British Museum Add. MS 15117 (1616 or earlier), which will
    be designated in this study as the London Book;
the Lodge Book (early 1570s); and
the Dallis Book (*ca.* 1583).

The London Book is justly famous, for it combines an extended text with an instrumental accompaniment. Aside from musical considerations, this manuscript offers the best gloss on Shakespeare's text, as well as an insight into his dramatic method. The subtle changes wrought on the popular model are revealed; at the same time the text enables us to correct the misprints in the F text and to supply the missing lines.

The first stanza reads

> The poor soul sat sighing by a sycamore tree
> With his hand in his bosom and his head upon his knee

---

[1] A comparable problem would exist if, in time to come, the popular songs of today were to be revived from mere piano versions.

[2] Cf. S. Beck, 'The Case of "O Mistresse mine" ', *Renaissance News*, VI (1953), 19–23; Mr. Beck's version is used by Alfred Deller in his gramophone recording. Cf. also *Renaissance News*, VII (1954), 98–100.

Uncorrected formes of sheet such as the one bound with the Chatsworth copy (facs. Clarendon Press, 1902) print

> The poore Sonle set sining, by a Sicamour tree.

Of the three misprints the printer properly amended 'Sonle' and 'set' but seems to have had insufficient familiarity with balladry to recognize the error in 'sining'. Later formes like that bound with the Huth copy (facs. Yale Press, 1954) have

> The poore Soule sat singing . . .

a pardonable mistake that was not corrected until the eighteenth century.[1] But these are trivia. The remaining seven stanzas of the London Book read:

II He sighed in his singing, and made a great moan, sing etc.
    I am dead to all pleasure, my true love she is gone, etc.

III The mute bird sat by him was made tame by his moans, etc.
    The true tears fell from him, would have melted the stones,
    sing etc.

IV Come all you forsaken and mourn you with me,
    Who speaks of a false love, mine's falser than she, sing etc.

V Let love no more boast her in palace nor bower,
    It buds, but it blasteth ere it be a flower, sing etc.

VI Though fair and more false, I die with thy wound,
    Thou hast lost the truest lover that goes upon the ground, sing

VII Let nobody chide her, her scorns I approve,
    She was born to be false, and I to die for her love, sing etc.

VIII Take this for my farewell and latest adieu
    Write this on my tomb, that in love I was true, sing etc.

Stanzas II, V, VI and VIII are missing from Desdemona's song, and their absence confirms the suspicion that Shakespeare omitted still others for the sake of dramatic expedience. It is obvious from the graphic arrangement in the London Book that the scribe was cramped for space; moreover, a greater number of stanzas is to be found in the *Roxburghe Ballads* and Percy's *Reliques*.

[1] Q_2 of 1630 has 'sighing', but most eighteenth-century editions have 'singing', as do Johnson-Steevens (1785) and also Knight (1839–42). The proper emendation, 'sighing', was first made by Capell (1768) and Malone (1790).

Stanza III is revised slightly (lines 45, 47) and is followed after the refrain by a variation of the first line of stanza VII (line 52). So far, the audience had heard two and a half stanzas and, assuming that they knew the song, no startling change had taken place. Had Desdemona continued with several consecutive stanzas to a suitable conclusion of the lyric, the audience would have received the welcome relief of a vocal divertissement. But Shakespeare deliberately avoids any semblance of a concert interlude. Following line 52 his heroine first scrambles, then distorts her lines, and with the piece in a shambles, the singing stops abruptly. In her final stanza

> I called my love false love, but what said he then?
> If I court moe women, you'll couch with moe men

Desdemona begins with a variant of the second half of Stanza IV of the London Book and grafts upon it the acid reproach of promiscuity, thereby destroying the lyrical integrity of the original. This is the *raison d'être* of lines 64 and 68, that the minds of Desdemona and Othello are obsessed with the frailty and temptations of the flesh. One suspects, moreover, that this theme was one of Shakespeare's chief concerns at this stage of his writing.

Whether the music in the London Book is the same melody which 'once "sighed along" the traverses of the Globe Theatre' we do not know. In its interplay of short lines and long lines[1] it has a charming poignancy. But if we are correct in assuming that Desdemona sings on the spur of the moment an old song, unaccompanied, the dramatic context does not permit a lute accompaniment. It would not be feasible, either for Desdemona or for Emilia to manage a lute while Emilia undresses her mistress. The entire character of her recitation, the spontaneous way in which she breaks into her swansong, modifies and breaks it off, precludes forethought or an elaborate instrumental accompaniment where phrases in the lute complement phrases in the voice. The version in the manuscript is by a professional musician;[2] the accompaniment, as at bars 2–4, goes beyond

[1] 'Sing Willow Willow Willow', bars 7–9 in Music Example 2, and 'O, willow, willow, willow, willow', bars 14–16.

[2] Peter Warlock, *The English Ayre*, London, 1926, p. 128, offers the hypothesis that the anonymous song 'might conceivably be the work of Robert Parsons who died in 1570'.

mere harmonization and is of a complexity that qualifies it as a concert piece, in which capacity it has been performed and recorded. Its vocal part, on the other hand, would be suitable in the stage performance of the tragedy once it is adapted to Shakespeare's text.

Apart from its fitness in musical terms, this composition would have been eligible for use by Shakespeare's company in a chronological sense as well, for the manuscript contains several layers of songs which were universally popular in the early seventeenth century. The mixture of psalms and playhouse songs suggests that its owner or user was a professional musician rather than one performing exclusively in the theatre. The manuscript is written in various hands and the inclusion of 'Have you seen but a white lily grow' from Jonson's *The Devil is an Ass* implies that it was not completed until 1616, whilst another song, 'Come my Celia', from *Volpone* may be dated as of 1606. But there are included as well compositions which originated before 1600: Richard Edwards's 'Awake ye woeful wights' from *Damon and Pythias* and the anonymous 'O death rock me asleep', which has been attributed alternately to Edwards and to Rochford. 'In youthful years', which is certainly by Edwards, was printed, along with two other lyrics in the London Book,[1] in an early miscellany, *Paradise of Dainty Devices*, 1576. There are several compositions by Byrd and one by his teacher Tallis, 'I call and cry to thee o Lord'. It is certain proof of the popularity of these ancients to find them in company with the later work of Jonson and Campion.

The scribe of the London Book and the printer of the Folio were each concerned with compressing all of the Willow Song onto one page, with consequent inconsistencies in both the Folio and the manuscript. As a result, the adaptation of the melody to Shakespeare's words has raised difficulties on which no general agreement has been reached. The three and a half couplets which Desdemona sings and which comprise the stanzas proper are accurate and complete in F, but the refrain does not go beyond noting that there is a burden. This burden is, as we have seen, rather summarily indicated in most stanzas. The printing is more detailed when there are several spoken asides (lines 48

[1] Hunnis's 'Alack when I look back' and (?) Kinwelmarsh's 'O heavenly God', both with music by William Byrd.

and 50) but even these sparse indications are not consistent. The refrain after the first line of the stanza reads 'sing all a green willow', at line 42; 'sing willow etc.' at 46 and 'sing willow etc.' at 56. Either phrase will fit the tune, as we have seen, and it seems extremely doubtful that a Jacobean audience would have taken any notice of the slight verbal difference in this half-line. But in the London Book the refrain after the first line in stanza II reads 'sing etc.', in stanza III, merely 'etc.', and in stanzas IV–VIII there are no indications at all.

The problem of adapting an abbreviated verbal refrain to a piece of music has but one solution, to expand the text. This exercise is not restricted to the Willow Song. Thomas Morley's famous

> It was a lover and his lass
> With a hey, with a ho, and a hey nonie no,
> And a hey nonie nonie no,
> That o'er the green cornfields did pass

is longer by one line (And a hey nonie nonie no) than Shakespeare's F text.

In the present adaptation (Music Example 3), Desdemona's Willow Song has been fitted to the music in such a way that the full refrain is sung after the first two stanzas. Only then, it is felt, does the brusque way in which the singing stops at

> If I court moe women, you'll couch with moe men

make its full dramatic impact.

The Lodge Book, now in the Folger Library, Washington, D.C., contains a lute solo with the marginal rubric, 'All of green willow'. The late Otto Gombosi described this version as 'one of the oldest and most appealing musical settings of the "Willow" song'.[1]

Unlike the London Book, the Lodge Book is purely instrumental, and the modern student is obliged to fit the text to the three strains as best he can. Shakespeare's first stanza has been adapted to the music (Music Example 4 below). Among other

---

[1] *Renaissance News*, VIII (1955), 13; cf. also *Shakespeare Quarterly*, IX (1958), 419–420. The shelf mark in the Folger Library is MS V.a.159 (olim 448.16). 'All of green willow' occurs on f. 19, and the section of the MS comprising ff. 13ᵛ–21ʳ dates from the 1570s.

anapaestic willow songs that are easily accommodated by the tune is that of John Heywood (given on page 30).

The Dallis Book, which is housed in the library of Trinity College, Dublin, consists of two portions, the so-called 'Dublin Virginal Manuscript', compiled about 1570, and the lute book of Dallis, usually dated as of 1583. This date was arrived at from a note in the Book, 'Incepi nonis Augusti praeceptore M[agis]tro. Thoma Dallis. Cantabrigia, Anno 1583'.[1] We may safely assume, then, that this music, too, is older than Shakespeare's *Othello*.

The Dallis lute book contains a tablature with the rubric 'All a green Willow T. Dallis'. The piece is so close to the Willow Song in the Lodge Book that it might be termed a variant. The first four bars of Dallis and Lodge are nearly identical, though Dallis omits the two bars to accommodate the short refrain line, 'Sing all a green willow'. Music for this line is essential if Shakespeare's lyric is to be sung and for this reason Bars 4–6 of the Lodge Book have been inserted in Music Example 5 in square brackets.

The enigmatic identity of Thomas Dallis is discussed in the Appendix to this chapter.

In all likelihood it is to a fragment of one of the three melodies discussed here that the dying Emilia alludes:

> What did thy song bode, lady?
> Hark, canst thou hear me? I will play the swan,
> And die in music: *Willow, Willow, Willow*.

From the italic type we may assume that Emilia sings the refrain. The first short refrain line from either the Lodge Book (bars 4–6) or the London Book (bars 7–9) would lend itself well to the purpose, as illustrated in the music example on page 29. This is the only instance where Shakespeare quotes a melody that had been sung earlier in the play. His device fulfils a dramatic function, for now that Othello's mind is purged of the false accusations brought against Desdemona, her distortion of the old song has relevance no longer. Emilia's quotation of the traditional refrain recalls to the minds of the audience the main

---

[1] Cf. H. M. Fitzgibbon, 'The Lute Books of Ballet and Dallis', *Music & Letters*, XI (1930), 71–77; *Dublin Virginal Manuscript*, ed. J. Ward, Wellesley (Mass.), 1954; *Le Luth et sa Musique*, ed. J. Jacquot, Paris, 1958, pp. 184–187.

theme of a well-known lyric, and at the end of the tragedy the spectator is made to remember the willow as an emblem of sorrow, and Desdemona's act of singing as an analogue to the dying swan.

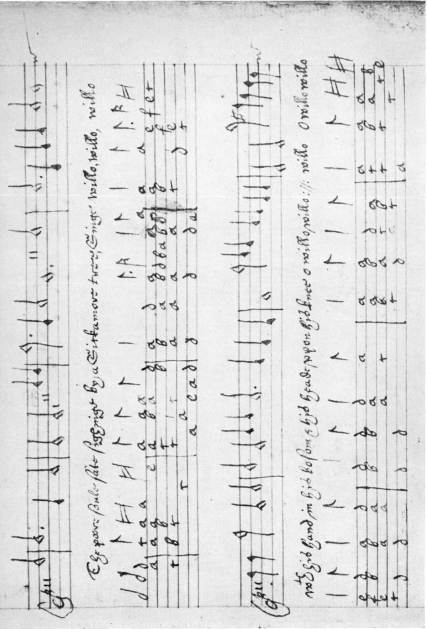

Facsimile 1a. The Willow Song, London Book.

willo willo, Fare well my garland Singe all agreene willo, willo willo, willo willo, Sing me...

All greene willo, must be my garland

NOTES ON TRANSCRIPTIONS

Appendix I

LONDON BOOK (British Museum Add. MS 15117, f. 18)

The melody has been printed by both Chappell and Wooldridge though with nineteenth-century harmonizations. Complete transcriptions of the original were made, amongst others, by Peter Warlock, E. H. Fellowes and J. P. Cutts. They appear in the following manner: Peter Warlock, ed., *English Ayres*, 6 vols., I.19 (1st edn., London: Enoch, 1922; 2nd edn. London: Oxford Press, 1927); E. H. Fellowes, 'The Willow Song', in Noble, pp. 152–154; J. P. Cutts, 'A Reconsideration of the Willow Song', *Journal of the American Musicological Society*, X (1957), 14–24.

In the London Book the music is notated on four braces, each brace composed of a five-line staff for the voice, with words beneath, and a six-line lute tablature. The fourth brace fills only half the width of the page, and into the remaining space the scribe compressed seven couplets representing stanzas II–VIII. For obvious limitations of space no refrain is given except 'sing etc.' or 'etc.'.

The first brace contains one scribal problem concerning the signs which give the length of notes above the lute tablature. In the early seventeenth century length was indicated either by stems and flags without heads or by conventional notes (semi-breves, minims, etc.). Here we have the usual stems and flags, but a second hand added two minims to bar 1. The voice has two minim rests in the first bar (indicated by strokes) and presumably the second scribe wished to indicate their length by the familiar note sign. It would make no musical sense to interpret these signs as anything but rests (in spite of their resemblance to the letter 'd'), and Warlock's example has been followed in the present transcription.

The second brace contains a scribal error in the voice part. At bar 16 the two notes for the word 'willow' should be placed one line higher. This emendation was made by Warlock and later editors.

The third brace contains a scribal error in the lute tablature. At bar 21 the first chord on the word 'all' reads

39

```
  a
  b
  a

  d
```

The third letter from the top should be 'b', not 'a'.

Another letter has been misplaced in the fourth brace of the lute tablature. At bar 27, the chord under the word 'must' puts the letter 'a' on the next to the bottom line, when it should be on the bottom line. This correction, too, was made by Warlock and followed by his successors.

In substance Warlock made an accurate and musicianly transcript of the Willow Song from a manuscript of the early seventeenth century. The task still remained to fit Shakespeare's folio text to the music, and to this exercise Fellowes addressed himself. His endeavour to 'conform strictly to Shakespeare's text and to carry the words through in song as they stand in the Play' was exemplary but, as we have noted, a refrain abbreviated in a verbal text may, and indeed frequently must, be expanded in the musical text if words and music are to be happily matched. Fellowes concluded the first stanza at bar 16 and did not include the full refrain until the end of the second stanza, lines 48–51. In following this procedure he showed his reluctance to use any words in the refrain which are not in F, and equally his reluctance to omit any of the music of the London Book. He therefore allotted the notes of the phrase 'shall be my garland' (bars 18–20) to the lute accompaniment alone, since the F text, line 48, has merely 'Sing willow, etc.'. But this method brings us back full circle to the question of the concert interlude versus dramatic sense.

J. P. Cutts agrees that Fellowes breaks off the singing of the first stanza too soon (at bar 16); nevertheless he does not himself carry through in the first stanza beyond bar 20. His expansion of the abbreviated phrase, 'Sing, etc.' to groups of three and six lines in alternate stanzas seems equally extraordinary.

In Music Example 2, the pitch has been transposed down a fourth, from g minor to d minor, both to accommodate a medium voice range and to facilitate comparison with the Dallis book. The upper line of verbal text is that of the London Book, the lower line gives those few verbal variants required by the first stanza of Shakespeare's text.

Music Example 3 gives the voice part only (without accompaniment); it has Shakespeare's complete text, indicating the spoken

interruptions and the two places where the singing breaks off altogether. Example 3 is intended for a performance of the play.

LONDON BOOK

Ex. 2.

The poor soul sat sigh-ing by a sy - ca-more tree, sing wil - low, wil-low, / all a green wil - low; with his / her hand in his / on her bo-som and his / her

LONDON BOOK

Ex. 3.

I   The poor soul sat sigh - ing   by a
II   The fresh streams ran   by her,   and
III Let no - bo - dy   blame him,   his
IV   I call'd my love   false love;   but

I   sy - ca - more   tree,   sing all   a green wil-low;
II   mur - mur'd her   moans,
III scorn I ap - prove, 3
IV   what said he   then?

I   her hand on her bo - som, her head on her
II   her salt tears fell from her, and sof - ten'd the
IV   If I court moe wo - men, you'll couch with moe

I   knee, sing wil - low, wil-low, wil-low, wil - low; sing
II   stones,   [stanza 2] 1
IV   men. 4

I   wil - low, wil-low, wil-low, wil - low shall be my gar -
II

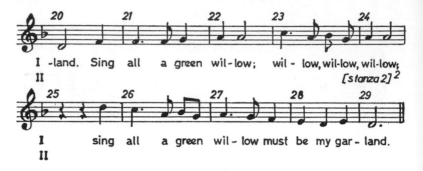

I -land.   Sing   all   a   green   wil-low;   wil - low, wil-low, wil-low;

II   [stanza 2] 2

I   sing   all   a   green   wil - low   must   be   my   gar - land.

II

1. [stanza 2, bar 16, singing interrupted:]
    Lay by these,

2   [stanza 2, bar 24, singing interrupted:]
    Prithee, hie thee; he'll come anon.

3   [stanza 3, bar 6, singing stops here:]
    Nay, that's not next. Hark! who is't that knocks? It is the wind.

4   [stanza 4, bar 14, singing stops here:]
    So get thee gone; good night. Mine eyes do itch. Doth that bode
    weeping?

Appendix II

LODGE BOOK (Folger Library, MS v.a.159, f. 19)

In modern transcription the instrumental piece, entitled 'All of green willow', is thirty bars long. It consists of three strains. The first strain (bars 1–6) is followed by a division, or variation, upon that strain (bars 6–12). The second strain (bars 12–18) is again followed by its division. But this time the division (18–22) is short of two bars, probably due to scribal omission. For the sake of symmetry, an editorial addition (marked by square brackets) has been made. The third and final strain (bars 22–26) is followed by a full division (bars 26–30). In Music Example 4, the pitch has been transposed up a tone, from c minor to d minor, to facilitate comparison with the London and Dallis Books. Shakespeare's text of the first stanza has been fitted to the three strains, but not to the divisions. These are not suitable for singing, due to the insertion of ornamental notes. In a vocal performance they could be omitted or played as instrumental postludes after each strain.

There are a few scribal errors in the lute tablature. At bars 13 (last note) and 14 (first two notes) the three letters denoting the bass were placed one string too high; and at bar 28 the rhythmic sign above the letters is incorrect: in modern notation semiquavers (sixteenth-notes), not quavers (eighth-notes) are called for. These matters have been emended in the modern transcription.

LODGE BOOK

Ex. 4.

The poor soul sat sigh-ing by a sy - ca-more tree, sing all a green wil-low; her hand on her bo-som, her head on her knee, sing

Appendix III

DALLIS BOOK (Trinity College, Dublin, MS D.3.30, p. 26)

We know little about the reputation of Dallis as a composer, except that he is honourably mentioned by Meres in his *Palladis Tamia*

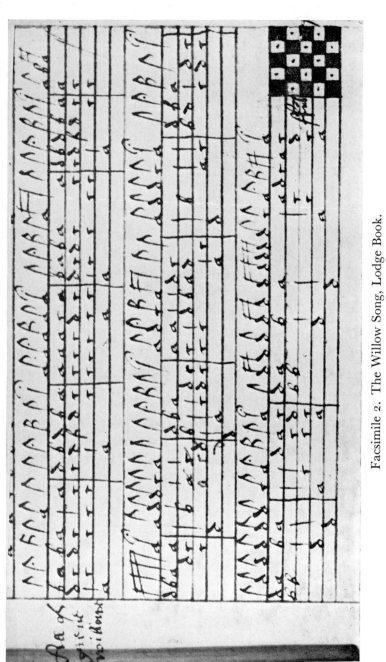

Facsimile 2. The Willow Song, Lodge Book.

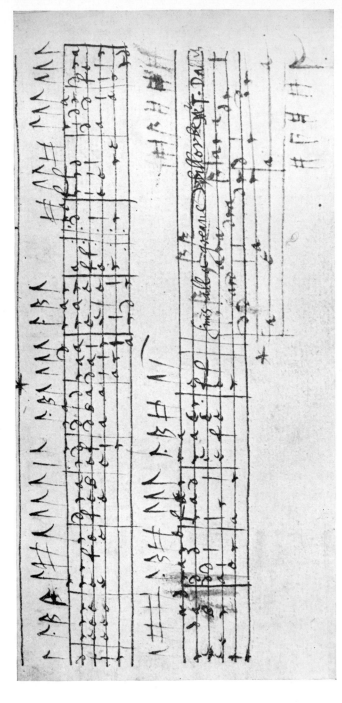

Facsimile 3. The Willow Song, Dallis Book.

of 1598. Meres's book is known to every student of Shakespeare for the very good reason that it contains, in the section on English poets, the paragraph quoted in Chapter I. The relevant sentence on music reads:

As Greece had these excellent musicians: Arion . . . Timotheus . . . Terpander . . . so England hath these: Master Cooper, Master Fairfax, Master Tallis, Master Taverner, Master Blitheman, Master Bird [Byrd], Doctor Tie [Tye], Doctor Dallis, Doctor Bull, M. Thomas Mud [Mudd], sometimes fellow of Pembroke Hall in Cambridge, M. Edward Johnson, Master Blankes [Blancks], Master Randall, Master Philips, Master Dowland, and M. Morley.

The list contains masters of the first rank, also lesser composers still fairly well known to students of the Fitzwilliam or Mulliner books; in any case, none so obscure that he is not listed in either the 1954 edition of *Grove's Dictionary* or Pulver's *Dictionary of English Musicians* of 1927, with the sole exception of 'Doctor Dallis'. Recently there has come to light a list similar to that of Meres, written down about 1592. It occurs in the manuscript autobiography of Thomas Whythorne, mentioning among the more prominent musicians of recent times (and in that order) Dr. Bull, Dr. Dally of Trinity College, Cambridge, Master Morley and Master Dowland.[1] The third and last mention of Dallis so far discovered occurs in a supplication of 1594 to Cambridge University by Edward Johnson, to be examined for his bachelor of music degree by Dr. Bull and Dr. Dallis. Confusion with Tallis is untenable since that composer had died some years before Johnson's supplication.

No scribal errors have been detected, and no emendations have therefore been necessary. The melody was transcribed by Wooldridge (I.110) with his own harmonization and adapted to Heywood's verse. Wooldridge remarks that 'the two concluding bars were probably different in the tune from these of the lute setting'. The words at bars 10–12 fit quite well, however, particularly if one sings 'must be my garland' instead of Heywood's 'Is my garland'. It is an open question whether or not the singing should cease at bar 12. If 12–16 are sung it may be preferable to employ all three quavers (eighth-notes) for the last syllable in bar 12 (f–g–b-flat). (The use of square brackets to mark the editorial addition of two bars from the Lodge Book after bar 4 of Dallis has been explained on page 37.) As in the case of the Lodge Book, the melody in Dallis easily fits a

---

[1] Cf. James Osborn, ed., *Autobiography of Thomas Whythorne*, Oxford, 1961, p. 302. Whythorne's list also includes Byrd, Tallis and Taverner. The name Dallis (or Dally) is not listed in the *Dictionary of National Biography* or *Alumni Cantabrigienses*, or the *Grace Book . . . containing the records of the University of Cambridge . . . 1542–1589.*

number of anapaestic willow songs. Accordingly, Shakespeare's first stanza and that of John Heywood have been adapted to the melody in Example 5.

DALLIS BOOK

Appendix IV

DREXEL FRAGMENT (New York Public Library, Drexel MS 4183, fly-leaf)

In the Drexel Collection of the New York Public Library several fragments of early Tudor music have come to light in the binding of a set of seventeenth-century part books. Of particular interest is the fragment on the verso of the fly-leaf of Drexel MS 4183, which consists of the treble part of a song beginning with the words (modernized)

> . . . when I have pleased my lady now and then

and ending

> for all a green willow is [my garla]nd

49

This version was recently discovered by Mr. John Stevens.[1]

The frequent and extensive rests between the musical phrases would suggest that this is the treble part of a part song, perhaps a song of three parts, not dissimilar in style to the version of 'Come o'er the burn Bessy', described in Chapter VII, Appendix IV. Both the nature of the extant music and the manner of notation suggest a date in the first half of the sixteenth century, that is to say, the same period as 'Come o'er the burn Bessy'. The sheet has been cropped, and as a result it is illegible in several places, notably at the beginning and end. In the following transcription modern bar-lines have been inserted, there being no bar-lines in the original. The metre of the verse is iambic, and the melody is in triple rhythm. It should be noted that the only place where there are six syllables of text under six notes of music is in the refrain. This suggests that the popular anapaestic refrain concluded an otherwise iambic song. It is unlikely that the melody of this fragment was ever used to accompany Desdemona's lyric. But because of its antiquity and the light it sheds on the age of the willow refrain and its widespread use, it deserves our attention.

> ... when
> I have pleased my lady now and then
> But now she loveth another man
> Because I cannot as he can
> A little age but late befell
> Which out of s[ervice] did me expel
> Now youth is come that beareth the bell
> Because I can not do so well
> Now all ye lovers take heed of me
> For once I was as lusty as ye
> And a[s I] am all ye shall be
> Therefore come after and dance with me
> For all a green willow is [my garla]nd

[1] *Music & Poetry in the Early Tudor Court*, London, 1961, p. 426. I am indebted to Mr. Stevens of Magdalene College, Cambridge, for lending me his photostats of the song fragments listed in his book. I am also indebted to Mr. Sydney Beck of the Music Division of the New York Public Library for providing me with the photograph from which the accompanying plate was made, for permission to reproduce and transcribe the photograph, and for various items of information.

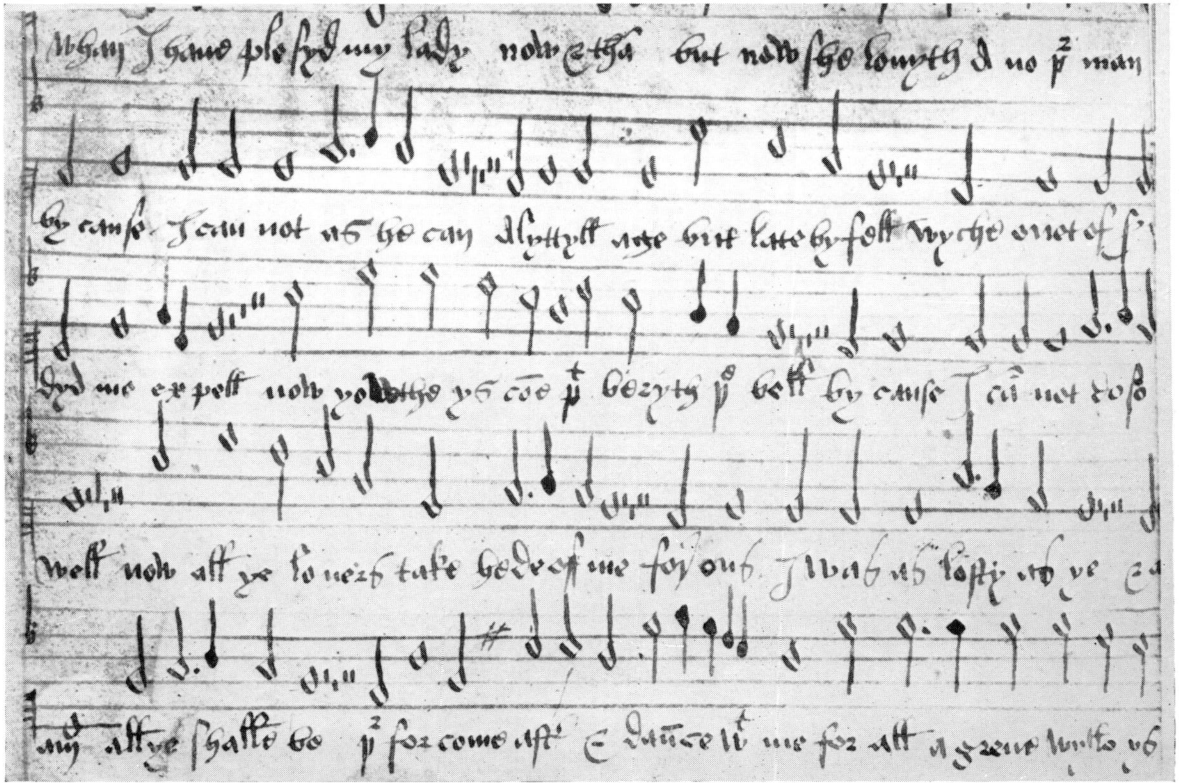

Facsimile 4. The Willow Song, Drexel Fragment.

Ex. 6.

WHEN I HAVE PLEASED MY LADY NOW AND THEN
BUT NOW SHE LOVETH ANOTHER MAN

Be - cause I can not as he can. A lit - tle age but late be-fell which out of s[er-vice] did me ex - pel, now youth is come that bea-reth the bell, be-cause I can not do so well. Now all ye lo - vers take heed of me, for once I was as lus - ty as ye, and a[s I]

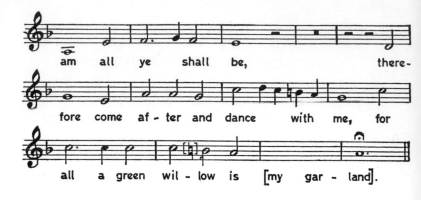

am   all   ye   shall   be,   there-

fore   come   af - ter   and   dance   with   me,   for

all   a   green   wil - low   is   [my   gar - land].

III

OPHELIA'S SONGS

AMONG the more perceptive critics of Elizabethan drama, Coleridge brought his poetic insight to bear on sundry aspects of Shakespeare's tragedies, including his use of music. Largely owing to his observations critics of the last century have become sensible of the unity that binds the separate strands of Shakespeare's art. In this respect the lyrics of Desdemona and Ophelia are masterpieces. Because they are integral parts of the plot in a dramatic sense and of the surrounding dialogue in a verbal sense, they show to great advantage Shakespeare's resourcefulness in his use of song. Coleridge contrasts his method with that of the eighteenth century librettist Metastasio who disposed his *scena* into neat divisions: 'at the end of the scene comes the *aria* as the exit speech of the character'.[1] Opposing this, Shakespeare's 'interfusion of the lyrical in and through the dramatic' is to be commended for its subtle concordance of plot and character development. Only Mozart can approach or equal Shakespeare's talent for integrating passages of dramatic action with lyrical utterances, in consequence of which his works soar above contemporary eighteenth-century Italian opera in the same way that Shakespeare's tragedies out-distance their Elizabethan counterparts.

Ophelia, like Desdemona, begins by singing 'old things'. Her anxieties and forebodings multiply as she proceeds from one

[1] *Coleridge's Shakespearean Criticism*, ed. T. M. Raysor, 2 vols., London, 1930, I.33 & 226.

53

lyrical fragment to the next. Coleridge perceived two strands 'floating on the surface of her pure imagination', 'the love for Hamlet and her filial love' and the fears for her chastity, 'not too delicately avowed by her father and her brother concerning the dangers to which her honour lay exposed'. Ophelia and Desdemona are pawns in tragedies where the main characters arc men of affairs: Hamlet and Claudius, Othello and Iago. The pathos of Desdemona's song resides in her incomprehension of Othello's lack of faith in one he professed to love and who loved him. In her extreme misery she sings an old song in the privacy of her bed-chamber with only her maid as an involuntary audience. The scene justifies Coleridge's observation that 'songs in Shakespeare are introduced as songs only, just as songs are in real life'. But Ophelia sings one ditty after another before the Court of Denmark. Such behaviour was strange, indeed, and contrary to all sense of propriety for an Elizabethan gentlewoman—or man, for that matter.

Thomas Morley's affable remarks implying that 'the art of singing was cultivated with equal zeal and discernment in every grade of social rank'[1] have long since been dismissed as without proper foundation. These comments are at variance with contemporary writings on etiquette which governed the behaviour of nobility and gentry. Castiglione's *Cortegiano* was first published in Venice in 1528, and its translation by Sir Thomas Hoby appeared in London in four editions between 1561 and 1603. The frequent and unsolicited performance of music by members of the aristocracy is vigorously condemned, with a reminder that, were such activity to be pursued, class distinctions between a nobleman and his music-performing servants would be broken down.

The like judgment I have in music: but I would not our courtier should do as many do, that as soon as they come to any place . . . without much entreating set out themselves to show as much as they know . . . so that a man would wean they came purposely to show themselves for that, and that it is their principal profession. There-

---

[1] *Plain and Easy Introduction to Practical Music* (1597), ed. R. A. Harman, London, 1952, p. 9; W. Woodfill, *Musicians in English Society*, Princeton, 1953, pp. 201 ff. and 223 ff.; J. A. Westrup, 'Domestic Music under the Stuarts', *Proceedings of the Royal Musical Association*, LXVIII (1941–42), 19–53.

fore, let our courtier come to show his music as a thing to pass the time withal, and as he were enforced to do it, and not in the presence of noble men, nor of any great multitude . . . Now as touching the time and season when these sorts of music are to be practiced: I believe at all times when a man is in familiar and loving company, having nothing else ado. (Book II.)

This was the code that permitted Desdemona to sing in the familiar and loving company of Emilia. But it is a symptom of Ophelia's derangement that she sings before an assembly of the Court without being encouraged to do so. To ensure the proper attitude in ladies as well as gentlemen, Castiglione offers this additional advice in the Third Book:

Therefore when she cometh to dance, or to show any kind of music, she ought to be brought to it with suffering herself somewhat to be prayed, and with a certain bashfulness . . .

None of the etiquette books condemns music altogether, but the restrictions imposed seem to fall under three main headings. First, a nobleman should not display his accomplishments in public (the performances of Nero are usually taken as signal tokens of his unfitness to be emperor); secondly, to indulge in such indoor recreations as the performance of music or other studious pursuits tends to corrode a warrior's virility; and, lastly, a gentleman must beware of excessive practice in any drawing-room accomplishment, a general proviso which often subsumes the earlier reservations.

Elyot's *Book of the Governor* which could boast ten editions between 1531 and 1600 dwells on the first recommendation:

But in this commendation of music I would not be thought to allure noble men to have so much delectation . . . that in playing and singing . . . they should put their whole study . . . as did the emperor Nero, which . . . in the presence of all the noble men and senators, would play on his harp and sing without ceasing . . . O, what misery was it to be subject to such a minstrel . . . King Philip when he heard that his son Alexander did sing sweetly and properly he rebuked him gently, saying 'But Alexander be ye not ashamed that ye can sing so well and cunningly?' Whereby he meant that the open profession of that craft was but of a base estimation.

Roger Ascham insisted with fine alliterativeness, that 'much music marreth men's manners' and, further, that too much music made man soft.[1] Nor did the opinions of Ascham and Elyot lapse with the death of Queen Elizabeth. In keeping with these conventions, songs in Elizabethan plays were generally performed by servants or 'minstrels' after the manner of Homer. The famous scene in the *Iliad* (IX.186), where Achilles is discovered singing to his harp as Agamemnon's embassy approach him and Patroclus, served as a shining example of the demoralizing effect of such behaviour on the great warrior and his soldiers. Stephen Gosson, a professed enemy of plays and music cited this incident as an example.[2]

Shakespeare's first deviation from the established custom occurs in *Much Ado About Nothing* (1598–99) with Balthasar's song, 'Sigh no more, Ladies'. The social prejudice is carefully acknowledged: Balthasar, a gentleman attendant on the Prince of Aragon, protests that his notes are not worth the noting, and his master entreats him, 'Why these are very crotchets that he speaks'. The role of Amiens in *As You Like It* (1599) seems to be an extension of the experiment. The dialogue lays emphasis on the etiquette to be observed by noblemen in contrast to the behaviour of professional musicians. The noble Amiens protests that his voice is ragged, that he sings only at the request of Jaques, but not to please himself, and is urged that 'tis no matter how it be in tune so it makes noise enough'. But the two singing boys who perform 'It was a lover and his lass' gloat over their professional status: they deliberately poke fun at the courteous disclaimers prescribed by Castiglione and Elyot and proceed to give the song:

Shall we clap into it roundly, without hawking or spitting or
saying we are hoarse, which are the only prologues to a bad voice?

Shakespeare's readiness to ignore the conventions which governed the use of music in tragedy is shown in *Troilus and Cressida* (1602), where he assigns a song to a major character of good social station. The noble Pandarus, like Balthasar and Amiens, is reluctant to behave in a manner that would identify him with a common minstrel. He protests to Paris that he is not full of harmony and to Helen that his art is rude, and he dallies

---

[1] *Toxophilus* (1545) and *Schoolmaster* (1570). Both books achieved three editions in the sixteenth century.
[2] *Shakespeare Society Publications*, 1841, II.39.

some seventy lines before obliging. Ophelia not only prattles incoherently but sings lyric upon lyric without restraint, and it is not surprising that such behaviour moves Claudius to ask, 'How long hath she been thus?' As she sings alternate snatches about love and death, the king continues:

> First, her father slain;
> Next your son gone . . .

The audience is made aware, through the concern of the spectators, of the hopeless misery which this double loss inflicts upon Ophelia. The profusion of her songs, unmatched in the canon of Shakespeare's tragedies, is but a symptom of her pathetic state. It is this condition upon which Shakespeare focusses attention, without giving any indication of courage or strength on the heroine's part. Ophelia's outpouring on Laertes' return mingles a requiem for her father's death with unrelated and incongruous burdens of popular songs. She begins

> They bore him barefac'd on the bier
> Hey non nony nony hey nony
> And on his grave rain'd many a tear
> Fare you well, my dove

The nonsense syllables of the second line, reminiscent of the famous lyric in *As You Like It*, relate more logically to lads, lasses and springtime than to lamentation and tears. The same may be said of the next prose line, 'You must sing "down-a-down" . . .', with its pastoral associations and its similarity to such popular burdens as 'with a hey down and a derry' or 'hey down-a-down'. Florio called it 'the burden of a country song, as we say hay doune a doune douna'.[1] But the sad remembrance of her bereavement returns as Ophelia dispenses rue and rosemary, fennel and columbine, only to shift abruptly with the singing of the third refrain:

> There's fennel for you, and columbines.
> . . . I would give you some violets, but they withered
> all when my father died. They say he made a good end.
> *For bonny sweet Robin is all my joy.*

[1] *World of Words . . . Dictionary in Italian and English*, London, 1598, s.v. 'Filibustacchina'; Nashe III.10; *Deloney*, ed. Mann, p. 305; Chappell 348–353, 391, 677; *Merry Wives of Windsor*, I.iv.44; *Two Noble Kinsmen*, III.v.140.

With this last snatch the true bent of Ophelia's mind is revealed, and Coleridge's opinion is sustained that Ophelia's fears 'concerning the dangers to which her honour lay exposed' were the cause of her insanity. These are, indeed, 'mad songs', not only because their performance in itself is improper but also because their subject matter is unbecoming to a maiden. 'Bonny Robin' songs deal with lovers, unfaithfulness and extra-marital affairs, as

> Love-passions must not be withstood
> Love everywhere will find us.
> I lived in field and town and so did he;
> I got me to the woods; Love followed me!
> Hey, jolly robin . . .[1]

Ophelia's Saint Valentine's Day lyric is in the same vein:

> Let in the maid, that out a maid
> Never departed more.

The incoherence, abrupt alternation between prose and verse, speaking and singing, and the lack of continuity and congruity serve the dramatist's purpose well. It would have been surprising had the company of the King's Men not repeated this successful formula. The role of the jailer's daughter in *Two Noble Kinsmen* is a case in point. Critics generally agree that the play was the joint product of 'Mr. John Fletcher and Mr. William Shakespeare', as the title-page of the quarto proclaims, although the precise distribution of the authorship remains in question. But there is no doubt that the character of the jailer's daughter, driven to madness by unrequited love and taking recourse in singing snatches of song, derives from the theatrical vogue initiated by the role of Ophelia. Her wooer reports, 'she sung much, but no sense . . . then she sung nothing but "Willow, willow, willow" '. (IV.i.66, 80). The jailer's daughter boasts furthermore that she can sing 'Bonny Robin' (IV.i.108), that hers is 'a fine song' and that she 'can sing twenty more'. Finally, her eagerness to 'call the maids and pay the minstrels; for I must lose my maidenhaid by cocklight' (IV.i.106, 112) completes the allusions to *Hamlet*. But in this much-discussed later play the background is of a different order. The heroine's fitness to sing does not come into question. A jailer's daughter would not be

---

[1] Robert Jones, *Fourth Book of Airs*, 1609, No. 19.

subject to the rigorous decorum weighing upon one who, the queen hoped, might be wedded to her son, the Prince of Denmark.

When Ophelia sings consecutive stanzas Shakespeare portrays her madness by a fickle change of thought which fluctuates between her concern for Hamlet's affection and her misery over her father's death.

> How should I your true love know
>   From another one?
> By his cockle hat and staff,
>   And his sandal shoon.
>
> He is dead and gone, lady,
>   He is dead and gone;
> At his head a grass-green turf,
>   At his heels a stone.
>
> White his shroud as the mountain snow
>   Larded all[1] with sweet flowers;
> Which bewept to the grave did not go
>   With true-love showers.

The first stanza is a variant of the old Walsingham song

> As ye came from the holy land
>   Of blessed[2] Walsingham,
> Met you not with my true love
>   By the way as you came?
>
> How should I know your true love,
>   That have met many a one
> As I came from the holy land,
>   That have come, that have gone?

Ophelia's second and third stanzas mourn her father's death, but the phrase 'true love' reappears in the final line of her lyric and again betrays her innermost anxiety.

[1] The word 'all' occurs in Q_2, but not in Q_1 or F_1.

[2] The word 'blessed' occurs in Percy's *Reliques* but not in the Percy Manuscript. Cf. Wheatley's edition of the *Reliques*, II.102 ff.; Kittredge SP 1084; Chappell 122; Wooldridge 69. The poem is sometimes attributed to Sir Walter Ralegh, cf. J. W. Hebel *et al.*, *Tudor Poetry and Prose*, New York, 1953, pp. 414 & 1253; *Poems of Ralegh*, ed. A. M. C. Latham, London, 1951, pp. 120–122.

The music for 'How should I your true love know' did not occur in print until the nineteenth century, although it has been fairly well established that the tune derived from Elizabethan sources. In his *Pictorial Edition of Shakespeare* (1839–42) Charles Knight invokes the reliability of the oral tradition and offers the following account:

> The music, still sung in the character of Ophelia, to the fragments of songs in the Fifth Scene of Act IV, is supposed to be the same, or nearly so, that was used in Shakespeare's time, and thence transmitted to us by tradition. When Drury-lane theatre was destroyed by fire, in 1812, the copy of these songs suffered the fate of the whole musical library; but Dr. Arnold noted down the airs from Mrs. Jordan's recollection of them . . .

Knight drew largely on the knowledge of Samuel Arnold (1740–1802), who shared the honours of conducting at the Drury Lane Theatre with the older Linley and Linley's son William (1771–1835).

William Chappell attempted, wherever possible, to provide tunes from proved Elizabethan sources for the section of his valuable book entitled 'Illustrating Shakespeare'. Where none were available he reprinted the traditional tunes as recorded by Arnold and Linley, relying as well on his wide knowledge of Elizabethan melodies and his sense of style. For Chappell was an 'antiquarian' in the finest sense of the word. He observed that Arnold, following Mrs. Jordan, recorded the tune of 'True love' in common time, whereas Linley, following the interpretation of another actress, gave the same melody in triple time. He also noted that in the *Beggar's Opera* of 1728 the tune occurs in common time to the words 'You'll think ere many days ensue'.[1] Since many of the airs in Gay's famous ballad opera are of considerable age, this correspondence supported Knight's claim of an oral tradition, and Chappell reprinted Arnold's tune. Later scholars have been more circumspect in their use of material from nineteenth century editions and, in fact, Wooldridge's revision of Chappell's standard work omits all tunes based on the Drury Lane tradition. Noble observed tersely of Ophelia

[1] Air 32. Unlike most other airs in the opera, it does not bear a name. Cf. the vocal score, ed. E. J. Dent, London, 1954, pp. xi and 45; also *Ninth Music Book*, ed. M. Hinrichsen, London, 1956, p. 45.

that 'unfortunately, we are unable to trace the originals of all her songs'. Naylor,[2] on the other hand, reprinted the music from Knight and Chappell, with the shrewd comment:

This is a striking example of corruption by stage use. It is a badly damaged version of 'Walsingham', given by Bull and Byrd in the *Fitzwilliam Virginal Book*. See also Dowland's setting of 'Walsingham' for lute . . .

Knight's *Pictorial Shakespeare* makes no pretense of documentation prior to the Drury Lane fire of 1812, but in the absence of material from Shakespeare's own epoch one cannot dismiss later practice altogether.

The following music examples reproduce: (a) Bull's Walsingham tune (Fitzwilliam No. 1) to which the text from the Percy manuscript has been fitted; (b) Air No. 32 from the *Beggar's Opera*; (c) the tune printed in the *Pictorial Shakespeare*.

Ex. 1(a)

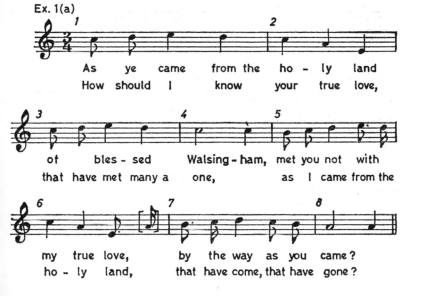

As ye came from the ho - ly land
How should I know your true love,

of bles - sed Walsing - ham, met you not with
that have met many a one, as I came from the

my true love, by the way as you came?
ho - ly land, that have come, that have gone?

2 Chappell 236, Noble 119, Naylor 190.

Ex. 1(b)

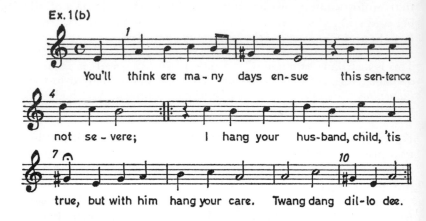

You'll think ere ma-ny days en-sue this sen-tence not se-vere; I hang your hus-band, child, 'tis true, but with him hang your care. Twang dang dil-lo dee.

Ex. 1(c)

How should I your true love know from a-no-ther one? By his cock-le hat and staff and his san-dal shoon.

The dialogue that ensues between Ophelia and Claudius leads unexpectedly to her rendition of 'Tomorrow is Saint Valentine's day'. In this lyric of four quatrains there is no evasion of the torment that possesses her soul.

> Tomorrow is Saint Valentine's day,
>   All in the morning betime,
> And I a maid at your window,
>   To be your Valentine.

> Then up he rose and donn'd his clothes
>   And dupp'd the chamber door,
> Let in the maid that out a maid
>   Never departed more.

By Gis and by Saint Charity,
   Alack and fie for shame!
Young men will do't if they come to't,
   By Cock, they are to blame.

Quoth she, Before you tumbled me,
   You promis'd me to wed.

(He answers:)[1]

So would I ha' done, by yonder sun,
   An thou had'st not come to my bed.

Lacking an authentic Elizabethan source for this lyric we turn again to the Drury Lane Theatre, whose tradition favoured a melody that was used in several ballad operas of the early eighteenth century, strikingly similar to an older tune called 'Soldier's Life'. This ballad, though not printed until 1651, was referred to by playwrights and ballad writers of Shakespeare's time.[2] The following music example gives two versions of the tune as they appear in Playford's *Dancing Master* of 1651 and the *Pictorial Shakespeare*:

Ex. 2(a)

The Folio describes Ophelia's first entrance in Act IV, scene v as 'distracted'. A more detailed stage direction appears in the first Quarto, 'Enter Ofelia playing on a lute, and her hair down,

---

[1] This rubric occurs only in Q_2, but not in Q_1 or F_1.

[2] W. Linley, *Shakespeare's Dramatic Songs*, 2 vols., 1815–16, II.50; C. Knight, *Pictorial Edition of Shakespeare*, 8 vols., 1839–42, Tragedies, I.152; Chappell 144, 227; Naylor 190. Playford 54 (p. 65 of original edition).

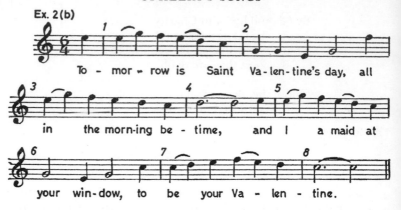

Ex. 2(b)

To-mor-row is Saint Va-len-tine's day, all in the morn-ing be-time, and I a maid at your win-dow, to be your Va-len-tine.

singing'. The lute may have been a useful stage accessory[1] in early performances at the Globe, and later casting difficulties may have caused its omission. But there can be no doubt that Ophelia sings, that she does so in great profusion, and that the playwright is at pains to emphasize this aspect of her behaviour. The first twenty lines of Act IV, scene v are largely devoted to a description of Ophelia's madness, before she enters 'distracted' and sings three quatrains of one song and four of another. She then exits with her famous four-fold 'good night' (line 74). The scene takes shape in a way that is significantly different from the musical scenes in other Elizabethan tragedies of the adult companies, for in *Hamlet* song, *per se*, becomes an integral part of the tragic scene. Ophelia does not content herself with one song, and the proportion of song to spoken lines is truly exceptional. In the succeeding fifty lines after Ophelia's re-entry at line 154, she quotes fragments of five further lyrics (listed in Appendix I).

The true Elizabethan heroine would regard with the utmost disdain such uncontrolled behaviour. Marlowe's Helen, Kyd's Bel Imperia, Webster's Vittoria, Fletcher's Evadne are proud creatures. They do not entertain with song, but they command their servants to do so. Nor do they arouse our sympathy in the way we might feel compassion for a small child or a bird. Gertrude may err, suffer and even squirm, but she remains a queen, and she most certainly would fall out of character were

[1] Cf. H. Granville Barker, *Prefaces to Shakespeare*, 5 vols., London, 1927–47, III.137: 'Modern Ophelias have an ineffective habit of drifting vaguely about the stage. A lute is at least an admirable anchor.'

she to sing. Later in the century Racine created Phèdre, who would be as incapable of song as the Oedipus of Greek antiquity. These personages of royal stature forged their own destinies. But it is precisely Ophelia's characterization as a helpless and powerless creature that makes her so poignantly pathetic, and this condition is emphasized by her singing. In both *Hamlet* and *Othello* the pathetic heroine complements the tragic hero. Ophelia betrays her nobility when she allows herself to be defeated by her fate and becomes its pawn; she is thus the object, not the subject of tragedy. The pathos of the weak is that they are wronged, whereas Lady Macbeth and Gertrude wrong themselves. (Cordelia's unwillingness to flatter is another matter.) But the designs of Hamlet, Polonius and Claudius are of a size that Ophelia can neither comprehend nor resist. In her distraught state she reverts to the songs a nurse may have taught her; not the aristocratic ayre, but crude songs of the common folk. There is an interesting eighteenth-century footnote to this situation, for Goethe went a step further and made his famous heroine (Ophelia's descendant in several ways) a poor girl of the lower classes. When Gretchen sings her song at the spinning wheel she does not quote the song of the poor, she is of the poor herself.

Shakespeare expounds the nature of Ophelia's performance in the course of Gertrude's account to Laertes at the end of Act IV: '. . . she chaunted snatches of old tunes // As one incapable of her own distress . . .'.[1] Then:

> . . . her garments heavy with their drink
> Pull'd the poor wretch from her melodious lay[2]
> To muddy death.

Here is another parallel with *Othello*, for Ophelia dies in song, like the swans of Apollo, 'who, when they perceive they must needs die, though they have been used to sing before, sing then more than ever, rejoicing that they are about to depart . . .'.[3]

[1] Scene vii, lines 178–179. Q_1 has 'sundry tunes', Q_2 'old laudes', F 'old tunes'.

[2] Q_2, 'melodious lay'; F_1, 'melodious buy'. 'Buy' would seem a misprint for 'lay'.

[3] Cf. *Oxford Dictionary of English Proverbs* and M. P. Tilley's *Proverbs in England in the 16th and 17th Centuries* for Plato, Aristotle, Cicero, Chaucer, Lydgate and Erasmus. In addition to *Hamlet* and *Othello* references occur in *King John*, *Merchant of Venice*, *Rape of Lucrece* and *Phoenix and the Turtle*.

The very pathos of the scene provoked some Jacobean satire. The jailer's daughter in *Two Noble Kinsmen* all but perishes singing madly; and there is an unmistakable reference to Ophelia in Beaumont and Fletcher's *Scornful Lady*:

> I will run mad first, and if that get not pity
> I'll drown myself, to a most dismal ditty.[1]

However dissimilar the circumstances of their respective fates, Desdemona and Ophelia die transfigured by the same poetic image of the willow tree.

> Your sister's drown'd, Laertes ...
> There's a willow grows aslant a brook
> . . .
> There on the pendent boughs her coronet weeds
> Clamb'ring to hang an envious sliver broke
> When down her weedy trophies and herself
> Fell in the weeping brook . . .[2]

In *Hamlet* and *Othello* the image transcends the traditional symbol of the forsaken paramour; it evokes death's doom and recalls

> ... in such a night
> Stood Dido with a willow in her hand ...
> (*Merchant of Venice* V.i.9)

Ophelia's songs may be inappropriate to her social station but they have an important function in helping to achieve the apotheosis of 'the poor wretch'.

---

[1] Fletcher I.272; according to Chambers the play was first produced between 1613 and 1617.
[2] ll.165-176. The first Quarto reads: Sitting upon a willow by a brook
    The envious sprig broke, into the brook she fell...

Appendix I

Songs Sung by Ophelia in Act IV, Scene 5

Lines

23 'How should I your true love know'
(Discussed above, p. 59.) Another use of the tune 'Walsingham' is discussed below, s.v. line 164.

48 'Tomorrow is Saint Valentine's Day'
(Discussed above, p. 62.)

164 'They bore him barefaced on the bier'
No Elizabethan music is known for this lyric. It is sung traditionally to an adaptation of the tune 'Walsingham' which serves also for 'How should I your true love know'. At other times, the tune for 'And will he not come again' (line 190) has been used, as shown in Music Example 3 (b), lower text.[1]

165 'Hey non nony nony hey nony'
This incongruous line obviously does not belong to lines 164 and 166, cf. page 57. It is omitted in Q_2, but occurs in F_1.

170 'You must sing down-a-down'
Another incongruous refrain line, discussed p. 57.

187 'For bonny sweet robin is all my joy'
Discussed pages 57–58. The music appears in Appendix II.

190 'And will he not come again'
Again, no Elizabethan music is known. The traditional tune is recorded in Knight's *Pictorial Shakespeare*, based on the Drury Lane tradition (Music Example 3b). The melody sounds like a variant, in the minor mode, of 'The Merry Milkmaids', printed in 1651 in Playford's *English Dancing Master* (Example 3a). Ophelia's second stanza seems to have been a target for satire, as can be seen from *Eastward Ho*, a play of joint authorship, produced in 1605.[2]

[1] Caulfield II.87; Naylor 191; Naylor SM 38.
[2] C. Knight, *Pictorial Edition of Shakespeare*, 1839–42, Tragedies, I.153; Playford 29; Naylor 191; Jonson IV.559 and IX.641 and IX.661.

Hamlet
And will he not come again?
And will he not come again?
  No, no, he is dead,
  Go to thy death-bed,
He never will come again.

His beard as white as snow,
All flaxen was his poll,
  He is gone, he is gone,
  And we cast away moan,
Gramercy on his soul![1]

Eastward Ho
His head as white as milk,
All flaxen was his hair:
  But now he is dead,
  and laid in his bed,
And never will come again.

Ex. 3 (a)

Appendix II

The music for 'Bonny sweet Robin' occurs in thirty contemporary sources, six of which were printed between 1597 and 1621, and the remainder are in manuscript. Moreover, the tune was used for a variety of other lyrics between 1594 and 1690 (sources 37, 31, 36). There also survive several Scottish variants of text and tune, printed

[1] Line 195: Q2: His beard was as white as snow
Line 199: Q2: God-a-mercy on his soul

Ex. 3(b)

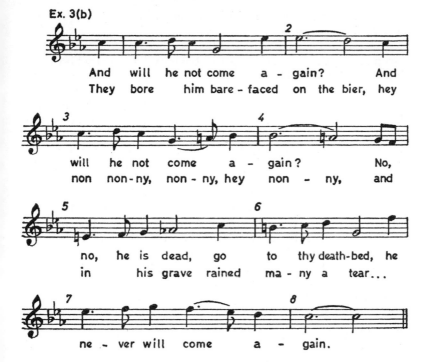

And will he not come a - gain? And
They bore him bare - faced on the bier, hey

will he not come a - gain? No,
non non - ny, non - ny, hey non - ny, and

no, he is dead, go to thy death-bed, he
in his grave rained ma - ny a tear...

ne - ver will come a - gain.

in the eighteenth century (sources 33, 34). In Shakespeare's age the popularity of this simple ditty excelled by far that of 'Greensleeves' which is so much better known today as an example of Elizabethan song. To account for this widespread favour by a single reason would be difficult. While the music itself is both attractive and easily adapted to different lyrics, the subject matter of 'Robin' songs probably played its part too. 'Robin' was a term of endearment, whether it referred to a popular outlaw or to a favourite bird. Needless to say, terms of endearment were frequently the occasion of punning and double-entendre, and in this connection the 'wake-robin' or 'long purple' flower was both known to Shakespeare and relevant to Ophelia's situation (source 38).

The majority of the musical sources are scored for lute, though some are for cittern (source 2), some for bandora (source 12), some for viol (sources 14, 18), others for a consort of instruments (sources 6, 26). The instrument most frequently used for these transcriptions, apart from the lute, was the virginals (sources 16, 17, 27).

Melodically the pieces are largely variants of the same tune. The simple version of Example 5 (source 20) is the paradigm for the most elaborate arrangements, of which the composition by John Dowland[1] is justly famous (sources 11, 24, 25).

There is in the tune a nice difference between the first and the second half (bars 1–8 against 9–16). Each half achieves coherence by internal repetition. The correspondence between bars 1–4 and 5–8 is obvious. In the second half the melodic similarity between bars 11–12 and 13–14 is more subtle but not less effective. Two melodies introduce a chromatic variation (sources 2 and 28) in that the tune descends a semitone at bars 4 and 8, namely d–c sharp instead of a fourth, d–a (cf. upper half of Example 6). This gives the piece a characteristic Elizabethan flavour. One version (source 5) is related more by harmony than by melody; it is reprinted in Example 6, lower half. To facilitate comparison, these two pieces (sources 28 and 5) have been printed below each other in Example 6. (They also provide two attractive instrumental numbers for a Shakespearean production using Elizabethan music.) The version preserved in sources 12, 19, 30 and 3 is not related: the number of notes (and therefore syllables) does not fit Ophelia's ditty. All thirty pieces are instrumental and, therefore, wordless.[2]

Since Ophelia 'chaunted snatches' her line can be accommodated either by the first or the last strain of the complete melody given in Example 5. It is interesting that a comparatively rare interval in vocal music, the leap of an ascending seventh (bars 2–3 and 12–13) occurs in each of these strains.

Ex. 4.

For bon - ny sweet Ro - bin is all my joy

For bon - ny sweet Ro - bin is all my joy

---

[1] Dowland's variations on 'Robin' have been performed by Julian Bream on the Third Programme of the BBC. The music is to be published in the forthcoming edition of the 'Lute Works of Dowland', edited by Mrs. Diana Poulton. I am indebted to Mrs. Poulton for many helpful suggestions.

[2] The one exception is source 3 which is not related, cf. Wooldridge I.273. Another song, similarly unrelated, is 'A robin, gentle robin' in British Museum, Add. MS 31922, cf. Naylor SM 25. It provides music for Thomas Wyatt's poem used in *Twelfth Night*, IV.ii.78–85, but not for Ophelia's fragment.

The very character of the tune, and the dramatic exigencies of Ophelia's mad scene demand that the song of 'Robin' be sung. But by an accident of transmission, the extant music books provide us with tunes but not with a text. This is contrary to the usual situation which confronts the student of these works. The late E. W. Naylor supplied some lines of his own[1] to make up the deficiency. But a verse in Robert Jones's *Fourth Book of Airs* of 1609, of which one stanza was quoted earlier in this chapter, has the advantage of being contemporary with Shakespeare's play. Its refrain of four lines[2] echoes several different titles by which the same tune is designated in various music books: 'Jolly Robin', 'Robin Hood', 'Follow me to the greenwood'.[3] But beyond this Jones's music also imitates some of the prominent musical phrases from Example 4, notably bars 1 and 13:

> Hey jolly robin, Ho jolly robin
> Hey jolly Robin Hood,
> Love finds out me as well as thee,
> To follow me, follow me to the greenwood.

It is this text that has been fitted to Example 5. Jones's own music is given in Example 7.

The lute music of source 20 (Dublin, Trinity College) is reproduced in Example 5, and the following emendations have been made, after comparison with other sources:

Bar 5, melody: auxiliary note 'g' added;
Bar 7, bass: original has 'f', emended to 'c–b flat';
Bar 13, melody: passing notes 'b flat' and 'g' added;
Bar 15, melody: passing note 'f' added.

At bars 3 and 7 the notes 'e' and 'd' have been added in square brackets to make the chords less bare for performance on a modern piano.

The lute music of source 28 (London, British Museum) is reproduced in Example 6, upper half. The only emendation necessary was to halve the time values of the first two melody notes in bar 15. The lower half of Example 6 gives the variant of source 5 (Robinson's *Schoole of Musicke*). Finally, Example 7 gives the refrain from the lute song 'In Sherwood lived stout Robin Hood' from Jones's *Fourth Book of Airs*. Example 5 is in the original key of d minor; Examples 6 and 7 have been transposed to the key of D.

[1] Naylor SM 39.
[2] *English School of Lutenist Song Writers*, ed. E. H. Fellowes, 2nd Series, 16 vols., London, 1920–32, XIV.55–57; original edition: sig. L.i.v.
[3] The bewildering variety of titles for this song, ranging from a simple 'Robin' to 'Robin Hood is to the Greenwood gone' has no further significance than that it represents different versions of the same music.

Ex. 5 (Dublin, 'Ballet Book', p. 113)—original key;

Ex. 6, upper half (London, Add. MS 31392, f. 25)—transposed from c minor to d minor;

Ex. 6, lower half (Robinson, *Schoole of Musicke*, sig. M.ii)—transposed from c minor to d minor;

Ex. 7 (Jones, *Fourth Book of Airs*, No. 19)—transposed from G Major to D Major.

Ex. 5.

Hey jol-ly Ro - bin, ho jol-ly Ro-bin,

hey jol-ly Ro - bin, Ro - bin Hood,

love finds out me as well as thee, to

fol - low my sweet Ro - bin to the green wood.

Ex. 6.

M S. Add. 31392

Robinson

Ex. 7.

PRINTED SOURCES

(1) Georg L. Fuhrmann, *Testudo gallo-germanica*, Nürnberg,
  1615   sig. K.iii.v.
  title: Galliarda J[ohn] D[owland]
(2) Anthony Holborne, *Cittharn Schoole*, London, 1597   sig. D.ii.r.
  title: Bonny sweet Robin
(3) Thomas Ravenscroft, *Pammelia*, London, 1609   sig. F.i.v.
  title: A Round of three Country Dances in One
  text of tenor: Robin Hood, Robin Hood, said little John
(4) Thomas Robinson, *Schoole of Musicke*, London, 1603   sig. I.ii.v.
  title: Robin is to the greenwood gone
(5) Thomas Robinson, *Schoole of Musicke*, London, 1603   sig. M.ii.r.
  title: Bonny sweet boy
(6) Thomas Simpson, *Taffelconsort*, Hamburg, 1621   No. xxix.
  title: none
  reprinted: *Jacobean Consort Music*, edd. R. T. Dart &
  W. Coates, London, 1955, pp. 195–198.

MANUSCRIPT SOURCES

(7)	Cambr. Un. Libr.	Dd.2.11.		f. 53.r.
	title: Robin		anon.	
(8)	Cambr. Un. Libr.	Dd.2.11.		f. 66.r.
	title: Robin		composed by Dowland	
(9)	Cambr. Un. Libr.	Dd.2.11.		f. 66.r.
	title: Bonny sweet boy		anon.	
(10)	Cambr. Un. Libr.	Dd.3.18.		f. 11.r.
	title: Robin is to the greenwood gone	anon.	
(11)	Cambr. Un. Libr.	Dd.9.33.		f. 29.v, 30.
	title: Robin		composed by Dowland	
(12)	Cambr. Un. Libr.	Dd.9.33.		f. 81.v.
	title: Robin Hood		anon.	
(13)	Cambr. Un. Libr.	Dd.9.33.		f. 82.r.
	title: Bonny sweet boy		anon.	
(14)	Cambr. Un. Libr.	Nn.6.36.		f. 19.v, 20.
	title: Robin		anon.	
(15)	Cambr. Un. Libr.	Add. 3056.		f. 32.v.
	title: Robin Galliard		anon.	
(16)	Cambr. Fitzw. Mus.	'Fitzwilliam Book'	reprinted: Fitzwilliam
	title: Robin		composed by J. Munday	No. 15.
(17)	Cambr. Fitzw. Mus.	'Fitzwilliam Book'	reprinted: Fitzwilliam
	title: Bonny sweet Robin		composed by G. Farnaby	No. 128.

APPENDIX

(18)	Dublin, Trinity College	'Ballet Book' D.1.21.	p. 27.
	title: Bonny sweet Robin	anon.	
(19)	Dublin, Trinity College	'Ballet Book' D.1.21.	p. 104.
	title: none	anon.	
(20)	Dublin, Trinity College	'Ballet Book' D.1.21.	p. 113.
	title: Robin Hood is to the greenwood gone		
		anon.	
(21)	Glasgow Un. Libr.	'Euing Book' R.d.43.	f. 31.r.
	title: none	anon.	
(22)	Glasgow Un. Libr.	'Euing Book' R.d.43.	f. 46.v, 47.
	title: Robin Hood	composed by Ascue	
(23)	Kassel, Landesbibliothek, 4°, Mus. 1081.		f. 3.v.
	title: Schön wär ich gern	anon.	
(24)	London, Brit. Mus.	'Pickering Book' Eg.2046.	f. 22.v.
	title: Sweet Robin	anon.	
(25)	London, Brit. Mus.	'Pickering Book' Eg.2046.	f. 35.r.
	title: Sweet Robin	anon.	
(26)	London, Brit. Mus.	Add. 17786.	p. 15.r.
	title: My Robin is to the, etc.	anon.	
(27)	London, Brit. Mus.	Add. 23623.	f. 13.v.
	title: Bonn well Robin	composed by J. Bull	
(28)	London, Brit. Mus.	Add. 31392.	f. 25.r.
	title: Jolly Robin	anon.	
(29)	Washington, Folger Libr.	'Dowland Book', 1610.1	f. 16.v.
	title: Robin is to the greenwood gone	anon.	
(30)	Washington, Folger Libr.	V.a.159 (olim 448.16)	f. 5.r.
	title: Robin Hood	anon.	

OTHER REFERENCES

(31) R. Johnson, *Golden Garland of Princely Pleasures*, 3rd edn., London, 1620, sig. D.8.v.: 'Fair Angel of England, thy beauty so bright', rubric: to the tune of Bonny sweet Robin [Pollard STC, 14674; reprinted 1690: Wing STC, J 804A].

(32) R. Johnson, *Crown Garland of Golden Roses* [3rd edn.], London, 1659, sig. F.5.v.: 'Fair Angel of England, thy beauty most bright', rubric: to the tune of Bonny sweet Robin [Wing STC, J 791; reprinted 1662: Wing STC, J 792; the poem does not occur in the 1612 or 1631 edns. of the *Crown Garland*, Pollard STC, 14672, 14673].

(33) A. Stuart, *Music for the Tea Table Miscellany*, Edinburgh, 1725, p. 40, 'There Nancy's to the greenwood gane'.

(34) Robert Bremner, *Thirty Scots Songs, for a Voice and Harpsichord*, 2 vols., Edinburgh, 1757, I.17, 'There Nancy's to the greenwood gane'.

(35) *Roxburghe Ballads*, edd. J. W. Ebsworth and W. Chappell, 9 vols., London, 1871–99, I.181: 'Fair Angel of England, thy beauty most bright', rubric: to the tune of Bonny sweet Robin.

(36) Roxburghe Ballads, VII.785, No. 9: 'Now farewell, good Christmas', rubric: tune of Bonny sweet Robin.

(37) H. E. Rollins, *Analytical Index to the Ballad-Entries . . . in the Stationers . . .*, Chapel Hill (N.C.), 1924, p. 58 (No. 617), s.v. 'April 26, 1594': 'Doleful adieu to the last Earl of Derby', rubric: to the tune of Bonny sweet Robin.

(38) H. Morris, 'Ophelia's "Bonny sweet Robin"', *Publications of the Modern Language Association*, LXXIII (1958), 601–603.

(39) E. S. LeComte, 'Ophelia's "Bonny Sweet Robin"', *Publications of the Modern Language Assn.*, LXXV (1960), 480.

IV

MAGIC SONGS

In his mature plays Shakespeare uses song in two forms: songs to express the character of the singer or the dramatic situation; and songs to influence the disposition, that is, magic songs. Magic songs were usually allotted to boy singers.

We may assume, according to Noble, that over a period of three years, from 1601 to 1604, Shakespeare's company had a leading boy capable of singing and playing the lute[1] which would explain the abundant use of song in the roles of Desdemona and Ophelia. For his male roles Shakespeare favoured adult actors for character songs and boys (in minor roles) for magic songs. Two important exceptions to this general rule are the lyrics of Desdemona and Ophelia, which are, in fact, character songs. The playwright had no choice in the casting of his heroines, however, since Elizabethan practice required that feminine roles be acted by boys.

The songs of the elves and fairies in *Midsummer Night's Dream* and *Merry Wives of Windsor* upheld the tradition that magic events were associated with music. When a court performance or other circumstance made necessary a large cast Shakespeare was quick to take advantage of a chorus of boys' voices. There is a tradition, first recorded in 1702, that the *Merry Wives of Windsor* was written by order of Queen Elizabeth. This may explain the elaborate, masque-like splendour of the closing scene with its spectacle and musical trappings. Likewise, the profusion

---

[1] Noble 80.

of masque-like scenes, with music, in the *Tempest* is favourable to the hypothesis that the play was presented at Court in honour of the wedding festivities of Princess Elizabeth. The present text probably derives from that performance of 1612–13. Ariel's 'Come unto these yellow sands' is both a boys' song and a magic song *par excellence*. It is a veritable pied piper's lay, and the spell-bound Ferdinand must follow it into Prospero's realm, meditating as he goes that its power was such that

> This music crept by me upon the waters
> Allaying both their fury, and my passion.

The power of music is likewise invoked in the *Midsummer Night's Dream* when the elves charm Titania with their lullaby, and at the conclusion of the *Merry Wives of Windsor*, when the fairies surround Falstaff to pinch him and disillusion him and to create the merry confusion in which Fenton gains Ann Page. The song which chastens Falstaff, 'Fie on sinful fantasy' was probably modelled on a similar pinching song in Lyly's *Endymion*. But it is worthy of notice that the Folio text of 1623 contains the text of the song, in accordance with Shakespeare's habit; whilst the first edition of *Endymion* merely has a stage direction that 'the fairies dance and with a song pinch him'.[1]

It may be argued that these three comedies, with their courtly splendour and wealth of song, are not typical of Shakespeare; but magic songs also occur in the plays where music is infrequent. There is an early example in *Julius Caesar* (1599) whereby a clear contrast is established between Cassius, with his lean and hungry look, and gentle Brutus, the noblest Roman of them all. Cassius 'loves no plays' and 'hears no music', and Shakespeare's portrayal recalls Lorenzo's warning in the *Merchant of Venice* against the man that is 'not mov'd with concord of sweet sounds, . . . Let no such man be trusted'. But the gentleness of Brutus, manifest in his kindness to Portia and Lucius, is sustained by his great fondness for music. Brutus's plea

> Canst thou hold up thy heavy eyes awhile,
> And touch thy instrument a strain or two?

[1] Quarto of 1591, sig. G.3.r.; Lyly, *Works*, ed. R. W. Bond, 3 vols., 1902, III.59. In 1632, twenty-six years after Lyly's death, a song was inserted (cf. Chapter I, p. 22). There is no 'good' quarto of *Merry Wives of Windsor*, and the Folio text of 1623 is generally considered a reliable source.

ushers in a scene of dramatic importance and poignancy. The stage direction reads 'Music and a Song', but the text of the song is unhappily lacking. Several references to Lucius and his lute (lines 256 to 292), whether concrete or allegorical, underscore the 'mood-music'. We are told that the tune is sleepy and Lucius plays to the god of slumber. On being awakened, his startled

> The strings, my lord, are false

is a prophetic utterance. Little does the boy apprehend the profound irony of his remark, as he speaks of the physical properties of music. For whereas Brutus hopes to be quieted and consoled Lucius's lute unwittingly becomes the prelude to the ghostly apparition which is truly

> Thy evil spirit, Brutus.

In this respect, Lucius's song may be compared to the mysterious strains that presage the fall of Antony in the later tragedy (IV.iii).

A song from *Henry VIII*, 'Orpheus with his lute made trees' is often employed in modern performances to serve as Lucius's strain. There are settings by Matthew Locke and Thomas Arne, but their later musical style is understandably out of step with Shakespeare's verse. Dowland's 'Weep you no more sad fountains' is sympathetic to the scene as a whole and its contemporaneous flavour would seem more suitable.[1]

There is a companion piece to Lucius's song, both in function and genre, in another Roman tragedy based on Plutarch, *Antony and Cleopatra*. 'Come thou monarch of the vine' (II.vii. 118) is also the only lyric in the drama and Enobarbus's command (line 115), 'the boy shall sing', indicates the singer's minor role in the play. These boys' voices are the means of invoking the traditional power of music to assist the development of the plot. They do not express the character of the singer. Caesar asserts the effectiveness of the old magic:

> . . . we have burnt our cheeks. Strong Enobarb
> Is weaker than the wine, and mine own tongue
> Splits what it speaks; the wild disguise hath almost
> Antick'd us all.

[1] H. Granville-Barker, *Prefaces to Shakespeare*, 5 vols., 1927–47, I.130; Noble 16.

The term 'antick'd' divulges the fact that several magic forces, beside song, are exercising their enchantment on the three rulers of the world. The entire banquet scene is in the nature of a masque with its attendant antics—a Bacchanalian dance with clasped hands, to the accompaniment of instrumental music; the boy's singing and, finally, the triumvirs joining in the 'holding'. (A holding–or burden–is a refrain.) It is worth noting that the cautious Caesar does not participate in the conversation which precedes the song and that he begs off after the singing. Like Cassius of the lean and hungry look he does not seem to be very fond of music and revels, though he is not averse to participating when they can further his plans.

> *Eno.* [to Antony]   Ha, my brave emperor,
> Shall we dance now the Egyptian Bacchanals,
> And celebrate our drink?
> *Pom.*   Let's ha't, good soldier.
> Come, let's all take hands,
> Till that the conquering wine hath steep'd our sense
> In soft and delicate Lethe.
> *Eno.*   All take hands,
> Make battery to our ears with the loud music:
> The while I'll place you, then the boy shall sing.
> The holding every man shall bear as loud
> As his strong sides can volley.

> [Music plays. Enobarbus places them hand in hand]

> [The Song]

> Come thou monarch of the vine,
> Plumpy Bacchus with pink eyne!
> In thy fats [i.e. vats] our cares be drown'd,
> With thy grapes our hairs be crown'd.
>   Cup us till the world go round,
>   Cup us till the world go round.

> *Caes.* What would you more? Pompey good night. Good brother,
> Let me request you off: our graver business,
> Frowns at this levity. Gentle lords, let's part,
> You see we have burnt our cheeks . . .

The singing, dancing, drinking and the loud music of 'these drums! these trumpets, flutes!' (line 136) combine to produce the magic. Pompey observes earlier in the scene (line 101) 'This is not yet an Alexandrian feast', to which Antony replies 'it ripens towards it'.

Song as an agent to influence the disposition of men is only one of the manifestations of the ancient Greek 'ethos' of music. The Greek word has challenged translators for centuries and has never been successfully put into the vernacular. Its meaning clearly includes 'custom, habit, and disposition' and in the ethical concept of music it is the soul, the 'humour' of man that becomes enthralled. Hence Shakespeare's aphorism that 'music oft hath such a charm to make bad good, and good provoke to harm'. The Greek theory of Ethos is only a particular instance of a universal human attitude that may be discerned in primitive magic as well as in some of the therapeutic notions of modern times. But it is clear that the articulation of this attitude in ancient Greek philosophy was of considerable importance to the poets, playwrights and aestheticians of the sixteenth century. The transmission of this concept from Athens to Alexandria, to Rome and thence to the Christian world at large, succeeded in maintaining, with undiminished vigour, the Greek concept from Plato's *Republic* to Milton's *Paradise Lost*. In view of its unique connotations, clarity can be served best by retaining the original Greek term.[1]

In the Middle Ages writings on the Ethos of music were largely influenced by Boethius, whereas in the period of the Renaissance the main sources, besides Cicero, were Plutarch and the Neo-Platonic writers. The gradual decrease of classical learning and a growing antipathy to notions of magic tended in time to stifle certain ideas that had been common property among schoolboys in Elizabethan times. But, for the poets, the ancient philosophy has remained ageless and has been honoured since Shakespeare's time by Herder and Goethe, Coleridge and Shelley, Yeats and Eliot.

As Shakespeare shaped the story of *Antony and Cleopatra* he relied on certain ancient formulations: that Dorian music inspired men to be disciplined, martial and courageous and in doing so strengthened church and state; while Lydian music had the demoralizing effect of making a man effeminate and

[1] H. Abert, *Die Lehre vom Ethos in der griechischen Musik*, Leipzig, 1899; O. Gombosi, *Tonarten und Stimmungen der antiken Musik*, Copenhagen, 1939.

unfit for political and military discipline. In spite of misconceptions concerning the ancient Greek modes and scales the Elizabethans were sensitive enough to distinguish between music that was sumptuous or ascetic, sensual or disciplined, abandoned or controlled. Nietzsche's antithesis of Apollonian and Dionysian art would have been understood by the Elizabethans because of their familiarity with the legends of Apollo and Dionysos and their respective worshippers. Apart from its employment in connection with instrumental music the Ethos of music could as well be invoked in song. In the Christian era, as in Plato's time, the resultant censorship led to a general distrust of this potent art, which received such epithets as 'lascivious', 'effeminate', 'too artful', 'popish' and a variety of other labels, according to the prejudices of the censor. The Roman Catholic church took great pains in the sixteenth century to discuss the dangers of introducing secular and vulgar tunes into the liturgy, and the Council of Trent exercised its influence on the future course of church music. But the Calvinist opposition to pomp and circumstance affected secular music as well, primarily in Holland and Scotland, though also in England and New England. In the final analysis, it was felt that music in general nourished the dangers to which a soft society was prone. Spenser is explicit in his description of this state of affairs in his allegorical poem, the *Faerie Queene*. On Phedria's island (Second Book) there is

> No bird but did her shrill notes sweetly sing,
> No song but did contain a lovely ditt,
> Trees, branches, birds, and songs were framèd fit
> For to allure frail mind to careless ease.

When the Elizabethan poet moralizes on the temptations that assail a 'frail mind' he rarely fails to emphasize the threat to military pursuits. A second temptress, Acrasia, was equally cunning in weakening the manly resolutions of valiant knights through a style of living in which song is prominent:

> ... more sweet than any bird on bough
> Would oftentimes among them bear a part
> And strive to pass (as she could well enough)
> Their native music by her skillful art:
> So did she all that might his constant heart
> Withdraw from thought of war-like enterprise.

But Spenser's Guyon, unlike Antony, resists temptation, though not before he is witness to a most seductive consort:

> For all that pleasing is to living ear,
> Was there consorted in one harmony . . .
> . . . The joyous birds, shrouded in cheerful shade,
> Their notes unto the voice attempered sweet;
> Th'angelical soft trembling voices made
> To th'instruments divine respondence meet;
> The silver sounding instruments did meet
> With the base murmur of the water's fall . . .

Spenser, the epic poet, merely *describes* the singing of

> lascivious boys,
> That ever mixed their song with light licentious toys.

But Shakespeare and Fletcher felt free to present the actual singing on the stage. The fastidious Ben Jonson was loath to introduce actual song into the genre of tragedy but he, too, aired the antithesis between valiant courtiers and lascivious boys in his *Catiline*, castigating those who never

> In riding or in using well their arms,
> Watching or other military labour,
> Did exercise their youth; but learned to love,
> Drink, dance, and sing, make feasts . . .

With characteristic learning Jonson derives his description of the Ethos theory from an ancient source: 'to dance and sing' is a translation of the dangers of 'cantare et saltare'.[1]

Once a ruler yielded his mind to pleasure, his downfall was certain. Caesar and Antony or Valentinian III and Maximus were ostensibly concerned with Roman affairs but the parable was clear to the audience who were mindful of Elizabeth and Essex, and James I and his minions. In Beaumont and Fletcher's *Valentinian* the new emperor, Maximus, meets his death in the course of a lavish banquet during which a boy sings to the god of wine, who frees from care:

> God Lyaeus ever young,
> Ever honoured, ever sung,
> Stained with blood of lusty grapes . . .[2]

[1] Jonson V.528; also X.151, where the Latin reference is given.
[2] Set to music by John Wilson, *Cheerful Ayres*, 1659, cantus, p. 130.

Loud instrumental music and dancing is added to the boy's song, as in the case of 'Come thou monarch of the vine'. But the human voice, as the myth of Orpheus reminds us, is ever the crowning power in the Ethos of music, and the Elizabethans usually joined song to instrumental music and other allurements to gain their effects.

The text of the song from *Antony and Cleopatra* contains an appeal to a deity and is couched in lines of four stresses. Its first word, 'Come', suggests the popular hymn for Whit Sunday:

Hrabanus Maurus, ninth century

> Veni Creator Spiritus,
> Mentes tuorum visita:
> Imple superna gratia
> Quae tu creasti pectora.

The English version of the ever-popular liturgical poem figures prominently in the 'Books of Psalms' of the sixteenth and seventeenth centuries. It is in iambic meter:

Sternhold-Hopkins *Psalter*, London: Day, 1562

> Come holy ghost, eternal God,
> Proceeding from above,
> Both from the father and the son,
> The God of peace and love.

But to a poet writing in the vernacular, in a system of accentual rather than quantitative metrics, the opening word 'Veni' suggests a trochaic rhythm,[1] as evidenced by the lyrics of Dowland, Heywood, Shakespeare and Campion:

Dowland, *Second Book of Ayres*, 1600

> Come, ye heavy states of night,
> Do my father's spirit right.
> Soundings baleful let me borrow
> Burthening my song with sorrow.

Heywood, *Rape of Lucrece*, 1603–08

> O thou Delphian God, inspire
> Thy priests, and with celestial fire
> Shot from thy beams crown our desire,
> That we may follow,

---

[1] It is interesting that in the twentieth century the composer Gustav Mahler began in trochaic scansion when he set the Latin hymn to music.

Shakespeare, *ca.* 1606–07

> Come thou monarch of the vine,
> Plumpy Bacchus, with pink eyne!
> In thy fats our cares be drowned,
> With thy grapes our hairs be crowned.

Campion, *Third Book of Ayres, ca.* 1617

> Come, o come, my life's delight,
> Let me not in languor pine,
> Love loves no delay; thy sight
> The more enjoyed the more divine.

The transmutation of a hymn addressed to the holy spirit into a poem supplicating Bacchus was only one instance of the many wandering melodies (contrafacta) that were characteristic of the interplay between sacred and secular Renaissance poetry.

The lyric by Thomas Heywood is the most relevant since it occurs in a Roman tragedy. Heywood's priest uses song to implore Apollo to lend his guidance through the oracle. In the ethical concept this prayer elevates and its derivation from a sacred hymn of the Christian church is all the more appropriate. Heywood was both too voluble and too undiscriminating, however, to restrict his use of song in a manner befitting the Elizabethan concept of tragedy. The title page of the *Rape of Lucrece* informs us that the printed copy is complete 'with the several songs in their apt places by Valerius, the merry lord among the Roman peers'. But the twenty songs Valerius sings are so slightly relevant to the plot that they seem more in the nature of a comic interlude. If Shakespeare was less circumspect than Jonson in his use of music, he was considerably more fastidious than Heywood, and his feeling for dramatic integrity would not permit him to include divertissements such as these for the sake of the groundlings.

Although no contemporary melody survives for 'Come thou monarch of the vine' there is no lack of music to fit Shakespeare's stanza. Three of the lyrics noted above have contemporary musical settings, and apart from these there is the lyric, with musical accompaniment, by John Wilson (born 1595), 'Come thou father of the spring'. Although slightly later than Shakespeare, this melody is musically both apposite and attractive.

The tragedy of *Macbeth*, written in 1605/06, contains no songs which can fairly be attributed to Shakespeare. The lyrics are unusually dreary, and the dramatic justification of the two Hecate songs as transmitted in the Folio is so slight as to be almost non-existent. On the other hand, there is no denying that three witches, played by boys and performing their songs on the heath to cast their spell over Macbeth, would provide excellent illustrations of the category of magic song. One is inclined to feel, however, that the absence of music at the appearance of Hamlet's Ghost or Macbeth's witches is symptomatic of Shakespeare's tragic approach. In his discrimination he stands halfway between the austerity of his Senecan predecessors and the musical opulence of his Jacobean followers.

There is fairly general agreement that 'Come away, come away, Hecate' and 'Black spirits' were interpolations from Middleton's *Witch*. In all probability the witches' dance in IV.i is a similar interpolation from Jonson's *Masque of Queens*. This leaves *Macbeth* as the only tragedy or tragi-comedy written between 1600 and 1606 to contain neither an adult song nor a boys' song. In view of the lyrics in *King Lear* and *Othello* one can scarcely attribute this lack to casting difficulties, and it seems a fair assumption that Shakespeare wished the stark and inevitable unfolding of his Scottish tragedy to proceed uninterrupted by song.

The dialogue which follows the boy's song in *Measure for Measure* shows that this song was intended to invoke the Ethos of music. Mariana confesses that the tune had assuaged her sorrow, had 'pleased my woe'; and the Duke, given to didactic statements, replies

> 'Tis good; though music oft hath such a charm
> To make bad good, and good provoke to harm.

Mariana's purpose is 'to make bad good' as the boy's song of deserted love consoles her. In the same way, Brutus, in his sorrow, seeks comfort from the lute song of Lucius. But to give oneself up to this melancholy stanza with its emphasis on the doleful phrase 'seal'd in vain' is also an act of self-indulgence and therefore likely to provoke good to harm. Seemingly Mariana realizes this. When the Duke enters the garden she prevents the boy from continuing, is impatient to be relieved of his embarrassing presence, and apologizes for having been discovered 'so musical', that is, for having had recourse to the palliative of a melancholy song. True, her discontent is 'brawling'—a poignant epithet after one of Shakespeare's loveliest songs. But like the biblical Saul, Mariana's real need is not so much for music to relieve her dejected spirit as for advice based on the law of God, which the Duke disguised as the 'man of comfort' offers her:

> [Enter Mariana, and Boy singing]

> Take, o take those lips away,
>   that so sweetly were forsworn,
> And those eyes: the break of day,
>   lights that do mislead the morn;
> But my kisses bring again, bring again,
> Seals of love, but seal'd in vain, seal'd in vain.

> [Enter Duke]

> *Mar.* Break off thy song, and haste thee quick away,
>   Here comes a man of comfort, whose advice
>   Hath often still'd my brawling discontent.
>   I cry you mercy, Sir, and well could wish
>   You had not found me here so musical.
>   Let me excuse me, and believe me so,
>   My mirth is much disples'd, but pleas'd my woe.
> *Duke* 'Tis good; though music oft hath such a charm
>   To make bad good, and good provoke to harm.

The repetition of 'bring again' and 'seal'd in vain' is similar to the arrangement in 'Come away, come away death'. Of either song it might be said that

> it is silly sooth,
> And dallies with the innocence of love,

for both the Duke in *Twelfth Night* and Mariana in *Measure for Measure* pamper themselves with these magic songs. One should note in passing that 'Come away' was originally assigned to a boy and later given to the clown's part in a revision of the play.[1] The typical Elizabethan comedy was full of song, and each song usually had several stanzas. In this respect 'Come away, come away death' is representative. But it is in keeping with the tragic and cynical overtones of *Measure for Measure* that its lyric

[1] *Twelfth Night*, NS 91; Greg FF 297; Noble 83.

should be cut short by dramatic exigencies.[1] Fletcher's play *The Bloody Brother* (*ca.* 1624/25, published 1639) has a second stanza which appears as well in the posthumous edition of Shakespeare's *Poems* (published 1640) and in John Wilson's musical setting (published 1652):

> Hide, o hide those hills of snow,
>   that thy frozen bosom wears,
> On whose tops the pinks that grow,
>   are yet of those that April wears;
> But first set my poor heart free,
> Bound in those icy chains by thee.

Although Mariana's bidding 'Break off thy song' hints at another stanza, there is no certain evidence that Fletcher's poetically inferior second stanza was written by Shakespeare. It is more likely that Fletcher wrote it to extend Shakespeare's single stanza.[2] John Wilson composed music for the King's Men from about 1615 to 1634, when he was succeeded by William Lawes. He may well have composed the song for Fletcher or for a revival of Shakespeare's play; however, the absence of Shakespeare's repeated 'bring again' and 'seal'd in vain' in both Wilson and Fletcher makes the first hypothesis more likely. Wilson's tune is the oldest surviving music for Shakespeare's stanza, and is reprinted in an appendix to this chapter.

It is another token of the importance of Latin literature for the schooling of Elizabethan and Jacobean poets that the two stanzas are freely derived from a popular Latin lyric, 'Ad Lydiam'. Several Renaissance editors have reprinted the Latin lyric which also elicited praise from Julius Caesar Scaliger. Its 'labra' and 'basia' are echoed in the first stanza and its 'papillae quae sauciant luxu nivei pectoris' in the second.[3]

---

[1] The 'Willow Song' in *Othello* is interrupted in a similar way. Both plays are based on Giraldi Cinthio's collection *Hecatommithi* and were written about the same time, 1603/04.

[2] Cf. E. F. Hart, 'The Answer-Poem of the Early 17th Century', *Review of English Studies*, VII (1956), 19–29, particularly 25.

[3] Stephen Gaselee, *Anthology of Mediaeval Latin*, London, 1925, p. 68; F. K. Vollmer, 'Zum Homerus Latinus', *Bayrische Akademie*, Sitz.-Ber., Philos.-Hist. Cl., 1913, 3. Abh.; Petronius, *Satyricon*, Paris: Pattisson, 1587, p. 169; Scaliger, *Poetice*, Lyons: Vincent, 1561, p. 328; Homerus, *Pyndari bellum Troianum*, Fano: Soncino, 1505, sig. D.ii.v; Homerus, *Pyndari bellum Troianum*, Fano: Soncino, 1515, sig. H.ii.v.

'In no other comedy of Shakespeare is there quite the same sense of tragedy averted, and to this fact are closely related the peculiar tone and technique of the play.'[1] This remark by a recent editor of *Measure for Measure* applies as well to the musical procedure. The economy, poignancy and integration of the music into the dramatic structure is in accord with Shakespeare's observance in the tragedies.

The bitterness and cynicism, the sense of tragedy and failure, in the plays written between *Julius Caesar* and *King Lear* have received critical attention from scholars since the turn of the century. In 1896 F. S. Boas perceived that in *Hamlet, Measure for Measure, Troilus and Cressida* and *All's Well that Ends Well* 'we move along dim untrodden paths, and at the close our feeling is neither of simple joy nor pain; we are excited, fascinated, perplexed, for the issues raised preclude a completely satisfactory outcome. . . . Dramas so singular in theme and temper cannot be strictly called comedies or tragedies. We may therefore borrow a convenient phrase from the theatre of today and class them together as Shakespeare's problem-plays'.

In 1896 the 'theatre of today' spelled Ibsen and his predilection for social reform—overtones that are discernible as well in the 'problem plays' of Shakespeare. Under the impact of Ibsen's ideas students of the theatre realized that the decadence of Denmark and Troy, Vienna and Venice not only portrayed the social shortcomings of Elizabethan England but was also a fable of their own day. In 1898 George Bernard Shaw lamented that Shakespeare 'could not pursue a genuinely scientific method in his studies of character and society, though in such unpopular plays as *All's Well that Ends Well, Measure for Measure* and *Troilus and Cressida* we find him ready and willing to start at the twentieth century if the seventeenth would only let him'. The prolonged unpopularity of the so-called problem comedies[2] is difficult to resolve. It is true that Shakespeare's criticism of human

---

[1] R. C. Bald, ed., *Measure for Measure*, Baltimore, 1956, p. 20. There are few recent editions of this play. J. D. Wilson's edition appeared in 1922.

[2] F. S. Boas, *Shakspere and his Predecessors*, London, 1896, p. 345; G. B. Shaw, *Three Unpleasant Plays*, London, 1898, p. xxi; W. W. Lawrence, *Shakespeare's Problem Comedies*, New York, 1931; O. J. Campbell, *Shakespeare's Satire*, New York, 1943; E. M. W. Tillyard, *Shakespeare's Problem Plays*, London, 1950.

nature and institutions has a sting in these plays that is lacking in the earlier comedies and in the later romances. To this hardness, jarring the public palate, should be added another serious handicap, namely, the absence of great and predominant parts. Such lack is not true of *Hamlet*, whose sweet prince will always command the centre of affection; but who can deny that Hector's death dwarfs the part of Troilus, and that Isabella's high moral purpose has few opportunities for great acting after the peripeteia (III.i.152)? It seems equally valid that another element which hinders the popularity of the problem comedies is their lack of music, that traditional asset of the genre of comedy. There are no wedding marches, no serenades, no lullabies, no choruses of elves or spirits, no festive processions. And when there is a charming lyric, there is no second stanza. Shakespeare, emerging as a mature artist with his production of *Hamlet* about the turn of the century, seemed determined to employ music only where it fitted his tragic or tragi-comic purpose.

Appendix

Julius Caesar, IV.iii.264.

(Discussed on p. 81.)

S.D. 'Music and a song': 'Weep you no more sad fountains', Dowland.

Antony & Cleopatra, II.vii.118.

(Discussed on pp. 87.)

'Come thou monarch of the vine': John Wilson, *Cheerfull Ayres*, 1659, cantus, p. 80: 'Come thou father of the spring' (Bodleian MS Mus. b.1, f. 128).

Measure for Measure, IV.i.1.

(Discussed on p. 90.)

'Take, o take those lips away':

Printed Sources:

(1) John Playford, *Select musicall ayres*, 1652, p. 2 (Wing STC, P 2502).
(2) Playford, *Select musicall ayres*, 1653, p. 24 (Wing STC, P 2503).
(3) Playford, *Select Ayres*, 1659, p. 1 (Wing STC, P 2500).
(4) Playford, *Treasury of Musick*, 1669, p. 1 (Wing STC, P 2504).
(5) Fletcher, IV. 307 (A. R. Waller's edn. of 1906).
(6) Fletcher, *Rollo, Duke of Normandy, or The Bloody Brother*, ed. J. D. Jump, Liverpool, 1948, pp. 67 and 106.

Manuscript Sources:

(7) London: British Museum, Add. 11608, f. 56.
(8) New York: Public Library, Drexel 4041, f. 32.
(9) New York: Public Library, Drexel 4267, f. 16.
(10) Oxford: Bodleian, Mus. b.1, f. 19ᵛ.
(11) Oxford: Christ Church, Mus. 434, f. 1.

The earliest printed version appears in Playford's anthology of 1652. It contains a few verbal variants. In the last line Shakespeare's F text reads

> Seals of love, but seal'd in vain, seal'd in vain

whereas Wilson-Playford, 1652, reads

> Seals of love though seals in vain.

The second 'seals' is probably a misprint for 'seal'd'; 'though' instead of 'but' appears in most manuscript sources. The first four lines in Wilson-Playford, 1652, read

Ex. 1.

Take, O take those lips a - - -

way that so sweet - ly were for - sworn,

and those eyes, that break of day, lights that do mis-

lead the morn, but my kis - ses bring a - gain,

seals of love, though seals in vain.

Take, o take those lips away
that so sweetly were forsworn,
And those eyes that break of days,
light that do mislead the morn.

The printer seems to have misplaced the plural at the end of the third line, where the rhyme demands 'day'; and 'those eyes' are 'lights', not 'light'. The following music example is a reprint of the 1652 version. It consists of the voice part, and the unfigured bass of the accompaniment. The harmony must therefore be supplied for active performance, whether on the lute or on the keyboard.

The manuscript in the Bodleian Library (Source No. 10) was carefully prepared under John Wilson's supervision. Although it, too, gives only the bass of the accompaniment one or two useful emendations of the bass line may be derived from it.

Music Example 2 offers a performing version. Chords have been supplied above the unfigured bass and the song has been transposed to the key of C minor to accommodate the average vocal range. Two emendations in the bass, apart from occasional octave leaps, have been made after collation with the Bodleian manuscript:

bar 4, 4th crotchet: passing notes 'g–f' instead of descending leap to 'e-flat'
bar 8, 4th crotchet: passing note 'b-flat' inserted before the 'a-flat' of bar 9.

In the printed version there is a double bar, separating the final couplet, 'But my kisses . . .' from the remainder. In the Bodleian manuscript a repetition of the final couplet (bars 11–14) is indicated.

Ex. 2.

APPENDIX

Macbeth

(Discussed on p. 88.)

Regarding comment on the interpolations in *Macbeth* and reprints of such music as may have been used in Middleton's *Witch* and Jonson's *Masque of Queens*, cf. the following editions:

1873 (rev. 1903): H. H. Furness, NV 235 and 253.
1940 (reprinted 1946): G. L. Kittredge, SP 878 & 938, 879 & 941.
1946: J. D. Wilson, NS 51 & 144, 54 & 149.
1951 (rev. 1957): K. Muir, NA xxxv & 103 & 111.
1956: A. Harbage (Baltimore, Maryland): pp. 20 & 76 & 80.

Cf. also: J. S. Smith, *Musica Antiqua*, London, 1812, pp. 48–59; W. W. Greg & F. P. Wilson, edd. *The Witch by Thomas Middleton* (Malone Society Reprints for 1948), London, 1950, pp. x, 57, 87; J. P. Cutts, 'Original Music to Middleton's *Witch*', *Shakespeare Quarterly*, VII (1956), 203–209; A. J. Sabol, *Songs and Dances of the Stuart Masque*, Providence (Rhode Island), 1959, pp. 121 & 169; R. Flatter, 'Hecate, "the other three witches", and their songs', *Shakespeare-Jahrbuch*, XCV (1959), 225–237.

V

ADULT SONGS AND ROBERT ARMIN

The circumstances that guided Shakespeare's development and produced a remarkable maturing of his art about the year 1600 remain a matter for speculation. The acquisition in 1599 of a better playhouse and a sympathetic musician-actor could be counted on to assist the playwright's growth. Shakespeare exhibited a confident technique in his use of music after the Chamberlain's Men had moved to the newly-built Globe Playhouse and it was about this time that he began to employ Robert Armin to sing the adult songs. Boy-singers and their magic songs were not cast aside, however, and at the end of his career Shakespeare gave some of his loveliest lyrics to Ariel in the *Tempest*. But in the period of his mature tragedies most of the songs were assigned to adult actors; their function was not to enchant but to characterize.

William Kemp and Robert Armin were the leaders among the 'Principall Actors' named in the Folio of 1623 who were accomplished singers and of whose appearance in the plays before 1611 we may be certain. Armin succeeded Kemp in 1599 as the new clown of the company. If the careers of playwrights may be taken as a guide, theatre and acting personnel may well have determined Shakespeare's course in the use of character songs by adult actors. The evolution was a gradual one, however, and a consideration of the earlier plays is necessary to gain perspective.

The absence of song in *Titus Andronicus* (1594) derives from its subject-matter and the Senecan precedent. This early work is one of the 'tragedies of blood' ridiculed by Jonson when he deplored the delight of audiences in the excess of bloodshed, so crudely presented. Shakespeare's first adult song occurs in a comedy. It is the famous serenade, 'Who is Silvia' in the *Two Gentlemen of Verona* (1594). (The *Comedy of Errors* of 1592/93 contains no songs.)[1] An element of persuasion, if not of enchantment, is never wholly absent from the comedy songs. Yet, when the lyrics are performed by adults, the Ethos of music is of secondary importance and when it is invoked its effect is unsuccessful. That the serenade to Silvia is designed to influence her disposition is clear from the dialogue. Thurio is advised to 'lay lime to tangle her desires by wailful sonnets', and when the Duke speaks of 'the force of heavenbred poesy' Proteus is quick to supply the standard humanist example of the power of music, 'Orpheus' lute . . . whose golden touch could soften steel and stone; make tigers tame . . .'. Scheming Proteus adds practical advice:

> Visit by night your lady's chamber window
> With some sweet consort, to their instruments
> Tune a deploring dump . . .

The performers are 'gentlemen', that is to say, adults[2] (unlike the boy-singers in *Midsummer Night's Dream* and the *Tempest*). The suit is singularly unsuccessful:

Silvia. Thinkst thou, I am so shallow, so conceitless,
   To be seduced by thy flattery . . . ?

But though the song fails to win Silvia's heart it affords Julia an opportunity to observe the treachery of Proteus. In the course of the scene Shakespeare employs a good many puns on musical terms:

Host.   The music likes you not.
Julia. You mistake, the musician likes me not.
Host. Why, my pretty youth?
Julia. He plays false, father.
Host. How, out of tune on the strings?

[1] The dates for *Titus* and *Comedy of Errors* are those given in Greg FF. Concerning Jonson's remarks cf. Chambers WS II.206.
[2] *Gent.* III.ii.92; IV.ii.24 and 86; Noble 43.

Julia. . . . so false that he grieves my very heartstrings.
Host. You have a quick ear.
Julia. Ay, I would I were deaf . . .
Host. I perceive you delight not in music.
Julia. Not a whit when it jars so.

Musical terms offered Shakespeare a favourite means for double-entendre, and he was at no loss for dramatic irony, whether it concerned the lute lesson in the *Taming of the Shrew* or Cassio's serenade in *Othello*. Though neither of these examples involves song, Shakespeare makes use of song in *Romeo and Juliet* (1595) to convey dramatic irony on two levels. In the brief scene in Act IV between the serving man Peter and the musicians there are puns on 'note', 'case', 'dump', 'crotchet' and 'silver sound'. Of greater dramatic importance, the low comedy of this scene serves as a foil to Juliet's supposed death in a manner that could not fail to add depth to the tragedy. It is one more invasion of lyricism and music into the essentially non-musical genre of classical tragedy and is an anticipation of the ironic pathos of the grave-digger's scene in *Hamlet* where, in an antiphonal arrangement of dialogue and song, the clown's low comedy becomes Shakespeare's means of intensifying a tragic situation. That Shakespeare should interrupt the Capulet plot with a comic scene for the clown-singer and his assistants was bound to shock the scrupulous critics of the eighteenth century. Voltaire and Jonson expressed their disapproval and Goethe felt the humour of the musicians to be so incongruous that he omitted scenes iv and v when he arranged the tragedy for the Weimar theatre in 1811.

In this early tragedy Will Kemp's scene was most likely written to fit the talents of the clown; its primary purpose was to present him with an effective bit of foolery, to provide relief from tension, and to fill a necessary interval of time. Shakespeare's mastery of the tragic genre made great strides between his writing of *The most excellent and lamentable Tragedie of Romeo and Juliet* and *Hamlet*. Yet, the former already displays a major characteristic in the songs, namely, their significance on two levels: while the clown engages in a battle of wits with lesser actors—the quibble on 'silver sound' which presumes to talk about money—the dialogue suggests traditional poetic epithets of the art of music, calling to mind well-established humanist theories. Allusions to the silver strings of Apollo's lyre, the muse, or song, were familiar utterances to an audience whose contemporary literature abounded in such classical phrases as 'silver-tuned strings', 'silver sound', 'silver voice' and 'silver-sounding tales'. Music in this vein was presumed to have the power to lead the soul to higher things, to Apollonian calm. It avoided the adverse effect which Lydian and Phrygian music were believed to invoke according to the Ethos theory:

This silver-sounding tale made such sugared harmony in his ears, that . . . he could have found in his heart to have packed up his pipes, and to have gone to heaven . . . he was more inflamed and ravished . . . than a young man . . . was with the Phrygian melody, who was so incensed and fired therewith, that he . . . set a courtesan's house on fire that had angered him.[1]

Since praise of the power of music was a favourite topic of the time, Elizabethan poets rarely failed to invoke the well-known examples: Orpheus and the underworld, Arion and the dolphin, Cadmos and the walls of Thebes. Perhaps the most famous passage is contained in Lorenzo's speech in the *Merchant of Venice* glorifying

> . . . the sweet power of music: therefore, the poet
> Did feign that Orpheus drew trees, stones, and floods . . .
>
> V.i

The lines which Old Capulet speaks in *Romeo and Juliet* at the beginning of Act IV, scene iv are preceded in the F text by the stage direction 'Play music', to indicate that the musicians are heard off-stage. In the following scene one of the musicians makes apt comment on their untimely and inappropriate arrival:

Musician. Faith we may put up our pipes and be gone.
Nurse. Honest good fellows, ah, put up, put up!
For well you know this is a pitiful case.
Musician. Ay, by my troth, the case may be amended.

These feeble puns on putting up pipes, that is, to 'shut up' or to pack away the instruments, and on the pitiful case, referring both to Juliet and the instrument-case, are followed by the entry of the group's chief wit. The F text reads 'Enter Peter' while Q_2

---

[1] Nashe II.222 and IV.262. Cf. also *Rom.* II.ii.166.

(1599) has 'Enter Will Kemp'—the immortal clown who, as a
member of Shakespeare's company, played Peter and Dogberry
and, quite probably, Falstaff. By his allusion in the ensuing
dialogue to several currently popular songs the clown under-
lines the unsuitable presence of merry musicians.

> *Peter.*   Musicians, o musicians,
> 'Heart's ease', 'Heart's ease',
> O, an you will have me live, play 'Heart's ease'.
> *Musician.* Why 'Heart's ease'?
> *Peter.*   O musicians, because my heart itself
> plays 'My heart is full of woe'. O play me
> some merry dump to comfort me.

Of 'Heart's ease' we have the music but no text; of 'My heart is
full of woe' the text without the music. Neither lyric was apparently performed, however.[1] The phrase 'merry dump' is
intentionally self-contradictory since 'dump', possibly related to
the French 'tombeau', is traditionally sad. Proteus's advice in
the *Two Gentlemen of Verona* to 'tune a deploring dump' is the
equivalent of the Duke's 'wailful sonnets'. But 'merry dump' is
the clown's way of emphasizing Capulet's earlier remarks (line
84)

> All things that we ordained festival
> Turn from their office to black funeral—
> Our instruments to melancholy bells,
> . . .
> Our solemn hymns to sullen dirges change.

In effect, Peter's mention of 'My heart is full of woe' and 'When
griping grief the heart doth wound / And doleful dumps the
mind oppress' is his own comical way of introducing a not so
'sullen dirge'. After some puns on 'sound' and 'crotchets' he
poses a riddle to the three musicians. In expounding it Peter,
the singer, is careful to address them as instrumentalists, using
names that are self-explanatory: 'Catling', a string made of cat-
gut; 'Rebeck', a stringed instrument; and 'Sound-Post', a small

---

[1] Tunes for 'Heart's ease' will be found in Playford 46 and Naylor SM,
p. xi; for 'My heart is full of woe', see Chappell 210. Concerning the 'merry
dump', cf. also John Ward, 'The "Dolfull Domps" ', *Journal of the American
Musicological Society*, IV, No. 2 (1951), 111–121.

piece of wood to counter the pressure of the bridge of a stringed instrument.

Peter.	When griping grief the heart would wound,
	And doleful dumps the mind oppress,
	Then music with her silver sound—
	Why 'silver sound'? Why 'music with her silver
	sound'? What say you, Simon Catling?
1st Mus.	Marry, sir, because silver hath a sweet sound.
Peter.	Pretty! What say you, Hugh Rebeck?
2nd Mus.	I say, 'silver sound' because musicians sound for silver.
Peter.	Pretty too! What say you James Sound-Post?
3rd Mus.	Faith, I know not what to say.
Peter.	O, I cry you mercy! You are the singer. I will say for
	you. It is 'music with her silver sound' because
	musicians have no gold for sounding.
	Then music with her silver sound
	With speedy help doth lend redress.

The lyric around which this banter spins survives for us both in text and music. A poem by Richard Edwards, printed posthumously in an anthology of 1576, begins

> Where griping grief the heart would wound
> And doleful dumps the mind oppress
> Then music with her silver sound
> Is wont with speed to give redress,
> Of troubled mind for every sore,
> Sweet music hath a salve therefore.

The music is preserved in two manuscripts.[1]

For a dramatic evaluation of the scene it becomes necessary to speculate whether Peter's quotation is sung or spoken. No stage direction in either the F text or the Q text gives an indication, though the context clearly implies that Peter sings. For one thing, the F text is very summary, it prints only:

> When griping grief the heart doth wound, then music
> with her silver sound.

And later in the scene:

> Then music with her silver sound, with speedy help
> doth lend redress

[1] Sources 2 and 3. The literary and musical sources of this song are listed in the Appendix to this chapter and there discussed.

As W. W. Greg remarks, 'Shakespeare in quoting a popular song from *The Paradise of Dainty Devices* did not trouble to write more than the first and the last lines'. The omission of the line

> And doleful dumps the mind oppress

in the F and Q_2 texts (1599) has no significance since it occurs in Q_1 (1597),[1] and the absence of explicit stage-directions has as little importance here as in the case of the Willow Song and the songs of Ophelia where the F text depends on italics to indicate that the lyrics are to be sung.

The poem which Peter quotes bears the title 'In Commendation of Music'. Edwards, himself an Elizabethan playwright, includes this stanza:

> For as the Roman poets say,
> In seas whom pirates would destroy,
> A dolphin saved from death most sharp,
> Arion playing on his harp.

Thomas Lodge argues in the same vein, in glorifying the power of music:

Do not the spheres move? . . . David rejoiceth, singeth, and praiseth the Lord by the harp . . . Pluto cannot keep Proserpina if Orpheus record. The seas shall not swallow Arion whilst he singeth, neither shall he perish while he harpeth, a doleful tuner, if a dying musician, can move a monster of the sea . . . a dolphin respecteth a heavenly record. . . .[2]

Finally, Sir John Davies proceeds much as Lodge and Edwards do:

> If music did not merit endless praise
> Would heavn'ly spheres delight in silver round
> . . .
> When antique poets music's praises tell,
> They say, it beasts did please and stones did move.[3]

---

[1] Cf. *Rom.* NS, 210, s.v. line 126; Kittredge SP 1434, s.v. line 129.

[2] *Defence of Poetry, Music, and Stage Plays, ca.* 1579. (*Publications* of the Shakespeare Society, London, 1853, XLVIII.17 f.) Other references to Arion and the Dolphin in Elizabethan plays may be found in *Twelfth Night*, I.ii.15; Heywood, *English Traveller*, II.i.

[3] 'Hymn in Praise of Music'. *Poetical Rhapsody*, 1602, ed. H. E. Rollins, 2 vols., Cambridge (Mass.), 1931/32, I.201 and II.176.

There is, in addition to the subject matter, another common element which unites these poems, and that is their humanist rhetoric. Lodge's 'doleful tuner' and Peter's 'doleful dumps'; Davies's 'silver round' and music's 'silver sound'. Thus, an audience might well be reminded of the elevating powers of music on hearing a popular song about the redress afforded by music with her silver sound. The lamentable fate of the lovers, and, to a lesser extent, the grief of Juliet's parents, merited dulcet and refined strains, not the loud merriment of the clown and his consort; and the pitiful case of Juliet demanded that Peter and the musicians put up their pipes. Instead, they lingered, joked, punned and listened to Peter's song. But by the very text of the song and the subtle emphasis of the pun their performance was appropriate to the festival turned funeral. In its oblique way the merry dump became the requisite dirge.

Amusing, even poignant, as the insertion of the clown's scene into a tragedy proved, the main opportunity for adult song between the writing of *Romeo and Juliet* and *Hamlet* lay in the comedies. Here the gradual evolution of Shakespeare's mastery in that genre is evident as one studies the *Merchant of Venice* (1596), *Much Ado about Nothing* (1598/99) and *As You Like It* (1599). 'Tell me where is fancy bred', sung by one of Portia's attendants while Bassanio makes his choice, is by its context an adult song.[1] The singer is an anonymous attendant of no dramatic importance and, in fact, he has no speaking lines. On the other hand, his audience includes two protagonists, whereas Peter's remarks were addressed to supernumeraries, and possibly the nurse. The song in the *Merchant of Venice* has both a descriptive and a dramatic function. It does not charm Bassanio but conveys the happy fairyland of love and comedy:

> How sweet the moonlight sleeps upon this bank!
> Here will we sit and let the sounds of music
> Creep in our ears . . .   V.i.54

The 'touches of sweet harmony' in the household of Belmont are

---

[1] E. J. Dent, 'Shakespeare and Music' in *Companion to Shakespeare Studies*, edd. H. Granville-Barker and G. B. Harrison, Cambridge, 1934, pp. 137–161, particularly 154; cf. also *Merchant of Venice*, NS, pp. xxx, 47, 149; also Greg FF, 257, s.v. III.ii.60; also C. Ing, *Elizabethan Lyrics*, London, 1951, p. 222.

in vivid contrast to the mercenary wrangles of Shylock's sur-
roundings, so wholly devoid of music. In dramatic terms, the
song is a hint to Bassanio to choose the leaden casket: the lines
rhyming with 'lead', the dying fancy remindful of a leaden
coffin, and the general tenor of the song censuring 'outward
shows' such as caskets adorned with gold and silver.

Balthazar, who renders 'Sigh no more, ladies, sigh no more'
in *Much Ado about Nothing* (II.iii.64) is socially and dramatically
in a superior category to the attendant in Portia's household.
He serves the Prince of Aragon and has courted Margaret, one
of the gentlewomen attending Hero. His protestations, in accordance with aristocratic prejudice, that 'there's not a note of
mine that's worth the noting' have already been mentioned.[1]
He puns on the same musical terms as those used by Peter, 'note',
'crotchet'—another proof, if one were needed, that the scene in
Romeo and Juliet belongs, by spirit and vocabulary, to the genre
of comedy. The Ethos of music is referred to in *Much Ado* but,
again, its operation is not successful in an adult song. True, the
Prince of Aragon 'will so practise on Benedick that . . . he shall
fall in love with Beatrice', and that is the purpose of Balthasar's
song. But Benedick is too well aware of the intention. Before the
lyric he comments, 'Now divine air! Now is his soul ravished!
Is it not strange that sheep's guts should hale souls out of
men's bodies?' And his first comment when the song is finished
is 'An he had been a dog that should have howl'd thus, they
would have hang'd him'. The subsequent dialogue between the
Prince, Leonato, and Claudio now puts the idea of Beatrice's love
into Benedick's mind, and the music once more emphasizes the
atmosphere of romantic comedy in which young gentlemen and
gentlewomen are destined to wed. It is to the life-force, to use a
term of George Bernard Shaw, that Benedick eventually sur-
renders. In the Elizabethan theatre it is represented by merry
music. In *Romeo and Juliet* the musicians are told to put up their
pipes, but in *Much Ado about Nothing* Benedick concludes the
comedy in a different vein:

> Strike up, pipers!   [Stage direction- Dance]
>
> FINIS

Merriment is the keynote, and the ladies are to 'sing no moe of

1 Chapter III, p. 56.

dumps so dull and heavy' but to convert their 'sounds of woe into hey nonny, nonny'. We do not know for certain who the adult singer was. The F text of 1623 has the stage remark

Enter Prince, Leonato, Claudio and Iacke Wilson.

Accordingly, at some point before 1623 an actor named John Wilson must have played the part of Balthasar. The Quarto of 1600 does not mention Wilson but reads merely

Enter Prince, Leonato, Claudio, Musicke.[1]

and a few lines later

Enter Balthaser with musicke.

There is a musical setting for 'Sigh no more Ladies' that is nearly contemporary. Thomas Ford was born in 1580 and published a collection of songs in 1607. His composition survives in a manuscript in Christ Church, Oxford.[2]

As You Like It boasts three adult songs, 'Under the greenwood tree', 'Blow, blow, thou winter wind' and 'What shall he have that killed the deer'. Amiens, the singer, is neither a clown nor an anonymous attendant but, like Balthasar, a nobleman. His speaking part is of no dramatic importance, but he has more lines than Balthasar and the increase in the number of songs cannot be ignored. They are not magic songs, for they treat of life in the Forest of Arden, and may be termed lyrical extensions of the Duke's speech at the opening of Act II:

---

[1] The question of Jack Wilson is too complicated to be dealt with here *in extenso*. As late as 1954 Bruce Pattison (*Shakespeare's Complete Works*, ed. C. J. Sisson, London, 1954, p. li) stated that the stage direction naming Wilson occurred in the Q text of 1600. This is erroneous. But even had the name appeared in print as early as 1600, John Wilson (born 1595, professor of music at Oxford 1656–61) could not have been the actor; cf. Greg FF 280, who suggests John Wilson, son of Nicholas Wilson, christened in 1585. Cf. also: E. F. Rimbault, *Who was Jack Wilson?*, London, 1846; V. Duckles, 'The curious art of John Wilson', *Journal of the American Musicological Society*, VII, No. 2 (1954), 93–112; modern editions of *ADO*, particularly NV 109, NS 128, Kittredge SP 122; *Malone Society Collections*, VI. 141.

[2] Set for two tenors and bass and not for solo voice, as required by the context of the play. A suitable arrangement for solo voice was published by Peter Warlock, *Four English Songs of the Early Seventeenth Century*, London, 1925, pp. 7–10.

Hath not old custom made this life more sweet
Than that of painted pomp? . . .
Here we feel but the penalty of Adam,
The seasons' difference; as the icy fang
And churlish chiding of the winter's wind . . .
Come, shall we go and kill us venison? . . .

The happy atmosphere of the arcadian, or pseudo-arcadian, existence is unfolded and developed in two succeeding acts with the help of additional lyrics dwelling on the same bucolic themes. It has been argued that Shakespeare increased the number of his songs because of competition with the boys' companies which emerged with new force after a lengthy silence. (Children were not acting at Court between the years 1590 and 1601.) Edward J. Dent acknowledges this as one factor but offers the musicality of the genre of comedy as a more basic reason:[1]

> There are two dances in *Much Ado about Nothing*, and in *As You Like It* two boy singers besides Amiens. Touchstone can sing also; and there is a masque, which demands 'still music'. It has been suggested that . . . the competition . . . of the little eyases who so plagued Hamlet's actor-visitors was beginning to be felt. Be that as it may these two comedies are made for the help of music . . . *Twelfth Night* follows close upon them, and again abounds in music.

The role of Touchstone is of compelling interest, for it was in this role that Robert Armin probably first earned his spurs as a member of Shakespeare's company. Armin seems to have possessed qualifications which attracted Shakespeare and which most likely were lacking in his predecessor: his jokes were of a more sophisticated nature; he was a 'wise' fool; he respected the playwright's 'true copy' and forbore extemporization; and, finally, as a clown and singer he felt a natural opposition to those men, be they Puritans or others, who were excessively serious and opposed to music.

It was to be expected that the 'fellowship' of share-holders in Shakespeare's company were likely to consider each other's talents and that Shakespeare in allotting his parts after 1599 would take Armin's qualities into account. The change from the serving-man as fool, played by Kemp, to the court-fool, clad in motley and played by Armin, is noticeable. The phrase 'wise

[1] Op. cit., p. 155.

fool' (as opposed to a burlesque clown) occurs many times both in Armin's own writings and in the roles Shakespeare created for him (Touchstone, Feste, Lear's Fool). Perhaps we have here an echo of the biblical 'Let him become a fool that he may be wise' (I Corinthians III.18); whatever the source,[1] the frequency of the seeming contradiction cannot be ignored. Touchstone is the witty, though critical, chorus in *As You Like It*, and his wisdom is referred to more often than his motley coat. It is a 'pity that fools may not speak wisely', he is a 'material fool', that is, of a mind full of substantial matter. He himself informs us, V.i.32:

> I do now remember a saying: 'The fool doth think he is wise,
> but the wise man knows himself to be a fool'.

Perhaps the most outspoken praise of Armin is recorded in *Twelfth Night* (III.i.67) when Viola says of Feste

> This fellow is wise enough to play the fool,
> And to do that well craves a kind of wit.

And of Lear's fool, Kent remarks early in the tragedy (I.iv.165)

> This is not altogether fool, my lord.

We can trace this thought in Armin's own publications (four of which are jest-books, records of the sayings and doings of clowns) as early as 1600. In his *Quips upon Questions*,[2] he comments:

> He plays the wise man then, and not the fool
> That wisely for his living can do so . . .

The drama of Queen Elizabeth's day developed with such speed that the clown's jigs and improvisations which took place as a rule after the performance must already have seemed quite old-fashioned by the time the Chamberlain's-King's Men performed *Hamlet*, *Othello* and *King Lear* (1600–06). But as late as 1599 a performance of *Julius Caesar* was succeeded by the

---

[1] Cf. also M. P. Tilley, *Dictionary of Proverbs*, Ann Arbor (Mich.), 1950; s.v. M 321, M 428, *et passim*.

[2] In older library catalogues this work is frequently credited to John Singer, but it has been unequivocally established as Armin's (Chambers ES II.300). A bibliography of the sources relevant to Robert Armin is given in Appendix II to this chapter.

customary jig.[1] Even the bit of 'fat' given to Kemp in *Romeo and Juliet*, though related to the tragic plot, seems clumsy from the vantage point of the early 1600s. The art of the playwright had reached a stage where the author's text demanded respect and faithful observance. Consequently, the clown's improvisations on which the older school of Tarleton and Kemp had thrived were superseded and Shakespeare could confidently voice his attitude through Hamlet (III.ii.42–50):

> And let those that play your clowns speak no more than is set down for them. For there be of them that will themselves laugh, to set on some quantity of barren spectators to laugh too, though in the meantime some necessary question of the play be then to be considered. That's villainous, and shows a pitiful ambition in the fool that uses it.

This new approach was accepted by Armin who wrote (*Quips upon Questions*):

> True it is, he plays the fool indeed,
> But in the play he plays it as he must . . .

Now with an intelligent and reliable clown at hand the playwright was able to integrate that character more harmoniously into the total structure. The fool's lively wit and quick responses served as a means of measuring a play's principal characters. Touchstone in *As You Like It*, Feste in *Twelfth Night*, the fool in *King Lear* are each the means of testing, respectively, the sentimentality of Rosalind, the stodginess of Malvolio and the rashness of Lear. They are touchstones in the same way that music becomes the 'pierre de touche' in Ronsard's famous preface, addressed to the King of France in 1560:[2]

Sire, tout ainsi que par la pierre de touche on esprouve l'or s'il est bon ou mauvais, ainsi les anciens esprouvoyent par la Musique les

---

[1] Chapter I, p. 3.

[2] *Livre de Meslanges contenant six vingtz chansons*. Cf. *Oeuvres Complètes*, ed. Laumonier, 8 vols., Paris, 1914–19, VII.16 & VIII.117; *Oeuvres Complètes*, ed. Cohen, 2 vols., Paris, 1938, II.979; G. Thibault & L. Percey, *Bibliographie . . . de Ronsard*, Paris, 1941, p. 24; Julien Tiersot, 'Ronsard et la musique', Internationale Musikgesellschaft, *Sammelbände*, IV (1902–03), 70–142 (particularly 82); F. Lesure & G. Thibault, *Bibliographie . . . Le Roy . . . 1551–1598*, Paris, 1955, pp. 92 (No. 68) and 156 (No. 165): No. 68 of 1560 is addressed to François II; No. 165 of 1572 is addressed to the succeeding monarch, Charles IX.

esprits de ceux qui sont genereux, magnanimes, et non forvoyans de leur premiere essence, et de ceux qui sont engourdiz, paresseux, et abastardiz en ce corps mortel, ne se souvenant de la celeste armonie du ciel . . .

The roles played by Armin differ from those of Peter in *Romeo and Juliet* and Dogberry in *Much Ado about Nothing* in that there is greater participation in the action of the play and an easier exchange of remarks with important characters. Furthermore, there is a greater use of comment and characterization. Peter's quatrain from a lyric by Edwards, interspersed with ten lines of prose, was the most extensive bit of singing Shakespeare entrusted to Kemp. By contrast, following his trial role as Touchstone, Armin was assigned four sizeable lyrics in *Twelfth Night*; he then played the fool in *King Lear*, which is so 'full of songs' (I.iv.186) and the part of Autolycus in the *Winter's Tale*.

A number of these songs mock the over-serious Puritan, the kill-joy of innocent pleasure. Hostility towards the man 'who hears no music' and 'hath no music in himself' was traditional. To quote Ronsard once more:

. . . celuy . . . lequel oyant un doux accord d'instrumens ou la douceur de la voyx naturelle . . . ne s'en esmeut point . . . doucement ravy, et si ne sçait comment dérobé hors de soy, c'est signe qu'il a l'âme tortue, vicieux, et dépravée, et duquel il se faut donner garde . . .

There can be no doubt that Lorenzo speaks for the playwright when he counsels:

> The man that hath no music in himself,
> Nor is not moved with concord of sweet sounds,
> Is fit for treasons, stratagems, and spoils,
> . . .
> Let no such man be trusted . . .

While Shakespeare and Jonson protest from time to time against an excessive indulgence in stage-plays and song they have no sympathy for the man who is wholly opposed to drama and music, such as the lean Cassius or Malvolio or Zeal-of-the-Land-Busy in Jonson's *Bartholomew Fair*. Still, one cannot claim that all the enemies of music were puritans in the term's narrow sense. Cassius and Shylock were not. Nor could this classification be applied to Stephen Gosson who published a tract in 1579 against 'poets, . . . jesters and such like caterpillars of a commonwealth'. But, the puritans who succeeded in closing the theatres in 1642 were so voluble in their attacks on the pleasurable arts that to an Elizabethan audience the skirmishes in *Twelfth Night* between the pompous Malvolio and the musical Feste the Jester were in the nature of a combat between Puritanism and Shakespeare's 'fellow', Robert Armin.

Malvolio's antipathy toward music appears in Act II, scene iii. To begin with, Feste sings the love song, 'O mistress mine' (lines 40–53). Then a catch is sung, 'Hold thy peace' (line 75). Toby, who is not much of a singer, proceeds to quote single lines from five different songs: 'Peg-a-Ramsey', 'Three merry men', 'Tilly-vally', 'There dwelt a man' and 'On the twelfth day of December' (lines 81–92). Such an abundance of musical conviviality goes too far for the staid steward. Malvolio asks Toby, Andrew and Feste whether they are mad. He continues

> Do ye make an alehouse of my lady's house, that ye squeak out your coziers' catches without any mitigation or remorse of voice?

After the usual puns about 'keeping time' Malvolio warns Toby that Olivia wants him to reform or else 'she is very willing to bid you farewell'. This unfortunate remark prompts Toby and Feste to further mockery with the singing of an entire stanza of Robert Jones's 'Farewell dear heart'.[1] The clown's thoroughgoing chastisement of Malvolio occurs in Act IV, scene ii, when he twits the unhappy steward and sings two songs. Disguised in gown and beard he announces himself as 'Sir Topas the curate who comes to visit Malvolio the lunatic' (line 25), only to appear shortly in his natural state, singing (lines 78–85)

---

[1] For the music to these songs, cf. 'O Mistress mine', *Renaissance News*, VI (1953), 20 and VII (1954), 98; 'Hold thy peace', T. Ravenscroft, *Deuteromelia*, 1610; edited by P. Warlock in *T. Ravenscroft: Pammelia and other Rounds*, London, 1928, p. 29, No. 5; cf. also J. Vlasto, 'An Elizabethan Anthology of Rounds', *Musical Quarterly*, XL (1954), 228, No. 32 and 231, Ex. 5. 'Peg-a-Ramsey' and 'Three Merry Men', Chappell I.220 and 216; 'Tilly-Vally', *Music & Letters*, XXXV (1954), 101; 'There dwelt a man' and 'Farewell dear heart', Naylor SM 24 f.; 'On the twelfth day', Kittredge SP 398.

> Hey Robin, jolly Robin
> Tell me how thy lady does . . .
> My lady is unkind . . .[1]

The five lines from Wyatt's poem emphasizing the unkindness of Olivia contain a variant of Armin's Christian name Robert. The same nickname was used by John Davies of Hereford in a poem which he addressed to Armin in 1610:

> But (honest Robin) thou with harmless mirth
> Dost please the world . . .
> . . . men dost school
> To do as thou dost—wisely play the fool.

When, after further taunting, Malvolio orders the clown to be gone, Feste dances off, singing

> I am gone, sir;
> And anon, sir,
> I'll be with you again,
> In a trice,
> Like to the old Vice,
> Your need to sustain;
> Who with dagger of lath,
> In his rage and his wrath,
> Cries 'aha!' to the devil.
> Like a mad lad,
> 'Pare thy nails, dad,'
> Adieu, goodman devil.
> [Stage direction: Exit.]

The 'old Vice' (buffoon) of the earlier Tudor stage was the predecessor of the Elizabethan fool,[2] and the Vice twitting the devil was a thinly veiled form of the Elizabethan jester mocking the Puritan—a musical jester goading an anti-musical puritan. The connection had been carefully established by Shakespeare when Toby questioned Maria about Malvolio (II.iii.150 ff.):

Toby. Tell us something of him.
Maria. Marry, sir, sometimes he is a kind of Puritan.

---

[1] For the music to this lyric, cf. *Music & Letters*, XXXVII (1956), facsimile facing p. 320 and Naylor SM 25; cf. also *Collected Poems of . . . Wyatt*, ed. K. Muir, London, 1949, p. 42.
[2] E. K. Chambers, *Mediaeval Stage*, 2 vols., London, 1923, II.203–205; Kittredge SP 419.

Andrew. O, if I thought that, I'd beat him like a dog!
Toby. What, for being a Puritan? . . .
Maria. The devil a Puritan that he is, or anything
constantly but a time-pleaser! . . .

No music survives for 'I am gone, sir'.[1] We are more for-
tunate in possessing Touchstone's lyric in *As You Like It*, 'Sweet
Oliver'. The 'most wicked Sir Oliver . . . a most vile Martext'
(V.i.5) is depicted as self-righteous and fussy in his refusal to
marry Touchstone, because there is no man to give Audrey
away (III.iii.71), yet he is willing to marry the fool 'under a
bush like a beggar'. This moves Jacques to counsel Touchstone
to 'get you to church, and have a good priest', which the clown
heeds (III.iii.100):

Touchstone. Come, sweet Audrey.
. . . Farewell, good Master Oliver: not
O sweet Oliver,
O brave Oliver,
Leave me not behind thee:
but—
Wind away,
Begone, I say,
I will not to wedding with thee.[2]

The analogy between the musical chastenings of Malvolio
and Martext and the contemporary literary battle raging between the friends and enemies of plays-and-music is only too
clear. At Oxford 'the divergence of opinions became most
articulate'.[3] The protagonists were John Rainolds who represented the Puritan party at the Hampton Court Conference in
1604, Stephen Gosson who, though not a member of the party,
followed the Puritan line of attack, and William Prynne whose

---

[1] Naylor SM 25; Noble 84; the tune quoted NV 271 is from the eighteenth century.

[2] The Elizabethan melody to this lyric is variously known as 'Pescod
Time', 'Hunts up' or 'Sweet Oliver'. It is reprinted in Wooldridge I.86–90;
B. Pattison, *Music and Poetry of the English Renaissance*, London, 1948, p. 171;
cf. also Jonson III.361 and IX.379 (s.v. III.vii.63). Wooldridge refers to the
Leyden Lute Book. The manuscript is now usually called the 'Thysius Lute
Book', cf. *Le Luth et sa Musique*, ed. J. Jacquot, Paris, 1958, p. 180, footnote 9.
The song 'Brande Soet Oliver' occurs on f. 472 of the manuscript.

[3] E. K. Chambers, ES I.250.

Puritan pamphlet was the most voluminous (and on account of which he lost both his ears and his university degree). The defence, led by William Gager and John Case, was spirited, but history is indebted to the writings of the attacking parties for the more useful details. Throughout the dispute stage-plays and music were coupled; sometimes the argument was concerned with biblical and classical authorities, at other times with personalities of the sixteenth century. The prohibition of the Old Testament that

woman shall not wear that which pertaineth unto a man, neither shall a man put on a woman's garment

was discussed by Calvin, Stephen Gosson and Ben Jonson.[1] It was plainly inimical to the dramatic and musical accomplishments of the boy-actors. The Platonic and Aristotelian notions of the false and true 'imitation' of poetry occurs in Stephen Gosson's *School of Abuse* as well as in *As You Like It*. The scene in which Touchstone sings 'O sweet Oliver' contains the lines

Audrey. I do not know what 'poetical' is, is it honest . . .?
Touchstone. No, truly: for the truest poetry is the most feigning . . .

When Rainolds and Gager debated whether all actors were *infames*, Gager of Christ Church professed to be stung by the reflection that such occasional stage-performers as the honest youths of Christ Church and so well-voiced a musician as their Master of the Choristers, should partake of the 'infamy' about which Rainolds argued.

That drama and music were contiguous territories is also driven home in the *Return from Parnassus*, Part II (a Cambridge play of 1601/02) where poets disgusted with the task of playwriting decide to take to the road:

Better it is 'mongst fiddlers to be chief
Than at a player's trencher beg relief. . . .

Their disgust grew out of the attitudes of such actors as William Kemp who endeavoured to be the playwrights' masters rather than their servants. (This casts yet another light on the superiority of the literate Robert Armin over the improvising Kemp.) There can be no doubt however that Burbage, Kemp and

[1] Cf. *Bartholomew Fair*, V.v.99 and Jonson X.214.

Armin were equally opposed to the Puritan position which postulated that acting and music-making in the theatres or the halls of colleges should be prohibited without exception as time-wasting and demoralizing. Shakespeare shared the humanist belief that

> the purpose of playing . . . was and is, to hold, as 'twere, the mirror up to nature; to show virtue her own feature, scorn her own image. . . .
>
> *Hamlet* III.ii.22

Gosson expressed himself in similar terms in 1579:

Now are the abuses of the world revealed, every man in a play may see his own faults, and learn by this glass [i.e. mirror] to amend his manners. . . .

The Puritans were unwilling to show 'scorn her own image' on the stage and were equally careful to distinguish between good and bad music within the classical theory of Ethos. The clearest formulation was given by Prynne in his *Histriomastix* (p. 274):

That music of itself is lawful, useful, and commendable, no man, no Christian dares deny . . . But that lascivious, amorous, effeminate, voluptuous music (which I only here encounter) should be either expedient or lawful unto Christians, there is none so audacious as to justify it, since both Scripture, Fathers, modern Christian writers, yea and heathen nations, states, and authors, have passed a doom upon it.

This learned and overblown pamphlet of 1633 does not command our admiration but it more than deserves our attention, for it epitomizes a tendency which Elizabethan and Jacobean playwrights were constantly combatting and which, in the end, was to achieve its short-lived triumph in the closing of the theatres.[1]

To sum up, the adult songs rendered by Robert Armin in the four plays discussed so far come under the heading of character songs rather than magic songs. Whether they taunt an enemy or please a patron or present the clown's own views their function is never to enchant. One might argue that 'Come away,

---

[1] A bibliography on the topic 'Puritans and Music' will be found in Appendix III.

come away, death' is the one exception that affords the Duke (*Twelfth Night*, II.iv.51) the same opportunity for self-indulgence as Mariana seeks from the boy-singer in *Measure for Measure*. There is ample evidence that the song was originally intended for a boy and it is understandable, therefore, that the lyric approaches the character of a magic song more than any of Armin's other tunes. There is yet the difference that whilst Mariana would presumably be comforted if the song were not interrupted, Duke Orsino, after listening to a full rendition of two stanzas, fulfils his social obligation of recompensing the singer but shows no sign of having been soothed. The melancholy god, far from protecting him (line 75) still pursues him. Orsino dismisses Feste and the attendants, and returns to his objective, never to be achieved in the play:

> Once more Cesario,
> Get thee to yond same sovereign cruelty.

Admittedly, the song has a subsidiary function, in that it is not addressed solely to the Duke but affects the audience as well. The element of 'mood music' in a comedy whose first line is

> If music be the food of love, play on . . .

is not to be discounted. But a careful study convinces one that the songs in Shakespeare are primarily addressed to the protagonists on the stage and that this function was understood by the audience. The playwright does not endeavour to condition his audience by music in a manner comparable to that employed in the modern theatre or cinema.

Equally noticeable with Armin's advent is the increase in the number of songs. Shakespeare abandoned his method of assigning the adult songs to protesting gentlemen of no dramatic stature; instead, he developed the role of the clown who was eager for music and for whom song was a natural occupation. The creation of Touchstone was an experimental step in the direction of the musical clown who would break into song at slight provocation and who, at the same time, would perform a function of some importance in the play. After 1599 Robert Armin became the principal instrument in Shakespeare's orchestra. That he could sing easily and intelligently was an important attribute, and in addition to these qualities he had an attractive personality. He was the 'wise fool' of Shakespeare and of John Davies of Hereford; he was an author in his own right and mindful of other authors' texts; and he was, as a matter of course, opposed to the Puritan attack and clever at satirizing the enemy.

Appendix I

'When Griping Grief the Heart Doth Wound'

[Title: 'In Commendation of Music']

The sources for this lyric are as follows:

(1) A printed anthology of poems, 1576: *Paradise of Dainty Devices*, ed. H. E. Rollins, Cambridge (Mass.), 1927, pp. 63, 227–229.
(2) A keyboard manuscript *ca.* 1550–85: *Mulliner Book*, ed. D. Stevens (*Musica Britannica*, II), 2nd rev. edn., London, 1954, No. 113, pp. 83, 96.
(3) An Elizabethan lute manuscript now in the National Library of Wales, Aberystwyth; shelf mark Brogyntyn MS 27, formerly Porkington MS 11.
(4) John Hawkins, *General History of Music*, 5 vols., London, 1776, V.444–45.
(5) James Hutton, 'Some English Poems in Praise of Music', *English Miscellany*, ed. Mario Praz, II (Rome, 1951), 1–63, particularly 32.
(6) Richard Newton, 'In Commendation of Music', *Lute Society Journal*, No. 6 (December, 1958), 138, 144. An edition of source 3.
(7) Taitt MS, a Scottish MS of the late seventeenth century, now at the University of California Library, Los Angeles. Recently discovered by Walter Rubsamen, who is preparing an edition of the transcription of the MS. A brief report appears in the *Festschrift für Heinrich Besseler*, Leipzig, 1961.

Source (1) attributes the poem to Richard Edwards, and it is reasonable to credit Edwards with the music as well.

The Brogyntyn Lute Book (source 3) belongs to a collection which was deposited in the National Library of Wales by the present Lord Harlech and takes its name from Lord Harlech's former home at Brogyntyn, later anglicized to Porkington, near Oswestry, Salop.

The Brogyntyn Book contains two items with relevant titles. That on pp. 126–27 may be disregarded as the music has no recognizable relationship to the well-known setting in the Mulliner Book, source (2) or the music example presented here. It is a wordless piece for solo lute, entitled 'The gripinge griefe that'. However, on p.125 there is another short, wordless piece for solo lute which is the basis of the present transcription. The title (rubric) is written in an enigmatic cipher and the vowels must be decoded from various half-circles and dots as follows: the half-circle with 2 dots equals 'e', with 3 dots 'i', with 4 dots 'o'. Thus decoded, the title reads 'where gripinge griefe the hare [*recte:* heart] woulde', insofar as it is legible at all.

Ex. 1.

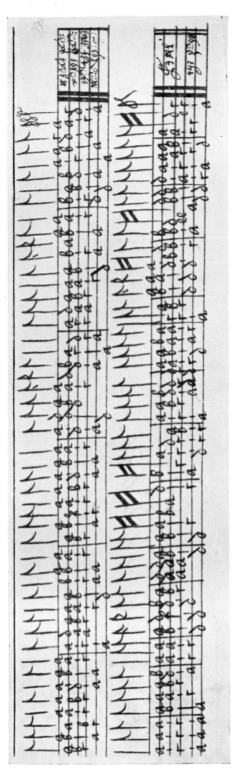

Facsimile 1. 'When griping grief the heart doth wound', Brogyntyn Book.

The Mulliner Book (source 2) gives the melody with accompaniment, the Brogyntyn Book (source 3) gives the accompaniment only. Both sources give the music without words. The rubric in the Mulliner Book is 'When griping griefs', that of the Brogyntyn Book 'Where griping grief the [heart] would'. In the Mulliner Book the key is d-minor, in the Brogyntyn Book c-minor. The present transcription has been transposed to a-minor and all subsequent remarks have reference to the transposed pitch. Mr. Newton (source 6) has made

a few emendations, which have been followed in our transcription. The most important of these changes consists in omitting the note g-sharp in the first chord of bar 17, thus reading (in ascending order) e–b, not e–g-sharp–b. As amended, the clash between g natural in the voice and g sharp in the accompaniment is avoided and bar 17 corresponds, as it should, to bar 5. Musically, sources 2 and 3 are very close; in fact, the bass, apart from occasional octave transposition, is identical. The following music example is based on source (3) since, clearly, it is intended for singing. Only the first 16 bars are sung by Peter in *Romeo and Juliet*, and Shakespeare's text has been fitted to the melody; bars 17–24 have Edwards's original text. The differences are slight:

EDWARDS

line 1   *Where* griping grief the heart *would* wound
line 3   *There* music with her silver sound
line 4   Is wont with speed to give redress

SHAKESPEARE

line 1   *When* griping grief the heart *doth* wound
line 3   *Then* music with her silver sound
line 4   With speedy help doth lend redress

Since the setting preserved in the Mulliner and Brogyntyn manuscripts is the only music for the text surviving from Shakespeare's age, it is likely that the clown sang some version of the melody of the first sixteen bars. The dramatic context calls for unaccompanied singing. The two strains, bars 1–8 and 9–16 fit well into the dialogue. When sung without interruption the relationship between the first strain (bars 1–8) ending in a half cadence and the second strain (bars 9–16) ending in a full cadence is in the customary harmonic form. Peter interrupts his singing at bar 12 to set a riddle, that is, he completes the first strain at bar 8, and the second strain is left incomplete at bar 12. When he resumes singing after the riddle has been solved he goes back to bar 9. The fact that bars 9–12 are identical with the opening bars 1–4 facilitates the new start. This time the second strain concludes with a full cadence at bar 16, as one would expect. Since the final eight bars (17–24) are omitted by Peter it seems preferable to end at bar 16 on c-natural rather than c-sharp, particularly as there is no instrumental accompaniment.

Appendix II

Bibliography of Sources Relevant to Robert Armin

(1) *Quips upon Questions*, London: Ferbrand, 1600, Pollard STC 22573: Brit. Mus.

(2) *Fool upon Fool*, London: Ferbrand, 1600, Folger Library (not recorded in Pollard STC).[1]

(3) *Fool upon Fool*, London: Ferbrand, 1605, Folger Library (not recorded in Pollard STC).[1]

(4) *Nest of Ninnies*, London: East, 1608, Pollard STC 775: Bodleian.

(5) *History of the Two Maids of Manchester*, London: Okes, 1609, Pollard STC 774: Bodleian.

(6) *Italian Tailor and His Boy*, London: Pavier, 1609, Pollard STC 774: Bodleian.

(7) *Valiant Welshman or Chronicle History* . . . London: Pursloe, 1615, Pollard STC 16: Brit. Mus., Bodleian. (This work by 'R. A., Gent' may or may not be by Armin.)

(Reprints and Discussion)

(8) Baldwin, T. W., *Organization and Personnel of the Shakespearean Company*, Princeton, 1927.

(9) Baldwin, 'Shakespeare's Jester', *Modern Language Notes*, XXXIX (1924), 447–55.

(10) Bradley, A. C., 'Feste the Jester', in *Miscellany*, London, 1929, pp. 207–217.

(10a) Busby, O.M., . . . *Development of the Fool in the Elizabethan Drama*, London, 1923.

(11) Chambers ES II.299 f.

(12) Chambers WS I.79 f.

(13) Collier, J. P. ed., *Fools and Jesters, with a reprint of* . . . *'Nest of Ninnies'* (Shakespeare Society Publications), London, 1842.

(14) Denkinger, E. M., 'Actors' Names in the Register of St. Bodolph Aldgate', *Publications of the Modern Language Association*, XLI (1926), 91–109.

(15) Felver, C. S., 'Robert Armin's Fragment of a Bawdy Ballad of "Mary Ambree" ', *Notes & Queries*, N.S., VII (1960), 14–16.

---

[1] In the forthcoming revision of Pollard STC by W. A. Jackson (Houghton Library, Harvard University) STC numbers 772.5 and 772.52 have been assigned to these two works.

(15a) Felver, C. S., *Robert Armin, Shakespeare's Fool: A Biographical Essay* (Kent State Univ. Bull., Research Series V), Kent (Ohio), 1961.

(16) Gray, A. K., 'Robert Armine, the foole', *Publications of the Modern Language Association*, XLII (1927), 673–685.

(17) Greg FF 285, 297, 386.

(18) Grosart, A. B., ed. *Works of Robert Armin*, London, 1880.

(19) Hotson, L., *Shakespeare's Motley*, London, 1952, p. 104 *et passim*.

(20) Hotson, L., *First Night of Twelfth Night*, London, 1954, pp. 83, 121, 149.

(21) Munro, John, *Shakespeare Allusion-Book*, 2 vols., London, 1909, I.83, 121, 149.

(22) Murray, J. M., 'A Fellow of Shakespeare: Robert Armin', *New Adelphi* I (1927–28), 251–253.

(23) Murray, J. T., *English Dramatic Companies, 1558–1642*, 2 vols., London, 1910, II.31.

(24) Nosworthy, J. E., ed. *Cymbeline* (New Arden Edition of Shakespeare), pp. lvii and 162.

(25) Nungezer, E., *Dictionary of Actors*, New Haven, 1929, pp. 15–20.

(26) Ouvry, Frederic, ed. *Quips upon Questions by John Singer . . .*, London: Privately printed, 1875.

(27) E. Welsford, *The Fool: His Social and Literary History*, London, 1935, pp. 162, 244 *et passim*.

(28) Wilson, F. P., 'English Jestbooks of the 16th and Early 17th Centuries', *Huntington Library Quarterly*, II (1938–39), 121–158, particularly 151–152.

(29) Wilson, J. D., ed. *Twelfth Night* (New Shakespeare Edition), 2nd edn., Cambridge, 1949, pp. 93–97, 101 *et passim*.

Appendix III

Puritans and Music—A Bibliography

John Case, *Speculum moralium quaestionum*, Oxford: Barnes, 1585; Pollard STC 4759: British Museum; Bodleian.

John Case, *Praise of Music*, Oxford: Barnes, 1586; Pollard STC 20184, s.v. 'Praise': British Museum; Bodleian.

William Byrd, *Gratification unto Master John Case*, London: East, 1589; Pollard STC 4246: Bodleian (bassus); Cambridge (cantus secundus); Royal Coll. Music MS 2041, f. 37r (superius).

John Rainolds, *Overthrow of Stage-Plays*, London, 1599; Pollard STC 20616: Bodleian. 1629 edn.: Pollard STC 20618: Bodleian.

William Prynne, *Histriomastix: the player's scourge*, London, 1633; Pollard STC 20464a: British Museum; Bodleian.

Gregory Smith, 'The Puritan Attack', in his *Elizabethan Critical Essays*, 2 vols., London, 1904, pp. xiv–xxxi.

E. K. Chambers, 'Humanism and Puritanism' in Chambers ES (1924), I.236–268.

P. A. Scholes, *The Puritans and Music in England and New England*, London, 1934.

W. Haller, *The Rise of Puritanism*, New York, 1938.

W. Ringler, *Stephen Gosson*, Princeton, 1941.

W. Ringler, 'The Praise of Musicke by John Case' in *Papers of the Bibliographical Society of America*, XLIV (1960), 119–121.

The word 'puritan' occurs in five of Shakespeare's plays. In its context, the sense may be uncomplimentary or merely matter of fact; but the term is never used approvingly. Cf. *TW N*, II.iii.152, 155, 159; NS pp. xxiv and 130; Kittredge SP 400. *All's W*, I.iii.56, 98; NA 23 and 25. *Wint*, IV.iii.46; NS 163. *Per*, IV.vi.9; NS 65. Concerning *AYL*, III.iii.101, cf. NS 105 and 143 (Kittredge SP 332, s.v. line 43).

VI

ADULT SONGS FROM
HAMLET TO *OTHELLO*

THE clown in Shakespeare's plays performs the role of a chorus as he comments on the pretences and follies of his fellow characters. The extent to which such a 'chorus of wit' functions depends on the author's dramatic plan. There are two clowns in *King Lear*, the professional fool and Edgar, disguised as Mad Tom. As far as Act III they are Lear's 'philosophers', a term he repeatedly bestows on Edgar. The lesson once learned, Lear's fool fades out of the play, and Edgar's role is concerned solely with the sub-plot of the blinded Gloucester. In at least three of Shakespeare's plays, *As You Like It, Twelfth Night* and *All's Well that Ends Well*, the chorus of wit, performed respectively by Touchstone, Feste and Lavache, functions throughout the play, since none of the protagonists have the impartiality or nimbleness of mind to fathom their own problems. In Touchstone's view, whoever 'hath learned no wit by nature or art' was a natural philosopher. By his learning Touchstone added to a natural bent the sharp edge of wit and the ability to improvise verse. He and Lear's fool excel in inventing rhymes, and Touchstone is quick to detect the 'false gallop' of Orlando's verses.

But, whereas in the tragedy of *Lear* the old King needed a philosopher-chorus to guide him, Hamlet was himself that very philosopher, and there was no need for a clown to unmask the foppery of courtiers, the garrulity of old men, the sensuality of 'this too, too solid [?sullied] flesh'. Hamlet had the intellectual insight to apprehend the conduct of Polonius, Ophelia and Laertes, not to mention Claudius and Gertrude, and so the tasks customarily performed by the clown could be discharged by the tragic hero. He perceives false pathos and improvises verse at several stages of the play. With his devastating wit, his personality is in sharp contrast to the characters of Othello and Lear, who are not quick-witted. Othello is noble and Lear every inch a king, but their minds do not display 'an almost enormous intellectual activity', to quote Coleridge once more. No wonder, then, that the tragedy of *Hamlet*, which is unique within the Shakespeare canon, left little room for the talents of Robert Armin. He was not omitted entirely, for it is generally agreed that he played the grave-digger.[1]

In the grave-digger's song in *Hamlet* Shakespeare re-orchestrates a theme that he had earlier treated with less subtlety in Peter's song in *Romeo and Juliet*. Neither Juliet's supposed death nor Ophelia's suicide should be the occasion for a clown's song. This seeming impropriety is a dramatic topic in the richer texture of Hamlet:

> *Hamlet.* Has this fellow no feeling for his business,
>   that he sings at grave-making?
> *Horatio.* Custom hath made it in him a property of easiness.
> *Hamlet.* 'Tis e'en so. The hand of little employment hath
>   the daintier sense.

On the surface, song should not be merely 'custom', a sensitive singer should discriminate. But the Elizabethan belief that singing reveals a kindly and compassionate nature must also be considered. Contrary to the impression made on Hamlet and Horatio the clown's singing betrays some feeling, though it is by no means 'dainty'.

The warnings in Ronsard which condemn the man that hath no music in himself have their positive pendant in the theatre: a kindly man is fond of song. The humble, compassionate Lear says to Cordelia in Act V,

---

[1] Throughout this study the author has endeavoured to regard the parts played by Burbage, Kemp and Armin in accordance with the general consensus of scholarship. Leslie Hotson has put forward the additional hypothesis that Armin also played Polonius. But here, as in most instances, one must rely on internal evidence for allotting a particular part to a particular actor.

> So we'll live,
> And pray, and sing, and tell old tales . . .

This contrasts with the rash Lear of Act I, who asks somewhat archly, 'When were you wont to be so full of song, sirrah?' As a king, Lear does not engage in song on the stage, but the grave-digger conforms to convention, 'for it is an old proverb

> They prove servants kind and good
> That sing at their business like birds in the wood'.[1]

The first scene of Act V of *Hamlet* may be regarded as a requiem in several movements. It is a sermon on death and the transitory character of human existence. The clown-gravedigger takes part in over 200 of the 300-odd lines in this scene: his dialogue with the assistant clown; his song and the remarks of Hamlet and Horatio; and his dialogue with Hamlet. The remainder of the scene contains the well-known struggle between Hamlet and Laertes in Ophelia's grave. The clown establishes the key:

> [S.D. Enter two Clowns]
> *Clown.* Is she to be buried in Christian burial when she
>   wilfully seeks her own salvation?

The theme is expanded when the Priest tells the angry Laertes

> . . . Her death was doubtful . . .
> We should profane the service of the dead
> To sing a requiem. . . .

Even so, Ophelia is to have her requiem. The clown's very song, 'In youth when I did love' precedes Hamlet's exclamation

> I lov'd Ophelia. Forty thousand brothers
> Could not (with all their quantity of love)
> Make up my sum . . .

as a long chorale prelude may lead into a short hymn tune. But it is not only Ophelia's requiem, it is also a funeral oration for Yorick, harking back to Hamlet's youth and the persons and ideas whose memory he treasures. In this sad scene with its frivolous overtones the role of the clown is vital. His discussion of the propriety of a Christian burial for a suicide and 'that

---

[1] Thomas Deloney, *Works*, ed. F. O. Mann, Oxford, 1912, p. 110.

great folk should have count'nance in this world to drown or hang themselves more than their even-Christen' shows a sure grasp of legal and social issues. His riddles and jokes about grave-diggers and grave-makers are relevant to the main theme, as is the song. The resemblance to a chorale prelude is not so much in its character as in its extensive dimensions—with the interspersed prose it occupies sixty lines. In the discussion with the assistant clown and in his battle of wits with Hamlet the grave-digger is 'not altogether fool', and in his own gruff manner, he is not without compassion for Ophelia's young love and for Hamlet, 'he that is mad and sent into England'. To be sure, he is of low station and quite naturally resents the fact that Ophelia is not treated like an ordinary Christian. In his own way, this rough and witty fool shares with his prince the antic disposition: he is fond of quibbles, quick repartee, and the world of verse. As the scene wears on the relationship between the lowly fool and the fool royal becomes increasingly clear, and it is significant that Yorick 'a mad rogue', the 'King's jester', 'of most excellent fancy' is the final topic of conversation between Hamlet and the grave-digger. When the prince addresses Yorick's skull

> Where be your gibes now? your gambols? your songs?
> your flashes of merriment . . . ?

he invokes his own youth. If death is the main topic, song and requiem its ceremonial attributes, several subsidiary motifs appear to pull the strands together. Madness is one, mingling the world of fools and jesters with the distressed minds of Ophelia and Hamlet. The artistic temperament, with its fondness for improvisation, is another. For Hamlet breaks into verse and delivers snatches from ballads and songs as 'unreasonably' as the grave-digger who sings while engaged in his labours. He taunts Polonius with the ballad of Jephtah's daughter (II.ii.426), madly quotes to Ophelia and the court 'For o, for o, the hobby horse is forgot' (III.ii.143), and presumably quotes ballads after the play scene or else improvises as-if ballads (III.ii.282 and 304). As befits his station, as well as the abilities of the actor Burbage, he speaks rather than sings these lines. But the lyrics are as much a token of his assumed madness as are those of Ophelia in her famous scene. When Hamlet pays tribute to the infinite jest and excellent fancy, the gambols and songs of 'a mad rogue', he reminds us that madness may not merely harbour method; it is also related to the divine madness of inspiration. Appropriately enough, Hamlet ends the discussion with an impromptu quatrain on 'imperious Caesar, dead and turn'd to clay'. Gilbert Murray has this to say of the dramatic propriety of this scene:

'It is very remarkable that Shakespeare who did such wonders in his idealized and half-mystic treatment of the real Fool should also have made his greatest tragic hero out of a Fool transfigured.'[1]

Shakespeare

1st stanza:
In youth when I did love, did love,
  Methought it was very sweet:
To contract-o-the time for-a-my behove,
  O methought there[-a-][1] was nothing[-a-] meet.

British Museum, Add. MS 4900
{ I loathe that I did love,
  In youth that I thought sweet:
As time required for my behove:
  Methink they are not meet.

Thomas Vaux—1st stanza
I loathe that I did love,
  In youth that I thought sweet:
As time requires for my behove
    Methinks they are not meet.

Thomas Vaux—2nd stanza
My lusts they do me leave,
  My fancies all be fled;
And tract of time begins to weave
    Gray hairs upon my head.

2nd stanza:
But age with his stealing steps
  Hath [clawed][2] me in his clutch:
And hath shipped me intil the land,
  As if I had never been such.

Thomas Vaux—3rd stanza
For age with his stealing steps,
  Hath clawed me with his crutch:
And lusty life away she leaps,
  As there had been none such.

Thomas Vaux—13th stanza
For beauty with her band
  These crooked cares hath wrought:
And shipped me into the land,
  From whence I first was brought.

3rd stanza:
A pickaxe and a spade, a spade,
  For and a shrouding sheet,
O, a pit of clay for to be made,
  For such a guest is meet.

Thomas Vaux—8th stanza
A pickaxe and a spade,
  And eke a shrouding sheet,
A house of clay for to be made,
  For such a guest most meet.

---

[1] *The Classical Tradition in Poetry*, London, 1927, p. 113.

[2] In Shakespeare's first stanza the two drawling or singing syllables 'a', marked by square brackets, occur only in Q_2 but not in F. Concerning these extra syllables cf. *Sound and Poetry, English Institute Essays: 1956*, New York, 1957, p. 35. In Shakespeare's second stanza, F has 'caught' but Q_2 has 'clawed' which agrees with Vaux. In the same line Shakespeare's 'clutch' seems an improvement on Vaux's 'crutch' of old age.

Thomas Lord Vaux's 'I loathe that I did love' was first printed in 1557 in a miscellany entitled *Songs and Sonnets written by the right honourable Lord Henry Howard late Earl of Surrey, and other*. This famous collection, named variously as 'Tottel's Miscellany' and 'The Earl of Surrey's Poems' was generally known to the Elizabethans simply as *Songs and Sonnets*. Slender 'had rather than forty shillings I had my book of Songs and Sonnets here'. Jonson's character Downright criticizes 'ballads and roguery . . . and Songs and Sonnets . . .' and at another time the poet directs 'no more of thy Songs and Sonnets'.[1] Nine editions of this collection appeared in the thirty years following their initial publication. Later the *Songs and Sonnets* could boast such learned editors as Bishop Percy in the eighteenth century and Hyder Rollins in the twentieth.[2]

Vaux's songs were so popular that their texts were widely adapted and parodied by versifiers, and echoes of his lyrics appear in other poems of the time. The alliteration 'loathe-love' of Vaux's first stanza appears in several later collections. A volume of 1578 has 'leave that I did love, Or loathe the thing that lik'd me so . . .'; another of 1606: 'not that I loathe, where I so long did love'. The alliteration 'stealing steps' in Vaux's third (and the grave-digger's second) stanza seems to have been equally attractive to Elizabethan writers. It appears between 1560 and 1577 as 'with stealing steps she followed fast', 'now hoared age with stealing steps', and 'old crooked age with stealing steps'. The charm of the original obviously lay in the sentiment of the lyric as a whole, a renunciation of youth, life and love, and in its neat and felicitous turns of phrases. In the three stanzas selected for the grave-digging scene Shakespeare has contrived to include both of these features.

A song of quite different character, sung by Pandarus in *Troilus and Cressida*, has been hailed as 'one of the very greatest dramatic song masterpieces in our language'.[3] Like the lyrics of

---

[1] Shakespeare, *Merry Wives of Windsor*, I.i.206; Jonson, *Every Man in his Humour*, IV.iii.17; *The Case is Altered*, IV.v.1. The shortened title was also used by Greene, Nash, Dekker and Fletcher.

[2] *Songes and Sonnettes*, ed. H. E. Rollins, 2 vols., Cambridge (Mass.), 1928–1929, I.165 f. and II.283 ff. lists the sources in detail.

[3] Noble 129.

Peter in *Romeo and Juliet* and of the gravedigger in *Hamlet* it is a section of verse embedded in a prose scene. It was sung by an adult actor whom we cannot identify, though it is tempting to speculate that about this time Shakespeare promoted Armin to a more challenging and rewarding part and that Armin did, in fact, play Pandarus.

Coleridge called *Troilus and Cressida* a 'grand history-piece in the robust style of Albrecht Dürer'. But whereas the Folio speaks of 'Mr. William Shakespeares Comedies, Histories and Tragedies', 'history' is not a generally accepted category of drama. 'Histories' and 'tragedies' deal alike with kings and generals, war and peace. The distinction implied in the Folio seems to be that the histories treat of English kings, the tragedies of Greek, Roman, Italian, Danish, Scottish and ancient British matters, as in the case of *King Lear*. This vexatious problem of definition, whether *Troilus and Cressida* is a tragedy or a comedy, is inescapable in a study of Shakespeare's use of music in tragedy. Both Q and F have been cited in the controversy which has attended the question of the play's status. The preface of Q 'from a never writer to an ever reader' mentions 'comedy' frequently and compares Shakespeare to Terence and Plautus. On the other hand, in editing the F text Shakespeare's fellows Heminge and Condell, together with Jaggard, their printer, clearly regarded the play as a tragedy. E. K. Chambers calls it a 'tragedy of disillusionment' but O. J. Campbell terms it a 'comical satire'. Elements of satire are inevitable in a play whose cast includes Thersites, yet, 'if the play began as a satire . . . it ended by being something very different. There are in the play two potential tragedies—a tragedy of war and a tragedy of love. . . .' F. P. Wilson continues this discussion with a note on the construction of the drama which suggests a chronicle play. Dryden had this form in mind when he opined in 1677

. . . the latter part of the tragedy is nothing but a confusion of drums and trumpets, excursions and alarms.

In qualifying the genre of tragedy, as presented in *Troilus and Cressida*, the terms 'chronicle' or 'history' would be proper.

Three scenes in Act V emphasize more than any other the play's tragic aspects. The death of Hector at the instigation of the treacherous Achilles may be compared to the assassination of Julius Caesar. This scene, in particular, has no counterpart in any of the comedies since death, murder and assassination are, *per se*, alien to the stuff of comedy. Then the disenchantment of Troilus with the faithless Cressida rings a note that is close to the disappointment of Hamlet in Ophelia and of Othello in Desdemona. Finally, the anger and hope of revenge of Troilus could not be conceived as the concluding note in any of the fourteen plays which the Folio groups as comedies.[1] The elements of exaggeration and ludicrousness are balanced by such intensity of feeling and bitterness in the entire emotional climate that any resemblance to pure comedy is destroyed. It may be that this acrimonious note has tempted some scholars to define *Troilus and Cressida* as a dark comedy, a problem play, or a satire. Shakespeare and Mozart have this in common, that their works frequently defy neat classification, and for this reason we ought to observe the tragic elements in *Troilus and Cressida* and to pay tribute to the play's greatness *sui generis*.

We have remarked that in *Hamlet* the prince's native wit obviates the need for a chorus which, according to custom, would function through one or more of the minor characters. In contrast, *Troilus and Cressida* may be said to possess three lesser characters who perceive the turn of events and the predicaments of the major personalities. One of these is the sagacious and statesman-like Ulysses, who redresses the balance when Troilus exaggerates:

Ulysses.   Cressid was here but now.
Troilus. Let it not be believed for womanhood!
       Think we had mothers . . .
Ulysses. What hath she done, prince, that can soil our mothers?

The wisdom of Ulysses is not that of a court-fool; it is more penetrating, while his understanding resembles that of an imperturbable courtier like Horatio. Thersites, on the other hand, functions as court-fool much like Lavache or Lear's fool; he is both amusing and perspicacious, as well as of a merciless acidity. His puns on the 'fool' are reminiscent of Touchstone and Feste:

[1] For a more detailed account of the views of Dryden, Coleridge, Campbell (1938), Chambers (1940), F. P. Wilson (1945), and others, cf. NV edition (1953). Cf. also Greg FF 338 ff. and 445 ff.

Thersites.   . . . he is Ajax.
Achilles.   I know that, fool.
Thersites.   Ay, but that fool knows not himself.
Ajax.   Therefore I beat thee.
Thersites.   . . . what modicums of wit he utters . . .
Achilles.   Peace, fool!
Thersites.   I would have peace and quietness, but the fool
                 will not—he there . . .
Ajax.   O thou damned cur! I shall—
Achilles.   Will you set your wit to a fool's?   (II.i.64)

Yet, Thersites is so reckless and ill-tempered and so irritating that he becomes more the caricature of a court-fool than a chorus of wit. The indulgent (if not endearing) qualities lacking in Thersites are supplied by Pandarus who sees through the exaggerations of Troilus quickly enough. His faculty of criticism is vitiated by excessive softness, however, for he accommodates rather than corrects. The role of the pander is dramatically relevant throughout the play, and the function of his song is to emphasize the decadence of Paris and Helen. That Pandarus partakes of some of the traditional characteristics of the stage-fool is obvious, even though he is presented as of noble birth. Like Sir Jeffrey Balurdo in *Antonio's Revenge* he is a fool *de facto*, if not according to social position. He is, at all events, a pander and a go-between, and the epilogue he speaks is similar to the appeals for applause by Puck and Feste. One line, oddly enough, calls to mind the clown-gravedigger of *Hamlet*. The Folio of 1623 reads

> Why should our endeavour be so desired
> and the performance so loathed?

But the Quarto of 1609 has 'loved' instead of 'desired', and with this variant a reference to 'I loathe that I did love' may be surmised. Indeed, Pandarus's song has a closer kinship to the lyrics of the grave-digger and of Lear's fool than to any lyric occurring in the comedies, which may be adduced as further evidence of the temper of the play as a whole. The subject matter of the song itself is not tragic, but its function in the general context is both ironic and tragic.

The fact that Pandarus alone sings does not only exhibit his kindlier nature. It offers yet another illustration of the Ethos theory: the provider of soft luxuries, the pander, is characterized by music that is luxuriant beyond measure, a symbol of debauchery. Pandarus's initial reluctance to play the minstrel by obliging Paris and Helen with a public performance has been discussed earlier as a reflection of a general social attitude. This sophisticated, lecherous song portrays the ills with which the court is beset, as surely as Amiens traces the outdoor life of the Forest of Arden. It is not only the clever song of a pander; Shakespeare establishes with elaborate care how aptly it suits the Trojan aristocracy and, by analogy, the object of his satire, the Elizabethan gentry.

The consort of (instrumental) music emanating from Priam's palace where Paris and Helen, those prototypes of depravity, are feasting, is interrupted by Pandarus's arrival. Paris demands that he and his mistress be compensated for this deprivation by a song from Pandarus's own lips. His flattering praise that Pandarus is 'full of harmony' implies that he is expected to produce music of some complexity and that he is to accompany himself in a song as euphonious and voluptuous as the banquet music the courtiers had been enjoying. Helen, with playful petulance, persists in Paris's request against all protestations of the pander's assumed modesty, and to the detriment of the immediate business, namely, the message from Troilus which Pandarus is to convey to Paris. Helen prescribes the theme of the lyric:

> *Helen.* Let thy song be love; this love will undo
> us all. O Cupid, Cupid, Cupid!

Paris confirms the theme and names a presumably well-known song:

> *Paris.* Ay, good now, 'love, love, nothing but love'.
> *Pandarus.* In good troth, it begins so.
>
> [S.D. Sings]
>
> Love, love, nothing but love,[1] still more!
> For, O, love's bow
> Shoots buck and doe;
> The shaft confounds
> Not that it wounds,
> But tickles still the sore.

[1] This is the F reading. The Q inserts an extra 'still love'.

> These lovers cry, O ho! they die!
>   Yet that which seems the wound to kill,
> Doth turn O ho![1] to ha! ha! he!
>   So dying love lives still.
> O ho![1] awhile, but ha! ha! ha!
> O ho![1] groans out for ha! ha! ha![2]

Pandarus accompanies himself on the lute, the Elizabethans' aristocratic instrument, as the dialogue confirms:

> Come, give me an instrument. Now, sweet queen.

Here, in contrast to the performances of Peter and the grave-digger, the social position of the singer is emphasized. Pandarus is truly 'full of harmony' in that a harmonic accompaniment supports his song, whereas in *Romeo and Juliet* and *Hamlet* the dramatic context and the status of the singers would make the use of a lute ridiculous. Pandarus's public performance as vocalist and instrumentalist enhances the Italianate, luxuriant impropriety of this court scene. Moreover, the metrical complexity of the song is such that an accompaniment, though not obligatory, would aid the performance. There is a neat description of the song in the dialogue which precedes the singing of 'O Mistress Mine' in *Twelfth Night*:

> *Toby.*   ... there is sixpence for you. Let's have a song ...
> *Clown.*   Would you have a love song, or a song of good life?
> *Toby.*   A love song, a love song.
> *Andrew.*   Ay, Ay! I care not for good life.
>   [S.D. Clown sings.]

The prose dialogue which frames Pandarus's song stresses its decadence by the excessive repetitions of certain descriptive adjectives. In seven lines the word 'fair' is bandied about our ears eleven times. This is succeeded by seventeen employments of 'sweet', beginning with the passage where Helen prevents Pandarus from delivering his message to Paris.

> *Helen.*   We'll hear you sing certainly.
> *Pandarus.*   Well, sweet queen ... But, merry, thus, my lord ...
>   your brother Troilus—

---

[1] Again the F reading, the Q has 'Oh, oh'.
[2] Both F and Q add 'hey ho' to the line. But this seems metrically unlikely. Ritson and later commentators assign 'hey ho' to the subsequent dialogue.

Helen. My Lord Pandarus; honey-sweet lord—

Pandarus. Go to, sweet queen, go to—commends himself most
affectionately to you—

Helen. You shall not bob us out of our melody . . .

Pandarus. Sweet queen, sweet queen; that's a sweet queen, i' faith.[1]

Helen. And to make a sweet lady sad is a sour offence.

In the dialogues that concern music Shakespeare's aptitude
for punning invariably comes to the fore, as we have seen. But
whereas he generally distinguishes between sweet and sour
music as concordant and discordant, the constant repetition
here suggests a sickly sweetness. The melody which Helen craves
and which Pandarus eventually provides belongs to the soft
Lydian airs in the Ethos theory of music.

When it is over, the song is analysed and yet another epithet
conveys the sensuousness of the Trojan court.

Helen. In love, i'faith, to the very tip of the nose.

Paris. He eats nothing but doves, love, and that breeds hot
blood, and hot blood begets hot thoughts, and hot
thoughts beget hot deeds, and hot deeds is love.

Pandarus. Is this the generation of love? Hot blood, hot thoughts,
and hot deeds?

Thus, the excessively sweet music becomes a symbol of excessively hot love and, in general, of the depravity of the gentry.
At first bidding Pandarus is, quite properly, reluctant to sing
and quite improperly he finally yields to the entreaty and sings.
The scene is, in fact, pure comedy, as were the scenes of Peter
and of the grave-digger. At the same time, it is an important
illustration of the play's principal theme, for the ironic relevance
of the attitudes of Pandarus and Paris to the fate of Troy and
Hector is important in the structure of the play.

The melodies employed in the plays preceding and including
Hamlet were probably of a simple and popular cast. But the
satirical shafts aimed at the aristocracy were unsuited to popular
ballad tunes. The elaborate air, with its greater musical complexity, was on that account introduced. 'Love, love, nothing
but love, still more' begins with a line of five stresses, which is
followed by two lines of two stresses each. With its plentiful
exclamations of 'o ho', 'ha ha he' and 'ha ha ha', the stanza

---

[1] Cf. Dryden's *Troilus and Cressida*, II.ii. '. . . 'Tis a sweet queen, a sweet
queen, a very sweet queen. . . .'

does not lend itself to easy duplication, unlike the more conventional lyric of three and four stress lines. Like Jonson's 'Slow slow fresh fount' it consists of a single highly irregular stanza. By contrast, it is characteristic of the metrical regularity of Edwards's 'Where griping grief the heart would wound' and Vaux's 'I loathe that I did love' that these lyrics each consist of several stanzas. Pandarus's song is prosodically closer to a madrigal than to ballad poetry; its formal shape has more exceptional proportions than any other lyric in Shakespeare's plays. This bizarre pattern is well suited to the decadence it expresses.

A comparison with the corresponding lyric in Dryden's *Troilus and Cressida* of 1679 is worth observing. In the later work hired musicians perform a love song, in keeping with the aristocratic convention, while Pandarus listens. The song is in two stanzas, and no such irregular mixture as that of two-stress and five-stress lines occurs. Although there are similarities, as when Shakespeare has 'cry', 'die', and 'groans', and Dryden gives us 'anguish', 'languish' and 'torment', the character of the Restoration song is so changed that it is metrically and socially unexceptional. Whatever daring it exhibits is an arranged pose, while the irregularity of the Elizabethan lyric is a token of the command with which Shakespeare modified the traditions of manners as well as verse to suit his purpose.

The effeminate and sentimental atmosphere of John Wilson's setting of 'Take, o take those lips away' would be representative of the kind of music required. A comparison of the greater musical complexity called for in *Troilus and Cressida* with the boy's song in *Measure for Measure* poses a final question of dramatic analysis. In Elizabethan and Jacobean drama song had two main functions: to characterize and to influence the disposition of men. In Pandarus's air these functions are interwoven. On the one hand it represents the kind of Italianate music that was said to debase an Italianate English gentry.[1] On the other

---

[1] It is not within the scope of this study to show how rigid the Elizabethan prejudice against Italy was. Playwrights and critics were predisposed to bring in the bias whenever an opportunity offered itself. Some good examples appear in Marlowe and Ascham: the scheming Gaveston, planning to corrupt the wanton Edward II with Italian masques; the reckless Machiavel, in the prologue to the *Jew of Malta*, prepared 'to read a lecture here in Britain' after his assassination of the Duc de Guise. In Ascham's *Scholemaster* (ed. J. E. B. Mayor, London, 1863, pp. 78, 223) a discussion of Italian vices culminates in the proverb: *Inglese Italianato e un diabolo incarnato.*

1. 'Broken Consort', playing for a masque, *ca.* 1596.

2. Unknown lady with an archlute, *ca.* 1620.

3. Isaac Oliver, 'Love Theme', showing lutenist and flautist, *ca.* 1590.

4. Nicholas Hilliard, Queen Elizabeth I playing a lute, *ca.* 1580.

Painted frieze showing (*above*) a tenor violin and a cittern; (*below*) a treble violin and a pandora, 1585.

6. Young girl with Italian music-book, 1567.

7. Lady Grace Talbot with virginals and a book of the Psalms in French, 1591.

By three famous Masters: William Byrd: D: Iohn Bull, & Orlando Gibbons,
Gentilmen of his Ma:ties most Illustrious Chappell.
Ingrauen
by William Hole.
Dedicated To all the Masters and Louers of Musick.
for
DORETHIE EVANS.
Cum
Priuilegio.

8b. William Hole, Lady playing the virginals, *ca.* 1613.

8a. Jacob Matham, Saint Cecilia playing the organ, *ca.* 1588.

hand, that gentry was well disposed towards its own destruction before the first note of music sounded. Decadent knights had been habitually exposed to this voluptuous euphony and had thereby lost their honour and ceased to heed the traditional customs, morals and courage expected of them. We may say that the song truly expresses the tempers of the ruling class with uncanny accuracy, and thus Shakespeare blends the magic and character-defining powers of music.

Pandarus's lyric is another one of the many songs in Shakespeare for which no contemporary music is known and to which we are obliged to adapt an Elizabethan or Jacobean melody. The 'Good Shepherd's Sorrow' which begins 'In sad and ashy weeds' was popular in the early seventeenth century and seems to have been set to a variety of texts, particularly when their subject was melancholic. It was sung to a text lamenting the death of Prince Henry in 1612 and again at the death of Queen Anne in 1619. To this rather mournful ditty 'Love, love, nothing but love' yields its syllables and stresses without undue clumsiness.[1]

> The Good Shepherd's Sorrow
> for the death of his beloved son.
>   // To an excellent new tune.
>
> In sad and ashy weeds
> I sigh, I pine, I grieve, I mourn;
> My oats and yellow reeds,
> I now to jets and ebon turn.
>   My urged eyes
>   Like winter skies
> My furrowed cheekes o'erflow,
>   All heav'n knows why
>   Men mourn as I,
> And who can blame my woe.

---

[1] Cf. Richard Johnson's lyrical anthology *A Crown Garland of Golden Roses* of which editions appeared in 1612 (Pollard STC, 14672), 1631 (Pollard STC, 14673), 1659 (reprinted by W. Chappell, *Percy Society Publications*, XV, London, 1845) and 1662 (Wing STC, J 792). Our poem occurs in the 2nd, 3rd and 4th editions, sig. D.8^r. Cf. also sig. D.5^v for another poem to the same tune. Cf. also *Pepys Ballads*, ed. H. E. Rollins, 8 vols., 1929–32, I.32; *Roxburgh Ballads*, ed. W. Chappell & J. W. Ebsworth, 9 vols., VII.785 (No. 10); *Cavalier and Puritan*, ed. H. E. Rollins, 1923, p. 60; Bodleian MS Rawl. poet. 160, f. 26^r; Bodleian MS Don.d.58, f. 21^v.

The music is recorded in a virginal manuscript from the first half of the seventeenth century, transcribed by Sir John Hawkins.[1]

The following adaptation reduces the compass of the tune to an octave, to facilitate the casting of Pandarus. An accompaniment could easily be fitted to the melody.

Ex. 8.

Love, love, no-thing but love still more! For, O, love's bow shoots buck and doe; the shaft con-founds not that it wounds, but tick-les still the sore. These lo-vers cry, o-ho, they die! Yet that which seems the wound to kill, doth turn, o ho, to ha, ha, he! So dy-ing love lives still. O ho, a while, but ha, ha, ha! O ho, groans out for ha, ha, ha!

The date usually assigned to *All's Well that Ends Well* is 1603/04, which would place it after *Troilus and Cressida* and before *Measure for Measure*. Of the three tragicomedies—or problem plays or satires—this drama is furthest removed from

[1] Now in the New York Public Library, Drexel MS 5609, p. 143. The original form of 'In sad and ashy weeds' from which Hawkins made his copy is in Paris Conservatoire, MS Réserve 1186 (olim 18546) f. 60. Cf. Chappell I.202; Wooldridge I.156; also J. M. Gibbon, *Melody and the Lyric*, London 1930, p. 158.

tragedy. Death and revenge were the final note in the Trojan play, while in *Measure for Measure* the Viennese scene is oppressively clouded throughout by the threat of Claudio's execution. No threat of death enters into the story of Bertram and Helena. The fate of the two protagonists is settled by the king and anticipated by the audience early in the play. Only the immaturity of Bertram holds up the denouement for several acts. To many commentators the play is a failure, in spite of several great speeches, Helena's beguiling character, and some witty comments by the clown Lavache, a part 'obviously designed for Robert Armin'.[1] The elements of human stubbornness and divine order form a jarring discord rather than a dramatic antithesis; and whereas the *deus ex machina* solution points to the extraordinary redeeming grace of the last plays it never reaches their perfection.

In addition to his function as a critical chorus, Lavache also sings a song in Act I, scene iii. The lyrical verse is in sharp contrast to the surrounding prose[2] and, true to custom, the verbal music with its puns and other witticisms leads into the actual music of the song:

Countess. Sirrah, tell my gentlewoman I would speak
with her—Helen I mean.
[S.D. Sings]
Clown. Was this fair face the cause, quoth she,
Why the Grecians sacked Troy?
Fond done, done fond,
Was this King Priam's joy?
With that she sighed as she stood, *bis*[3]
And gave this sentence then:
Among nine bad if one be good,

---

[1] According to G. K. Hunter, the play's latest editor (1959), NA xxi and xxxiv. I am indebted to Mr. Hunter for several ideas which he sets out in his introduction.

[2] Lines 67–76 against lines 1–222. Whether the quatrain at lines 58–61 was spoken or sung is uncertain.

[3] The F text of 1623 is our only authority, since there is no Q. F prints the word *bis* in italics at the end of the line to denote repetition. In the case of the slightly shorter line 'Among nine bad . . .' the repetition is printed in full. The *Oxford English Dictionary* describes 'bis' as a musical direction but quotes no instance of its use before the early nineteenth century.

Among nine bad if one be good,
There's yet one good in ten.
Countess. What, one good in ten? You corrupt the song, sirrah.
Clown. One good woman in ten, madam, which is a purifying
a' th' song.

It would be grudging to deny the agreeableness of Lavache's song and the humour of his jokes. His perversion of the original ballad[1] in which Hecuba presumably laments the behaviour of her depraved son Paris is but a thin disguise for Shakespeare's unceasing concern with Trojan and Greek morality. But Lavache's lyric cannot be compared, in dramatic importance, to those in *Hamlet* or *Troilus and Cressida*. No contemporary music is known.

The singularity of Desdemona's performance has already been noted. That she would seek solace in music is understandable. But that she would sing herself rather than call an attendant was distinctly unconventional. Nor does the irregularity of *Othello* in respect of the use of music end there. The play is equally exceptional in regard to adult song. Othello's clown-servant has no song, whereas Iago, the bluff soldier, sings twice (II.iii). Iago's performance raises several questions to which no generally agreed answers have been found. Who was the first Iago? What were his motives and what sort of character and personality lay behind them? Finally, what kind of a tragedy is *Othello*?

In an assessment of Iago's mental constitution Coleridge's description of 'motiveless malignity' aptly complements Bradley's designation of Iago's deadly coldness and his 'gaiety in destruction': malice becomes its own reward. His intellectual delight in his own clever manoeuvres was shared by an audience that was half delighted, half aghast. Bradley's comments on the difference between Milton's Satan and Shakespeare's Iago conclude:

It is only in Goethe's Mephistopheles that a fit companion for Iago can be found. Here there is something of the same . . . gaiety in destruction.

In both cases there are overtones of the elegant court fool who

---

[1] Malone notes 'The Lamentation of Hecuba and the Ladyes of Troye' (entered Stat. Reg. 1586) as possibly the original from which the Clown quoted.

holds in his bag of tricks the resort to song as one of the means of duping his victim. The 'gulling' and 'bleeding' that characterize Iago's treatment of Roderigo was a frequent device in Jacobean comedy. It may also be observed in the relationship between Autolycus and the young shepherd in the *Winter's Tale* (IV.iii) or Subtle and Dapper in Jonson's *Alchemist* (III.v).

The King's Men performed both Jonson's *Alchemist* and *Othello* at Oxford in 1610. Armin's name appears in the list of actors appended to the published version of the *Alchemist*. This lends some support to the hypothesis that Armin played the part of Iago from its inception until the winter of 1610/11 when, to all appearances, he retired from the company. (It is also likely that he played the part of Autolycus in the winter of 1610 and that the part was, in fact, written for him.) A comprehensive monograph by T. W. Baldwin, dealing with the probabilities of casting,[1] gives full credit to Robert Armin's achievement:

As soon as Kemp leaves the company in 1599 the clown changes notably into the sly, roguish, jesting fool of court. As Armin says of himself in his *Nest of Ninnies*, 'I goe in Motly'. It is immediately evident that Touchstone, Feste, the Clown in the present form of *All's Well* or the Fool in *Lear* are of another guess from the pompous, countrified, blundering clown of Kemp.

Nevertheless, Baldwin allots several parts which are humorous, though not clown-like, to John Lowin who joined the company in 1603. Among them are Jonson's Volpone and Mammon; and Shakespeare's Falstaff, Parolles and Iago. That Lowin played Falstaff some time after Kemp has been proven. But the hypothesis that Armin played the part of Iago deserves credence. Admittedly, the two drinking songs in Act II could be sung, after a fashion, by most actors. Still, among the principal actors named in the Folio of 1623 Armin was clearly the best adult singer up to 1610/11. The pompous part of Falstaff apparently fitted both Kemp and Lowin; the sly, insinuating part of Iago would have favoured, one ventures to think, the character and slight size of Armin.

Whether Iago was played by Armin or Lowin, the hypothesis that a comic actor took the role raises the question of the comic

[1] *Organization and Personnel of the Shakespearean Company*, Princeton, 1927, particularly pp. 244–248.

element in this tragedy. Its frame differs significantly from the historical grandeur of *Hamlet, King Lear* and *Macbeth*, and the contemporary *mise-en-scène* in which Shakespeare chose to present the play is peculiar to its mixture of the tragic and comic. For the dukes and kings of the comedies belong to a happy fairyland, whereas the destinies of Hamlet and Fortinbras, Caesar and Brutus, Macbeth and Banquo, Antony and Octavius, are of a majestic order. Schoolboys and play-house audiences accepted these characters as the stuff of remote history. But the date of the Turkish attack on Cyprus had been as recent as 1570,[1] and there was nothing ancient, much less hallowed, about the fates of Othello and Iago. The final tribute to King Lear would be out of place in this company:

> The oldest hath borne most: we that are young
> Shall never see so much, nor live so long.
> > [Exeunt with a dead march]

Once Iago determines on a 'stoup of wine' to

> > put our Cassio in some action
> > That may offend the isle   (II.iii.63)

the business in hand is vigorously pursued to the point where Montano challenges Cassio to a fight:

> *Montano.*   Come, come, you're drunk!
> *Cassio.*   Drunk?   (line 156)

That a song should function as wine's proverbial ally is to be expected, but the contrast with the drunken scene in *Antony and Cleopatra* is worth noting. In the Roman play a 'boy' is directed to sing a song on the galley of Pompey who

> doth this day laugh away his fortune.

But it is part of Iago's skill and cunning that he does not depend on an attendant. By himself performing and thereby precisely timing his own adult songs Iago becomes, not fortune's fool, but the master of his fate. (That he is not important or rich enough

---

[1] On the contemporary quality of *Othello* cf. A. C. Bradley, *Shakespearean Tragedy*, London, 1904, Lecture V; cf. also the comment by Helen Gardner on the hero's combination of tragic and comic qualities in the 'Annual Shakespeare Lecture of the British Academy' for 1955.

to command a boy-singer is by the way.) Moreover, by pretending to be full of song, as good-natured and kindly people were supposed to be, 'honest' Iago disarms any suspicion Cassio may have harboured. Iago breaks into his first song without warning:

line 66 *Cassio.* Fore God, they have given me a rouse
  already.
  Montano. Good faith, a little one; not past a pint,
  as I am a soldier.
  Iago. Some wine, ho!
  [sings] And let me the canakin clink, clink;
  And let me the canakin clink.
  A soldier's a man;
  O, man's life's but a span,
  Why, then, let a soldier drink.
  Some wine, boys!
  Cassio. Fore God, an excellent song
  Iago. I learn'd it in England, where indeed they
  are most potent in potting. Your Dane . . .

The prose dialogue is interrupted by the verse of the song which has the obvious characteristics of a stanza intended for singing: the extra 'clink' in line 71, the manner in which line 72 repeats 71, the sudden reduction to a two-stress line in 73, and the return to the opening length and rhyme in line 75. In Q_1, of 1622, lines 73–74 have a more symmetrical pattern:

> A soldier's a man
> A life's but a span

But in the 1600s the insertion of extra syllables was one of Shakespeare's methods of adapting verse for singing; witness, for instance, the grave-digger's song in *Hamlet*. There seems no good reason why the compositor of the F text should have printed a metrically more irregular line for Iago's song unless an authoritative copy had so instructed him. The Q reading would seem to be based on an actor's remembering a standard version rather than the playwright's variant.

Despite the fact that several parallel passages[1] in the con-

---

[1] Quoted in H. C. Hart's edn., London, 1903, p. 97; cf. also NV (1886), p. 130; NS (1957), p. 171; *The Knave in Grain*, ed. R. C. Bald (Malone Society Reprints), Oxford, 1961, lines 1616–19. T. Ravenscroft, *Pammelia*, ed. P. Warlock, London, 1928, p. 16, No. 68.

temporary literature mention carousing, canakins and clinking, neither the text nor the music of the original drinking song have so far been discovered. Among possible tunes that could be fitted to Iago's words 'Joan Sanderson'[1] seems to offer one of the best adaptations. Certain sections of it have been set below to accompany the song.

The fifteen lines of prose that intervene between Iago's first and second lyric deal with two themes: first, Iago ostensibly extols the virtues of the 'pottle', though the subsequent dialogue makes clear that Iago, Cassio and Montano one and all condemn drunkenness as a vice; the second theme, which is stressed with equal insistence, gives the origin of the song as English and commends the English, from whom Iago had learned the song, for their extraordinary capacity for drinking. Danes, Germans and Hollanders 'are nothing to your English' and 'your Englishman . . . drinks you with facility your Dane

---

[1] An alternative title is 'Cushion Dance'. Several variants were printed between 1615 and 1686, cf. Chappell I.153; Wooldridge I.287; *Grove's Dictionary of Music* . . ., 5th edn., 1954, s.v. 'Cushion Dance'; G. Bontoux, *La chanson en Angleterre au temps d'Elisabeth*, Oxford, 1936, p. 149. The variant preserved in Playford's *Dancing Master* of 1686 fits the words best and has been used here. Another suggestion, made by D. C. Greer, is to use the tune 'Soldier's Life', printed and discussed as Music Example 2 (a), Chapter III, p. 63.

dead drunk'. Indeed, the last line before the singing resumes is a jocular thrust in the same direction:

Cassio.   To the health of our General!
Montano.   . . . I'll do you justice.
Iago.   O sweet England!
        [Sings:] King Stephen was and a worthy peer,
              His breeches cost him but a crown. . . .

Iago sings the complete seventh stanza of this well-known Scottish ballad entitled variously 'Bell my wife', 'Tak your auld cloak about thee' or simply 'The Old Cloak'.

Modern commentators are inclined to think that the ballad is Scottish in origin and that the words 'lown' and 'auld' are reminiscent of its northern ancestry. Both Scottish and Irish tunes were so popular in Shakespeare's England that they often became indigenous to the English repertory through their adaptation to the English texts. The 'King Stephen' variant occurs in several sources, though the majority of the collections in which the lyric is preserved is Scottish. (A list of sources and references for the text and music will be found in Appendix II.)

While the primary function of this song is to bring about Cassio's disgrace, in the process it reveals aspects of Iago's and Cassio's personalities. In order to achieve his purpose Iago assumes a bonhomie that mingles banter, drinking and singing. Like Goethe's Mephistopheles in Auerbach's cellar the evil agent must wear a clown's disguise to ensnare his victim. It is, indeed, unfortunate that though the ballad was apparently well known in the sixteenth century the earliest preserved musical text is no older than Oswald's mid-eighteenth-century collection of Scottish tunes which contains 'Tak your auld cloak about you' in a wordless instrumental arrangement for flute. The version printed by Bremner for voice and keyboard accompaniment, with the words from Ramsay's anthology, provides a good basis for comparison with Shakespeare, as the following stanzas show:

Shakespeare:
King Stephen was and a[1] worthy peer,
    His breeches cost him but a crown,
He held them sixpence all too dear,
    With that he call'd the tailor lown;

[1] Q_1: a; F: and-a; Q_2: and a.

He was a wight of high renown,
　　And thou art but of low degree;
'Tis pride that pulls the country down,
　　Then take thine auld[1] cloak about thee.

Ramsay-Bremner:
In days when our King Robert rang,
　　His trews they cost but haff a crown;
He said they were a groat o'erdear,
　　And ca'd the tailor thief and loun.
He was the king that wore a crown,
　　And thou the man of laigh degree,
'Tis pride puts a' the country down,
　　Sae tak thy auld cloak about ye.

The following two music examples reprint the instrumental version by Oswald and the vocal version by Bremner. The first and fourth stanzas of Ramsay are set below the Bremner rendering and below these stanzas is printed Shakespeare's text. When Bremner reprinted his *Thirty Scots Songs* in 1770 he changed the

Ex. 10

---

[1] Q_1: Then take thine owd.
F: And take thy awl'd.
Q_2: Then take thine auld.
Concerning the extra syllable in the first line see the discussion of 'And let me the canakin clink' and 'In youth when I did love' above.

notes in bar 15 slightly to form a descending figure, whereas the corresponding notes, in the 1757 version, ascended. The older

Ex. 11.

In   win - ter when   the   rain rain'd cauld,   and
In   days when our   king Ro - bert rang,   his
King Ste - phen was   and a wor - thy peer,   his

frost and snaw on   il - ka hill,   and Bo - ras with his
trews they cost but haff a crown,   he said they were a
bree - ches cost him but a crown;   he held them six - pence

blasts sae bauld, was threat-'ning a'   our   ky to kill, then
groat o'er dear, and ca'd the tai - lor thief and loun. He
all   too dear,   with that he call'd the tai - lor lown; he

Bell my wife,   wha loves na strife,   she said to me   right
was the king   that wore a crown, and thou the man of
was a wight of high re - nown, and thou art but of

ha - sti - ly,   get   up, good - man, save Cro - my's life, and
laigh de - gree, 'tis pride puts a'   the coun - try down, sae
low de - gree; 'tis pride that pulls the coun - try down, then

tak   your auld   cloak   a - bout   ye.
tak   thy   auld   cloak   a - bout   ye.
take thine auld   cloak   a - bout   thee.

printing seems the more proper and was preferred by Robert Chambers (1862) and John Greig (1893). However, the descending figure was printed by James Johnson in 1790, and Joseph Ritson in 1794, and is therefore reproduced here as an alternate ending.

Appendix I

'In Youth when I did Love'—
'I Loathe that I did Love'

The *Songs and Sonnets*, which included a number of Thomas Lord Vaux's lyrics besides 'I loathe that I did love', were well known to the Elizabethans.[1] 'I loathe that I did love' survives in six other sources, four of which give the words only, two of them the music. Moreover, its tune accompanies yet another lyric, 'You graves of grisly ghosts'.[2] The version sung in *Hamlet* and the song of the Lemures in Goethe's *Faust* (derived from Shakespeare) are two further variations of Vaux's ballad.

Two musical settings are known of 'I loathe that I did love'. The first of these was written (not printed) in the margin of a copy of the edition of *Songs and Sonnets* which was printed in 1557. This copy is no longer extant, but the melody had been transcribed from it in the nineteenth century and preserved in Nott's edition of the collection of 1814. The second setting is to be found in British Museum, Additional Manuscript 4900.

George Frederick Nott consulted many sources in preparing his critical edition, including the copy now lost. His musical collaborator was William Crotch who transcribed twelve tunes from this valuable source of the sixteenth century. It must be stressed, however, that the sole authority for this setting at present is Crotch's transcription

---

[1] Certain lyrics of Thomas Lord Vaux were in great public favour. One of them, 'How can the tree but waste' appeared in numerous editions of another miscellany, the *Paradise of Dainty Devices*; it has been transmitted in six texts, four of them with music. There is also a lyric by Deloney to be sung to the tune of it. *Paradise of Dainty Devices*, ed. H. E. Rollins, Cambridge (Mass.), 1927, pp. 72 f. and 236 f. lists the sources in detail. Thomas Deloney, *Works*, ed. F. A. Mann, Oxford, 1912, p. 405. O. F. Emerson, 'Shakespeare's Sonnetteering', *Studies in Philology*, XX (1923), 111–136.

Music for 'How can the tree' may be found: (1) W. Barley, *Book of Tablature*, London, 1596; (2) British Museum, Add. MS 24665; (3) Edinburgh, Adv., MS 5.2.14; (4) Cambridge, MS Dd.4.23. (5) Oxford, Christ Church, Mus. MS 984-8.

[2] *Gorgeous Gallery of Gallant Inventions*, ed. H. E. Rollins, Cambridge (Mass.), 1926, p. 35.

which was published in 1814.[1] Crotch gives the melody only, as reprinted in our Music Example No. 1 below. Strangely enough, only one copy of Nott's edition *with music* is known to exist. This unique copy is in the Library of the Duke of Norfolk in Arundel Castle.[2] Crotch's transcription does not accommodate itself to regular metrical barring. This may be due to the rhythmical freedom with which the music follows the accents of the words, or it may be due to a scribal error in the sixteenth-century volume, or an error in transcription. In any case, the melodic line in the examples which follow is nearly identical, and the differences lie in the degree of regularity of the metrical rhythm. Examples 3 and 4 maintain the same measure in each bar, in the manner of a hymn tune of the eighteenth or nineteenth century. But in Example 2, offered as a working hypothesis, bars of four minims and bars of three minims alternate freely. This entails only two emendations: to lengthen both in bar 3 and in bar 7 the last note by a crotchet. The transcriptions of Chappell and Wooldridge are offered as Examples 3 and 4. Finally, Example 5 gives both Vaux's and Shakespeare's text, fitted to Example 2. In the latter case a good deal of rhythmical freedom would be required in performance.[3]

The second musical setting, preserved in the British Museum Additional Manuscript 4900, dates from the early seventeenth century. On two facing pages f. 62v and 63r, there are to be found the voice part and the lute accompaniment of three songs, among them

Ex. 1.

[1] Both Nott and Crotch were contemporaries at Christ Church, Oxford, in the closing decades of the eighteenth century. Nott received his B.A. in 1788, M.A. 1792; Crotch became organist in 1790 (and professor of music in the University in 1797).

[2] Four other copies of the 1814 edition are in the British Museum: shelf marks 11604.ff.4; 11607.i.7; 11623.ff.1; C.60.o.13. None of these four copies have the music plates, which are to be found in the Arundel copy between pages 4 and 5 and pages 154 and 155. Nott's edition of 1815 contains no music.

[3] Chappell I.217, harmonized by G. A. Macfarren; Wooldridge I.52, harmonized by himself; R. Hughey, 'The Harington Ms at Arundel Castle and Related Documents', *Library*, XV (1934–35), 388–444, particularly 394 f.

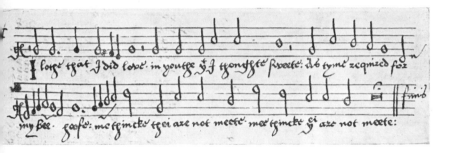

Facsimile 1. 'I loathe that I did love'.

Ex. 2.

Ex. 3.

Ex. 4.

Ex. 5.

I loathe that I did love, in
In youth when I did love, did love, me -

youth that I thought sweet: as time re-quires for
thought it was ve - ry sweet: to contract o the time for a

my be - hove me - thinks they are not meet.
my be - hove, O me thought there a was no-thing a meet.

Ex. 6.

'I loathe that I did love'. A complete transcription, transposed a third downward from C Major to A Major, is given in Example 6.[1] This version is not suitable for performance by the gravedigger for several reasons. The lute accompaniment is out of place, as are also the elaborate melismas on the words 'behove' and 'methink'. Accordingly, a simplified voice part has been prepared and is given in Example 7.[2] (Upper text, Vaux; lower text, Shakespeare.)

Ex.7.

1   2
I   loathe   that   I   did   love,   in
In   youth   when   I   did   love,   me -

3   4   5
youth   that   I   thought   sweet: as   time   re- quir'd   for
thought   it   was   ve - ry   sweet: to   con-tract   o   the   time   for a

6   7
my   be - hove,   me -   think   they   are   not
my   be - hove,   O   me -   thought   there   a   was   nothing a

8   9   10
meet,   me - think   they   are   not   meet.
meet,   me - thought   there   a   was   nothing a   meet.

[1] Two emendations have been made in the transcription of the lute tablature. At bar 3, 4th quaver (eighth-note), the manuscript, as transposed, reads 'f sharp-b', which has been emended 'g sharp-b'. At bar 7 the note values for the fourth crotchet (quarter-note) have been transcribed at half the value: manuscript has dotted crotchet (quarter-note) plus quaver (eighth-note), emended as dotted quaver plus semiquaver.

[2] Chappell I.216 f. gives the tune, harmonized by G. A. Macfarren. Chappell changed a few accidentals, and allotted the text differently to the notes, to avoid the melismas. Wooldridge I.52 did not transcribe the music, but commented that 'it is more scholastic and evidently a piece of chamber music'. That the manuscript preserves a more complex setting than that transcribed by Crotch is quite true, though the term chamber music is misleading in regard to a song. The voice part of Example 6 is correctly transcribed in B. Pattison, *Music and Poetry of the English Renaissance*, London, 1948, p. 167.

Appendix II

King Stephen was and a Worthy Peer

Since certain of the sources listed below are rare the shelf-mark of copies in the Bodleian or the British Museum, abbreviated as O and L, has been indicated.

TEXT

ca. 1650   Bishop Percy's Folio MS. Cf. J. W. Hales & F. J. Furnivall, *Bishop Percy's Folio Manuscript*, 3 vols., London, 1867–68, II.320.

1730   Allan Ramsay, *Tea Table Miscellany* . . ., London, 1730, p. 113; O: 12.Θ.1338.

1765   Thomas Percy, *Reliques of Ancient English Poetry*, Book the Second: Containing Ballads that Illustrate Shakespeare, No. 7.

REFERENCES TO TEXT

1592   R. Greene, *Quip for an Upstart Courtier*, '. . . it was a good and blessed time here in England when King Stephen wore a pair of cloth breeches. . . .'

1600/10   The jig of 'Michael and Frances'. Cf. C. J. Sisson, *Lost Plays of Shakespeare's Age*, Cambridge, 1936, pp. 137, 207.

> *To the tune of 'Take thy old coat about thee'*
> 'What news?', quoth he, 'my pretty peat,
> me thinks thou looks full merrily . . .'
> *Original spelling*
> What newes quoth he my prettie peate
> mee thinks thou lookes full merely

1609   T. Dekker, *The Gull's Hornbook*, '. . . his breeches were not so much worth as King Stephen's, that cost but a poor noble . . .'

1611   *The Tempest*, IV.i.222: O King Stephano! O peer! O worthy Stephano, look what a wardrobe here is for thee!

MUSIC

1750/60   James Oswald, *Caledonian Pocket Companion . . . Scotch tunes . . . for the German flute . . .*, 8 vols., London, n.d., II.29; L: Hirsch.M.1443.

1757   Robert Bremner, *Thirty Scots Songs, for a Voice and Harpsi-*

156

chord . . . the words from Allan Ramsay, 2 vols., Edinburgh, n.d., I.14; O: Mus. 2.c.92 (3).

1790   James Johnson, *Scots Musical Museum*, 6 vols., Edinburgh, n.d. [1787–1803], III.258.

1794   Joseph Ritson, *Scottish Songs*, 2 vols., London, 1794, I.219.

1859   Chappell, II.505.

1862   Robert Chambers, *Songs of Scotland prior to Burns*, Edinburgh, 1862, p. 113.

1893   John Greig, *Scots Minstrelsie*, 6 vols., Edinburgh, 1893, II.194.

1900   John Glen, *Early Scottish Melodies*, Edinburgh, 1900, p. 144.

VII

BLANK VERSE, PROSE AND
SONGS IN *KING LEAR*

S<small>HAKESPEARE</small>'s celebrated blank verse found its glorious
expression in the dignified speech of his tragedies. This fact is
well known and in itself needs no emphasis. But in his prosody,
as in other aspects of his works, Shakespeare developed a
technique peculiarly his own; in particular, his unorthodox
inclusion of lyrics offered relief from and a contrast to the preponderant blank verse. Allowing that song was, to begin with,
an unconventional element in tragedy, there were yet differences
in the degree to which the use of lyrics would appear as incongruous. Generally speaking, the verse of a song deviated
from the surrounding blank verse only in its shorter lines (and
usually by end-rhyme), but the iambic metre prevailed and
verse was encased by verse. This was certainly true of the boys'
songs. As a rule, these were performed by an attendant at the
behest of some superior. Since the song in Act IV of *Measure for
Measure* opens the scene it is followed by blank verse; the drinking scene in *Antony and Cleopatra*, II.vii, with its boy's song, is also
in verse (lines 60–119 and 126–142), as is the scene in *Julius
Caesar*, IV.iii, where Lucius sings for Brutus. The two exceptions
where boys' songs are allotted to heroines, not attendants, show
some variation in the metrical shape of the surrounding dialogue. In the case of the Willow Song, the unusual domesticity
of the occasion and the wholly unheroic and matter-of-fact
attitude of Emilia evoke some prose lines (38–40, 53–54, 72–88);

but the lyric proper is framed by verse (lines 11–37 and 59–71) and the scene as a whole is enclosed in verse (1–10, 89–108). In the mad songs of Ophelia the case differs according to the speaker of the dialogue. When the heroine's songs break in upon the lines of the queen or Laertes, the verse of balladry succeeds the blank verse of tragedy. When, on the other hand, Ophelia proceeds from her own speech (lines 41–47) to song, her lyric is framed by prose, an exceptional case brought about by her exceptional state of mind.

Although Shakespeare appears to have observed the accepted rules in regard to boys' songs or simply songs of attendants, he flouted tradition when he permitted clowns to mingle with kings. 'We that are young' are inclined to smile at Sidney's injunction. But it is as well to remember that as late as the nineteenth century so brilliant a poet and so perceptive a critic as Coleridge questioned the authenticity of the porter's speech in the tragedy of *Macbeth*. Thus, the adult songs in Shakespeare's tragedies must take their place within the framework of the character's role, and the lyrics of the clown in *Romeo and Juliet*, of the grave-digger, of Pandarus, of Lavache and of Iago are accordingly enveloped in prose. It is also true of *King Lear*: of the eighteen pieces of verse given to the fool and to Edgar all but one occur within prose passages. This procedure is too consistent to be explained as accidental. There is no doubt that the prose of the comic and tragi-comic scenes interrupts the lofty structure of tragedy, where the characteristic and traditional mode of expression is blank verse; and one surmises that our modern audiences who take raucous and indecorous speech as a matter of course miss some of the pungency of Shakespeare's drama when they ignore the irregularity of his procedure.

Shakespeare's artistry in the comic scenes resembles a prism whose many facets surprise and delight the onlooker: the shock of the unexpected is followed by the delight of discovery. The puns and jokes, trivial and lewd as they may be, throw an ironic but also deeply moving light upon the central tragic theme. We no sooner come to accept this jocular prose when we suffer another sea-change, for in the hands of a great dramatic poet the occasional infusion of song partakes of magic. This effect of verse within prose, of surprise within surprise, is comparable to the dramatic illusion of the play within the play. After the

success of *Hamlet* both devices were overworked to cheap purpose, but rarely has the verse of adult song within the prose of
the clown's scene been handled in more masterly fashion than in
Hamlet and *King Lear*. In this respect it is instructive to compare
Shakespeare's tragedy with his source, the anonymous *Chronicle
History of King Leir* of 1605, where the king is never insane and
there is no fool or mad Tom. *The Chronicle . . . of . . . Leir* contains
prose only occasionally, as in the scenes of the messenger; the
king speaks exclusively in verse. Moreover, as befitting the genre
of tragedy, there are no songs whatever.[1]

The course of Lear's development from king to madman and
his recovery to true regal stature is mirrored in the prosody.[2]
His momentous decision in the opening scene

> To shake all cares and business from our age,
> Conferring them on younger strengths . . .

is expressed in traditional verse. In the fourth scene the king
shows concern for the first time over the treatment he is receiv-
ing at the hands of Goneril and her steward Oswald. This per-
turbation is expressed in prose (particularly lines 68 ff.). As the
prose scene proceeds it is interspersed by seven lyrics in which
the fool shows his perspicacious grasp of the king's plight. He
instructs the former king by his song:

Fool. . . . thou hadst little wit in thy bald crown when thou
gav'st thy golden one away. If I speak like myself in
this, let him be whipped that first finds it so.

[Sings]

> Fools had ne'er less grace in a year;
> For wise men are grown foppish,
> And know not how their wits to wear,
> Their manners are so apish.

---

[1] Statistics about the proportion of blank verse and prose in *Hamlet, King
Lear, Troilus and Cressida* and other plays are given in Appendix VIII to this
chapter.

[2] Both Q_1 of 1608 and F of 1623 are careless about the printing of verse,
so that unusual discretion must be exercised by modern editors. There is also
the need to decide whether verse is spoken or sung, since none of the lyrics
are marked as songs in the Q or F texts. Throughout this chapter the consensus of modern editorial practice has been followed, notably NS, ed.
Duthie, 1960. A complete list of the eighteen pieces of verse given to the fool
or Edgar appears in Appendix I to this chapter.

Lear. When were you wont to be so full of songs, sirrah?
Fool. I have used it, nuncle, e'er since thou mad'st
    thy daughters thy mothers—for when thou gav'st them
    the rod and putt'st down thine own breeches,

                                   [Sings]

        Then they for sudden joy did weep,[1]
          And I for sorrow sung,
        That such a king should play bo-peep,
          And go the fools among.

    Prithee, nuncle, keep a schoolmaster that can teach
    thy fool to lie: I would fain learn to lie.

But throughout his role the fool does not lie; he teaches the king
the bitter lesson of truth; he is, as Kent observes to Lear, 'not
altogether fool, my Lord'.

There are many transitions from verse to prose as Lear is
taught humility and compassion by painful degrees. But no-
where are these prosodic changes more revealing than in the
storm scenes of Act III. Lear opens the second scene in blank
verse:

    Blow, winds, and crack your cheeks! rage! blow!
    You cataracts and hurricanoes, spout
    Till you have drenched our steeples, drowned the cocks!

But the fool cautions practical wisdom, prosaic in more than one
sense:

    O nuncle, court holy water in a dry house is
    better than this rain-water out o'door. Good nuncle,
    in, ask thy daughter's blessing!

Again the king apostrophizes the elements:

    But yet I call you servile ministers,
    That will with two pernicious daughters join
    Your high-engendered battles 'gainst a head
    So old and white as this. O, ho! 'tis foul!

only to have his fool rejoin

    He that has a house to put's head in has a good
    head-piece.
          The cod-piece that will house
          Before the head has any,

[1] Music for this quatrain is transcribed and discussed in Appendix II.

> The head and he shall louse:
> So beggars marry many.
> . . .

This mixture of prose and lyric with its indecorous frankness is characteristic of a clown's role. Invariably the connection between dialogue and poem is a single word whose sound evokes the lyric which consequently borders on a pun. The old and white head of Lear leads to the head and head-piece of the fool. 'Wit' acts as a lever for the next lyric:

Lear.   My wits begin to turn.
> Come on, my boy. How dost, my boy? Art cold?
> I am cold myself . . .
> Poor fool and knave, I have one part in my heart
> That's sorry yet for thee.

Fool. [Sings]
> > He that has and a little tiny wit—
> > > With heigh-ho, the wind and the rain—
> > Must make content with his fortunes fit,
> > > Though the rain it raineth every day.

Lear. True, boy. Come, bring us to this hovel.
Fool. This is a brave night to cool a courtesan! I'll
> speak a prophecy ere I go:
> > When priests are more in word than matter;
> > When brewers mar their malt with water;
> > . . .
> > Then comes the time, who lives to see't,
> > That going shall be used with feet.
> This prophecy Merlin shall make, for I live before his time.

In this scene Lear's mind has not been driven from sanity to insanity, from royal blank verse to prose, and the fool's verse follows immediately upon the king's speech. Consequently we have the first (and only) example in *King Lear* where the fool's song is preceded by verse. It is significant, dramatically, that Lear is sufficiently composed to 'have one part in my heart that's sorry yet for thee'. For, in spite of his keen discernment of the king's situation, the fool still depends on Lear. At the same time, he speaks more wisely than appears on the surface. The 'rain it raineth every day' is not only a philosophical maxim of sorts but such an obvious fact that a miraculously humble and considerate king is induced to seek shelter in 'this hovel'.

In the fourth scene of Act III the insanity of Lear reaches its culmination when he strives to tear off his clothes. He now has for company, in addition to the court fool, Edgar, masquerading as mad Tom. They sing their lowly snatches of song at him. He is still composed (line 6) when he observes

> Thou think'st 'tis much that this contentious storm
> Invades us to the skin: so 'tis to thee;
> But where the greater malady is fixed,
> The lesser is scarce felt.

And there is some royal stance in his speech (line 60) when he pities poor Tom:

Edgar. .... Bless thy five wits! Tom's a cold.[1] O, do de, do de, do de, bless thee from whirlwinds ...
.... and there, and there again, and there.
[S.D. storm still]

Lear. What, has his daughters brought him to this pass? Could'st thou save nothing? Would'st thou give 'em all?
...
Kent. He hath no daughters, Sir.
Lear. Death, traitor! Nothing could have subdued nature To such a lowness but his unkind daughters.

By the end of the scene (line 100) the king is reduced to 'the thing itself':

Edgar. .... Keep thy foot out of brothels, thy hand out of plackets, thy pen from lenders' books, and defy the foul fiend.
Still through the hawthorn blows the cold wind,
Says suum, mun, hey nonny nonny.
Dolphin my boy, boy! sessa! let him trot by.
[S.D. storm still]

---

[1] The lunatic bedlam beggars of London traditionally complained of being cold and blessed the wits of their prospective donors. In all probability we have here a fragment of a traditional song, 'Poor Tom'. Music for a quatrain which begins 'Poor naked Bedlam, Tom's a-cold' and concludes 'God almighty bless thy wits' survives in a composition of Orlando Gibbons and is transcribed and discussed in Appendix III. Concerning Robert Armin as a possible source of information on the mad Bedlam (Bethlehem Hospital) Beggars and their songs, cf. A. K. Gray, 'Robert Armine, the foole', *Publications* of the Modern Language Association, XLII (1927), 673–685.

Lear. Thou wert better in a grave . . .
       . . . thou art the thing itself; unaccommodated
man is no more but such a poor, bare, forked
animal as thou art. Off, off you lendings! Come,
unbutton here!

              [S.D. Strives to tear off his clothes]

Lear's prose following upon Edgar's ditty is both startling and pathetic. The king who attempts to tear off his clothes and demands 'Come, unbutton here!' must suffer the humiliating and purging experience of madness before he can resume his royal status.[1] At the play's conclusion a humble monarch graciously asks (in his former blank verse)

       Pray you, undo this button: thank you, sir.

This line is doubly remarkable in its moderation and self control, for it follows his anguished lamentation over Cordelia's death with the famous five-fold 'never' which stretches blank verse to its utmost desolation.

The printing of the F text in Act III, scene iv is unfortunately slipshod and there are several points of uncertainty, such as where mad Tom begins to sing or, indeed, whether he sings at all. The refrain 'hey nonny nonny',[2] also quoted by Ophelia in her mad scene, makes actual singing probable.

In scene vi the exiled king is still attended by the fool and mad Tom and hears songs by both. The fantastic criss-cross of ideas which emerges from this mingled web of prose and verse has its poetic attractions, but the comprehensive dramatic purpose is to reduce the haughty Lear to the humanity of the fool and Tom. Like proud Oedipus, he must fall before his redemption, and fall he does, before Gloucester, Kent and the fool carry him off the stage.

In reply to the fool's question, Lear declares that he knows himself to be part of the company of madmen:

Fool. Prithee, nuncle, tell me whether a madman be
      a gentleman or a yeoman.
Lear. A king, a king!

---

[1] NS, xxxvii.

[2] F: sayes suum, mun, nonny; Q: hay no on ny; 1790, Malone: says suum, mun, ha no nonny; 1892, Wright: says suum, mun, ha no nonny; 1960, Duthie: says suum, mun, hey nonny nonny.

Lear still speaks either in very short lines or in verse.

> *Fool.* ... he's a mad yeoman that sees his son a
>   gentleman before him.
> *Lear.* To have a thousand with red burning spits
>   Come hizzing in upon 'em!

In the course of the mock trial which follows, Lear and Kent speak in stately blank verse but the fool and Tom have prose, except when they sing or quote a lyric. After the second lyric Lear's composure breaks down again and the effect of his speech is pathetic rather than grandiose, it 'moves our pity, but does not strike awe'.[1] (III.vi.20)

> *Lear.* It shall be done, I will arraign them straight.
>   ...   Now,
>   you she-foxes—
> *Edgar.* [regarding an imaginary fiend]
>   Look where he stands and glares! Want'st
>   thou eyes at trial, madam?
>   [Sings]
>   Come o'er the burn, Bessy, to me.[2]
>
> *Fool.* [Sings] Her boat hath a leak,
>   And she must not speak
>   Why she dares not come over to thee.
> *Edgar.* The foul fiend haunts poor Tom in the voice of a
>   nightingale ...
> *Kent.* How do you, sir? ...
>   Will you lie down and rest upon the cushions?
> *Lear.* I'll see their trial first. Bring in their evidence.
>   ... You are o'th'commission ...
> *Edgar.* Let us deal justly.

---

[1] G. W. Knight, *Wheel of Fire*, 4th edn., London, 1949, p. 168.

[2] The passage occurs only in Q and not in F. Q: come ore the broome Bessy to mee. Malone, 1790: Come o'er the bourn, Bessy, to me. It was Capell (1768) who first emended 'broome' to 'boorne', and all subsequent editors have followed him. Whatever the spelling, 'boorne', 'bourn' or 'burn', the meaning is 'brook', 'rivulet'. Cf. NV (1880), 207. In the *Merry Wives of Windsor* Brook's name is spelled 'Broome' in the F text.

> Sleepest or wakest thou, jolly shepherd?[1]
> Thy sheep be in the corn;
> And for one blast of thy minikin mouth
> Thy sheep shall take no harm.

> Purr the cat is gray.

Lear.   Arraign her first; 'tis Goneril. . . .
 . . . she kicked the poor king, her father.

With all this torment of the storm within and the storm without Lear has acquired a new humility. Duthie persuades us that when, in this scene, the king speaks in enigmatic and ironic paradoxes he is at last

able to speak in an idiom that has been used by the Fool all along . . . In the dramatic design, the tutor-fool is no longer required; and Shakespeare boldly dispenses with him.

Indeed, with the fool's exit singing disappears altogether from the tragedy. The king of Act I employed a fool who sometimes sang for him; the Lear of Act IV

> was met even now
> As mad as the vex'd sea, singing aloud,

and the wheel has turned full circle when Act V presents the king and Cordelia as prisoners, and he exclaims

> Come, let's away to prison:
> We two alone will sing like birds i' th' cage;
> When thou dost ask me blessing, I'll kneel down
> And ask of thee forgiveness. So we'll live,
> And pray, and sing, and tell old tales, and laugh . . .

The dramatic function of the songs and the unconventional prose scenes which add grotesque and bizarre elements to the tragedy proper have been fulfilled when arrogant Lear has become 'wise enough to play the fool'. The fear of madness haunts the king from the first Act onward

> O let me not be mad, not mad, sweet heaven!   I.v.49
> O Fool, I shall go mad!   II.iv.288
> My wits begin to turn.   III.ii.67

[1] Malone (1790) and Muir (1952) have 'Come o'er the burn Bessy to me' and 'Sleepest or wakest thou, jolly shepherd' in italics, indicating that the verses are to be sung. Duthie and Wilson (1960) have the stage direction 'sings' for the first lyric, but not for the second.

By entering the lunatic fraternity of mad Tom, Lear is able to view the world's play with good grace: his wise laughter, gaiety and humanity transcend the routine course of tragedy and chronicle history. The singing fool teaches a lesson that concerns not only an ancient King of Britain. In our own century William Butler Yeats has apostrophized the gospel of gaiety:

> . . .
> All perform their tragic play,
> There struts Hamlet, there is Lear,
> That's Ophelia, that Cordelia;
> Yet they, should the last scene be there,
> The great stage curtain about to drop,
> If worthy their prominent part in the play,
> Do not break up their lines to weep.
> They know that Hamlet and Lear are gay;
> . . .
> All things fall and are built again,
> And those that build them again are gay.
>
> Two Chinamen, behind them a third,
> Are carved in lapis lazuli,
> . . .
> The third, doubtless a serving-man,
> Carries a musical instrument.
> . . .
> There, on the mountain and the sky,
> On all the tragic scene they stare.
> One asks for mournful melodies;
> Accomplished fingers begin to play.
> Their eyes mid many wrinkles, their eyes,
> Their ancient, glittering eyes, are gay.

Of the eighteen lyrics which are sung or recited in *King Lear*, 'Come o'er the burn, Bessy' (III.vi) seems to have had an unabated popularity for well over three centuries, to judge from the several sources available to us today. The earliest probably dates from the first quarter of the sixteenth century, about a century before Shakespeare's play.[1] The music of this early

---

[1] British Museum, Add. MS 5665, f. 143^v; reproduced in facsimile in J. O. Halliwell-Phillipps, ed., *Works of Shakespeare*, 16 vols., London, 1853–1865, XIV.466; a transcription of the music is given in Appendix IV to this chapter. Further discussion of this lyric has appeared in John Stevens's *Music & Poetry in the Early Tudor Court*, London, 1961, 435 (No. 66).

setting is scored for three voices. It differs substantially from the melody transmitted in lute books contemporary with Shakespeare. But the verbal text is remarkably close to that of all the other versions:

> Come o'er the burn Bessy,
> Thou little pretty Bessy,
> Come o'er the burn Bessy to me.

> The burn is this world blind,
> And Bessy is mankind,
> So proper I can none find as she.
> She dances and leapes
> And Christ stands and clepes.
> Come o'er the burn Bessy to me.

The figure of speech, persuading Bessy, as mankind, to come to the Saviour, is not unusual among the sacred *contra-facta* of the sixteenth century.

Two other manuscripts[1] give much the same text without music. Verbal differences are negligible, and the basic conceit of converting a love-song to a spiritual theme is clearly conveyed.

It was natural that the occasion of young 'Bess' acceding to England's throne should induce another topical application of the lyric. In an undated ballad, in the Harleian collection,[2] of *ca.* 1558 England woos Queen Elizabeth:

> 1st stanza
> Come over the born, Bessy,
> Come over the born, Bessy,
> Sweet Bessy come over to me;
> And I shall thee take,
> And my dear lady make,
> Before all other that ever I see.

---

[1] Oxford, Bodleian, MS Ashmole 176, f. 100ʳ; Cambridge, Emmanuel College, MS 263, fly-leaf.

[2] Cf. *Harleian Miscellany*, ed. T. Park, London, 1808–1813, X.260; *Tudor Poetry and Prose*, edd. Hebel-Hudson-Johnson-Green-Hoopes, New York, 1953, pp. 408 and 1252. It is interesting to note that the same William Birch published an adaptation of another ballad which occurs in *Much Ado About Nothing*, V.ii.26. Cf. *The Times*, 17 November 1958, p. 11 and *Journal of the American Musicological Society*, X (1957), 164.

Last stanza
> All honour, laud, and praise
> Be to the Lord God always,
> Who hath all princes' hearts in his hands;
> That by his power and might
> He may guide them right
> For the wealth of all Christian lands.

> *Finis, quod* WILLIAM BIRCHE,
> *God save the Queen.*

Shortly after the accession of Queen Elizabeth W. Wager wrote the 'very merry and pithy comedy, called *The Longer thou Livest . . .*', wherein a foolish character sings fragments from several songs 'as fools were wont'. Among them we find:

> Come over the born Bessy,
>   My little pretty Bessy,
> Come over the born Bessy to me.

Since the fragment, as printed, does not extend beyond these three lines, we cannot say whether it is the original love-song or another adaptation, but the former supposition is more likely.[1]

Except for the stanza in *King Lear* no amorous version of 'Come over the Burn' survives unless we consider the burden of a poem (without music) preserved in the British Museum.[2] Although the number of syllables in the two opening lines is curtailed, the poem can be made to fit the Elizabethan tune.

> My proper Bessy,
> My pretty Bessy,
> Turn over again to me;
> For sleepest thou, Bessy,
> Or wakest thou, Bessy,
> Mine heart, it is with thee.

The continued popularity of the basic image is upheld in a Scottish version printed in the eighteenth century

---

[1] Cf. Pollard STC, 24935; the edition by J. S. Farmer in *Tudor Facsimile Texts*, London, 1910, sig. A.ii. leaf 2r. Chambers ES III.504; Kittredge SP 1191.

[2] British Museum, Harley MS 2252, f. 135r.

> Blink over the burn, sweet Betty,
> It is a cauld winter night.[1]

Essentially these poems are uniformly cast into stanzas made up of two sections, each section being accommodated by one musical strain. Where the text of either section consists of only three lines the strain may be repeated; where of six lines, repetition becomes obligatory to take in the words. In the printed text of *King Lear* only one line of the old song is given but in view of the striking conformity of manuscript and printed sources, whether spiritual or political, there seems to be good reason for completing the verbal refrain (or burden, holding, or foot) by expansion:

> Come o'er the burn, Bessy,
> [My little pretty Bessy,
> Come o'er the burn, Bessy] to me.

In the music example given in Appendix V, these lines have been fitted to the first strain of the melody.

The second half of the stanza is sung by the Fool who, responding to Mad Tom's snatch, improvises his own version:

> Her boat hath a leak,
> And she must not speak
> Why she dares not come over to thee.

The rhyme scheme of these lines is not far removed from Birch's political ballad on Queen Bess

> And I shall thee take,
> And my dear lady make,
> Before all other that ever I see.

There is nothing delicate about the Fool's improvisation but this is only the obverse side of the coin. Again the clowning scene and its song provide an oblique comment on the all-powerful emotion of love which ennobles the dying Lear and which, in its curious yet touching way even, softens the heart of the Macchiavellian Edmund as he lies dying.

Two lute books provide instrumental versions of the Elizabethan melody for 'Come over the burn Bessy'. One is at Cam-

---

[1] A. Stuart, *Music for the Tea Table Miscellany*, Edinburgh [1725], p. 50; R. Chambers, *Songs of Scotland*, Edinburgh, 1862, p. 283.

bridge, the other is in the Weld Lute Book in the possession of Lord Forester.[1] Both versions are transcribed and discussed in Appendices V and VI respectively.

The Fool's 'He that has and a little tiny wit' introduces a phrase that was popular in Elizabethan jest books. It was natural enough that the Fool, by pose or actual disposition more or less out of his wits, should dally with the expression. The lyric in *Lear* is closely related to the epilogue of *Twelfth Night* and it is likely that both were sung to the same tune.

> *King Lear*, III.ii.74
>> He that has and a little tiny wit—
>>> With heigh-ho, the wind and the rain—
>> Must make content with his fortunes fit,
>>> Though the rain it raineth every day.

> *Twelfth Night*, V.i.398
> (first of five stanzas)
>> When that I was and a little tiny boy,
>>> With hey, ho, the wind and the rain,
>> A foolish thing was but a toy,
>>> For the rain it raineth every day.

These two versions of a simple quatrain pose several questions. Do we deal here with a popular song, adapted to two different plays? If this was so, was the adaptation made by Robert Armin who impersonated both Feste and Lear's Fool or by Shakespeare? (Several phrases from the lyric occur in Armin's printed works.) Did the stanza in the tragedy give rise to the extended lyric in the comedy? In such a case, the chronology of the extant texts of *King Lear* and *Twelfth Night* would be affected. Is Feste's epilogue merely another merry song in a comedy or is it a song by a wise fool with tragic overtones? The earliest extant music, transcribed and discussed in Appendix VII, is for Feste's lyric; no music for the stanza of Lear's Fool has come to light so far.

The title page of one of Armin's books, printed in 1600, announces *Quips upon questions . . . shewing a little wit, with a great*

---

[1] Folio 6ʳ. The manuscript was known to Wooldridge in 1893, but subsequently lost. It was recently re-discovered by Robert Spencer, cf. *Lute Society Journal*, I, No. 6 (1960), 121–134. I am indebted to Mr. Spencer for providing me with a microfilm from which the transcription, offered in Appendix VI, was prepared.

deal of will. . . . Such phrases as 'much wit', 'no wit left' occur half a dozen times in one of the 'quips'. Another expression which seems to have been one of Armin's favourites, 'but that's all one' appears in the final stanza of *Twelfth Night* following several employments of the same phrase in the course of the comedy. It is also used three times by Armin in his jest-book, *Nest of Ninnies,* in the edition of 1608. As a result of these and other phrases which occur both in *Twelfth Night* and in Armin's works several scholars have attributed Feste's song to Armin[1] or at least denied it to Shakespeare. On the other hand, Bradley, Kittredge and Noble see no reason to question Shakespeare's authorship. One is inclined to agree with their view. Shakespeare went out of his way to compliment the 'wise fool' throughout the play; he would not hesitate to make use of some of Armin's phrases or those of Elizabethan fools in general, since borrowings of this nature were considered a tribute to the author borrowed. Moreover, the phrases in question are fairly common in the literature of the period. Some examples, to be found in Donne and Heywood, also involve the notion of the fool's singing. It does not seem, therefore, that a neat allocation of authorship is possible until the lost popular song of the wind and the rain, which may have served both Armin and Shakespeare at different times, is discovered.

The dramatic significance of Feste's epilogue is another matter. If we assume that Shakespeare's art in mingling the tragic and comic developed significantly between the writing of *Hamlet* and *King Lear* and that this development represents a major aspect of his stature as a playwright in this period, we cannot view Feste's song as either clumsy or irrelevant foolery.

There is the further conjecture that *Twelfth Night*, as printed in the Folio of 1623, does not date from 1600/02, but that it was revised after the first performance of *King Lear*. Much of the chronological argument rests on musical grounds.[2]

---

[1] NS 96, which quotes, in addition to J. D. Wilson's own opinion, Warburton, Capell, Farmer, Steevens and Aldis Wright.

[2] Richmond Noble, in collaboration with A. W. Pollard, helped in the formulation of interlocking hypotheses, presented in the NS edition of *Twelfth Night*, p. 101. Cf. also Noble 80, 87, 148. A cautious summary of the hypotheses was given by Greg FF 297, in 1955: 'There is some force in the argument that Feste's closing song . . . and its echo in *King Lear* . . . are likely

The original version of *Twelfth Night*, now lost, seems to have employed a leading boy with a singing voice in the part of Viola. There can be no doubt that the company which supplied the roles of Ophelia and Desdemona would also provide a Viola to sing 'Come away, come away, death'. But when the comedy was revised, probably in 1606, the song was transferred to Feste. Noble surmises that the company had lost its singing boy and that the adult singer Robert Armin proved an excellent 'draw'. These are reasonable suppositions, but one may add that beginning with the gravedigger's song in *Hamlet* the dimensions of Shakespeare's adult songs increased and the boys' songs decreased. No role comparable to Ophelia is created until we reach that of Ariel in *The Tempest*. One is reluctant to ascribe a consistent development in Shakespeare's tragic period exclusively to practical considerations. The tragi-comic method of integrating songs into plays must have been a complementary reason for employing an actor of Armin's maturity and sagacity. Indeed, to several observers, tragi-comedy rather than unalloyed merriment is the keynote of Feste's epilogue. His position in Olivia's household is far from secure when the play opens and it is even more in abeyance when the comedy comes to an end. His musings that the rain raineth every day are neither foolish nor particularly hilarious, they draw a philosophical and somewhat quizzical *summa* of the entire proceedings, worthy of him wise enough to play the fool. When the last stanza opens 'A great while ago the world began' we agree with Shakespeare's singer that foolishness, disguises and sudden changes of fortune are part and parcel of a greater design. The vicissitudes of Viola and Lear's wheel of fire are seen through the poetic imagination of the mature Shakespeare, and the song that reminds us that there is nothing new under the sun is appropriate to both.

to be close in date, and it has been even argued that the snatch in *King Lear* was the germ out of which the song in *Twelfth Night* grew, probably under the fostering care of Robert Armin, who is supposed to have played the fool in both plays. . . . Since some alteration is admitted . . . 1606 is as likely as any other date.'

Tabulation of Lyrics in
King Lear

Below are listed eighteen pieces of verse which are allotted to the fool and Edgar. The three modern editions chiefly consulted were those of G. L. Kittredge (1940; reprinted Kittredge SP, 1946), K. Muir (NA 1952, rev. 1957) and G. I. Duthie (NS 1960). As indicated at the beginning of this chapter most modern editors agree on the division between prose and verse, and where verse is sung and not spoken. For example, Duthie has in four instances added a stage direction specifying that the lyric in question be sung. This stage direction corresponds in each case to the use of italics by K. Muir. Neither stage direction nor italic type-face occur in either the Q or F texts.

Line[1]		Folio or Quarto	NS page	NA page
	Act I, scene iv			
131	Have more than thou showest	288	24	42
154	That lord that counselled thee	Quarto[2]	25	43
181	Fools had ne'er less grace in a year	288	26	45
			Singing	Italics
191	Then they for sudden joy did weep	288	26	45
			Singing	Italics
217	He that keeps nor crust nor crumb	288	27	46
235	The hedge-sparrow fed the cuckoo so long	288	27	47
340	A fox, when one has caught her	289	31	54
	Act II, scene iv			
48	Fathers that wear rags	293	47	85
79	That sir which serves and seeks for gain	293	48	87
	Act III, scene ii			
27	The codpiece that will house	296	59	108
74	He that has and a little tiny wit	296	61	111
			Sings	Italics
81	When priests are more in word than matter	296	61	111

[1] Numbering according to Globe text.   [2] Not in Folio.

Act III, scene iv

125	S'Withhold footed thrice the 'old	298	67	123 Italics
143	Horse to ride, and weapon to wear	298	67	125 Italics
187	Child Roland to the dark tower came	298	69	128 Italics

Act III, scene vi

27	Come o'er the burn, Bessy, to me	Quarto[1]	71 Sings	132 Italics
43	Sleepest or wakest thou jolly shepherd	Quarto[1]	72	133 Italics
69	Be thy mouth or black or white	299	72	135

Appendix II

'Some Men for Sudden Joy did Weep'

This must be an old ballad, as H. E. Rollins shows (*Old English Ballads*, Cambridge, 1920, pp. 47–53). Various versions occur in *Certain most godly . . . letters* by Miles Coverdale, printed in 1564 (Pollard-Redgrave STC, No. 5886, p. 634) and in Thomas Heywood's *Rape of Lucrece*, printed in 1608 (*Works*, ed. Pearson, V.179). There are also several manuscript variants and two references by Thomas Nashe (*Works*, ed. McKerrow III.104 and V.196). Finally, there is also a version with music, discovered by Peter J. Seng, *Shakespeare Quarterly*, IX (1958), 583–585. On the blank page facing the printed preface of a copy of Thomas Ravenscroft's *Pammelia* of 1609 (Pollard-Redgrave STC, No. 20759) is a manuscript notation in an early seventeenth-century hand (British Museum, shelf-mark K.1.e.9).

Coverdale, *Certain most godly . . . letters . . .*

> Some men for sudden joy do weep,
> And some in sorrow sing:
> When that they lie in danger deep,
> To put away mourning.

---

[1] Not in Folio.

Heywood, *Rape of Lucrece*

> When Tarquin first in Court began
> And was approved King:
> Some men for sudden joy did weep,
> But I for sorrow sing.

Manuscript notation in Ravenscroft's *Pammelia*

> Late as I waked out of sleep
> I heard a pretty thing:
> Some men for sudden joy do weep
> And some for sorrow sing.

King Lear, I.iv.191

> Then they for sudden joy did weep,
> And I for sorrow sung,
> That such a king should play bo-peep,
> And go the fools among.

A facsimile of the two relevant pages from *Pammelia* accompanies Mr. Seng's article in the *Shakespeare Quarterly*. In the copy of *Pammelia* a repeat sign occurs after bar 7.

The first two lines of Heywood's lyric are obviously a variant of the well-known ballad (Wooldridge I. 92):

> When Arthur first in Court began,
> And was approvéd King,
> By force of arms great victories won,
> And conquest home did bring.

But the second half of Heywood's quatrain is related to 'Then they for sudden joy did weep'. Shakespeare knew the ballad 'When Arthur first in court began', for Falstaff quotes it in *2 Henry IV*, II. iv.36. The ballad of King Arthur was sung to the tune 'Flying Fame' (Wooldridge I. 91). This tune proved to be one of the most popular melodies of the time accommodating, among others, 'Chevy Chase' and the 'Lamentable Song of the Death of King Lear'. It seems reasonable therefore, to fit both Heywood's and Shakespeare's quatrains to this tune.[1]

Appendix III

'Tom's A-Cold . . . Bless Thy Wits'

We have no certain knowledge whether Mad Tom sings or speaks the lines derived from the traditional Bedlam call. A musical source for what must have been a well-known London cry is a composition by Orlando Gibbons (1583–1625) for voices and viols. It is entitled 'The London Cry' and survives in three different sets of part-books preserved in manuscript in the British Museum: Add. 17792–96

[1] I am indebted to D. C. Greer for the suggestion that 'Then they for sudden joy did weep' would fit the ballad tune, 'Flying Fame'. Mr. Greer has in preparation a more detailed article on the subject. Cf. p. 244, footnote 1, for references concerning the 'Lamentable Song of . . . Lear'.

29372–76, 37402–06. The complete verbal text of the relevant passage in Gibbons (source 1) reads

> Poor naked Bedlam, Tom's a-cold,
> a small cut of thy bacon
> or a piece of thy sow's side, good Bess,
> God Almighty, bless thy wits.

Gibbons's composition is an 'In nomine'. This was the generic name for an extremely popular type of English fantasia cultivated primarily in the sixteenth and seventeenth centuries, from Taverner to Purcell. These compositions are characterized by the liturgical chant (in slow notes, usually in the alto) around which the other voices weave their contrapuntal texture. The Latin text of the chant is

> Gloria tibi trinitas aequalis,
> una deitas, et ante omnia saecula,
> et nunc et in perpetuum.

Gibbons follows the usual pattern in placing the chant melody, the so-called *cantus firmus*, lower than the treble. The section which provides the notes for the Bedlam cry corresponds to the Latin words 'et nunc et in perpetuum'. Both the relevant portion of the chant and its adaptation by Gibbons are transcribed below. It will be seen that the street cry proper (bars 117–126) is chanted to the reciting note 'f', corresponding to the syllables 'et in per-' of the chant, the remainder of the melody being played by viols alone. Whether the composer was amused to frame so secular a text within a sacred melody or whether he merely used a popular contrapuntal tag without considering its origin, is difficult to determine today. The great majority of the extant compositions of this type (between 150 and 200) are purely instrumental.

Ex. 2.

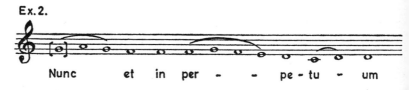

Nunc et in per - - pe - tu - um

Sources 2–4 and 7–9 preserve another lyric in which Tom of Bedlam, naked, begs for bacon and hopes that his potential donor will not lose his 'five sound senses'. The parallel is only verbal, however, and Shakespeare's line does not fit the extant music (sources 3, 8, 9) easily. The first eight lines in a manuscript of the first quarter of the seventeenth century (source 2) read as follows:

Ex. 3.

From the hag and hungry goblin,
    That into rags would rend yee,
And the spirit, that stands by the naked man,
    In the Book of Moons defend yee,
That of your five sound senses
    You never be forsaken,
Nor wander from yourselves with Tom
    Abroad to beg your bacon.

Obviously this lyric, and the fragment from Gibbons, quoted earlier, and the passage of Mad Tom in *King Lear*, are all related in vocabulary and atmosphere. The importance of source (1) for our understanding of Shakespeare has been argued by Bridge and Wilson (sources 10 and 17); that of source (2) by Graves and Wells (sources 12 and 18). On examination it is clear that source (1) provides the closer analogy, but there is no denying that both sources are deserving of a short gloss, and it is surprising that none is to be found in modern editions of the play.

SOURCES

(1) London, British Museum, Add. MS 17792, cantus, f. 110 r.
(2) London, British Museum, Add. MS 24665, p. 76.
(3) London, British Museum, Add. MS 38539, f. 14 r, rubric 'Tom of Bedlam'.
(4) Oxford, Bodleian, MS Tanner 465, p. 278.
(5) 1616: Jonson, *Devil is an Ass* (Jonson VI.254, X.251).
(6) 1656: *Wit and Drollery*, Wing STC, W 3131, London, p. 126.
(7) 1660: *Le Prince d'Amour*, Wing STC, R 2189, London, p. 167.
(8) 1859: Chappell I.335.
(9) 1893: Wooldridge I.175.
(10) 1919/20: F. Bridge, 'Musical Cries of London in Shakespeare's Time', *Proceedings of the Royal Musical Association*, XLVI.13–20.
(11) 1921: O. Gibbons, *The Cryes of London*, ed. F. Bridge (Novello's P.S.B. No. 1345), London.
(12) 1927: R. Graves, 'Loving Mad Tom', in *Common Asphodel*, reprinted in *Crowning Privilege*, (Pelican Books), Harmondsworth, 1959, pp. 247–266.
(13) 1933: O. Gibbons, *The Cries of London*, ed. F. Allinson & H. Just (Edition Schott No. 1628), Mainz.
(14) 1951: E. H. Fellowes, *O. Gibbons*, 2nd edn., London, p. 85.
(15) 1954: *Grove's Dictionary of Music*, 5th edn., s.v. 'In nomine'.
(16) 1956: O. Gibbons, *The Cries of London*, ed. D. Stevens (Novello's P.S.B. No. 1575), London.
(17) 1960: F. P. Wilson, 'Street-Cries', *Shakespeare Survey*, XIII.106–110.
(18) 1961: S. Wells, 'Tom o'Bedlam's Song and *King Lear*', *Shakespeare Quarterly*, XII.311–315.

Appendix IV

'Come O'er the Burn Bessy'

This song is transmitted in British Museum Add. MS 5665, ff. 143ᵛ–144ʳ. The manuscript dates from the early sixteenth century. The initial musical phrase which enters in imitation in all three voices (triplex, tenor, bassus) is not the same as the Elizabethan melodies transcribed in Appendices V and VI. A few emendations were required in the transcription.[1] At bar 4 of the triplex the scribe

---

[1] Kindly supplied by Dr. F. Ll. Harrison of the University of Oxford. The transcription differs in several details from that published in C. F. Abdy Williams and

has 'Come o'er the burn Bessy'. There are fewer notes than syllables, however, and, accordingly, the word 'Bessy' has been omitted in the transcription. At bar 7 (bassus, 3rd note) and bar 16 (bassus, 5th note), the context calls for crotchets, though the scribe has indicated the equivalent of quavers in modern transcription. At bar 13 the bassus reads 'pretty' while the two upper parts read 'proper', an incongruity removed in the transcription. Finally, at bar 19 the third note of the triplex reads b-natural. Considering the b-flat at this point in the bass, however, the upper part also demands b-flat.

Ex. 4.

C. W. Pearce, edd., *Madrigals by English Composers of the Close of the Fifteenth Century* (Plainsong and Mediaeval Music Society), London, 1893, No. 2.

Appendix V

'Over the Broom Bessy'

This piece for solo lute, without words, appears in MS Dd.2.11, f. 8ov of the Cambridge University Library. It bears the rubric 'Over the broom Bessy'. (It has been pointed out in the body of this chapter that 'broome' is a frequent misspelling for 'brooke' or 'boorne'.) The melody was first transcribed in Wooldridge I.121 with a harmonization by Wooldridge. A complete transcription was offered in Naylor SM 52, and the present transcription does not differ materially from Naylor's. Naylor states after bar 48 that 'the MS ends thus', though he rightly surmises that 'the composer . . .

probably meant either to finish with a big chord of G or to repeat...'. As in the case of the Willow Song, the scribe was obviously cramped for space in trying to finish the piece without starting a new line. For this reason he omitted one bar in the last line and noted it in the margin. Also, at the end of that line, he did not include the rubric, as was customary, but transferred it to the margin as well. The conclusion of the line is almost illegible but on careful examination one is impelled to feel that the rhythm sign above the six-line tablature clearly demands a 49th bar. Furthermore, an examination of the manuscript under a magnifying glass reveals a cipher that resembles the letter-notation 'c' on both the third and fourth course from the top. This would correspond to the notes 'd–b' in modern transcription.

The piece consists of two strains, the first appears at bars 1–8, the second at bars 17–24. There are two variations (or divisions) of the first strain (bars 9–16, 25–32) and two variations of the second (bars 33–40, 41–49). The strains are identified by Roman numerals in Music Example 5. The harmony of both strains is based on a rather curious ground bass. In modern terminology the last four bars present a clear cadence in G: tonic-dominant-tonic-tonic. But the first four bars reiterate the flattened leading note. It is this note (F rather than F sharp) that suggests some survival of the seventh of the mediaeval modes, the Mixolydian.

In Music Example 6, the melody has been fitted to the words sung by Mad Tom and the Fool in *King Lear*. The first half, the burden, is allotted to Tom and the second half to the Fool. Clearly, no accompaniment would be feasible in a stage performance. To facilitate comparison, a variant of the tune preserved in the Weld Manuscript (to be discussed in Appendix VI) has been transposed to the same pitch as Music Example 6. It is given as Music Example 7 and fitted to the same words from Shakespeare's tragedy. Further, to facilitate comparison between Examples 5, 6 and 7, the bar numbers from Example 5 have been transferred to Examples 6 and 7.

Appendix VI

'Brown Bessy, Sweet Bessy'

The Weld Manuscript or Weld Lute Book in Lord Forester's possession contains 'Brown Bessy, sweet Bessy, come over to me' on f. 6ʳ. The transcription of the two strains presents no difficulties. As in the case of Ex. 5 we have, harmonically, a ground bass charac-

terized by a flattened leading note which is sustained throughout the
first four bars. The second four bars proceed with tonic-dominant-
tonic-tonic. Example 5 is in the key of G while the present example

(continued next page)

(8) is in the key of C. But apart from this transposition of pitch, there is a harmonic difference: Example 5 is in the major, Example 8 in the minor. The transpositions of these two examples (6 and 7) are

(Ex. 5, continued)

Facsimile 1. 'Come o'er the burn'.

accordingly in G major and G minor. Only in the last bars of both
strains (7–8 and 15–16) does Example 8 introduce the major, the
so-called *tierce de Picardie*.

Ex. 8.

Appendix VII

'He that has and a Little Tiny Wit'

No source earlier than the eighteenth century is known for this lyric. In 1772 there appeared in London a volume of songs from the repertory of the famous Vauxhall Gardens, entitled *The New Songs in the Pantomime of the Witches; the Celebrated Epilogue in the Comedy of Twelfth Night . . . sung by Mr. Vernon at Vauxhall; composed by J. Vernon . . . Printed and Sold by John Johnston . . . Covent Garden, where may*

Ex. 9.

Ex. 10.

He that   has and a   lit - tle ti - ny wit, with a
When that I   was and a   lit - tle ti - ny boy, with a

heigh - ho, the   wind and the rain, must make con-tent with his
heigh - ho, the   wind and the rain, a   fool - ish thing was

for - tunes fit,   though the   rain   it   rain - eth
but   a   toy,   for   the   rain   it   rain - eth

ev' - ry   day,   with a   heigh – ho,   the
ev' - ry   day,   with a   heigh – ho,   the

wind and the rain, though the rain it rain-eth   ev' - ry day.
wind and the rain, for   the rain it rain-eth   ev' - ry day.

be had . . . King Arthur with Purcell's Chorusses. . . . The name of Purcell on the title-page reminds us that much of the music used at Vauxhall (or Drury Lane) in the eighteenth century was adapted from older sources. Whether Joseph Vernon (1738–82) composed a new tune for Shakespeare's comedy or whether he arranged a traditional melody, is difficult to determine now. In any event, an accurate transcript from the 1772 volume is given in Music Example 9.[1]

In 1859 William Chappell published a variation of Vernon's melody (Chappell I.225), though, curiously, he does not mention his source. His version is in G major, while Vernon's composition is in G minor, and there are several melodic variants, though none of them change the basic contours of the tune. Chappell said of his illustration that it was

still sung on the stage to this tune. It has no other authority than theatrical tradition.

Music Example 10 reproduces Chappell's version to which the stanzas from *King Lear* and below it that from *Twelfth Night* have been fitted. It will be observed that at the end of bars 2 and 8 Chappell inserted the extra syllable 'a' (as Vernon had done before him) which is, however, neither in Shakespeare's tragedy nor in his comedy. Still, this is a small detail in a tune which may well be traditional and which sounds—at least in its surviving shape—like a song from a ballad opera.

The lack of antiquity in the tradition of the tune induced Wooldridge, when he revised Chappell's standard work in 1893, to omit the song altogether, since no melody previous to Vernon's publication survives. But the lyric has been reprinted from Chappell as late as 1955 (J. H. Long, *Shakespeare's Use of Music*, Gainesville, Florida, p. 182) and is still widely used on the stage.

[1] In bar 13 the numeral '6' is printed under the note G, but the sixth-chord would seem to belong to the preceding F sharp.

Appendix VIII

Verse and Prose in
Hamlet, *King Lear* and *Troilus and Cressida*

The proportion of verse to prose is governed by the nature of the play and the characters it contains. Since the language of the clown is prose, the typical comedy contains a larger proportion of it[1] than most of the history plays which are, in fact, much longer than the comedies.

	Total	Prose
Much Ado about Nothing	2535	1808
As You Like It	2608	1438
Twelfth Night	2429	1485
Merry Wives of Windsor	2634	2307

The amount of prose in a history play is in direct ratio to the number of its comic scenes. The presence of a Falstaff or a Pistol has a direct bearing on the proportion of prose to verse:

	Total	Prose
Richard III	3600	69
2 Henry IV	3180	1860
Henry V	3166	1235

On the other hand, the typical tragedy is almost devoid of prose as it is of clowns and songs:

	Total	Prose
Julius Caesar	2450	160
Macbeth	2084	141
Antony and Cleopatra	3016	264

Those tragedies which contain an unconventionally large admixture of clowning and song are characterized by a different proportion. The following tabulation deals with Shakespeare's seven longest plays:

	Total	Prose
Hamlet	3762	1047
Richard III	3600	69
Troilus and Cressida	3329	1010
Coriolanus	3279	726
Cymbeline	3264	450
Othello	3229	591
King Lear	3205	844

The number of tragedies in this list of longest plays is impressive.[2] The effect of the roles of the grave-digger and Ophelia in *Hamlet*, of the Fool and Edgar in *King Lear*, is to increase the proportion of

[1] The following statistics are based on two articles of Alfred Hart, published in *Review of English Studies*, VIII (1932), entitled 'Number of Lines in Shakespeare's Plays' (pp. 19–28) and 'Length of Elizabethan and Jacobean Plays' (pp. 139–154).
[2] Cf. the discussion of magnitude (megethos) in Chapter I, page 1.

prose. In the case of the tragi-comedy of Trojans and Greeks the similarity to *Hamlet* and *King Lear* in the disposition of prose and verse should be noted. It supports the hypothesis, advanced earlier, that in many respects *Troilus and Cressida* should be evaluated within the frame-work of the tragic tradition and that it was likely that Armin played the part of Pandarus. The prose scenes of *Coriolanus* are largely connected with the citizens of Rome and the Volscian serving-men. These scenes contain no songs, but the humour of the Volscian serving-men is again reminiscent of Armin.[1] To the modern student *Cymbeline* (1609–10), like the *Winter's Tale* and *The Tempest*, is classed as a romance, not a tragedy. Yet it is remarkable that the editors of the Folio included it among the tragedies. It certainly is longer than the other romances and contains surprisingly large portions of 'the stately tent of war'. It is the serious political and military matter, as well as the presence of such humorous characters as Cloten and the jailer that give *Cymbeline* a place in the metrical tables among the tragedies.

A survey of this kind is necessarily in the nature of an over-simplification. Obviously, there are other and subtler reasons which occasionally call for prose within the blank verse of tragedy: the despair which drives Zabina out of her mind in Marlowe's *Tamburlaine* (Part I, Act V), the feigned madness of Hamlet, the real madness of Lear, are instances. Still, the majority of the prose passages occurs in comic scenes and the length and greatness of *Hamlet* and *King Lear* are related to Shakespeare's capacity to graft songs and clowning scenes upon the trunk of tragedy.

[1] Cf. Kittredge 924; also the S.D. 'Music plays' for the Volscian banquet at IV.v.1.

VIII

INSTRUMENTAL MUSIC: PART ONE

Tamburlaine, Richard II, Troilus and Cressida

THE range of instrumental music in Shakespeare's plays extends from the obvious and functional music of battles and banquets to the celestial music not ordinarily heard by mortal ears. At one extreme we have the herald's trumpet, the soldier's drum, the clown's pipe, the fiddler's 'noise' of the tavern; at the other extreme the music of the spheres

> Still quiring to the young-eyed cherubins;
> Such harmony is in immortal souls,
> But whilst this muddy vesture of decay
> Doth grossly close it in, we cannot hear it.

It is the playwright's task to make us listen, or, at the least, to suggest to our imagination the music of both worlds, to reflect in poetry and music the flesh as well as the spirit; to bring alive both the 'brazen din' and the 'tuned spheres'.[1] 'Brazen din' is a description more apt for the early tragedies, such as *Tamburlaine* and *Henry VI* and less for *Antony and Cleopatra*, where battle scenes give way in importance to character portrayal. The term refers not only to the stentorian voice of brass instruments but also to an unabashed, if not impudent, behaviour. Tamburlaine's progress towards the conquest of the world is punctuated by military flourishes to signify a succession of challenges and bouts that would become tiresome were it not for the poetic relief of

---

[1] *ANT*, IV.viii.36; V.ii.84.

Marlowe's blank verse. As early as the turn of the century, and before the accession of James I, Jonson and Shakespeare were able to caricature the incessant braying of trumpets and the tireless beating of drums. These military calls were but another aspect of the Ethos of music,[1] for the sound of wind instruments and drums was meant to induce a warlike spirit, intensified by the martial rhythm in which fanfares and drum-rolls were couched. Such signals also conveyed to the characters on stage a call to combat, or the arrival of important personages, and communicated to the audience what was happening on the stage.

Conforming to Elizabethan rules of conduct, the class of instrument employed was defined according to the character of a scene and the social position of its participants. A glance at some of the pre-Shakespearean tragedies reveals the importance of trumpets for the plays that were dedicated to the problems of the aristocracy and the commonwealth. In musical terms the 'stately-written', buskinned, tragedy could, if its author wished, dispense with songs and serenades of love, but not with the trumpet signals and fanfares to herald kings and marshals.

> *Balthazar.* Hieronimo, methinks a comedy were better.
> *Hieronimo.* A comedy?
> Fie! comedies are fit for common wits;
> But to present a kingly troop withal,
> Give me a stately-written tragedy;
> *Tragedia cothurnata*, fitting kings,
> Containing matter, and not common things.
> *The Spanish Tragedy*, Act V.

To employ trumpeters was among the carefully guarded privileges of the nobility and, by and large, only court trumpeters were allowed to perform on the instrument. They belonged to a special guild, and in view of their superior position rarely performed in combination with other instruments. In the language of military signals, drums belonged to the infantry, trumpets to the cavalry. The Trojans, Persians, Spaniards and Englishmen of the early tragedies engaged in wars that were fought before the cannon became an exclusive instrument of battle. Hence, we have drums for the commoner and trumpets for the nobleman. In *All's Well that Ends Well* nothing charac-

---

[1] See Chapter IV, 'Magic Songs' p. 83.

terizes Parolles so much as a person of 'common things' as his incessant prattle about a lost drum. In the *Spanish Tragedy* Kyd extols Orpheus's lute and the music of 'cherubins chanting heavenly notes', but the actual music is reserved for more penetrating strains. In the opening scene we have

[S.D. A tucket afar off]

King. What means the warning of this trumpet's sound?
General. This tells me that your grace's men of war,
. . .
Come marching on towards your royal seat
To show themselves before your majesty.

Equally imposing are the implications of the stage direction at the conclusion of the action

[S.D. The trumpets sound a dead march; the King of Spain mourning after his brother's body, and the King of Portugal bearing the body of his son.]

The term 'tucket' is but one of a bewildering variety of names (let alone doubtful meanings and etymologies) used to describe military signals. Both tucket and sennet probably derive from the Italian: 'toccare', 'toccata' and 'sonare', 'sonata' respectively. Both were trumpet flourishes. The term 'tucket' occurs seven times in Shakespeare and usually has reference to a particular person, such as Mountjoy or Aeneas. With few exceptions they are not English. The sennet differed from the ordinary trumpet flourish by its greater length. There are nine sennets in Shakespeare. At times the playwright distinguishes between a short fanfare and the more extended, processional composition for brass instruments. For instance, the stage direction in *1 Henry VI*, III.i, 'Sennet. Flourish. Exeunt.', implies that a sennet was sounded while the procession marched off and a flourish for the completion of the exit. Flourishes and alarums are met with more frequently in Elizabethan plays: there are some seventy occurrences in Shakespeare alone.[1] Even so, he employs the

---

[1] For further details and bibliographical references cf. Naylor; also P. A. Jorgensen, *Shakespeare's Military World*, Berkeley (Calif.), 1956. Florio's *Dictionary of the Italian and English Tongues*, 1611, s.v. 'toccare', 'toccata d'un musico', and 'tocco', supports the view that the verb meant to strike, to touch, to blow, whether a trumpet, a drum, or even a keyboard instrument.

tumult of military signals (as well as the simulation of divine music) with characteristic economy.

Marlowe notes in the Prologue to *Tamburlaine the Great, Part II* that he was induced to write a sequel to his earlier play in view of the success of Part I which

> Hath made our poet pen his Second Part,
> Where death cuts off the progress of his pomp, . . .

Trumpets continue to play their roles in Part II with customary splendour, although there is no dead march at the conclusion and frequently the signal 'alarum', not 'flourish', is given.[1]

'Alarums' were usually executed by drums which were, at times, accompanied by trumpets. One surmises that the greater prominence of the drum is a reflection of Tamburlaine's character, particularly as it is displayed in his behaviour toward his son and his enemies. But in the present context the main interest of Marlowe's tragedy is in the death scene of Zenocrate in Act II, scene iv. It portrays the emperor 'raving, impatient, desperate and mad' at the death of his Zenocrate. Following the example of Bel-Imperia in the *Spanish Tragedy* he invokes the music of the spheres

> The cherubins and holy seraphins,
> That sing and play before the King of Kings,
> Use all their voices and their instruments
> To entertain divine Zenocrate:
> And in this sweet and curious harmony,
> The god that tunes this music to our souls
> Holds out his hand in highest majesty
> To entertain divine Zenocrate.

The natural music of Marlowe's verse is later supplemented by actual music:

> *Zenocrate.* Sweet sons, farewell; in death resemble me,
> And in your lives your father's excellency.
> Some music, and my fit will cease, my lord.
> [S.D. They call music]

---

[1] V.iii.101 and 114, for instance. The line numbering is that of U. M. Ellis-Fermor's edn., London, 1930.

Tamburlaine.

> Proud fury, and intolerable fit,
> That dares torment the body of my love, . . .
> And had she liv'd before the siege of Troy,
> Helen, whose beauty summoned Greece to arms,
> And drew a thousand ships to Tenedos,
> Had not been nam'd in Homer's Iliads, . . .
> Nor Lesbia nor Corinna had been nam'd,—
> Zenocrate had been the argument
> Of every epigram or elegy.

This glowing eulogy of the beloved is followed by the stage direction, 'The music sounds and she dies'.

The 'god that tunes this music to our souls' did, indeed, endow Marlowe with the gift of re-creating its sonority for human ears. *Tamburlaine* and *Doctor Faustus* were worthy ancestors of Shakespeare's immortal verse, for Marlowe was among the first of the Elizabethan writers of tragedy to enhance the pathos of a mournful scene with instrumental music supplied by a consort of strings. The strange strains were a functional need to cure Zenocrate's fit; beyond this they both illumine and complement the threnody of Tamburlaine's lines. This poignant scene, together with the episode in *Doctor Faustus* when 'music sounds and Helen passeth over the stage', taught Shakespeare a lesson he never forgot: to underline miraculous events with music, not only in a prelude or dumb-show but in the very context of the spoken play.

The trial by combat in Act I, scene iii of Shakespeare's *Tragedy of King Richard the Second*[1] takes place to the accompaniment, in profusion, of the braying trumpet to underscore the giddy atmosphere of Richard's court. The scene is important for its characterization of Richard: his lack of judgment towards both friend and enemy, Mowbray, Duke of Norfolk and Bolingbroke, Duke of Hereford. As the play moves toward its tragic close, the tender tones of stringed instruments intrude upon Richard's solitude—the antithesis of his erstwhile glorious state.

In the earlier scene the sound of the trumpet is designed to

---

[1] The title of Q, 1597; the F title is: *The Life and Death of King Richard the Second.*

increase the ardour of these armed knights who stand ready to cross swords:

(line 6)   [S.D. Flourish, Enter King . . . Then Mowbray in armour, and Herald.]

(line 25)   [S.D. Tucket. Enter Hereford and Herald.]

(line 104) *1st Herald.* Harry of Hereford, Lancaster, and Derby Stands here . . .

2nd Herald. Here standeth Thomas Mowbray, Duke of Norfolk,
> . . .
> Attending but the signal to begin.

Marshal. Sound trumpets, and set forward, combatants.
> [S.D. A charge sounded]
> Stay, the king hath thrown his warder down.

Richard. Let them lay by their helmets and their spears
> . . .
> Withdraw with us and let the trumpets sound,
> While we return these dukes what we decree.
> [S.D. A long flourish]
> . . .
> And for our eyes do hate the dire aspect
> Of civil wounds ploughed up with neighbours' swords;
> . . .
> Which so roused up with boistrous untuned drums,
> With harsh-resounding trumpets' dreadful bray

(line 248) *Richard.* Cousin, farewell—and uncle, bid him so,
> Six years we banish him and he shall go.
> [S.D. Exit. Flourish]

This scene is revived in *2 Henry IV*, IV.i.122, when Mowbray's son reminisces and recreates the excitement of that moment when the two knights and their steeds responded to the trumpet's challenge:

> And then that Henry Bolingbroke and he,
> Being mounted, and both rousèd in their seats,
> Their neighing coursers daring of the spur,
> . . .
> And the loud trumpet blowing them together;
> Then, then, when there was nothing could have stayed
> My father from the breast of Bolingbroke,
> O when the King did throw his warder down,
> (His own life hung upon the staff he threw!)
> . . .

In *Richard II* Shakespeare dispensed with the horses, though Holinshed and other sources set the trial on horseback. Limitations of the stage may have been responsible, but trumpets assuredly could not be spared. Their sound was essential to convey a challenge that was to become senseless through the king's decision, whose 'own life hung upon the staff he threw'. The connotations of the 'untuned drums' and the 'harsh-resounding trumpets' are clear: they herald a civil war. In patriotic scenes of victory and in trials where virtue is honoured, Shakespeare employs the brazen signal, according to custom. But excessive fighting and excessive trumpeting is invariably censured and, more often than not, the descriptive adjectives which refer to trumpets and drums are intended to evoke fear on the part of the audience. That their sympathies were with peace and against strife hardly needs saying. Furthermore, an examination of the instrumental passages in the plays evinces the playwright's own preference for a soft voice, 'ever soft, gentle, and low, an excellent thing'—not only in woman, but also in music.

The soft music of a consort of strings reminds the deposed and captive Richard of the 'concord of my state and time':

> ... But whate'er I be,
> Nor I, nor any man that but man is,
> With nothing shall be pleas'd, till he be eas'd
> With being nothing.
>   [S.D. Music]
>   Music do I hear?
> Ha, ha! keep time—how sour sweet music is
> When time is broke and no proportion kept!
> So is it in the music of men's lives.
> And here I have the daintiness of ear
> To check time broke in a disordered string;
> But for the concord of my state and time
> Had not an ear to hear my true time broke ...
> This music mads me. Let it sound no more;
> For though it have holp madmen to their wits,
> In me it seems it will make wise men mad.
> Yet blessing on his heart that gives it me,
> For 'tis a sign of love ...

But whereas the right sort of music helps 'madmen to their wits', the chastened Richard, unlike Zenocrate, is not in a fit to be eased by music, his only cure is 'being nothing'. The music recalls to his mind the universal need for proportion, the concord of music reminds him of the concord of state and peace. Whether Richard observes time broke in the disordered strings because the consort plays in faulty rhythm or whether, in his self-searching mood, anticipating his impending murder, he reads this disorder into the music, is hard to say. One is inclined to assume the latter. In any case, the soft music of strings becomes a powerful agent in causing Richard to re-assess his position and in rousing the compassion of the audience.

Not every tragedy (or tragi-comedy) by Shakespeare contrasts the loud and boisterous music of war with the quiet order of a soft consort that represents peace and a harmonious commonwealth. As opposed to Zenocrate, Richard and Lear, Troilus's giddy flights are not eased by 'marvellous' music. Yet, there is hardly any play which articulates more clearly the relationship between the music of the spheres, the music of men's lives, and the consort of strings, than does *Troilus and Cressida*. The use of braying trumpets and references to well-proportioned music as a symbol of political harmony recur throughout the play. Of the many scenes which involve the music of war three are conspicuous: Hector's challenge delivered by Aeneas; Hector's duel with Ajax; and Hector's murder by Achilles.

The challenge delivered by Aeneas in Act I is brazen both in sound and meaning; it is boldly and confidently delivered and intended to provoke:

Agamemnon. What trumpet? look, Menelaus.
Menelaus. From Troy . . .
Agamemnon. What's your affair, I pray you?
Aeneas. Sir, pardon: 'tis for Agamemnon's ears.
Agamemnon. He hears nought privately that comes from Troy.
Aeneas. Nor I from Troy come not to whisper him;
    I bring a trumpet to awake his ear,
    To set his sense on the attentive bent . . .
          Trumpet, blow loud,
    Send thy brass voice through all these lazy tents;
    And every Greek of mettle, let him know,
    What Troy means fairly shall be spoke aloud.
                [S.D. Trumpet sounds]

We have, great Agamemnon, here in Troy
A prince called Hector . . .
                              . . . He bad me take a trumpet . . .
He hath a lady wiser, fairer, truer,
Than ever Greek did couple in his arms,
And will tomorrow with his trumpet call. . . .

The frequent repetitions of 'trumpet' and 'loud' are excessive,
as is, indeed, the entire tone of the challenge as the trumpet is
bid to send its 'brass voice through all these lazy tents'. There
is a disproportionate amount of chivalry and a corresponding
lack of statesmanship, as Hector is to discover to his own and
Troy's peril. When the actual duel takes place (IV.v), the
musical references savour more of sound than of sense.

Ajax.   Thou, trumpet, there's my purse.
          Now crack thy lungs, and split thy brazen pipe;
          . . .
          Come, stretch thy chest, and let thy eyes spout blood;
          Thou blow'st for Hector.
                                   [S.D. Trumpet sounds]
Ulysses.   No trumpet answers.
Achilles.   'Tis but early days . . .
                                   [S.D. Trumpet within]
All.   The Trojans' trumpet . . .
                                   [S.D. Alarum]
Agamemnon. They are in action . . .
                                   [S.D. Trumpets cease]

Shakespeare underscores the ludicrousness of this inconclu-
sive combat in the exaggerated instructions which Ajax gives to
the trumpeter. Moreover, while the beginning of the fight is
heralded by 'alarum', its conclusion is marked by 'trumpets
cease'. One may surmise from these stage directions that the
signal for combat is executed by both trumpet and drum, an
excess which here, as well as in *Henry VI*, paints an arrogant and
lavish society destroying itself in futile war.[1] There runs throughout the play a strong anti-foreign bias. We are made to feel that
this sumptuousness in chivalry and music is alien to the native

---

[1] Concerning an Italianate English gentry as the object of satire in both
plays, cf. *English Institute Essays, 1952*, ed. Alan S. Downer, New York, 1954,
p. 120.

English tradition, and that Trojans and Greeks are thinly disguised representations of the English gentry succumbing to foreign luxury. In Jonson as well as Shakespeare, the main objects of derision are Italianate manners and customs. The exaggeratedly ceremonious trials-by-combat in *Richard II* and *Troilus and Cressida* are caricatured with even greater force in Jonson's *Cynthia's Revels*, where a mock tournament in courtship (not in knightly combat) is punctuated by no fewer than twenty trumpet signals.[1] Jonson castigates the same fanciful speech of courtiers (the 'Solemn Address' and the 'Perfect Close') that Touchstone lampoons in his description of mincing courtiers arguing 'by the book' (the 'Retort Courteous' and the 'Quip Modest').[2] In *Troilus* Pandarus, Helen, Paris, the servant—the group as a whole seem to be engaged in a verbal display of clever affectations. In Act III, scene i there are some 150 lines of prose couched in elaborate, new-fangled courtiers' speech, accompanied by voluptuous instrumental strains that are succeeded by Pandarus's voluptuous song. It is the devil's music, appealing to the flesh, which characterizes the foreign Helen and her destructive influence.

The brazen din that was so prominent in Acts I and IV is noticeably absent in the final scene of the play where the unarmed Hector is murdered by Achilles' Myrmidons. There is no flourish for Hector, since he is not seeking battle, nor one for Achilles, who steals upon him. With its significant absence of trumpets the whole scene is lacking in aristocratic tone and is Macchiavellian rather than chivalrous. No dead march is sounded for Hector, and Achilles exhorts his soldiers to spread a lie. When the Greek and Trojan trumpeters sound a retreat they signal to lesser men, and 'the bruit is Hector's slain' is given out by common soldiers to the sound of drums.

Ulysses' famous speech on degree in Act I, scene iii, is one of the most comprehensive expositions of Shakespeare's beliefs concerning the interrelationship of the music of the spheres, the music of men's lives and the consort of strings.

---

[1] Jonson IV.142 ff. The French are also the subject of occasional ridicule: 'Your frenchified fool is your only fool'. But the main object of satire in these plays and in *Volpone* is Italian sumptuousness.

[2] *AYL*, V.iv.74 ff.

The heavens themselves, the planets, and this centre,
Observe degree, priority, and place, . . .
And therefore is the glorious planet Sol
In noble eminence enthron'd and spher'd
Amidst the other; whose medicinable eye
Corrects the influence of evil planets[1] . . .
. . . like the commandment of a king . . .
. . . O, when degree is shaked
Which is the ladder of all high designs,
The enterprise is sick! How could communities,
Degrees in schools, and brotherhoods in cities,
Peaceful commerce from dividable shores,
The primogenitive and due of birth,
Prerogative of age, crowns, sceptres, laurels,
But by degree, stand in authentic place?
Take but degree away, untune that string,
And hark what discord follows! . . .

These ancient Pythagorean and Platonic beliefs into which
the Ethos theory of music is woven, were transmitted largely
through Cicero's *Somnium Scipionis.* The main channels were
Macrobius's commentary on Cicero and the standard Latin
treatises on the art of music from Boethius and Cassiodorus to
Tinctoris and Glareanus. The philosophers asserted that the
music of the planets—*musica mundana*—was reflected in the
affairs of men—*musica humana.* This theory of the music of
the spheres had grafted upon it, by Platonists and Christians
alike, the Ethos theory, namely, that suitable music performed by
men—*musica instrumentalis*—would induce virtue and harmony
in human beings. The terminology of this hypothesis is inclined
to be misleading, in two respects: first, *musica instrumentalis* is not
restricted to instruments, and the performers may 'use all their
voices and their instruments'. Secondly, virtue and earthly
harmony do not invariably result from man-made music, since
music may degrade. The music that emanates from the Trojan
palace at the beginning of Act III of *Troilus and Cressida,* though
harmonious, does not reform Paris and Helen; rather, it appeals
to their depravity and confirms it. And this is true as much of
the instrumental 'broken consort' as it is of Pandarus's song
which succeeds it. The word 'broken' solicits puns on various

[1] F: 'ill aspects of planets evil'. Cf. NS 154, s.v. line 92.

levels, including musical. Richard 'had not an ear to hear his true time broke' and Pandarus, Paris and Paris's servant show other facets of the verbal prism.

> [S.D. Music sounds within]
>
> *Pandarus.* Friend, you, pray you, a word . . .
> . . . What music is this?
> *Servant.* I do but partly know, sir: it is music in parts.
> *Pandarus.* Know you the musicians?
> *Servant.* Wholly, sir.
> *Pandarus.* Who play they to?
> *Servant.* To the hearers, sir.
> *Pandarus.* At whose pleasure, friend?
> *Servant.* At mine, sir, and theirs that love music . . .
> . . . at the request of Paris my lord, who is there
> in person; with him, the mortal Venus,
> the heart-blood of beauty . . .
>
> [S.D. Enter Paris and Helen]
>
> *Pandarus.* Fair be to you, my lord, . . . Especially to you,
> fair queen . . . Fair prince, here is good broken music.
> *Paris.* You have broke it cousin; and by my life,
> you shall make it whole again: you shall piece
> it out with a piece of your performance. Nell, he
> is full of harmony . . .

The 'broken consort' was a mixture of the tone colours of stringed and wind instruments. Such a combination produced more expressive and exciting music than the 'whole consort' which was restricted to a single family of instruments, such as viols or recorders. For the sake of completeness it should be stated that any combination of instruments that went beyond a single family would be termed 'broken consort' as, for example, a combination of cornetts and flutes. But the only examples relevant to dramatic poetry concern the blending of wind and string families.

Elizabethan audiences, aware of the meaning attached to these different groups, associated the 'broken consort' with entertainment and lavish banquets. According to one contemporary source, the whole consort of viols was 'esteemed', but the broken consort 'much more delightful for the reception of guests'. It was for the louder, broken consort that Thomas Morley published his *Consort Lessons* which became so popular that they were reprinted in the course of Shakespeare's active theatrical career. Philip Rosseter, who was also associated with the theatre, published *Lessons for Consort* for the same combination.[1] Paris and Helen would unquestionably favour music that was delightful, not esteemed. Their broken music was 'broke', that is interrupted, by Cousin Pandarus. But he does not 'make it whole again' in the wholesome sense of the word, he merely replaces a sensuous piece of instrumental music with a sensuous song, which, as he is full of harmony, tends in a pleasure-loving direction. The scene as a whole has a clownish atmosphere and is couched in the manner Shakespeare used for his clown-scenes.[2] Unlike the blank verse of Ulysses' elevated speech on degree, it is written in prose. The servant's puns on music in parts, he knows but 'partly', played by musicians he knows 'wholly', are reminiscent of Peter's foolery in *Romeo and Juliet* and that of the grave-digger in *Hamlet*.

At least three treatises, Castiglione's *Courtier*, Montaigne's *Essays* and Bodin's *Republic*, were so highly esteemed and carefully studied by the Elizabethans that the Platonic beliefs which their pages contained were transmuted into commonplace aphorisms. In this way music was characterized as 'broken' when it reflected a politically unsound commonwealth and also when it tended to impel courtiers and citizens in that perilous direction. The acknowledgment of this presumptive influence added yet another overtone to the broken consort that was traditional for banquets and other lavish entertainments. Bodin's argument on the correspondence between the music made by men and 'the concord of my state and time' throws a conspicuous light on the nature of musical passages in Elizabethan and Jacobean tragedy where contemporary beliefs on the principles of kingship and statesmanship are aired.[3]

---

[1] For 'esteemed' vs. 'delightful', cf. W. H. McCabe, 'Music . . . on a 17th Century . . . Stage', *Musical Quarterly*, XXIV (1938), 313 ff. For the English genre of broken consort, cf. the historical introduction to *Morley's Consort Lessons*, ed. Sydney Beck, New York and London, 1959. Mr. Beck's edition and Mr. Thurston Dart's anthology of *Jacobean Consort Music*, London, 1955, are the most conveniently available reprints for the modern producer.

[2] See discussion of the role of clowns in Chapter VII, p. 159.

[3] The influence of Bodin was so well established that Burton quotes the French author (in company with the Bible and Cassiodorus) in his *Anatomy of Melancholy*, Oxford, 1624, as one of his authorities on the power of music.

But let us now come unto the opinion of Plato, who thought the changes and ruins of commonweals to ensue when as the consent of the sweetness which proceedeth from the harmony thereof is interrupted and broken . . . If therefore choice be had of such proportions as make a sweet consent . . . the commonweal shall so be everlasting: if so be that the state of commonweals depend of harmony. But that harmony (as saith Plato) is sometime broken, so that the sweet consent thereof must needs perish, and so commonweals at length come to ruin and decay.[1]

The convictions of Bodin and other humanists of the need for a centralized and effective sovereignty of state in the person and power of the monarch are reflected in the wish of Ulysses to see power and decision in the hands of Agamemnon. This necessity for a puissant sovereignty is the key-note of Bodin's political works, and their influence on the development of English political thought under Elizabeth and James I was inevitable. Bodin argues by analogy in the manner of Renaissance writers and rhetoricians. The monarchic commonwealth like musical harmony is

. . . tempered by sweet concord . . . .As the first interval, that is, the octave, with its one or two ratio, . . . embraces all the intervals, so in one and the same prince is the sovereignty, and from him it flows to all the magistrates.

Is it so remarkable, then, that Exeter should declare in Act I of *Henry V*

For government, though high, and low, and lower,
Put into parts, doth keep in one consent,
Congreeing in a full and natural close
Like music.

In an age when punning was a favourite form of humour, the homonym was also put to serious use. Clerics, courtiers and

---

[1] The main sources for Bodin's ideas on music and politics are his *Methodus ad facilem historiarum cognitionem*, 1566 (ed. B. Reynolds, New York, 1945) and his *Six Livres de la Republique*, 1576 (tr. R. Knolles, London, 1606). In 1581 the Duc d'Alençon, wooing the hand of Queen Elizabeth, visited London with Bodin in his train. To his delight Bodin discovered that his writings were being seriously studied at Cambridge University though in a poor Latin translation. He resolved to supply an authoritative Latin edition himself and did so in 1586. The foregoing quotation is from the *Republique*, tr. Knolles, p. 455. Cf. also Bibliography s.v. Bodin.

playwrights alike would buttress an argument on proportion by an obvious example from the art of tones,[1] as did Bodin in addressing the French monarch and Shakespeare in the discourses of Exeter and Ulysses. Following his exegesis of the monarchic government, Bodin proceeds to equate the harmonic proportion of music with peace:

. . . peace, fitting the harmonic ratio in the most remarkable way, is the most excellent and best objective of empires and states.

To seek in the concord of music a cure for civil and religious strife; to employ music for drawing down the influences of the heavens upon the royal house and the averting of war was a favourite theme of dramatic presentations in Paris and London.[2]

Bodin makes a further pertinent reference to the intrinsic power of music in his description of the public banquets, *epulones*, which were held by the Romans to induce a harmonious state of mind in the magistrates. On the occasion of these *epulones*, according to Cicero and commentators of the sixteenth century, the soft, dignified music of strings was the means of paying homage to the Deities and of inducing wisdom in the magistrates. But the achievements of heroes of battle were celebrated with music loud and wild. This contrast in the use of strings versus winds provides important clues for our understanding of Elizabethan drama.

[1] See the editions of *Henry V*, NS 127, NA 21, for references to Elyot's *Book of the Governor*, Shakespeare's most likely source in addition to Cicero and St. Augustine.
[2] Bodin, *Methodus*, ed. Reynolds, pp. 286 ff.; F. A. Yates, 'Dramatic Religious Processions in Paris', *Annales Musicologiques*, II (1954), 215-70, part. 254.

IX

INSTRUMENTAL MUSIC: PART TWO

Stringed versus Wind Instruments

I. Trumpets

Towards the conclusion of Shakespeare's most celebrated tragedy Horatio speaks the well-known lines:

> Good night, sweet prince,
> And flights of angels sing thee to thy rest!
> Why does the drum come hither?
> > [S.D. Enter Fortinbras, the English ambassadors,
> > with drum, colours, and attendants.]

Not only is the song of the angels—or the muses—interrupted by the music of war, but the play's apotheosis is pronounced in Martian tones:

> *Fortinbras.*   Let four captains
> Bear Hamlet like a soldier to the stage,
> For he was likely, had he been put on,
> To have proved most royally; and for his passage,
> The soldier's music and the rites of war
> Speak loudly for him.
> Take up the bodies. Such a sight as this
> Becomes the field, but here shows much amiss.
> Go, bid the soldiers shoot.
> > [S.D. Exeunt marching: after the which a
> > peal of ordnance are shot off.]

The 'soldiers' music and the rites of war' loom large in the mature tragedies—trumpets, drums and cannon (ordnance) being cognate to their subject-matter. By contrast, the soft and harmonious music of the well-ordered commonwealth, reflecting the harmony of celestial music, is likely to be evoked by verse alone. Towards the end of this stage of Shakespeare's development, notably in *King Lear* (1605/06) and *Pericles* (1607/08), the quiet, and quieting, music becomes actual sound on the stage, interpreted by strings. But the fullest use of the music of Apollo, as opposed to the music of Mars, is made in the last plays, the so-called Romances, to whose miraculous and happy surprises the whole consort of strings gives support.

With a striking difference, the noisy merriment of Claudius in the first and last acts of *Hamlet* evokes an ominous feeling. He, who has taken his sometime sister to wife (I.ii.12),

> With mirth in funeral, and with dirge in marriage

disports a jollity whose impropriety recalls 'our solemn hymns to sullen dirges change' in *Romeo and Juliet*. Cannon and trumpets supply the customary stage music for Claudius's rouses (carouses) which Hamlet censures for their excess and of which the audience would certainly disapprove.

Claudius. No jocund health that Denmark drinks today,
But the great cannon to the clouds shall tell,
And the king's rouse the heaven shall bruit again,
Re-speaking earthly thunder. Come away.
    [S.D. Flourish. Exeunt all but Hamlet]
                                                    I.ii.125
        [S.D. A flourish of trumpets, and
                two pieces go off]
Hamlet. The king doth wake to-night and takes his rouse,
Keeps wassail, and the swagg'ring upspring reels,
And as he drains his draughts of Rhenish down,
The kettledrum and trumpet thus bray out
The triumph of his pledge.
                                                    I.iv.8
Claudius. Let all the battlements their ordnance fire.
                        ... give me the cups;
And let the kettle to the trumpet speak,
The trumpet to the cannoneer without,
The cannons to the heavens, the heaven to earth,

'Now the King drinks to Hamlet.' Come, begin,
And you, the judges, bear a wary eye.
[S.D. Trumpets the while]

V.ii.281

Even if the unusually full stage directions of Q_2, the 'good'
quarto of 1604, were lacking, the verse of itself paints an eloquent picture, where kettledrum and trumpet 'bray', and noise
and mirth usurp the place of the 'dirge', which should have
taken place on the death of old King Hamlet. The fact that loud
music plays a part in this excessive and inappropriate revelry is
an obvious stroke of characterization and stage display. To use
Hamlet's phrase, it 'soils' the exalted office of Claudius. The
same kind of drunken revelry soils Antony, and wherever present it reflects, as well, on the commonwealth. In *Hamlet* the
Danes are

> . . . traduc'd and tax'd of other nations.

The instrumental noise that accompanies the carouses of
Claudius is paralleled by the Egyptian bacchanal in *Antony and
Cleopatra* (II.vii), whose function was to

> make battery to our ears with loud music.

Later (IV.viii) the incontinent Antony is strangely reminiscent
of Claudius whose rouses and cannonshots the 'heaven shall
bruit again':

> *Antony.* Through Alexandria make a jolly march,
> . . .
> And drink carouses to the next day's fate,
> Which promises royal peril. Trumpeters,
> With brazen din blast you the city's ear;
> Make mingle with our rattling tabourines,
> That heaven and earth may strike their sounds together,
> Applauding our approach.

Trumpet signals in the tragedies were not restricted to jolly
and noisy incontinence, however. The brazen call was also used
as a challenge to combat. Its use in the fourth act of *Othello* is
striking since in that domestic tragedy military or ceremonious
signals occur only rarely. In fact, there are but two trumpet fanfares in the entire drama; one to herald the arrival of Othello

in Cyprus (II.i.180), the other the arrival of Lodovico (IV.i.226). The second signal comes at an awkward moment, for Othello has just abandoned himself to Iago's diabolicism and a wretched Moor rouses himself to ask, 'What trumpet is that same?' 'Something from Venice, sure' he has to be told. Whereupon he endeavours to respond to the familiar sound which, in war, would incite valiant knights and their steeds to battle, and, in peace, put men of affairs on guard and at their ceremonious best. Othello makes two attempts to meet the challenge, each time in single lines. But his air is that of a tired animal, he cannot go on, and we are back at 'fire and brimstone', 'devil, devil', and 'crocodile's tears'. His degradation is complete when he humiliates Desdemona before Lodovico and attendants, and the ceremonious occasion, ushered in by the heralding trumpets, comes to a grievous end. Thus, the customary signal becomes a means of emphasizing that the noble Moor is unequal to the demands of a state occasion.

The writing of *King Lear* followed closely upon *Othello*, and the devilry of Edmund, bastard of Gloucester, has much in common with the character of Iago. In the final settlement of the tragedy of the house of Gloucester, the trumpet is once more brought into play to work its effect. At Edmund's encounter with Albany (V.iii.90) we hear

Albany. Thou art armed, Gloucester: let the trumpet sound;
If none appear to prove upon thy person
Thy heinous, manifest, and many treasons,
There is my pledge! . . .

Edmund throws down his glove, and a herald is called.

Albany. Come hither, Herald. Let the trumpet sound.
And read out this.
[S.D. A trumpet sounds]
Herald. [reads] If any man of quality or degree within
the lists of the army will maintain upon Edmund
supposed Earl of Gloucester, that he is a manifold
traitor, let him appear by the third sound of the
trumpet. He is bold in his defence.
[S.D. First trumpet]
Again! [S.D. Second Trumpet]
Again! [S.D. Third trumpet]
[S.D. Trumpet answers within]

The several repetitions of the phrase 'trumpet sound' within fifteen lines of dialogue prepare for the five signals actually sounded on the stage; the final trumpet, answering off-stage, comes as a surprise both to Edmund and the audience. Its mere sound signifies the arrival of justice: both the crime and the punishment of the protagonist are conveyed in these few strains. The following thirty-odd lines before Edmund falls are but an extension of the event, in the manner of a coda.

In this context the function of the trumpet is not musical, it is dramatic. We have only to consider Beethoven's opera *Fidelio*, written two centuries later, to realize the extra-musical quality of such a fanfare. An off-stage trumpet announcing the liberating arrival of the Governor at the prison intercepts the imminent murder of the hero, and the drama's peripeteia is brought about —a dramatic surprise within the musical organization. The impact of the signal in *King Lear* is comparable. Here, as elsewhere in the tragedies, Shakespeare uses the trumpet as a tool to convey his meaning more succinctly and unequivocally than words could do.[1]

II. Instrumental Interludes and Oboes

To employ the term 'interlude' in a discussion of Elizabethan tragedy does not necessarily imply that the musical scene is independent of the spoken play. The character of these shows within the show ranges from extraneous matter to building-stones closely integrated within the structure as a whole. Various pretexts are used to relieve the monotony of spoken verse by instrumental strains: a dumb-show as in *Hamlet* (III.ii) or *Macbeth* (IV.i); a banquet as in *Titus* (V.iii) or *Macbeth* (I.vii); a dance as in *Romeo* (I.v), or an ominous premonition as in *Antony* (IV.iii). Of these dramatic occasions the dumb-show is of particular importance since it indicates a significant departure in the Elizabethan drama of blank verse from the contemporary translations of Seneca's dramas. In this regard it is illuminating to compare Seneca's *Thyestes* 'faithfully Englished by Jasper Heywood' (1560), Norton's and Sackville's *Gorboduc* (1562), the

---

[1] The present analysis has profited much from the perspicacious comments on trumpet signals in H. Granville-Barker's *Prefaces to Shakespeare*, 5 vols., 1927–47. *King Lear* is treated in Vol. I, *Othello* in Vol. II.

earliest English tragedy to employ both blank verse and dumb-show with instrumental music, and Shakespeare's earliest tragedy, *Titus Andronicus* (?1590–94).

Heywood's *Thyestes* is a tragedy of revenge and blood which proceeds entirely without song or instrumental interlude. Its five acts are in iambic heptameters and at the end of each act there is a moralizing chorus in rhymed iambic pentameters. These choruses, extending from fifty-four to ninety-six lines, are too long to be sung, nor are they lyrical by nature. The only act which lacks a concluding chorus is the fifth, which offers instead an interlude in the form of Thyestes' soliloquy in rhymed iambic pentameters. The bloody banquet at which a father, unwittingly, feasts on his own murdered children might have provided an Elizabethan playwright (whose audience was ever eager for music) with at least two opportunities for its use: an instrumental accompaniment for the banquet, and a song for Thyestes. (In the preceding fourteeners Atreus informs the audience that Thyestes 'strains his voice and sings'.) Yet, so strong was the classical tradition of rhetoric without music that Thyestes' monologue of forty-nine lines is a rhetorical soliloquy of an unhappy man. Neither song, nor broken consort, nor even a whole consort of oboes, was brought into use to function as a background to the unhappy feast.

Atreus. . . .
> The father (mingled with the wine) his children's
> blood shall sup,
> That would have drunk of mine. Behold he now begins
> to strain
> His voice, and sings, nor yet for joy his mind he may
> refrain.

Thyestes. [alone] O beaten bosoms, dull'd so long with woe,
> Lay down your cares, at length your griefs relent . . .
> Why call'st thou me aback, and hindrest me
> This happy day to celebrate? Wherefore
> Bidst thou me (sorrow) weep without a cause?[1]

Gorboduc (1562) contains a great deal of cruelty: the younger brother kills the elder, the mother the younger, the people the

---

[1] *Seneca, his ten tragedies translated into English, edited by Thomas Newton, anno 1581,* intr. T. S. Eliot (Tudor Translations, 2nd series, ed. C. Whibley), 2 vols., London, 1927, I.87.

father and mother. The political and moral sentiments of the play are closely related to the Senecan model. But a new element appears in the dramatic scheme in the form of the dumb-show.[1] The source of this innovation is difficult to fathom; it may have derived from the Italian *intermedii* and French *entremets*, or from the native English tradition of city pageants and court masques; or, quite likely, from both.[2]

Whatever its origin, the dumb-show was one of the forms of relief from a preponderant diet of speech declaimed in verse. The battle scenes with drums and trumpets and the clown's prose scenes with adult songs were also useful, as we have seen. But the latter were rarely used before 1600, whereas the dumb-show appears to have been a regular feature in plays as early as *Gorboduc, Jocasta, Tancred* and *Appius*, all performed between 1562 and 1567. *Gorboduc* is particularly useful to the student of music in Shakespeare's plays because the symbolism of various groups of instruments, as they were characteristically used in dumb-shows, appears to be established quite early, and their significance remained the same throughout Shakespeare's tragedies.

The dumb-show preceding the first act of *Gorboduc* presents the fable of the faggot of sticks which cannot be broken while they are knit together, whereby 'was signified that a state knit in unity doth continue strong against all force'. This allegory was enacted to the accompaniment of strings, whose soft sound represented the united commonwealth according to ancient, mediaeval and Elizabethan beliefs. Violins, which often replaced viols in theatrical performances, were specified. But by the time the last act is reached, this harmony has been wholly undone, and 'drums and flutes began to sound during which there came

---

[1] Cf. the discussion of *Gorboduc* and dumb-shows in Chapter I.

[2] Cf.: *Early English Classical Tragedies*, ed. J. W. Cunliffe, Oxford, 1912, p. 298 f.; *Chief Pre-Shakespearean Dramas*, ed. J. Q. Adams, Boston, 1924, p. 503; F. S. Boas, *Introduction to Tudor Drama*, Oxford, 1933, p. 33 f.; B. R. Pearn, 'Dumb-Shows in Elizabethan Drama', *Review of English Studies*, XI (1935), 385–405; A. P. Rossiter, *English Drama from Early Times to the Elizabethans*, London, 1950, p. 134 f.; M. C. Bradbrook, *Themes & Conventions of Elizabethan Tragedy*, Cambridge, 1935; paper-back edn.: Cambridge, 1960, p. 27; D. Mehl, 'Zur Entwicklung des 'Play within a Play' im elisabethanischen Drama', *Shakespeare-Jahrbuch*, XCVII (1961), 134-152; D. Mehl, *Die Funktion des 'Dumbshow' im elisabethanischen Drama*, Dissertation, Munich, 1960.

upon the stage a company of harquebussiers and of armed men, all in order of battle. . . . Hereby was signified tumults, rebellions, arms and civil wars to follow'. These ominous events were already presaged in

'The Order and Signification of the
Dumb Show before the Fourth Act.'

First, the music of oboes began to play, during which there came forth from under the stage, as though out of hell, three furies . . . Hereby was signified the unnatural murders to follow . . .

That the squealing of oboes was held to be an ill omen is borne out by many stage directions in Elizabethan plays. One may assume that, essentially, all wind instruments were considered loud and piercing: trumpets, cornetts, oboes, pipes and even flutes. When the playwright wished to express an unusually soft quality by means of a wind instrument he spoke of 'still flutes' or 'still recorders'.

In any case, Shakespeare's earliest tragedy, *Titus Andronicus*, prescribes oboes for its most gruesome scene (V.iii):

Marcus Andronicus. Please you, therefore, draw nigh, and take
your places.
Saturnius. Marcus, we will.
[S.D. Oboes. A table brought in.
Enter Titus, like a cook, placing
the meat on the table and Lavinia
with a veil over her face.]

In the F text oboes are indicated to accompany the gruesome banquet where Titus kills his own daughter Lavinia and Tamora 'daintily has fed' on the flesh of her own children 'baked in this pie'. In the Q_1 text of 1594 the stage direction reads 'trumpets sounding'. Whatever the scoring, noisy instruments are now inserted to provide a background for this bloody action that is reminiscent of *Gorboduc*, the *Spanish Tragedy* and their prototype, the *Thyestes*. The verse declamation in Seneca's tragedy, Englished by Heywood, informs the reader of a bloody banquet and a song, but no music is heard. In *Gorboduc* the moralizing choruses at the conclusion of each act are balanced by the action and music of the dumb-shows which precede the act. In the *Spanish Tragedy* we have a banquet and a dumb-show in Act I, as well as the gruesome revenge in Act V: trumpets and drums are prescribed in the first act, but no stage directions for music complement Hieronimo's revenge.[1] In Shakespeare's *Titus*, however, banquet, music, and bloody revenge are combined in a melodramatic manner. There is a great deal of excess in this early tragedy, as its critics customarily declare, but there is no denying that the counterpointing of cruelty and music is an effective dramatic procedure.

The employment of the musical interlude in *Romeo and Juliet* is no less compelling, although it has not the blood-curdling atmosphere of its predecessor. Indeed, after his production of *Titus* Shakespeare's use of instrumental music in tragedy is more in the nature of foretelling crime and punishment than accompanying it. In the play of the starcrossed lovers, however, the ball-room scene is an effective way of bringing about the meeting of the protagonists. The use of music here is perhaps neither as essential nor as poignant as in some scenes of Marlowe and of the later Shakespeare. Yet, the device of the masked ball and its orchestra as the medium for love at first sight was both traditional and dramatically efficacious. The stage direction (I.v.30)

> Music plays and they dance . . .

is brief, both in the Q and the F texts. But an earlier remark of Benvolio (I.iv.10)

> We'll measure them a measure

and the entire tradition of stage and dance music makes it clear that after the conclusion of the Capulet banquet a broken consort plays a pavan, that is, a measure.[2]

The instrumental interlude in *Hamlet* (III.ii.145) is an integral part of one of the main stages of the action:

> Oboes play. The dumb show enters.
> Enter a King and a Queen, very lovingly; . . . Anon comes in a fellow, . . . pours poison in the sleeper's ears . . . The poisoner wooes the Queen . . . she . . . in the end, accepts his love.   [Exeunt.]

---

[1] For the dumb-show in Act I of the *Spanish Tragedy*, cf. C. Prouty's edn., 1951, p. 17, and P. Edwards's edn., 1959, p. 26; for another dumb-show at the conclusion of Act III, cf. Prouty p. 83, Edwards p. 99. There is no reference to musical instruments in the latter.

[2] A discussion of 'measure', 'passymeasure' and other musical terms for dancing will be found in Appendix I to this chapter.

On the surface it seems surprising that Hamlet would have the play

Wherein I'll catch the conscience of the King

preceded by a dumb-show, since shortly before, in the same scene (line 14) he has exclaimed against the cheap actor who will

. . . split the ears of the groundlings, who (for the most part) are capable of nothing but inexplicable dumb shows and noise.

The term 'noise', besides referring to trumpet, drums and cannon, included a band of musicians. The groundlings, then, or more generally speaking, the audience, clamoured for action, spectacle, and music, the very elements which Elizabethan dramatists added to the Senecan model.

The juxtaposition of Hamlet's criticism of inexplicable dumb-shows and the presentation of an actual dumb-show in the same scene has been variously interpreted.[1] It has been argued that Hamlet is not responsible for the dumb-show which the players present on their own initiative and which Claudius does not watch (otherwise he would have rushed from the room at this time instead of later when the poisoning is presented in the spoken tragedy). It has also been said that Hamlet chooses this means of criticizing inexplicable dumb-shows by presenting one that has a relation to the plot and thus acts as the first turn of the screw, to be re-inforced by the subsequent blank verse. This view seems the more reasonable, particularly since

The centre and focus of interest during the acting of *The Murder of Gonzago* must be—for Shakespeare's audience—not the actors in that play, but the guilty Claudius. We should therefore be enabled to follow the plot without attending too much to the players—and in this we are assisted by the dumb show, which is by no means 'inexplicable' . . .[2]

Whichever view is held, there is general agreement that one of Shakespeare's purposes in introducing the scene is to prepare the audience for what is to come. In this endeavour the squealing of the oboes offers assistance as it did in *Gorboduc* and in *Titus*.

---

[1] Cf. NS, 2nd rev. edn., 1954, pp. 196 (s.v. line 12) and 200 (s.v. line 133); Kittredge SP 1064 (s.v. line 13) and 1067 (s.v. line 145).

[2] Kittredge, op. cit.

The so-called 'bad' Quarto of 1603 merely calls for a dumb-show, indicating no instruments, the 'good' Quarto of 1604 has 'The trumpets sound. Dumb show follows', but the F text consistently employs oboes on these ominous occasions. It should be remembered, too, that the dumb-show with oboes is part of a larger scene, full of spectacle and 'noise', as is characteristic of the pomp and circumstance with which Claudius surrounds himself here, as well as in Acts I and V:

> [F text, III.ii.94]
> Enter King, Queen, Polonius, Ophelia . . . Danish March. Sound a Flourish.

> [Q₂ text]
> Enter Trumpets and Kettledrums, King, Queen, Polonius, Ophelia.

A flourish could be performed by either cornetts or oboes, and need not be played by brazen trumpets. In either case, a 'Danish March' (probably added after the accession in 1603 of James I, whose queen was Anne of Denmark) would be a piece of music of some length, comparable to the oboe accompaniment for the banquet in *Titus*.

When King Duncan comes to stay at Macbeth's castle (I.vi) the stage direction reads: 'Oboes and torches. Enter King . . .'. (Since there is no early Quarto, the Folio provides the only authoritative text.) The banquet scene that follows opens with the stage direction, 'Oboes. Torches. Enter a Sewer and diverse servants with dishes and service . . .'. The king, the courtiers and Lady Macbeth are at table in hall while Macbeth, having absented himself, delivers his soliloquy:

> If it were done, when 'tis done, then 'twere well,
> It were done quickly: if th'assassination
> Could trammel up the consequence . . .

The supper and the music of the oboes seemingly go on during this speech, for when Lady Macbeth joins her husband (at line 28) she reports that supper is almost but not quite completed. The sound of the oboes surely provides a grim counterpoint to Macbeth's deliberations and foreshadows his eventual decision to 'screw his courage to the sticking-place' and commit the contemplated regicide.

The most crucial employment of the oboes takes place in Act IV, scene i. Without considering the genuineness of this scene as a whole[1] one may certainly vouch for the authenticity of lines 44–124, for they contain two integral portions of the drama: the three warnings and the show of eight kings. The former (lines 69–94), like the terrifying storm scenes in *King Lear*, are accompanied by thunder:

[S.D. Thunder. 1st Apparition, an armed head]
. . .
1st App.   Macbeth, Macbeth, Macbeth: Beware Macduff . . .
    [S.D. Thunder. 2nd Apparition, a bloody child]
2nd App. Macbeth, Macbeth, Macbeth . . .
                      . . . For none of woman born
    Shall harm Macbeth . . .
    [S.D. Thunder. 3rd Apparition, a child . . . with a tree . . .]
. . .
3rd App. Macbeth shall never vanquish'd be, until
    Great Birnam Wood to high Dunsinane Hill
    Shall come against him.

These cryptic warnings and assurances receive an ominous emphasis from the off-stage thunder which here takes the place of the customary music of war, of the 'boistrous untun'd drums and harsh-resounding trumpets' dreadful bray'. Further terrors await Macbeth:

Macbeth.   Why sinks that cauldron? and what noise [i.e. music]
               [S.D. Oboes]   is this?
1st Witch. Show!
2nd Witch. Show!
3rd Witch. Show!
All.   Show his eyes and grieve his heart;
        Come like shadows, so depart.
              [S.D. A show (i.e. dumb-show)
      of eight kings, (the eighth) with a glass (i.e. mirror)
      in his hand, and Banquo last.]
Macbeth.   Thou art too like the spirit of Banquo: down!
        Thy crown does sear mine eye-balls . . .

This pantomime, commemorating the murder of Banquo and other victims, is accompanied by the same harsh, nasal oboes

---

[1] Cf. Chapter IV, pp. 88, 95.

which attended the dumb-show of the 'Murder of Gonzago' in *Hamlet*.[1]

In Thomas Middleton's *Hengist, King of Kent, or the Mayor of Queenborough, ca.* 1616-20, the murders of Constantius and Vortimer are acted out in the second and third dumb-shows of the play, both of which begin with the stage direction 'Oboes'. By contrast, the first dumb-show, which depicts a drawing of lots and a lovers' farewell, simply has 'Music'.[2]

The doomed career of Macbeth demands the presence of sinister oboes or instruments of a like character. In the tragedy of *Antony and Cleopatra*, however, emotional hues of another complexion predominate and other tone colours are therefore specified. The famous description of Cleopatra's lavish barge in North's *Plutarch* includes equally lavish music to set the rhythm of the oar's stroke:

> . . . the poop whereof was of gold, the sails of purple, the oars of silver, which kept stroke in rowing after the sound of the music of flutes, oboes, citterns, viols and such other instruments as they played upon in the barge.

Plutarch describes a broken consort composed of strings (citterns, viols) as well as winds (flutes, oboes). Within this combination the oboes would be not unduly prominent or sonorous. But Shakespeare, whose account otherwise follows his source rather closely, has reduced the band to a single family of instruments, the amorous flute (II.ii):

> The poop was beaten gold;
> Purple the sails, and so perfuméd that
> The winds were lovesick with them; the oars were silver,
> Which to the tune of flutes kept stroke, and made
> The water which they beat to follow faster,
> As amorous of their strokes. . . .

There is a similar musical economy in Shakespeare's treatment

[1] Kittredge SP 880 and 943; NS 151.

[2] Middleton's play, a tragedy or chronicle history with an extended underplot, provides many useful points of comparison with Shakespeare's tragic method. It survives in a manuscript, probably derived from an annotated prompt-copy, with unusually full stage directions. T. Middleton, *Hengist*, ed. R. C. Bald, London, 1938, pp. 12, 23, 69; S. Schoenbaum, *Middleton's Tragedies*, New York, 1955, pp. 86, 217.

of Plutarch in Act IV, scene iii, where supernatural strains presage that the gods are about to forsake Antony. In North's translation of the ancient source we have

... the self-same night within little of midnight, when all the city was quiet, full of fear ... it is said that suddenly they heard a marvellous sweet harmony of sundry sorts of instruments of music, with the cry of a multitude of people, as they had been dancing, and had song as they use in Bacchus feasts, with movings and turnings after the manner of the Satyrs: and it seemed that this dance went through the city unto the gate that opened to the enemies, and that all the troupe that made this noise they heard, went out of the city at that gate. Now such as in reason sought the depth of the interpretation of this wonder, thought that it was the god unto whom Antonius bare singular devotion to counterfeit and resemble him, that did forsake them.[1]

Here is Shakespeare's description:

2nd Soldier. Heard you of nothing strange about the streets? ...
3rd Soldier.   'Tis a brave army,
            And full of purpose.
                        [S.D. Music of the oboes is under the stage]
                        Peace! What noise?
1st Soldier.   List! list!
2nd Soldier. Hark!
1st Soldier.   Music i' th'air.
3rd Soldier.   Under the earth.
4th Soldier. It signs well, does it not?
3rd Soldier.   No.
1st Soldier.   Peace, I say!
            What should this mean?
2nd Soldier. 'Tis the god Hercules, whom Antony lov'd,
            Now leaves him.
1st Soldier.   Walk, let's see if other watchmen
            Do hear what we do.
2nd Soldier.   How now, masters?
Omnes.   How now?
            How now? Do you hear this?
1st Soldier.   Ay, is't not strange?
3rd Soldier. Do you hear masters? Do you hear?
1st Soldier. Follow the noise so far as we have quarter.
            Let's see how it will give off.
Omnes.   Content. 'Tis strange.   [Exeunt]

[1] Plutarch, VI.78.

One is aware that Plutarch, the historian, writes with the leisurely detail of an epic poet, whereas the playwright must restrict himself to a few significant details in order to create dramatic poetry. This is not to deny Shakespeare's debt to Plutarch. That he read the passage carefully is born out by the fact that several of the phrases, though not used in this scene, appear elsewhere in the tragedy and in other plays. The term noise is only too familiar in its connotation of loud music. Plutarch leads the way by describing 'the troupe that made this noise' and in adding a marginal rubric: 'Strange noises heard and nothing seen.' So it is of noise that Hamlet speaks in connection with dumb-shows; that Macbeth queries when he hears oboes for the show of eight kings; and that baffles Antony's soldiers who ask 'What noise?'. Plutarch's noise is not specified, however, it is performed by sundry sorts of instruments, which suggest a broken consort. Shakespeare, as in the description of Cleopatra's barge, reduces the instruments used to a single family, oboes under the stage. (In concealing the musicians under the stage the music was made to seem supernatural.) Plutarch's song 'as they use in Bacchus feasts' was suppressed in Shakespeare's transposition of the scene, but makes its appearance in the Bacchanalian song and dance in Act II, scene vii.[1]

Wholly absent from *Antony and Cleopatra* are Plutarch's 'marvellous sweet harmony of sundry sorts of instruments' and 'movings and turnings after the manner of the satyrs'. These phrases suggest masque and antimasque to a Jacobean ear, and thus they re-appear in Shakespeare's romances: a satyrs' dance in the *Winter's Tale* and the marvellous strains in *The Tempest* (III.iii.19):

> [S.D. Solemn and strange music; and Prospero on the
>   top (invisible).]
> *Alonso.*   What harmony is this? My good friends, hark!
> *Gonzalo.* Marvellous sweet music!

Keeping in mind Shakespeare's faculty for retaining verbal echoes from his various sources, one cannot help feeling that this particular passage from North's *Plutarch* bore abundant fruit. The notion of the supernatural, conveyed by such terms as 'marvellous sweet' and 'wonder' in the source leads to the 'strange'

---

[1] Discussed in Chapter IV on 'Magic Songs'.

noise that baffles Antony's soldiers; to the 'solemn and strange music' in *The Tempest*; and, finally, to Gonzalo's exclamation in which the phrase that proved unsuitable for the Roman tragedy re-emerges with literal accuracy. Shakespeare selects from his sources, and adds to them, in accordance with the need for apt characterization in a swiftly moving drama: for Cleopatra's barge the description is reduced to amorous flutes, and Antony's downfall is augured by shrill oboes.

Through the ages the circumstances associated with oboes have varied from the martial to the popular, but oboes were, before Shakespeare's day, considered neither amorous nor lofty on the whole. The Spartans marched to battle to the music of the 'aulos'[1] and from these early days the oboe and its kind were associated with war. During the Middle Ages and Renaissance the instrument fulfilled a variety of functions for which it was qualified because of its relative loudness: courtly entertainments, receptions, banquets, dances, hunts; also popular entertainment and music of shepherds. (In the latter case bagpipes frequently replaced the oboes.) Literary references to the oboe usually stress its shrillness. Thoinot Arbeau remarks in his *Orchésographie* of 1589 that it is 'bonne pour faire resonner un grand bruit', and Peter Leycester, as late as 1650 describes the oboe as 'loud and shrill'. This quality was its main usefulness for the city waits of England in the sixteenth and seventeenth centuries who relied largely on double-reed instruments.[2] The giant orchestras of the late nineteenth century have played their part in dulling the sensibilities of modern audiences to the tone colours of the oboe family. It is worth noting, though, that as late as Wagner's *Tristan* and Verdi's *Otello* the composers begin the last acts of their respective works with sombre melodies which presage death and which, in each case, are played by a member of the oboe family, the so-called English horn (actually an alto oboe).

Enough has been said to show the steady development and increasing significance of the instrumental interlude. Some further characteristics of the oboe will emerge in the contrast

[1] The 'aulos' is a double-reed instrument, and therefore of the oboe type. To call it a 'flute' is a mis-translation.

[2] Cf. W. Woodfill, *Musicians in English Society*, Princeton, 1953, pp. 84 and 370; the terms 'oboe' and 'shawm' were sometimes used interchangeably.

between the 'pipes' of Dionysus and the 'strings' of Apollo. Proceeding from the banquet in *Titus Andronicus* and the dance in *Romeo and Juliet*, which seem to have functioned as preliminary studies, Shakespeare achieves the utmost degree of relevance in his mature tragedies. In *Hamlet* the oboes are still functional, since music was required for the play within the play as much as for ballroom dancing and banqueting. But in the Scottish and Roman tragedies it is the supernatural and fantastic elements that call for music, and this tendency points towards the wondrous world of the *Winter's Tale* and *The Tempest*.

III. Pan's Pipes versus Apollo's Strings

This discussion so far has been concerned with specific instruments and the special tone colours and meanings attached to them. There exists, besides, the general antagonism between the wind and string families as a whole—an important element in classical mythology, folklore and proverbial lore and, last but not least, in the dramatic literature deriving from these sources.

The generic name 'pipe' was used by the Elizabethans for wind instruments as a class. It covered a wide range from the simple pipe in 'pipe and tabor' (small recorder and small drum) to flutes, military whistles, oboes, shawms, cornetts, bagpipes and what not. A band of 'pipers' or 'pifferari', as the Italians called them, did not refer to a specific instrument but to a whole class. Whether the particular tone colour is determined by the mouth-hole (flute) or the double-reed (oboe) would be of secondary interest to laymen in the sixteenth as well as the twentieth centuries. It was the sonority which decided the usefulness or the connotations of the instrument: wind instruments as a class were louder than strings, and in the popular imagination they were associated with entertainment, particularly with out-door entertainment. To the strings was allotted the music that had a spiritual message, whose effect was to be elevating or refined. There are, of course, many functional exceptions to this rule. For reasons of sonority, wind instruments were occasionally used in the church, and they appear repeatedly in Renaissance paintings of angels making music. (These angels are usually performing in what may be termed out-door concerts.) But regardless of the exceptions we may adduce, the fact remains that Elizabethans associated strings with the spirit and wind instruments with the flesh. If the acoustics of a public playhouse or an out-door pageant demanded a modification or exception it did not affect the rule.

The myth of the rivalry between Apollo and Pan, the god who could charm with his lyre, and the demigod who, with his pipe, made earthly not heavenly music, is as old as Western civilization. The English Renaissance made these beliefs so much their own that, at times, their transmutation into the vernacular had amusing results. Caxton, in 1480, translated Ovid's description of the contest between Apollo and Pan in this way:

> Pan piped and sprang vantage him of the
> hornpipe of Cornwall in amusing Midas . . .

An awareness of this ancient rivalry was ubiquitous and popular, not restricted to the discussions of the humanists. As late as 1662 Thomas Fuller, speaking of bagpipes and country clowns, said that

the bagpipe in the judgment of the rural Midas's carrieth away the credit of the harp of Apollo himself.

Whether the Englished account speaks of pipe or flute or hornpipe, bagpipe or cornett, the emphasis is invariably on popular entertainment, clowns and dancing. In the etiquette books the aspersions against wind instruments are also related to classical matter:

. . . all these instruments [lutes and viols], in the which I will have it sufficient that our courtier have an understanding. Yet the more cunninger he is upon them, the better it is for him, without meddling much with the instruments that Minerva and Alcibiades refused, because it seemeth they are noisome . . .

This reference in the *Cortegiano*, Englished by Thomas Hoby in 1561, is amplified in the *Galateo*, which was Englished by Robert Peterson in 1576. In this latter work 'very necessary and profitable for all gentlemen, or other' we have the fable of Minerva who, chancing to catch sight of herself as she played her cornett for her pleasure beside a fountain, was so ashamed when she beheld the 'strange gestures she must needs make with her mouth as she played . . . that she brake the cornett in pieces and cast it away'. The account goes on to say

And truly she did but well, for it is no instrument for a woman to use. And it becomes men as ill, if they be not of that base condition and calling, that they must make it a gain and an art to live upon it. And look what I speak, concerning the unseemly gestures of the countenance . . .[1]

The poems of Horace formed another group of ancient sources, quoted and echoed alike by rhetoricians and dramatists. There the 'pipe' is used frequently, if we translate thus the Roman 'tibia'. In the *Odes*, that fertile ground for apt phrases and ideas, the advice to Asteria is to avoid the lowly pipes

> Prima nocte domum // claude neque in vias
> Sub cantu querulae // despice tibiae.
> [At nightfall close thy dwelling and do not look
> into the streets at the music of the pining pipe]

This warning is echoed in Shylock's instructions to Jessica:

> What, are there masques? Hear you me, Jessica.
> Lock up my doors; and when you hear the drum
> And the vile squealing of the wry-necked fife,
> Clamber not you up to the casements then,
> Nor thrust your head into the public street . . .

Within the ethical concept the 'cantus querulae tibiae' is no more to be trusted than the 'vile squealing fife'. Moreover, Shylock's fife is 'wry-necked', that is to say, it contorts the features and body of the player.[2]

---

[1] Nietzsche's famous work, *Die Geburt der Tragoedie aus dem Geiste der Musik*, 1872, deals with the contrast between the moderation of Apollo and the orgiastic associations connected with Pan, Marsyas and Dionysos.

Cf. also Ovid's *Metamorphoses*, tr. W. Caxton, edd. S. Gaselee and H. Brett-Smith, Oxford, 1924, p. 32; T. Fuller's *Worthies of England*, ed. P. A. Nuttall, 3 vols., London, 1840, II.267; Castiglione's *Cortegiano*, tr. T. Hoby, intr. W. Raleigh (Tudor Translations, 1st ser.), London, 1900, p. 118; della Casa's *Galateo*, tr. R. Peterson, intr. J. E. Spingarn (Humanist's Library), London and Boston, 1914, p. 114.

Cf. also della Casa's *Galateo*, tr. R. S. Pine-Coffin, Harmondsworth, 1958, p. 101, where Athene-Minerva is playing the bagpipes, not the cornett. On pp. 105–131 there is a useful 'note on Books of Courtesy in England'.

[2] Cf. *Mer V*, II.v.30, NV 89, Kittredge SP 246; Horace's *Odes*, Bk. III, No. 7 (Loeb Library, p. 206 f.); Naylor 155 f.

Sometimes the Renaissance observed the antithesis between Apollo's strings and Pan's pipes more strictly than did the ancients. In another of his odes Horace describes both lyre and pipe as apt for the praises of gods *and* men:

> Quem virum aut heroa lyra vel acri
> Tibia sumis celebrare, Clio?
> Quem deum . . .
> [What man, what hero, dost thou take to herald
> on the lyre or sharp pipe, o Clio? What god . . .]

but certain commentators, among them Torrentius, Bishop of Amsterdam in the sixteenth century, insisted on making a distinction between the louder pipe (sonora magis et acutior), fit for the praises of men and war, and the softer lyre (gravior modestiorque) more apt for the praises of the gods.

In Othello's Farewell to Arms

> Farewell the neighing steed and the shrill trump,
> The spirit-stirring drum, th'ear-piercing fife, . . .

the ear-piercing fife is yet another echo of Horace, for the phrase 'acris tibia' was often singled out by commentators as an example of admirable diction. But Shakespeare's context suggests men and war, not Apollo's lyre or praise of the gods.[1]

The Elizabethan preference for the lute was not only learned and genteel, it was also functional. The difficulties arising in the use of pipes when casting a play are made evident in John Lyly's drama *Midas*, acted before Queen Elizabeth in 1590, and published in 1592.[2] In the musical contest between the god of the muses and the leader of the satyrs Apollo first sings his song, accompanying himself on the lute. In his turn Pan announces

> Now let me tune my pipes. I cannot pipe and sing,
> that's the odds in the instrument, not the art: but

---

[1] *Oth.* III.iii.352; Horace, *Odes*, Book I, No. 12 (Loeb Library, p. 34); Cicero, *Tusculanae Disputationes* (Loeb Library p. 330 f.); Quintilian, *Institutio Oratoria* (Loeb Library, III.200 f.); *Horatius*, ed. L. Torrentius, Antwerp, 1608, p. 45; A Dacier, *Remarques . . . Horace*, 10 vols. Paris, 1689–97, I.170.

[2] Chambers ES III.416. The quotation, including the stage direction, occurs in the quarto of 1592, sig. E.i.r. In view of the several additions which may not be by Lyly, in the edition of 1632, this is important. Cf. also Lyly's *Works*, ed. R. W. Bond, 3 vols., Oxford, 1902, III.142.

I will pipe and then sing; and then judge both of
the art and instrument.

[S.D. He pipes, and then sings]

The accent on *then* is significant: Pan will pipe and *then* sing,
Midas should *then* judge, and the stage direction once more em-
phasizes that a piper cannot play and sing at the same time.
Could Lyly, in writing this scene, have drawn from Plutarch?
There we learn from Sir Thomas North's translation that
Alcibiades, being put to school

... was very obedient ... saving that he disdained to learn to play of
the flute or recorder: saying, that it was no gentlemanly quality.
For, said he, to play on the viol with a stick, doth not alter man's
favour, nor disgraceth any gentleman: but otherwise, to play on the
flute, his countenance altereth and changeth so oft, that his familiar
friends can scant know him. Moreover, the harp or viol doth not let
[i.e. prevent] him that playeth on them from speaking, or singing as
he playeth: where he that playeth on the flute, holdeth his mouth so
hard to it, that it taketh not only his words from him but his voice.
Therefore, said he, let the children of the Thebans play on the flute
... as for us Athenians, we have ... for protectors ... the goddess
Pallas, and the god Apollo: of the which the one in old time ...
brake the flute, and the other pulled his skin over his ears, that
played upon the flute ...[1]

The limitations of the flute as Alcibiades describes them would
be obvious disadvantages to a player enacting a noble role in a
tragedy. Moreover, while the writings of Ovid, Horace, Plutarch
and the etiquette books were the common property of gentlemen and playwrights, the groundlings, through their attendance
at the theatre, would be equally aware of the conventions which
these teachings imposed. Such popular plays as the *Spanish
Tragedy* described Pan and Marsyas as 'harsh and ill' (II.i).
There were, besides, the ever popular picture books in which
the contrast between string and wind instruments was a traditional topic. The much-favoured *Ship of Fools* is a case in point.
There were woodcuts by Dürer in the German and Latin editions, and illustrations derived from Dürer in the five editions
published in London in the sixteenth century. In all of these the
fool plays the bagpipe while harp and lute lie neglected on the
ground, with this warning:

[1] Plutarch II.91.

Tibia cui fatuo tantum solatio praebet
  Nec curat cytharam: plectra et amoena lyrae:
Hic propere ascendat stultorum (posco) carinam:
  Et remos celeri concitet ille manu.

[That fool, to whom the pipe offers solace,
  Who does not care for harp, quill and the pleasures of the lyre,
He should properly board (I demand) the Ship of Fools
  And move the oars with quick hand.][1]

An extensive treatment of these beliefs occurs in Cassio's serenade in *Othello* (III.i), a scene that has, at times, unfortunately been dismissed by critics as a piece of irrelevant clowning. Most often it is the professional fool, as in the picture-books, or his descendant, the fool royal, as in Lyly's *Midas*, whose merrymaking and incontinence are associated with pipes. In characterizing the foolishness of the officer Cassio, Shakespeare employs the stage-clown who uses the musicians Cassio has hired as a foil. Having disgraced himself in a drunken brawl while on duty, Cassio now serenades Othello and Desdemona in the hope of recovering the Moor's favour.

> [S.D. Enter Cassio, Musicians, and Clown]
>
> *Cassio.* Masters, play here; I will content your pains;
>   Something that's brief; and bid 'Good morrow, General'.
>   [S.D. They play.][2]
> *Clown.* Why, masters, have your instruments been at[3] Naples,
>   that they speak i' th' nose thus?
> *Musician.* How, sir, how?
> *Clown.* Are these, I pray, call'd[3] wind instruments?
> *Musician.* Ay, marry, are they, sir.
> *Clown.* O, thereby hangs a tail.
> *Musician.* Whereby hangs a tale, sir?
> *Clown.* Marry, sir, by many a wind instrument that I know.
>   But, masters, here's money for you; and the General
>   so likes your music, that he desires you, of all loves,[3]
>   to make no more noise with it.

[1] Jacob Locher, *Stultifera Navis*, Basel, 1497, f. lxii.r; Alexander Barclay, *The Ship of Fools*, London, 1509, f. cvii.r; 2nd edn. 1570; 3rd edn. 1590; modern reprint, ed. T. H. Jamieson, London, 1874. For other iconographic and literary parallels, cf. *Annales Musicologiques*, III (1955), 273.

[2] This stage direction does not occur in Q_1 or F texts, but is supplied by most modern editors from Q_2 of 1630.

[3] The Q_1 reading. F has 'in Naples'; 'I pray you, wind instruments'; 'desires you, for love's sake'.

Musician. Well, sir, we will not.

Clown. If you have any music that may not be heard to't again; but, as they say, to hear music the General does not greatly care.

Musician. We have none such, sir.

Clown. Then put up your pipes in your bag, for I'll away. Go, vanish into air, away!

[S.D. Exeunt musicians.]

The dialogue between clown and musician, in straightforward prose, is set off, according to Shakespeare's custom, by the blank verse which precedes it and which follows the clown's exit. There are the puns and quips reminiscent of the scene in *Romeo and Juliet* where one of the musicians disappointedly exclaims 'we may put up our pipes and be gone'. The disrepute in which wind instruments were held is emphasized by the reference to the nasal tone-colour of tibia and oboe which 'speak i' th'nose thus', and by the lewd jokes which pipes, that is to say, wind instruments, invite. Intermingled with this earthy conversational sequence is the higher, abstruse level having to do with 'music that may not be heard', the celestial harmony that speaks for the spirit, as opposed to foolish pipes, to be put up in a bag. Othello's clown acts as the faithful and intelligent servant of his General who, according to tradition, would not care for the music of wind instruments, who in the circumstances would wish the musicians to 'make no more noise' (loud music) and who would not greatly care to *hear* music. This final phrase hinges on the concept of the music of the spheres. The clown's admonition, 'If you have any music that may not be heard, to't again' is a reference to Pythagorean ideas, frequently discussed in stage-plays and in the polemical literature about the theatres. In Dekker's play, *The Pleasant Comedy of Old Fortunatus* (1600), Galloway counsels the love-sick Orleans:

O, bid thy soul
Lift up her intellectual eyes to heaven,
And (in this ample book of wonders) read,
Of what celestial mold, what sacred essence,
Herself is formed, the search whereof will drive
Sounds musical among the jarring spirits,
And in sweet tune set that which none inherits.

The same concept was used as an argument in the war of the theatres. Stephen Gosson exclaimed in a pamphlet (1579):

Pythagoras . . . condemns them for fools that judge music by sound and ear . . .

and exhorted his readers

. . . look up to heaven: the order of the spheres, the unfallible motion of the planets . . . the politic laws in well-governed commonwealths . . . this is right music, this perfect harmony.

Thomas Lodge replied in another pamphlet of 1579/80:

Pythagoras, you say, allows not that music is discerned by ears, but he wisheth us to ascend unto the sky, and mark that harmony. Surely this is but one doctor's opinion (yet I dislike not of it) but to speak my conscience, methinks music best pleaseth me when I hear it . . . but as I like music, so admit I not of those that deprave the same: your pipers are so odious to me as yourself. . .

Lodge, then, does not follow Gosson in using the concept of the music of the spheres as an argument against all audible music, but even he agrees on the sensual nature of pipes. In this connection the very title of Gosson's pamphlet attacking plays and music is significant: *The School of Abuse: containing a pleasant invective against poets, pipers, players, jesters, and such like caterpillars of a commonwealth.*[1] One other passage from Gosson should be quoted here, since it contains yet another reference to the musical contest between Pan and Apollo:

When Anacharsis travelled all over Greece to seek out wise men he found none in Athens . . . but coming to Chenas, a blind village in comparison of Athens, a Paltock's Inn, he found one Miso . . . I speak not this to prefer Botley before Oxford, a cottage of clowns before a college of Muses, Pan's pipe before Apollo's harp, but to show you that poor Miso can read you such a lecture of philosophy as Aristotle never dreamed on.

Whether or not the concluding phrase hummed in Shakespeare's ear when he wrote of 'more things, Horatio, than are dreamt of in your philosophy' we do not know; references to the

---

[1] Cf. Gosson, *School of Abuse*, reprinted in the *Publications* of the Shakespeare Society, London, 1841, pp. 16 and 41; Lodge, *Defence of Poetry, Music, and Stage-Plays*, reprinted *Publications* of the Shakespeare Society, London, 1853, p. 20 f.

lowly pipes are not lacking in *Hamlet*. The prince praises
Horatio (III.ii.75) as one of

> ... those
> Whose blood and judgement are so well commingled
> That they are not a pipe for Fortune's finger
> To sound what stop she please ...

and later in the scene he returns more extensively to the subject
of wind instruments, when he teaches Rosencrantz and Guildenstern a lesson by way of the recorders (lines 354–389):

Hamlet. Sir, I lack advancement.

Rosenkrantz. How can that be, when you have the voice
of the King himself for your succession in Denmark?

Hamlet. Ay, sir, but 'while the grass grows'—the proverb
is something musty.

[S.D. Enter the Players with recorders][1]

O, the recorders! Let me see one. To withdraw with you,
why do you go about to recover the wind of me, as if you
would drive me into a toil?

Guildenstern. O my lord, if my duty be too bold, my love
is too unmannerly.

Hamlet. I do not well understand that. Will you play
upon this pipe?

Guil. My lord, I cannot.

Hamlet. I pray you.

Guil. Believe me, I cannot.

Hamlet. I do beseech you.

Guil. I know no touch of it, my lord.

Hamlet. It is as easy as lying. Govern these ventages
with your fingers and thumb, give it breath with
your mouth, and it will discourse most eloquent[2]
music. Look you, these are the stops.

Guil. But these cannot I command to any utterance
of harmony. I have not the skill.

Hamlet. Why look you now, how unworthy a thing you make
of me! You would play upon me; you would seem
to know my stops; you would pluck out the heart
of my mystery; you would sound me from my lowest
note to the top of my compass; and there is much music,

---

[1] This stage direction is taken from Q2. The F text reads: 'Enter one with
a recorder'. Cf. Greg FF 319.

[2] Q1 reads 'delicate'; F reads 'excellent'.

excellent voice in this little organ, yet cannot you make it speak. 'Sblood, do you think I am easier to be play'd on than a pipe?

The term 'stop' here denotes both the finger-holes of the instruments and the fingerings, that is the positions of the fingers by which the notes are produced. This second meaning is also employed in *2 Henry IV*, Induction, 17,

> ... Rumour is a pipe
> Blown by surmises, jealousies, conjectures;
> And of so easy and so plain a stop
> . . .
> The still-discordant wav'ring multitude,
> Can play upon it. . . .

The idea of comparing mastery of a mind with mastery of a wind instrument may be traced again to North's translation of Plutarch. Pericles is praised, for he alone knew

how to move passions and affections thoroughly, which are as stops and sounds of the soul, that would be played upon with a fine-fingered hand of a cunning master.

But Guildenstern cannot 'govern' the ventages, he is the man that hath no music, not even the comparatively simple cunning of the lowly pipe.[1]

IV. Tuning

The obvious contrast to untuned drums and harsh-resounding pipes were the stringed instruments; their music was considered an earthly representation of the music of the spheres. The strings were, as a rule, sweetly, not harshly, tuned and, indeed, the Elizabethan's concept of tuning provides the key to many of the musical passages in Elizabethan plays. Celestial harmony, the well-ordered commonwealth, and sweet music, that is, soft music in the proper tuning, stand at the one extreme. At the other we have the untuned sky—unpropitious constellation of planets, thunder, meteors—which is mirrored alike in the civil wars of states as well as the jangled, loud strains of musicians. References to harmonious or discordant tuning in men

[1] Cf. Christopher Welch, *Six Lectures on the Recorder and other Flutes in Relation to Literature*, London, 1911, pp. 157–183, 184–251; H. M. Fitzgibbon, *Story of the Flute*, London, 1914, pp. 16, 231; Plutarch II.22.

and music abound in the contemporary plays and continue to be a significant part of the poetic language of Milton and Dryden. The latter's 'Song for St. Cecilia's Day, 1687' concludes

> As from the power of sacred lays
> The spheres began to move,
> And sung the great Creator's praise
> To all the blest above;
> So when the last and dreadful hour
> This crumbling pageant shall devour,
> The trumpet shall be heard on high,
> The dead shall live, the living die,
> And Music shall untune the sky!

Dr. Johnson had wished that 'the antithesis of *music untuning* had found some other place' than the finale of this cantata; yet the juxtaposition of a blaring trumpet, crumbling pageant and 'untuning' seems proper for one versed in the tradition of Shakespeare and Jonson, as Dryden was.[1] Whether the poets praise a Christian Saint or a pagan god, divine order and its reflection in human order are at all times associated with tuning, variously termed celestial, sweet, or consenting in a full close. In *Tamburlaine*, as we have seen, God 'tunes' the music of the spheres to our souls; and Salomon tells us in Peele's *David and Bethsabe* that God's 'cunning tunes the music of my soul'. Following this statement David exhorts Salomon to be the perfect echo of God's heavenly voice.[2] In Lyly's *Midas* the god of the muses challenges the demigod of the satyrs:

Pan, wilt thou contend with Apollo, who tunes the heavens, and makes them all hang by harmony? Orpheus that caused trees to move with the sweetness of his harp, offereth yearly homage to my lute, so doth Arion, that brought dolphins to his sugared notes, and Amphion, that by music rear'd the walls of Thebes. Only Pan with his harsh whistles (which makes beasts shake for fear, not men dance for joy) seeks to compare with Apollo.

In our own age, where there is an ever widening rift between literary expression and the actuality which impinges upon the

---

[1] For an extensive discussion, cf. John Hollander, *The Untuning of the Sky*, Princeton, 1961, pp. 409 ff. *et passim*.

[2] Lines 1713 and 1755 in Ashley Thorndyke's *Minor Elizabethan Drama*, Vol. I, London, 1910, reprinted 1951.

senses, we are inclined to dismiss any allusion to celestial tuning as another felicitous phrase. But the Elizabethan poet had the gift of imbuing his symbolic expressions with the concrete experience from which they sprang, and this endowed the conceits with a wonderful vitality. Many of Shakespeare's metaphors take on added meaning and life once the tradition of sweet and harsh tuning is recognized. In the earlier tragedies it is the union of lovers that is well tuned, but once fate or intrigue drives them asunder the tuning is jarred or jangled. But in the later works the ideas of kingship and the well-ordered commonwealth take precedence, and the contrast is there established between proper and harmonious, as opposed to harsh and beastly, tuning.

An early example is Juliet's complaint at Romeo's parting:

> It is the lark that sings so out of tune,
> Straining harsh discords and unpleasing sharps.
> Some say the lark makes sweet division;
> This doth not so, . . .

The craftsmanlike terms that Shakespeare uses to express this thought—the sharps which mar a simple diatonic melody and the pleasant divisions (or variations) expected in well-tuned music, give added strength and meaning to the adjectives 'sweet' and 'harsh'. But the tuning passages in the subsequent tragedies become more bitter. There is the rejection of Ophelia by Hamlet which anticipates, in some ways, Othello's rejection of Desdemona. Once Hamlet suspects Ophelia to be Polonius's tool, or Othello believes Desdemona to be Cassios's mistress, their intimate communion is destroyed, and the outraged male orders Ophelia

> . . . To a nunnery, go.
>
> [S.D. Exit Hamlet]

Ophelia. O, what a noble mind is here o'erthrown!
> . . .
> And I, of ladies most deject and wretched,
> That suck'd the honey of his music vows,
> Now see that noble and most sovereign reason
> Like sweet bells jangled, out of tune and harsh.[1]

---

[1] Cf. Webster's *White Devil*, III.ii.96 for an echo of bells and inappropriate tuning:

> . . . What are whores?
> They are those flattering bells, have all one tune
> At weddings, and at funerals . . .

There is a similar concreteness about discord and harmonious tuning in *Othello*, a work in which both actual music and musical imagery are of vital importance. When Othello arrives at Cyprus, the short love scene between him and Desdemona culminates in the couplet (II.i.200):

> And this, and this, the greatest discords be
> That e'er our hearts shall make.

The F text has no stage direction, but in Q_1 we read 'they kiss', which yields the clue as to how the words 'And this, and this' are to be punctuated. The musical figure of speech is taken up by Iago in an aside:

> O, you are well tuned now!
> But I'll set down the pegs that make this music, . . .

The main merit of likening the kisses to discords is to facilitate Iago's mode of expression. His ironical observation that the lovers are well-tuned, and his vow to destroy the pitch and thereby the harmony of that tuning, is the keynote of the play. The tuning metaphor reappears twice at critical stages. Halfway through the tragedy (III.iv.123) Desdemona admits to Cassio that she cannot assist his cause, 'My advocation is not now in tune'. And at the end of the play, when Othello learns that Cassio is not dead, he exclaims (V.ii.115) 'Then murther's out of tune, And sweet revenge grows harsh'. Othello's outcry reflects the development of the play as a whole, and the lowering of his own stature. Iago had all too successfully set down the pegs.

At the same time Desdemona's and Othello's lines are indicative of the wide range encompassed by the notion of tuning: any aspect of man's character, relations, or even the milieu in which he lived, might be termed sweetly or harshly tuned. When Malcolm commends Macduff (IV.iii.235) he refers to courage and character:

Macduff.   Front to front

Bring thou this fiend of Scotland and myself;

> Within my sword's length set him; if he 'scape,
> Heaven forgive him too!

Malcolm.   This tune[1] goes manly.

Lear, when in accord with himself, his office of kingship, and the world in which he moves, is one (IV.iii.41)

> Who sometime, in his better tune, remembers
> What we are come about, . . .

Cleopatra, on the other hand, were she to be exhibited in Caesar's triumphal procession, would be 'out o'tune', off the key of true regal stature (V.ii.216):

> . . . saucy lictors
> Will catch at us like strumpets, and scald rimers
> Ballad us out o'tune, the quick comedians
> Extemporally will stage us . . .

Her misgiving that the memory of her rule with Antony will be satirized by base minstrels and actors—'pipers and players' Stephen Gosson would have called them—is epitomized in her fear of becoming notorious through cheapening song. Her better tune, to quote *King Lear*, would thus be forgotten. The model for Cleopatra's phrase again derives from Horace[2] whose 'insignis cantabitur' becomes 'ballad us out o'tune' in Shakespeare (and the 'sad burden to a merry song' in Pope).

Whether the ballad is off key or the burden inappropriate to the song, in some of the plays an attempt is made to restore the proper tuning. This usually involves an invocation of the music of the spheres in verse, or else a representation of that celestial harmony by actual music performed by strings. It should be noted that the very act of tuning suggests the adjustment of pitch by changing the tension of a string: the pegs must be set down or up. Concreteness of metaphor was another reason for favouring stringed over wind instruments in passages on tuning, heavenly or otherwise. We may say with Ulysses,

---

[1] The F text reads 'This time goes manly', but since Rowe most modern editors accept the emendation 'tune': Cf. NS 71, NA 140, Kittredge SP 885.

[2] *Satires*, Bk. II, No. 1, line 45; for Pope's translation of the passage cf. the *Twickenham Edition*, IV (2nd edn., 1953), p. 13.

Take but degree away, untune that string,
And hark what discord follows!...

And in the eighth sonnet Shakespeare extols 'the true concord of well-tuned sounds' and admonishes the young man to

Mark how one string, sweet husband to another,
Strikes each in each by mutual ordering;

A detailed exposition of the interrelationship of kingship, the music of the spheres, and the well-tuned consort of strings occurs in Samuel Rowley's history play (printed in 1605), *When you see me, you know me :*[1]

Prince Edward.   ...who's there? Doctor Tye,
    Our music's lecturer... Indeed I take much delight in ye.
Tye.   In music may your grace ever delight,
    Though not in me, music is fit for kings,
    And not for those, know not the chime of strings.
Prince.   Truly I love it, yet there are a sort...
    Calling it idle, vain, and frivolous.
Tye.   ... Music is heavenly, for heaven is music,
    For there the seraphims do sing continually...
Prince.   As music, so is man govern'd by stops,[2]
    Aw'd by dividing notes, sometimes aloft,
    Sometime below...
    Yet 'mongst these many strings, be one untun'd
    Or jarreth low, or higher than his course...
    Corrupts them all, so doth bad man[3] the best.

Whether music was in tune or out of tune was more keenly perceived by the Elizabethans than it is by modern listeners, since equal temperament did not come into universal use until the nineteenth century. From that time forward instruments with a fixed pitch, the piano and organ, tuned in equal temperament, have affected the acoustical properties of much of our musical diet. Thus, we hear a Bach fugue, a Beethoven sonata, a Schubert song, and a church anthem accompanied by organ, slightly out of tune. In Elizabethan days the situation differed in several ways. The occasions for hearing music without key-

---

[1] Malone Society Reprint, 1952, lines 2028 ff.
[2] As C. T. Onions in his *Shakespeare Glossary* points out 'stop' sometimes means the 'fret' of a stringed instrument.
[3] Original has plural: 'men'.

board were more numerous: choirs singing a cappella, consort music performed by strings, songs accompanied by the lute. (The main domestic instrument was the lute, not the virginals.) When keyboard instruments were used in churches, theatres or at home, they were, as a rule, tuned in 'mean' temperament,[1] which favoured the important consonances. The result was that for the keys most used the consonances were much purer, more close to perfect intonation. To hear these consonances jangled was, therefore, a more vivid acoustical experience, and the return to euphonious music, performed by a 'whole' consort of strings—free to play in perfect intonation—became a striking restoration of law and order.

V. Strings

The music of strings has been invoked to restore noble persons to their proper tuning ever since the Biblical David consoled Saul. David's and Orpheus's lutes were favourite topics of Elizabethan playwrights, witness Peele's *David and Bethsabe* and Rowley's *When you see me*. . . . In the induction to the anonymous *Mucedorus*[2] the 'silver tuned strings' of the muse are threatened by the martial strains of Envy who will 'fill the air with a shrilling [i.e. *acris*, ear-piercing] sound'. Kindred associations are to be found in the mystery plays and pageants which preceded the writings of the Elizabethan dramatists, and in the operas of the seventeenth and eighteenth centuries which were to follow. In the days of Chaucer and in the works of his French models the contrast between 'haut' and 'bas'—music high and low—simply referred to loud and soft.[3] In the mystery plays trumpets and

---

[1] Further details and bibliographies can be found in dictionaries of music, s.v. 'Temperament'. Cf. also Ll. S. Lloyd, *Music and Sound*, 2nd edn., 1951, s.v. 'Temperament', 'Tuning'.

[2] 1st edn., 1598, 5th edn. 1613, cf. *Shakespeare Apocrypha*, ed. C. F. Tucker Brooke, 2nd edn., Oxford, 1918, pp. 194, 424.

[3] Cf. three relevant articles by E. A. Bowles: 'Haut and Bas: the Grouping of Musical Instruments', *Musica Disciplina*, VIII (1954), 115–140; 'Instruments at the Court of Burgundy', *Galpin Society Journal*, VI (1953), 41–51; 'Musical Instruments in Civic Processions', *Acta Musicologica*, XXIII (1961), 147–161; cf. also O. Gombosi, 'Dance and Dance Music in the Late Middle Ages', *Musical Quarterly*, XXVII (1941), 289–305; J. Stevens, 'Music in Mediaeval Drama', *Proceedings* of the Royal Musical Association, LXXXIV (1957/58), 81–95; R. L. Weaver, 'Sixteenth-Century Instrumentation', *Musical Quarterly*, XLVII (1961), 363–378.

clarions were used for triumphal marches, military scenes, Judgement Day and feasting; drums and cymbals depicted the deeds of the devil; Herod commands 'Now blow up, minstrel, with all your might' but Death kills Herod while the royal party inappropriately makes merry (*dum buccinant*). On the other hand, stringed instruments and portative organs represented God the Father, Christ, the choir of angels and other religious or philo-sophical scenes; paradise is depicted by still flutes, harps, lutes, rebecs and vielles; the figure of Boethius, the philosopher-musician, is accompanied by strings and organ on the occasion of Henry VI's return to London in 1432.

The operas of the eighteenth century perpetuated the use of subjects taken from classical mythology. The symbol of the silver-tuned strings is still alive in Gluck's *Orfeo* (1762), where the hero's single dulcet harp triumphs over the grim, full orchestra with its cornetts. And in the allegorical prologue to the exotic *Les Indes Galantes* (1735) Rameau depicts the peaceful consort of nations (Scene ii) to the accompaniment of strings which are interrupted by Bellone's drums and trumpets (Scene iii).

In Shakespeare, where the dialogue calls for 'soft' instru-ments, strings are implied as a matter of course; in other cases they are specified. An analogy to the lute-song in *Julius Caesar* occurs in *Henry VIII*, when Queen Catherine directs

> Take thy lute, wench. My soul grows sad with troubles.
> Sing and disperse them if thou canst . . .

It may be argued that Brutus's and Catherine's attendants sing to the lute because, as the fable of Midas teaches, they could not accompany their song on a wind instrument. Yet, in view of the centuries-old tradition surrounding Shakespeare, the presumed healing power of the soft strings and their association with divinity in Classical and Biblical lore add symbolic strength to the functional need. In *2 Henry IV* (IV.v.1) the appeal for still-ness and quiet implies the use of strings; in this case the music is purely instrumental.

> *King.* Let there be no noise made, my gentle friends,
> Unless some dull and favourable hand
> Will whisper music to my weary spirit.
> *Warwick.* Call for the music in the other room.

King. Set me my crown upon my pillow here.
. . .

Warwick. Less noise, less noise! . . .
Not so much noise, my lords. Sweet prince, speak low.

In *Pericles* (III.ii. 88) Cerimon, whose magic powers anticipate
those of Prospero, brings Thaisa back to life in this fashion:

> The still[1] and woeful music that we have,
> Cause it to sound, beseech you.
> The viol[2] once more; how thou stirr'st thou block!
> The music there! I pray you, give her air.
> Gentlemen,
> This queen will live, . . .

Cerimon's exhortation, 'The music there!' we must interpret as
a command to the musicians to play louder. The aristocratic
strings were easily audible at the Blackfriars Theatre or in a
covered hall, but at the Globe Playhouse their softness constituted an acoustical hazard. 'Louder the music there' is the
corresponding phrase in the following quotation where the 'untuned and jarring senses' of Lear (IV.vii.15) are restored to
sanity:

> *Cordelia.* How does the King?
> *Doctor.* Madam, sleeps still.
> *Cordelia.* O you kind gods,
> Cure this great breach in his abuséd nature!
> Th'untuned and jarring senses . . .
> . . .
> *Doctor.* Be by, good madam, when we do awake him;
> I doubt not of his temperance . . .
> . . .
> Please you, draw near. Louder the music there![3]

[1] Q$_1$ reads 'rough and woeful music', which makes no sense. The sub-
stitution 'still' is suggested by a parallel passage in George Wilkins's *Pericles*,
1608, ed. K. Muir, Liverpool, 1953, p. 65:
. . . then calling softly to the Gentlemen who were witnesses about him, he
bade them that they should command some still music to sound. For certainly, quoth he, I think this Queen will live . . .
Among modern editors who emend 'still' are N. Delius (1872) and J. C.
Maxwell (1956).

[2] Q$_1$ reads 'viole', Q$_4$ has 'viall'. Most modern editors have, in modern
spelling, 'viol'.

[3] This line occurs in Q$_1$ but is omitted in F. Its authenticity has not been
doubted by modern editors, cf. NS 102; Kittredge SP 1207; NA 189.

The importance of this scene for Lear's physical and spiritual regeneration is only too obvious. His progress from feeling himself 'bound upon a wheel of fire' to his plea to Cordelia, 'Pray you now, forget and forgive; I am old and foolish' must produce in the emotions of the audience the tragic catharsis. It is therefore instructive to compare this scene with other contemporary treatments of the theme: *The True Chronicle History of King Leir and His Three Daughters*, printed 1605, and 'A Lamentable Song of the Death of King Lear and his three Daughters, to the tune of, When Flying Fame', printed in 1620.[1] The similarities between Shakespeare's tragedy, the Chronicle, and the ballad are many and striking. In the Chronicle the famishing Lear is revived by Cordelia's food, and when he recognizes her, he kneels, and she protests and kneels in turn many times. Shakespeare's eloquent and economical use of this gesture in the restoration scene has often been admired, but his introduction of music at this stage is the more remarkable, since it is lacking in both the Chronicle and the ballad: it is a dramatic stroke of considerable pathos and originality. The transition from chaos to cosmos, from untuned and jarring senses to recognition and self-knowledge is one of the great instrumental passages in verse tragedy.

VI. Heavenly Music on the Stage

> The ten-fold orbs of heaven are said to move
> By music; for they make harmonious din:
> And all the powers subordinate above
> Spend time, nay spend eternity therein.[2]

The writer of a philosophical poem could well afford to state that the orbs of heaven are *said* to move by music, but the play-

---

[1] *The Chronicle History*, Pollard STC, 15343, is available in a Malone Society Reprint, Oxford, 1907. 'A Lamentable Song' appeared in Richard Johnson's *Golden Garland*, 3rd edn., 1620, Pollard STC, 14674 (no previous edn. known); 13th edn., 1690, Wing STC, J 804A; reprinted NV 402–407. Both Chronicle History and Lamentable Song are discussed in Wilfrid Perrett, *Story of King Lear* (Palaestra XXXV), Berlin, 1904. The tune 'Flying Fame', also called 'Chevy Chase', is given in Wooldridge I.91.

[2] John Davies (of Hereford), commendatory poem from Thomas Ravenscroft's *Brief Discourse . . . in Measurable Music*, London, 1614, Pollard STC, 20756.

wright was frequently under compulsion to treat celestial music, and its intervention, as an actual part of the stage business. Theatrical tradition posited that the heavenly strains were audible only to those for whom the gods had a message, and for them it constituted a psychological reality that affected their behaviour. When Pericles exclaims (V.i.231)

> The music of the spheres! List my Marina.
> . . .
> Rarest sounds! Do ye not hear?
> . . .
> . . . most heavenly music!
> It nips me unto listening, and thick slumber
> Hangs upon mine eyes . . .

he is not merely delivering figures of speech. Pericles believes in celestial harmony, does fall asleep, and hears the oracle of Diana (or the voices of his intuition and conscience, if you will). To him the 'most heavenly music' is as real as the appearance of Banquo's ghost was to Macbeth or that of old King Hamlet to his son. In the same manner Queen Catherine in *Henry VIII* (IV.ii.77) sees and hears a heavenly ballet (or masque) after she has asked for actual music to put her into the proper spirit:

> Good Griffith,
> Cause the musicians play me that sad note
> I named my knell, whilst I sit meditating
> On that celestial harmony I go to.
> [S.D. Sad and solemn music]

The masque now enacted on the stage is for her alone, as she sleeps, and the celestial harmony audible only to her. 'Saw ye none enter since I slept?' she asks. 'None, Madam', replies Griffith. Nevertheless, this harmony is the dramatic agent that prepares for the death of the Queen. In like fashion, the 'solemn and strange music' to the accompaniment of which Ariel as a harpy enacts his masque-like interlude in *The Tempest*[1] (III.iii. 52), is heard by the three men of sin whom the God-like Prospero wishes to chastize, but it is not heard by the honourable Gonzalo.

Fletcher, who tends to be more melodramatic and less fastidious than Shakespeare, on occasion has the 'invisible fiddlers'

---

[1] Cf. p. 224 above.

heard by all characters on the stage. In his *Prophetess*, 1622, entitled a 'tragical history' (actually a tragicomedy with a strong admixture of masque and pastoral), the benevolent prophetess Delia, like Prospero, conjures up heavenly sounds:[1]

Delia. Strike music from the spheres.

                            [S.D. Music]

Drusilla. O now you honour me.
Diocles. Ha! in the air!
All. Miraculous!
Maximian. This shows the gods approve...
Geta. My master is an Emperor, and I feel
          A senator's itch upon me: would I could hire
          These fine invisible fiddlers to play to me
          At my instalment...

The idea that celestial music could also become audible was not restricted to playwrights, it provided an attractive conceit to music publishers who might find a lofty and, at the same time arresting title for anthologies of madrigals in the ancient tradition. There were published for example, *Musica Divina*, 1583; *Harmonia Celeste*, 1583; *Symphonia Angelica*, 1585; *Melodia Olympica*, 1591.[2]

The practices of the Jacobean stage and the beliefs of the age suggest that music presumably emanating from above was performed on strings by the theatre musicians. But the employment of this ethereal music, with its telling effect, was reserved for moments of climax, and its performance was probably improvised on the occasion in the same way that an organist improvises soft strains to create an unworldly atmosphere. The extant printed collections of consort music[3] are largely for combinations of wind and stringed instruments. Only John Dowland's *Lachrimae* (1604), containing music 'both grave and light', is exclusively scored for lute and viols (or violins). This situation creates a problem for the modern director who must provide an actual score for his theatre orchestra. Dowland's music for strings offers an excellent choice on occasion, but Jacobean theatres did not,

[1] Cf. Fletcher V.342; also E. M. Waith, *Tragicomedy in Beaumont and Fletcher*, New Haven, 1952, p. 129.

[2] Cf. *Journal of the American Musicological Society*, IV (1951), 123.

[3] Listed in Appendix II to this chapter, with bibliographical references and selected modern reprints.

as a rule, produce, nor did the audience expect, such demanding fare, and the same condition would apply to our theatre today. Producers will find it most convenient to have adapted for stringed instruments such music as was originally intended for broken consort, available in keyboard anthologies such as the Fitzwilliam Book, or in Jacobean theatrical manuscripts, notated for treble and bass. In the last category, the most important is British Museum Add. MS 10444, of which twenty-five pieces have been put into modern transcription.[1] It is possible that one of them, entitled 'The Tempest' may have been performed at some time when Ariel and his attendants enacted a masque. Though this cannot be proven, it is a fair assumption that the music usually performed was similarly simple and undemanding, and that the pieces in the British Museum MS are representative of the tradition of the Elizabethan playhouses. Occasional music in the theatre rarely displays the contrapuntal skill of the fantasias of Dowland or Coperario; it is more likely to meet the wishes of the playwright and the expectations of the audience by its extreme simplicity of contour and texture. 'C'est le ton qui fait la musique', as the proverb has it, and here the tone-colour of bowed stringed instruments, amplified by the sonority of chordal, plucked stringed instruments[2] is of the greatest usefulness. It is the *tone* of pipes or strings that informs the audience of the nature and character of the music. Apart from its use in spoken drama, we do well to recall Gluck's method in *Orfeo*, where the hero's harp-arpeggios, devoid of any melodic or contrapuntal interest, suggest by contrast and tone the nature of the victory which Orpheus's soft lute is to gain. And a few decades later Mozart highlights the sombre colour of the trombones to provide a sinister atmosphere when the ghostly statue in the churchyard scene is heard to speak. Here, too, voice and accompaniment are reduced to the simplicity of a litany.

It is also clear from the dramatic context that the stringed instruments were performed in a manner which concealed the

---

[1] Andrew Sabol, *Songs and Dances for the Stuart Masque*, Providence, 1959, Nos. 39–63; cf. also *Music & Letters*, III (1922), 49–58; XXXV (1954), 185–200; XL (1959), 397–399; *The Tempest*, ed. F. Kermode, NA 156–160.

[2] Such as lute or cittern; in modern performances it is often necessary to substitute guitar or harpsichord.

musicians, either behind a curtain or under a trap-door. This fashion of concealing miraculous music was much admired by Englishmen in such diverse places as the Villa d'Este outside Rome and King James's Banqueting House at Whitehall. Thomas Nashe's *Unfortunate Traveller*, 1594, recounts the wondrous experiences of an English traveller abroad. In a description, obviously modelled on the Villa d'Este, Nashe speaks of a

summer banqueting house . . . that was the marvel of the world . . . It was built . . . like a theatre without: within there was a heaven . . . wherein the sun and moon and each visible star had his true similitude . . . and by what enwrapped art, I cannot conceive, these spheres in their proper orbs observed their circular wheelings and turnings, making a certain kind of soft angelical murmuring music in their often windings . . . which music the philosophers say in the true heaven, by reason of the grossness of our senses, we are not capable of.[1]

The Banqueting House at Whitehall was also built like a theatre; in fact, it was a theatre in every respect save its name, and as such its influence on the masques of Daniel and Jonson and on Shakespeare's last plays, was considerable. In a masque at Whitehall or a play at the Blackfriars or the Globe the music of the spheres would be represented by the strings of Apollo or the organ of Saint Cecilia.[2] But within the conventions of tragedy it was also possible to work on the imaginary forces of the listener, and to invoke the heavenly harmony by means of blank verse. Proud as the musician may be to chronicle the many instances where the playwright asks for actual performance, he is bound, in modesty, to recognize that the most glorious music is the music of Shakespeare's verse:

> His legs bestrid the ocean, his rear'd arm
> Crested the world; his voice was propertied
> As all the *tuned spheres*, and that to friends;
> But when he meant to quail and shake the orb,
> He was as rattling thunder.

Antony, the king, and Cleopatra, the queen, redeemed through death, regain their regal stature. Their kingship on this earth is

---

[1] Nashe II.282; IV.284.
[2] Nashe's description refers to a hydraulic organ.

a reflection of the music of the spheres, with its solemn and glorious tuning. The progression from rattling thunder to tuned spheres, both in *King Lear* and in *Antony and Cleopatra* is a symbol of the hero's transfiguration, of the catharsis of tragedy.

Appendix I

Dances in the Plays

(1) PAVAN OR MEASURE

Among the publications[1] dealing with English dances in the sixteenth century, and their background, the writings of Otto Gombosi have been particularly helpful in establishing the meaning of 'measure' and 'passy measures pavin', terms which have continued to baffle Shakespearean commentators until the twentieth century. To begin with, the term 'measure' was the English equivalent of the French 'basse danse' in the earlier sixteenth century; it took on the meaning of 'pavan' in Shakespeare's day. The inherent ambiguity of the meaning of 'measure' must have been a delight to Shakespeare with his proverbial fondness for punning on musical terms, and the reader is often obliged to ponder whether the dialogue refers to an actual dance or whether it has to do with proportion in general. Moreover, a favourite subdivision of the pavan, namely, a particular kind of ground-bass on which the music for the dance was constructed, was called in Italy 'passamezzo antico' and in England 'passing measure pavin'. Understandably, these foreign terms were not always spelt accurately, let alone uniformly. With printers' errors in addition, we have 'passy measures panyn', for 'passing measures pavin [i.e. pavan]', which may well prove an enigma to those not familiar with the terminology of music and the dance. It is significant that 'measure' is used by Shakespeare more frequently than any other title of a dance.[2]

[1] Thoinot Arbeau [anagram for Jehan Tabourot], *Orchésographie* [1st edn. Langres, 1589; 2nd edn. 1596], tr. C. W. Beaumont, London, 1925; Mabel Dolmetsch, *Dances of England and France from 1450 to 1600*, London, 1949; Otto Gombosi, article 'Folia' in *Musik in Geschichte und Gegenwart*, ed. F. Blume, Cassel, 1949 ff., IV.479–484; 'Some Musical Aspects of the English Court Masque', *Journal of the American Musicological Society*, I, No. 3 (1948), 3–19; Naylor, p. 131 *et passim*; Gerda Prange, 'Shakespeares Äusserungen über die Tänze seiner Zeit', *Shakespeare Jahrbuch*, LXXXIX (1953), 132–161; Jeffrey Pulver, 'Dances of Shakespeare's England', Internationale Musik-Gesellschaft, *Sammelbände*, XV (1913–14), 99–102; A. F. Sieveking, 'Dancing', in Onions S.E., II.437–450; John Ward, 'The Dolfull Domps' *Journal of the American Musicological Society*, IV (1951), 111–121; 'The Folia', Internationale Musik-Gesellschaft, Congress Utrecht 1952, *Kongress-Bericht*, Amsterdam, 1953, pp. 415–422.

[2] Among fifty passages, measure occurs 17 times, jig 9 times, dump 5 times and galliard 4 times.

In *Romeo and Juliet* the term is introduced with the customary puns: (I.iv.9)

> *Benvolio.* But let them measure us by what they will,
> We'll measure them a measure, and be gone.

Romeo, on the other hand, does not pun, he is merely awaiting the end of the dance (I.v.52):

> The measure done, I'll watch her place of stand
> And touching hers, make blessed my rude hand.

The great bulk of extant Elizabethan and Jacobean music for solo instruments, such as virginals or lute, and for consorts, whole or broken, consists of dance music, largely in the form of pavans and galliards. Frequently the stately pavan, in duple time, is paired with the more animated galliard, in triple time, and the two are often connected by the same bass or treble or both. Two of the basses which were popular as harmonic skeletons for dances (as well as songs) were the passamezzo antico in the minor mode, and the passamezzo moderno in the major mode. Using Roman numerals to designate the seven steps of the scale these basses may be schematically represented as follows:

antico   I/VII/I/V//III/VII/I–V/I
moderno   I/IV/I/V//I/IV/I–V/I

Ex.1.

PASSAMEZZO ANTICO (PASSING MEASURE)

PASSAMEZZO MODERNO (QUADRAN PAVANE)

The single oblique line indicates the time unit, usually one or two semibreves; the double oblique line indicates the caesura after the half cadence. Thus, the whole pavan followed a rhythmical organization into units of eight bars, or multiples thereof, a characteristic it shares with modern dance music. It is only necessary to add that the English equivalents for antico and moderno were passing measure pavin and quadran pavin to have sufficient knowledge for understanding Shakespeare's puns in *Twelfth Night* (V.i.206), where the wounded Toby asks for the doctor:

Toby. Sot, did'st see Dick Surgeon, sot?

Clown. O, he's drunk, Sir Toby, an hour agone. His
eyes were set at eight i' th' morning.

Toby. Then he's a rogue and a passy measures
pavin: I hate a drunken rogue.

Toby, who prefers to cut a quick caper (I.iii.137), is inconvenienced by the delay of the surgeon, who is as slow as a pavan. Moreover, the surgeon is as drunk as his prospective patient habitually is, and his eyes are set as early as eight in the morning; the numeral eight provides another pun on the eights and fours into which the strains of a pavan are organized. Thomas Morley in his *Plain and Easy Introduction to Practical Music* emphasizes both the slowness of the pavan and its organization into groups of eight (or four) semibreves.[1]

The next in gravity and goodness unto this [the fantasia] is called a Pavan, a kind of staid music ordained for grave dancing and most commonly made of three strains . . . a strain they make to contain eight or twelve or sixteen semibreves as they list, yet fewer than eight I have not seen in any Pavan . . . you must cast your music by four, so that if you keep that rule it is no matter how many fours you put in your strain for it will fall out well . . . every reasonable dancer will make measure of no measure, so that it is no great matter of what number [of four semibreves] you make your strain.

Morley, too, cannot resist the temptation to pun on measure as dance and measure as proportion or number. In *Twelfth Night* it is the fact that the surgeon is drunk, that is, past measure, which suggests the passing measure pavin. Among the many examples of this favourite form the compositions by William Byrd and Peter Philips are particularly attractive. A vocal adaptation of the popular ground-bass occurs in a setting of Thomas Campion's poem, 'What if a day or a month or a year'.[2]

(2) GALLIARD, OR CINQUE PAS

The following two stanzas from Sir John Davies' 'Orchestra, or A Poem of Dancing', 1596, contrast the slow pavan (or measure)

[1] 1st edn. 1597; 2nd edn. 1608; 3rd edn. 1771; facsimile reprint, ed. E. H. Fellowes, London, 1937; ed. R. A. Harman, London, 1952. Here quoted from the 1952 edn., p. 296. Cf. also Malone's edn. of Shakespeare, 1790, IV.105 f., who recognized that 'panyn' in the F text was a misprint for pavin, that pavans were slow, and that passing measure is an anglicized form of passamezzo.

[2] The Passamezzo Pavans by Byrd and Philips are reprinted Fitzwilliam I.203 and 299. 'What if a day' from British Museum Add. MS 24665 is reprinted P. Warlock, *English Ayres*, 6 vols., London, 1927–31, VI.28. The particular variation of the passing measure pavin employed in 'What if a day' is called 'Folia', cf. D. C. Greer's 'What if a day', *Music & Letters*, 1962.

with the quick galliard (or cinque pas). The second stanza also explains why 'cinque-pas' or five steps were associated with the galliard.

> Not those young students of the heavenly book,
>   Atlas the great, Prometheus the wise,
> Which on the stars did all their lifetime look,
>   Could ever find such measures in the skies,
>   So full of change and rare varieties;
>   Yet all the feet whereon these measures go
>   Are only spondees, solemn, grave and slow.
>
> But for more divers and more pleasing show,
>   A swift and wandering dance he did invent,
> With passages uncertain, to and fro,
>   Yet with a certain answer and consent
>   To the quick music of the instrument.
>   Five was the number of the music's feet,
>   Which still the dance did with five paces meet.

Shakespeare usually stresses the quick pace of the galliard and its lighthearted associations. In *Henry V* (I.ii.252) the French ambassador warns the young English monarch that

>   There's nought in France
> That can be with a nimble galliard won;
> You cannot revel into dukedoms there.

The term 'cinque-pas' occurs only once in the tragedies, namely, in the 1603 quarto of *Hamlet*. In the scene in which Hamlet censures extemporizing clowns, the Quarto adds[1]

> *Hamlet.* And then you have some again that keeps one suit of jests
>   as a man is known by one suit of apparel, and gentlemen
>   quote his jests down in their tables before they come to
>   the play . . . and thus keeping in his cinquepace of jests . . .

There is no unanimity among editors whether this addition to the F text is actually by Shakespeare. Collier and Halliwell-Phillipps are among those who think that it is, but whatever its provenance, it is without doubt Elizabethan in origin. Certainly, the nimble galliard goes well with jests, as the example in *Henry V* shows; another instance occurs in *Twelfth Night*, I.iii.127, 139, 144.

---

[1] Cf. NS 197; NV I.230 and II.65; *Oxford English Dictionary* s.v. 'Cinquepace'; *Grove's Dictionary of Music*, 5th edn., s.v. 'sink-a-pace'; Naylor, 118, 137; Chappell, I. 156. Other spellings include 'sinke-a-pace' (*Twelfth Night*, I.iii.139) and 'sincopas' (Nat. Libr. of Scotland, Adv. Mus. MS 5.2.15, p. 161). The passage from Q_1 of *Hamlet* is not recorded in Bartlett's *Concordance*, but it is indexed in the 'Hamlet Appendix' of Charles Crawford's *Concordance to . . . Kyd*, Louvain, 1906–10, p. 504.

(3) JIG

Like the cinque pas of jests, the jig, too, was associated with clowns[1] and appropriately enough the term appears more frequently in Shakespeare's comedies. It occurs three times in *Hamlet*, however, though always in a disapproving sense. Of Polonius the prince remarks that

> . . . He's for a jig, or a tale of bawdry, or he sleeps. . . .

In the 'nunnery scene' Hamlet angrily reproaches Ophelia

> . . . God hath given you one face, and you,
> make yourselves another; you jig, you amble, and
> you lisp . . .

And preceding the play within the play he exclaims

> O God, your only jig-maker. What should
> a man do but be merry, for look you how
> cheerfully my mother looks, and my
> father died within's two hours.

This deprecation of the jig and its associations is fairly common among tragic playwrights. In his dedication of *Catiline* Jonson pleads for proper poetry 'in these jig-given times'. Marlowe begins the Prologue to *Tamburlaine* with

> From jigging veins of rhyming mother-wits,
> And such conceits as clownage keeps in pay,
> We'll lead you to the stately tent of war, . . .

(4) DUMP

The 'deploring dump' or the 'merry dump', as it is ironically called in *Romeo and Juliet* has been discussed in Chapter V (pp. 102 ff.) with reference to J. Ward's article on the subject.[2] The hypothesis that Mr. Ward offers, that the English 'dump' or 'domp' is the equivalent of the French 'deploracion' or 'tombeau', has much to

---

[1] In addition to the literature cited at the beginning of this Appendix (Naylor, Prange, Pulver, Sieveking), and to dictionary articles on 'jig', the following four monographs should prove helpful: C. R. Baskervill, *Elizabethan Jig and Related Song Drama*, Chicago, 1929; W. Danckert, *Geschichte der Gigue*, Leipzig, 1924; W. J. Lawrence, *Pre-Restoration Studies*, Cambridge (Mass.), 1927 [Includes an essay on the jig]; C. J. Sisson, *Lost Plays of Shakespeare's Age*, Cambridge, 1936 [Includes a chapter on the jig].

[2] Concerning the relationship of the 'Duke of Somerset's Dump' to the passamezzo antico, cf. O. Gombosi, ed., *Capirola Lute Book*, Paris, 1955, p. lxvii.

commend it. The term dump might well represent an anglicized form of 'tombeau' which originally meant a piece written in memory of a deceased person. In time it was applied to any mournful or pensive melody, performed as a dance or a song. Certainly Shakespeare's five uses of the term, three of them in *Romeo and Juliet*, all assume mournful overtones. When Balthasar implores the ladies in *Much Ado About Nothing* to

> . . . sing no moe
> Of dumps so dull and heavy . . .

he is articulating the traditional meaning in Shakespeare's day. In the anonymous *Chronicle History of King Leir*, 1605, Cornwall addresses his wife[1]

> My Goneril, you come in wishèd time,
> To put your father from these pensive dumps.

(5) OTHER DANCES

The remaining dance forms range, in alphabetical order, from the well-known Bergamasca in the *Midsummer Night's Dream* to the Volta (or Lavolta) in *Troilus and Cressida*. Troilus mentions the volta with its high leap as one of the temptations of the Grecian camp likely to attract Cressida (IV.iv.88):

> I cannot sing,
> Nor heel the high lavolt, nor sweeten talk,
> Nor play at subtle games . . .

But the significance of these passages in the tragedies does not merit detailed discussion. Contrary to the comedies, the dances are not actually performed, with the single exception of the measure in *Romeo and Juliet*, where the dance fulfils a functional need in the plot. Generally, they are mentioned in the dialogue, usually within the frame-work of the Ethos theory of music or with regard to traditional associations. The following tabulation of dance terms mentioned in Shakespeare may be helpful:

bergamasca, bergomask	1
branle, brawl	1
canary	3
cinque pas	[see galliard]
coranto, courante	3
dump, domp	5

[1] Malone Society Reprint, Oxford, 1907, line 830.

galliard, cinque pas	6
hay	1
jig	9
lavolta	[see volta]
measure	17
morris	2
pavan	[see measure]
volta	2
	——
	50

Of this total of 50 passages, 30 occur in the comedies, 10 in the tragedies, 7 in the histories, 3 in the poems.

Appendix II

Principal Collections of Consort Music Printed in England

Pollard
STC

153	J. Adson	Courtly Masquing Ayres . . . violins, consorts and cornetts Copies: DM, L, O	1621
7097	J. Dowland	Lachrimae . . . Pavans, Galliards, and Almains . . . lute, viols, or violons Copies: L, LINC	[1604]
13563	A. Holborne	Pavans, Galliards, Almains . . . viols, violins, or other musical wind instruments Copies: L	1599
13957	T. Hume	Poetical Music . . . principally . . . for two bass viols . . . upon sundry instruments . . . together with the virginals, or rather with a wind instrument and the voice Copies: L	1607
18131	T. Morley	Consort Lessons . . . treble lute . . . pandora . . . cittern . . . bass viol . . . flute . . . treble viol Copies: L, O, OCH	1599
18132	T. Morley	Consort Lessons . . . Copies: HN, L, LCM, NYP	1611
21333	P. Rosseter	Lessons for Consort . . . treble lute . . . pandora . . . cittern . . . bass viol . . . flute . . . treble viol Copies: LCM, O	1609

DM   Dublin: Marsh Library
HN   Huntington Library, California
L   London: British Museum
LCM   „   Royal College of Music
LINC   Lincoln Cathedral
NYP   New York Public Library
O   Oxford: Bodleian
OCH   Oxford: Christ Church

Dowland: Lachrimae, ed. P. Warlock, London, 1927.
Jacobean Consort Music, edd. T. Dart & W. Coates, 1955.
   [contains pieces by Adson, Dowland, Holborne, Hume, etc.]
Morley: Consort Lessons, ed. S. Beck, New York, 1959.
Holborne: Suite, ed. T. Dart, London, 1959.
   [excerpts from Holborne's *Pavans* . . .]
R. Donington, article 'Consort of Viols' in *Grove's Dictionary of Music*, ed.
   E. Blom, London, 1954.
T. Dart, article 'Consort' in *Musik in Geschichte und Gegenwart*, ed. F. Blume,
   1949 ff.

The articles and reprints listed above contain additional sources of English music printed abroad; there are also references and selected reprints of pieces from manuscript sources. Needless to say, the bulk of consort music survives in manuscript only.

X

A RETROSPECT OF SCHOLARSHIP ON SHAKESPEARE AND MUSIC

A CONSIDERATION of the role that music plays in the dramas of Shakespeare is to be found in reference works of all kinds from the comprehensive encyclopaedia to the brief article in a periodical. General, and specifically English histories of music include material on Shakespeare, and the forthcoming Volume IV of the *New Oxford History of Music* will deal with music for the theatre in Shakespeare's time.

The researches of eighteenth-century scholars provided the basis for subsequent research. It is, perhaps, not generally realized how many musical problems are touched upon in Bishop Percy's *Reliques of Ancient English Poetry* of 1765. Yet, the second book 'containing ballads that illustrate Shakespeare' was a pilot study that tried to illuminate the Shakespeare lyrics by reference to sources of the sixteenth and seventeenth centuries. This enthusiasm for the old ballads also distinguishes Thomas Warton's *History of English Poetry* (1774–81). The sympathies of Percy and Warton, harbingers of the coming Romanticism, differed widely from the antiquarian bent of a Joseph Ritson, yet the latter's *Ancient Songs* (1790; rev. W. C. Hazlitt, 1877) is also a standard source for the glosses of later commentators. The general histories of music by John Hawkins (1776) and Charles Burney (1776–89) paid particular attention to manuscript and printed collections. The authors also took advantage of their professional musicianship to reprint some of the music that had hitherto been merely mentioned. In this way Hawkins could add to Percy's discoveries the catch, 'Hold thy peace' from T. Ravenscroft's *Deuteromelia*, 1609, mentioned in *Twelfth Night* (II.iii.67). These collective discoveries were to bear fruit in various annotated editions of Shakespeare's plays, of which Malone's edition of 1790, in ten volumes, is particularly felicitous in its musical glosses. It was Malone's brilliant emendation that connected Pistol's 'calmie custure me' in *Henry V* (IV.iv.4) with a famous Irish song, recorded in many Elizabethan and Jacobean anthologics. His observant eye also caught in the first line of Desdemona's Willow Song the erroneous 'singing' as a misprint for 'sighing'.[1] (Boswell's revision of Malone in 1821 contains further emendations and discoveries.)

The roll-call of significant contributions in the nineteenth century begins with Douce's *Illustrations of Shakespeare* (1st edn., 1807) and takes us to Edward Woodall Naylor's *Shakespeare and Music* (1st edn., 1896). The former perpetuates the antiquarian tendencies of his predecessors, but Naylor, the modern scholar, happily puts to good use his competence to transcribe lute and cittern tablatures. Many basic sources were reprinted during the first half of the century, notably in the *Progresses* of Queen Elizabeth and King James, edited by John Nichols (1823, 1828); and the tracts and ballads made available in the *Publications* of the Shakespeare Society (1840–53) as, for instance, J. P. Collier's edition of Robert Armin's *Nest of Ninnies*. Granted that the work of a Nichols or a Collier should in time be revised, with attention paid to modern notions of accuracy, yet the impetus which these publications gave to further studies in the field can hardly be overestimated. When Edward Francis Rimbault published *Who was Jack Wilson?* in 1846, the first sentence significantly read:

In the second volume of the 'Shakespeare Society's Papers', Mr. Collier has communicated an article (p. 33) upon 'Jack Wilson', the performer of Balthazar in *Much Ado About Nothing*.

Rimbault, along with W. Chappell, was one of the founders of the Musical Antiquarian Society. His publications arc too

[1] Capell had made the emendation in 1768, but Steevens continued with 'singing' in 1785.

259

numerous to mention, but the *Musical Illustrations of . . . Percy's Reliques* (1850) deserves particular notice, with the reservation here, as elsewhere, that modern accuracy is not to be expected. Charles Knight's *Pictorial Edition of Shakespeare* (8 vols., 1839–42) was even richer in its musical illustrations than had been Boswell's revision of Malone. Knight frequently relied on stage tradition at the Drury Lane Theatre, with the result that he provides tunes from the age of Garrick and Sheridan, instead of Marlowe and Shakespeare. Still, his illustrations are sometimes the oldest versions extant, and therefore valuable.

The second half of the century produced a spate of indispensable monographs as well as the bulky editions of Shakespeare by Halliwell-Phillipps and Furness. Halliwell-Phillipps drew attention to and reproduced in facsimile a musical version of 'Come over the burn Bessy' from *King Lear* (III.vi.28) and Furness reprinted the findings of Chappell and others. Chappell opened new fields for the exploration of English balladry. His *Popular Music of the Olden Time* (2 vols., 1855–59), succeeding as it did his earlier collections and editions, was a masterly summary of extant knowledge to which were added many contributions of his own. Here was patient scrutiny of manuscripts at London, Cambridge and Dublin, as well as of early printed editions. When no early source could be found, Chappell searched for oral tradition in collections of the eighteenth and nineteenth centuries, never obscuring or falsifying the pedigree of a tune. His work was revised by H. E. Wooldridge in 1893 (under the title *Old English Popular Music*). Both Chappell and Wooldridge give the original melodies, though with nineteenth century accompaniments. The main value of their work lies in their lists of extant versions and their ability to detect a Shakespearean tune even when it was veiled below a variety of titles, first lines and other disguises. Chappell (jointly with J. W. Ebsworth) was also the editor of the *Roxburghe Ballads* (9 vols., 1871–99) which, though limited to the texts without music, throw a good deal of light on some of Shakespeare's songs. By contrast John Caulfield's *Collection of the Vocal Music in Shakespeare's Plays* (2 vols., 1864) is almost pointless since the author does not indicate his sources; yet this voluminous collection is very nearly a favourite with theatrical producers. F. J. Furnivall followed in the footsteps of Chappell and Ebsworth with his unbounded enthusiasm for the old ballads. Of his many publications we may single out the edition (jointly with J. W. Hales) of *Bishop Percy's Folio Manuscript*, which contains the earliest known version of 'King Stephen was a worthy peer' from *Othello* (II.iii.92). Furnivall was also one of the many contributors to the *Publications* of the New Shakspere Society (1874–92). No student of Shakespeare's songs can afford to ignore the many detailed glosses in the Society's *Transactions* or the various musical programmes, detailed in the Society's *Miscellanies*. No. 3 of the latter (rev. edn., 1884, edd. F. J. Furnivall and W. G. Stone) is both the most voluminous (xxxv plus 113 pp.) and the most helpful to the modern student, with its copious index and details of the contents of such earlier collections as J. Playford's *Select Ayres*, 1659; J. Vernon's *New Songs*, 1762; W. Linley's *Dramatic Songs*, 1816; and J. Caulfield's *Collection* of 1864, referred to earlier.

Before the end of the century there were further important contributions in the works of J. F. Bridge, W. Barclay Squire and E. W. Naylor. Bridge's *Songs from Shakespeare: The Earliest Known Settings* (London: Novello, n.d., ?1894) together with his later *Shakespearean Music in the Plays* (1923) offers early settings as well as some facsimiles not readily available elsewhere. Barclay Squire (with J. A. Fuller-Maitland) provided a modern edition of the *Fitzwilliam Virginal Book*, one of the most voluminous manuscript collections of the early seventeenth century, and of particular relevance for Shakespearean studies (2 vols., 1894–99). The first edition of Naylor's *Shakespeare and Music* (1896) made full use of the contributions of Chappell, Wooldridge and others, and, moreover, described the background of Elizabethan vocal and instrumental music to a general public.

The twentieth century has witnessed both the blessing and the curse of modern scholarship. One encounters research on the one hand that takes full advantage of bibliographical and photographic facilities, with a resultant degree of accuracy and detail that is novel in modern European history. On the other hand, the exigencies of commercial publishing and marketing have produced a kind of popular book, based on second-hand knowledge and marred by serious inaccuracies. Since both kinds of publications appear in a variety of comprehensive bibliographies, a separation of the sheep from the goats is clearly obligatory. Sir Walter Greg's *List of English Plays... before 1643*

(1900), based on authoritative knowledge, is exemplary of its kind. That it should now be superseded by the same author's *Bibliography of Printed English Drama* (4 vols., 1939–59) in no way detracts from its historical importance. Greg's numerous publications are an indispensable tool for musical research on Shakespeare: the chronological and bibliographical judgments are supplemented by many detailed comments on stage directions concerning music and on the different versions of lyrics in quartos and folios. Concerning these matters, the *Editorial Problem in Shakespeare* (3rd edn., 1954) and the *Shakespeare First Folio* (1955) are particularly helpful. But, in contrast to these trustworthy volumes, it must be said that Louis C. Elson's *Shakespeare in Music* (1901) and Charles Vincent's *Fifty Shakespeare Songs* (1906) are typical of glibly popular works, full of inaccuracies. They are neither as learned nor as helpful as Chappell was in 1859, let alone Wooldridge in 1893 or Naylor in 1896. Vincent's volume is a forerunner of several anthologies intended for the singer in quest of material for a recital to be entitled 'Shakespeare in Music'. Vincent's successors have improved somewhat upon his method, notably Vincent Jackson, *English Melodies from the 13th to the 18th Century* (1910) and Frank H. Potter, *Reliquary of English Song* (2 vols., 1915–16, accompaniments by C. Vincent). But none of these publications commands the authority of the best books of the nineteenth century, though Potter's reliquary includes useful facsimiles of the 'Willow Song' and of Jonson's 'Have you seen but a white lily grow'.

The need for authoritative reprints of old music, so forcefully stimulated by Squire's edition of the Fitzwilliam Book, was recognized by Naylor (d. 1934), whose researches persevered into the twentieth century and resulted in several standard works. His study of the Fitzwilliam Book (*An Elizabethan Virginal Book*, 1905) was followed by an anthology of Elizabethan music, entitled *Shakespeare Music* (1st edn., 1913, 2nd edn., 1928). Unlike his predecessors, Chappell and Wooldridge, Naylor did not feel impelled to provide modern accompaniments, but reprinted melody and accompaniment as he found them in the original scores. His transcriptions of 'A robyn, gentyl robyn' from British Museum, Add. MS 31922 and of 'Come over the burn Bessy' from Cambridge, MS Dd.2.11 are significant steps forward. Of Naylor's later work we may mention here his *Poets and Music*

(1928). The chapter on Shakespeare (pp. 89–130) contains a valuable discussion of passages in Shakespeare dealing with concrete musical instruments as well as with the music of the spheres. A revision of *Shakespeare and Music* appeared in 1931 and its excellence is a challenge to later scholars. G. H. Cowling's *Music on the Shakespearean Stage* (1913) is frequently referred to as a supplement to Naylor's standard work. Cowling discriminates nicely between the 'brazen din' of Marlowe and Shakespeare's more economical use of battle signals, but, unlike Naylor, he does not refer to sources where old music may be found. His discussion of the songs, moreover, is marred by his lack of appreciation of their dramatic function. It is fair to say that Naylor's volume remains the most serviceable treatment of the subject, though this is partly due to the fact that some of the most original contributions between the years 1900 and 1960 have appeared in the form of short articles. From a variety of periodical and composite publications which were produced before 1918 we may single out the following nine: The Malone Society was founded in 1906, and its earliest publications first appeared in 1907, stimulated by the bibliographical researches of Greg and others. Both its typographical facsimile reprints and the documents contained in its *Collections* make possible a study of lyrics sung and of musical stage directions under conditions which, even in this age of microfilms, are a blessing and a necessity. The fourth volume (1909) of the *Cambridge History of English Literature* contains H. H. Child's chapter on 'Song-Books and Miscellanies' which though now out of date should still be consulted.

The first volume of the *Musical Antiquary* appeared in 1909–1910, the fourth and last in 1912–13. But its early demise must not obscure its importance for Elizabethan studies: 'Music and Shakespeare' by E. W. Naylor, I.129–148; 'Early Elizabethan Stage Music', anonymous, I.30–40 and IV.112–117; 'Lists of the King's Musicians from the Audit Office Declared Accounts' by E. Stokes, I.56 *et passim* and IV.55 *et passim*. Another casualty of the First World War were the polyglot *Sammelbände* of the International Musicological Society containing, among others, a useful article on 'Dances in Shakespeare's England' (1913–14, XV.99–102) by Jeffrey Pulver, the author of the valuable *Biographical Dictionary of Old English Music* (1927). Pulver was also one of the contributors to *Proceedings of the Royal Musical Association* which published several articles of interest before 1918 (and continues to do so). G. E. P. Arkwright's 'Elizabethan Choirboy Plays and their Music' (1913–14, XL.117–138) is valuable not only for the light it throws on Pistol's 'O death, rock me asleep' but for his elucidation of the entire tradition as typified by Edwards's *Damon and Pithias* and parodied in Shakespeare's playlet 'Pyramus and Thisbe'. Arkwright belonged to a species, now almost extinct, the gentleman-scholar: his essay of twenty pages, if written today, might well have developed into a book of several hundred pages, with caustic footnotes. As it was, his article was supplemented by his labours as editor of the *Musical Antiquary* and of the *Old English Edition* (25 vols., 1889–1902) which reproduced Thomas Campion's *Lord Hay's Masque*. The *Proceedings of the Royal Musical Association* also counted among its contributors Percy Scholes, the well-known author of the *Oxford Companion to Music* and *The Puritans and Music*. His paper 'The Purpose behind Shakespeare's Use of Music' (1916–17, XLIII. 1–15) illuminates the consistent way in which the poet employed music to make manifest and effective the supernatural element in the plays. The divine interventions in *Pericles*, *Cymbeline*, *Winter's Tale* and *The Tempest* would be wooden without the support of musical accompaniment, and Scholes was the first among musical scholars to explain Shakespeare's method of employing music. If his understanding of the subject was not omniscient, Scholes nevertheless blazed a trail for later writers. The dissolution of the *Musical Antiquary* and the various publications of the International Musicological Society in 1914 was, perhaps, the final inducement for the founding in 1915 of the American periodical, *The Musical Quarterly*. It emphasized, as had the earlier *New Variorum Edition* of Furness, the importance of transatlantic publications. Edward Dent's article on the 'Musical Interpretation of Shakespeare on the Modern Stage' (1916, II.523–537) is only one of the many contributions on the subject which this doyen of English music historians was to offer. In this article Dent, a man of letters whose interests were by no means restricted to sharps and flats, distinguishes clearly between the roles played by music in spoken drama and in opera, and assesses the differences in kind between Shakespeare's plays and the later adaptations of Dryden and Purcell. Dent deals with the new methods of reviving Shakespeare which William Poel and Granville Barker initiated and himself provided Elizabethan music for the Marlowe Society when it produced *Doctor Faustus* in 1910 and the *Knight of the Burning Pestle* in 1911. This passionate enthusiasm of the scholar who helped to shape the policies of Sadler's Wells and Glyndebourne was bound to leave its mark also on musical scholarship in regard to Shakespeare. Of his later works we mention here only his *Foundations of English Opera* (1928) and his chapter on 'Shakespeare and Music' in the *Companion to Shakespeare Studies* (edd. H. Granville-Barker and G. B. Harrison, 1934). It is an incontrovertible fact that, between them, Naylor and Dent, in the twentieth century, have done more than any other two authors to present a clear and accurate picture of the role of music in the plays. This does not preclude mentioning that subsequent research has modified and revised several details in their accounts. Finally, there remain the shorter articles which appeared in several composite volumes before 1918. These and a variety of *Festschriften* and *Kongressberichte* which continue to appear with increasing frequency, are not easily located except in large national libraries and may therefore be easily overlooked. J. R. Moore's 'The Function of the Songs in Shakespeare's Plays' appeared in *Shakespeare Studies . . . University of Wisconsin* (1916, pp. 78–102), and A. C. Bradley's 'Feste, the Jester' in *A Book of Homage to Shakespeare* (ed. I. Gollancz, 1916; republished in Bradley's *A Miscellany*, 1929, pp. 207–217). The author of *Shakespearean Tragedy* scarcely needs an introduction yet the many fleeting observations on the art of music, in Bradley's classic book, barely suggest the detail and shrewdness with which the author examines the role of Robert Armin and his songs in *Twelfth Night*. By assigning full credit to Shakespeare (rather than to Armin) for the concluding song of the comedy Bradley joins the minority company of Charles Knight in the nineteenth century and Richmond Noble and George L. Kittredge in the twentieth, a group which scholars of recent vintage are inclined to support. Moore's article is one of several growing out of his doctoral dissertation, which also yielded 'The Songs of the Public Theatres in the Time of Shakespeare' (*Journal of English and Germanic Philology*, XXVIII (1929), 166–202) and 'The Songs in Lyly's Plays' (*PMLA* XLII (1927), 623–640). It is not possible to recount here the well-known controversy in regard to the authenticity of Lyly's lyrics; suffice it to say that no study of *Midsummer Night's Dream* or *Merry Wives of Windsor* can dispense with an examination of the earlier playwright's methods. Another composite publication, *Shakespeare's England* (edd. S. Lee, C. T. Onions, W. Raleigh, 2 vols., 1916), produced valuable articles by W. Barclay Squire on 'Music', C. H. Firth on 'Ballads and Broadsides' and a 'Glossary of Musical Terms' by C. T. Onions, whose labours on the *Oxford English Dictionary* and the *Shakespeare Glossary* are well known.

The majority of the publications mentioned so far deal, quite properly, with songs and ballads. Serious consideration of instrumental problems begins with the publication of Francis W. Galpin's *Old English Instruments of Music* (1910; 3rd edn., 1932) and Christopher Welch's *Six Lectures on the Recorder* (1911; the first three chapters, including 'Hamlet and the Recorder', reprinted 1961).

In the period between the two World Wars scholarly publications increased with such rapidity that it becomes necessary to exercise an even greater selectivity in a compilation of this kind. Therefore articles in periodicals, except *in extremis*, must give way to major books and reprints.[1]

No account of the 1920s, however brief, can omit the works of E. H. Fellowes, R. Noble, H. E. Rollins and P. Warlock. Fellowes wrote many books on music, among them monographs on *Byrd* and *Gibbons*, yet his lasting merit consists in his having reprinted the old music in modern editions, thus making it accessible to the ears and the minds of the general public. Recitals of Elizabethan music, whether in the concert hall or over the wireless or gramophone, would be unthinkable today without the industry and daring of Fellowes. There are some minor errors, certain sharps or flats incorrectly placed, some unacknowledged transpositions, some silent emendations. Yet, these details are insignificant compared with the total achieve-

---

[1] For sundry relevant articles, *Grove's Dictionary of Music* (5th edn., 1954) and the German encyclopaedia, *Musik in Geschichte und Gegenwart* (Cassel, 1949 ff.) should be consulted under such headings as Shakespeare, Byrd, Morley; lute, cittern, cornett, sackbut, tucket; ballad, folk music, ayre, etc. The subject headings of the British Museum and the Library of Congress are likewise useful. The most detailed bibliography is provided by the annual American publication *Music Index*.

ment. The *English Madrigal School* (36 vols., 1913–24) and *Songs . . . from Beaumont and Fletcher* (1928) were supplemented by the *English School of Lutenist Song Writers* (32 vols., 1920–32), a work that is indispensable to the student of spoken drama. There are two series to this *corpus*, a First Series giving both tablatures and modern transcriptions, and a Second Series giving transcriptions only. The First Series includes Dowland and Morley; Ferrabosco, Campion and Jones appear in the Second Series. To these must be added the *Complete Works of W. Byrd* (20 vols., 1937–50), containing Byrd's keyboard arrangements of popular tunes occurring in Shakespeare. On Fellowes's death in 1951 R. Thurston Dart succeeded him as editor of the *School of Lutenist Song Writers*. Volume 17 of the First Series reprints Giovanni Coperario (alias John Cooper) whose *Songs of Mourning* for Prince Henry and lyrics for Campion's *Somerset Masque* are of great interest. Volume 17 of the Second Series contains the songs of Robert Johnson whose cardinal importance for *The Tempest* and other plays is well known. A rival and critic of Fellowes, Peter Warlock nevertheless made an equally important contribution to Shakespeare studies. His taste and emendations were impeccable, his assessment of attributed and anonymous compositions very good indeed. His tantalizingly short book, *The English Ayre* (1926) is the best of its kind to appear so far, and his *English Ayres* (edited jointly with Philip Wilson, 4 vols., 1922–25; 2nd edn., 6 vols., 1927–31) is an indispensable anthology since it includes several important anonymous songs not transcribed by Fellowes. Among these 'I loathe that I did love' is relevant to the grave-digger's song in *Hamlet*. Warlock also edited *Elizabethan Songs . . . for . . . voice . . . and . . . stringed instruments*, (3 vols., 1926) and Ravenscroft's *Pammelia* (1928). That all of these works are now out of print is an indication of the vicissitudes of modern publishing.

Another great editor of the twenties, Hyder E. Rollins, provided a detailed census of relevant musical manuscripts. Rollins's edition of *Tottel's Songes and Sonnettes* (1928–29) brought to completion one of the tasks left unfinished by Bishop Percy in the eighteenth century. The *Analytical Index to ballad entries . . .* (Chapel Hill, N.C., 1924) is an indispensable aid to a study of the *Stationers' Registers*. Of the important contributions in this period there remains *Shakespeare's Use of Song* (1923) by

Richmond Noble, whose researches have contributed many a valuable footnote to John Dover Wilson's *New Shakespeare* edition. Noble, after Naylor, wrote the best monograph on Shakespeare and music to date.

The periodical *Music & Letters* was founded in 1920 and from its inception paid heed to Shakespeare research. Before the Second World War it published articles by W. J. Lawrence (1922),[1] H. M. Fitzgibbon (1930) and S. A. Bayliss (1934). Important essays of the period appearing in other periodicals and series were by E. Law (Shakespeare Association *Papers*, 1920), E. S. Lindsey (*Studies in Philology*, 1924), L. B. Wright (*Studies in Philology*, 1927), E. S. Lindsey (*Modern Language Notes*, 1929), Ernest Brennecke (*P.M.L.A.*, 1939). Books of the thirties, specifically dealing with musical problems, include J. M. Gibbon, *Melody and the Lyric* (1930), Scholes's *Puritans and Music* (already mentioned) and G. Bontoux's *Chanson en Angleterre* (1936). Gibbon's book is a useful digest of Chappell, Wooldridge, Naylor and others but, as such, it suffers from its neglect of original sources. Mlle Bontoux's sumptuous volume is to be commended for its facsimiles and other illustrations as well as for its unusually liberal transliterations of lute tablatures. Among general books that throw light on musical topics there are the standard reference works of E. K. Chambers and A. Nicoll, as well as the monographs of G. Wilson Knight.

The harvest of the forties proved more significant for specifically musical studies. Among the important periodical articles R. T. Dart's piece on 'Morley's Consort Lessons of 1599' (*Proceedings of the Royal Musical Association*, 1947–48) brought to the fore one of the most prominent authors, editors and performers of our age. Numerous articles, largely concerned with instrumental music, have appeared over Dart's name in *Music & Letters* and the *Galpin Society Journal*. His *Jacobean Consort Music* (edited jointly with W. Coates, 1955) is an indispensable reprint and equally valuable for the Shakespearean producer are two recent slim editions, the *Suite . . . Brass Music . . . James I* and the *Holborne . . . Suite for an Ensemble* (both 1959).

Otto Gombosi's 'Some musical Aspects of the English Court

---

[1] The many books published by W. J. Lawrence contain several valuable passages on music.

Masque' appeared in the *Journal of the American Musicological Society*, I (1948). Gombosi's knowledge of 'passamezzo antico' and 'passamezzo moderno', of Sir Toby Belch's 'passy-measures pavin' in *Twelfth Night* (V.i.206) remains unchallenged, and his knowledge of early lute books, such as the Giles Lodge Book at the Folger Library in Washington (containing an early musical version of the Willow Song) was equally profound. His untimely death in 1955 deprived music and letters of a first-rate scholar. Other relevant periodical articles are duly recorded in the *New Shakespeare* and the *New Arden* editions of the plays.

The major books of the forties include M. C. Boyd, *Elizabethan Music*, C. L. Day's and E. B. Murrie's bibliography, *English Song Books*, Bruce Pattison, *Music and Poetry of the English Renaissance*, Mabel Dolmetsch, *Dances of England and France, 1450–1600*. Of these Pattison's is the most important and should be read in conjunction with his chapters on 'Literature and Music' in V. de Sola Pinto's *English Renaissance* (2nd edn., 1951, pp. 120–138) and 'Music and Masque' in C. J. Sisson's one-volume edition of Shakespeare's *Works* (1954, pp. xlvii–lii). Pattison is one of the few major scholars in the field who followed E. J. Dent in focusing attention on the hybrid and difficult field of words-and-music. Critical evaluations will be found in John Stevens's *Music and Poetry in the Early Tudor Court* and in the present writer's review of Pattison's work in the *Journal of the American Musicological Society*, II (1949). The author emphasizes unduly the happy union of poetry and music and minimizes the inevitable conflicts which arise from time to time between these two arts. Nevertheless, his discussion of musical and poetical forms is a *sine qua non* for later research. Of general works bearing on music one may single out G. E. Bentley's *Jacobean Stage*, T. W. Baldwin's *Shakspere's Small Latine* . . . and W. A. Ringler's two monographs on *Rainolds* and *Gosson* respectively. The importance of music at the Blackfriars is considered in Bentley's article, 'Shakespeare and the Blackfriar's Theatre' in *Shakespeare Survey I* which is supplemented by the studies of Isaacs and Armstrong (*Shakespeare Association Papers*, 1933; *Society for Theatre Research Pamphlets*, 1958). Baldwin's work on the importance of classical sources for Shakespeare's musical passages follows his earlier monograph on the *Organization and Personnel of the Shakespearean Company*

(1927) which embarks on, though it does not settle, the all-important question of Robert Armin.

The decade of the 1950s produced the largest number of books either dealing with or reprinting music. W. R. Bowden's *English Dramatic Lyric, 1603–42* (1951) is a carefully documented study of the occasions when Stuart playwrights employed music. Utilizing the material that had been gathered in earlier collections (such as E. B. Reed, *Songs from the British Drama*, 1925; T. Brooke, ed. *Shakespeare Songs*, 1929) Bowden analyzes the functions of the lyric and the dramatic purpose underlying the categories most frequently used. His volume contains appendices to all of the songs in the plays of Armin, Beaumont and Fletcher, Chapman, Dekker, Heywood, Jonson, Marston, among others. Catherine Ing's *Elizabethan Lyrics* (1951) gives more consideration to Campion than to Shakespeare, though the section on Shakespeare (pp. 219–230) is valuable, and the general discussion of metrics and music the best to date. Denis Stevens's edition of the *Mulliner Book* (1951, rev. edn., 1954) makes available a collection of keyboard music of great worth for Elizabethan drama. Of an earlier date than the *Fitzwilliam Book* this anthology throws light on the lyrics of Richard Edwards and, in consequence, on 'Where griping grief the heart doth wound', which the clown sings in *Romeo and Juliet*. The *Mulliner Book*, in company with Thurston Dart's *Jacobean Consort Music* (mentioned earlier) is part of a monumental series of reprints of English music, which also includes John Stevens's edition of *Mediaeval Carols* (1952, rev. 1958). Both Denis Stevens and John Stevens persevere in their contributions to our knowledge of Tudor music. Walter Woodfill's *Musicians in English Society from Elizabeth to Charles I* (1953) is an indispensable source-book dealing with musicians of the city and of the court; it also offers an excellent bibliography (pp. 315–361). Two valuable reprints of music appeared in 1954, David Lumsden's *Anthology of English Lute Music* and John Ward's *Dublin Virginal Manuscript*, the latter an anthology of keyboard music. Lumsden and Ward are both authorities on lute music and have contributed important articles on that subject to learned journals. Their editions have been supplemented by three further reprints, enumerated below, and altogether the student of today has more music of the sixteenth and seventeenth centuries readily available than his forebears had. Margaret Dean-Smith's edition of *Playford's English Dancing Master, 1651* (1957) is a facsimile reprint of one of the main sources of Chappell and Naylor. The author's annotations and cross-references to other English and Dutch collections, as well as to standard reference works (such as Child's *English and Scottish Popular Ballads*) add value to the volume. Andrew Sabol's edition of *Songs and Dances for the Stuart Masque* (1959) makes available thirty-eight songs and twenty-five instrumental pieces. The latter are taken from British Museum, Add. MS 10444, an important theatrical source, which W. J. Lawrence had described in *Music & Letters* in 1922. The manuscript presents only treble and bass, so that modern editors must supply the harmony. One does not always agree with Sabol's solutions, but the edition, including the author's apparatus of notes and bibliography, is a valuable contribution to scholarship. Sydney Beck's edition of *The First Book of Consort Lessons, Collected by Thomas Morley* (1959) is one of the finest pieces of scholarly reconstruction to be reviewed in this retrospect. It bids fair to supplement Dart's *Jacobean Consort Music* as a major source of instrumental music for Shakespearean producers. Of its twenty-five numbers, 'O Mistresse Mine' is of particular interest to students of *Twelfth Night*.

Three further monographs complete the list of books exclusively concerned with music. John H. Long's *Shakespeare's Use of Music . . . Seven Comedies* (1955) consists largely of letterpress but contains thirty-five music examples. Included among these are several of the author's adaptations of Elizabethan melodies to Shakespeare's lyrics when no specific contemporary melody was known. Such adaptations are essential in the circumstances and Long's solutions are, on the whole, musicianly and helpful. Unfortunately, the work is based entirely on the researches of earlier scholars, such as Chappell and Naylor, and his discussion and bibliography are marred by serious errors. J. S. Manifold, in *Music in English Drama: From Shakespeare to Purcell*, casts a wide net and includes a discussion of Restoration music. The author's elucidation on the associations of 'high' and 'low' music are sound: the contrast between the loud music of winds and the soft strains of strings is important for Shakespeare and his contemporaries. Unlike Long, Manifold does not give music examples. By contrast, J. P. Cutts's *La Musique de*

Scène de Shakespeare: The King's Men sous le règne de Jacques Ier (Paris, 1959) contains fifty-three pieces of music (pp. 1–110) as well as a detailed critical commentary (pp. 111–189). The latter is most useful since its concordances list many manuscripts scattered in London, Dublin, New York and Washington. Cutts is a prolific writer, well known in the field, and between 1952 and 1962 he has published two books and some thirty articles. His *Seventeenth Century Books and Lyrics* appeared in 1959, and the articles are to be found in such standard publications as *Music & Letters* and *Shakespeare Survey*. Unfortunately, zeal and haste are no substitutes for accuracy, and whereas Cutts's work cannot be ignored, it cannot be trusted either.[1]

Only the briefest selection of periodical articles of the fifties can be offered here. Among foreign and less easily accessible sources the *English Miscellany*, edited by Mario Praz at Rome, contains a long and excellent essay by James Hutton (1951). Several symposia, edited by Jean Jacquot at Paris, include *Musique et Poésie* (1954), *Musique Instrumentale* (1955), *Fêtes de la Renaissance* (1956) and *Le Luth et sa Musique* (1958). These volumes contain much valuable information, bibliographically and otherwise. The German *Shakespeare Jahrbuch* contains several pertinent articles (Prange, 1953; Nicoll, 1958). Of American Journals we mention the *Musical Quarterly* (Vlastos, 1954; Long, 1958); *Shakespeare Quarterly* (Brennecke, 1953; Seng, 1958; Pafford, 1959; Seng, 1959; Waldo, 1959); *Journal of the American Musicological Society* (Ward, 1951; 1957); *Renaissance News* (Beck, 1953) and *Musica Disciplina* (Bowles, 1954). In England the obvious periodicals are *Music & Letters* and *Shakespeare Survey*. An index to the former covering 1920–1959, appeared in 1962, and Volume XI of the *Survey* contains an index to the first ten volumes, as well as an article on music by J. M. Nosworthy which supplements his edition of *Cymbeline* for the New Arden. It is also worth the student's while to check the *Galpin Society Journal* (Lumsden, 1953; Dart, 1958) and the *Lute Society Journal* (Newton, 1958; Spencer, 1958).

Of general works bearing on music three are relevant to boy

---

[1] For professional criticism see *Library*, 5th ser., X (1955), 55–57; *Shakespeare Quarterly*, IX (1958), 114–115; *Music & Letters*, XLI (1960), 300–303; *Notes* of the Music Library Association, XVIII (1961), 228–229.

singers and adult singers. Ronald Watkins (*On Producing Shakespeare*, 1950) agrees with T. W. Baldwin that Shakespeare's brother Edmund is a likely candidate for a singing boy named 'Ned'. Of Alfred Harbage's several books, *Shakespeare and the Rival Traditions* (1952) is particularly pertinent to a consideration of the musical resources available at the Blackfriars Theatre where the boy singers and instrumentalists so greatly excelled the performers in the adult playhouses. Leslie Hotson's *Shakespeare's Motley* (1952), on the other hand, concentrates on the main adult singer of Shakespeare's company, namely Robert Armin. Several hypotheses advanced by Hotson in this work have found wide acceptance, whereas *The First Night of Twelfth Night* (1954), also touching on Armin, remains highly controversial. Paul A. Jorgensen's *Shakespeare's Military World* (1956) includes a surprisingly detailed and knowledgeable account of battle music.

The major problems of the sixties and seventies will be editorial as well as analytical. Now that the Mulliner and Fitzwilliam books have been reprinted we sorely need editions of the major lute manuscripts in London, Cambridge and Dublin. For the writing of books and articles we are in urgent need of authors who will combine learning in literary and musical matters. Recent developments in international bibliography, as well as the increased availability of microfilms and xerographs, should be of aid.

BIBLIOGRAPHY OF SOURCES
PRINTED AFTER 1700

ABERT, H., *Die Lehre vom Ethos in der griechischen Musik*, Leipzig, 1899.

ADAMS, J. C., 'The Staging of "The Tempest", III.iii', *Review of English Studies*, XIV (1938), 404–419.

— *Globe Playhouse: Its Design and Equipment*, Cambridge (Mass.), 1942.

ADAMS, JOSEPH QUINCY, *Shakespearean Playhouses*, Boston, 1917.

— ed. *Chief Pre-Shakespearean Dramas*, Boston, 1924.

— 'A New Song by Robert Jones', *Modern Language Quarterly*, I (1940), 45–48.

ALEXANDER, PETER, *Shakespeare's Life and Art*, London, 1939.

— *Shakespeare Primer*, London, 1951.

— ed. *Shakespeare: Complete Works*, London, 1951.

American Garland, s.v. C. H. Firth.

Analytical Index to the ballad entries (1557–1709), s.v. H. E. Rollins.

Ancient Scottish Melodies, s.v. William Dauney.

Ancient Songs and Ballads, s.v. J. Ritson.

ANDERS, H. R. D., *Shakespeare's Books*, Berlin, 1904.

ARBEAU, THOINOT, pseud. [Jehan Tabourot], s.v. C. W. Beaumont.

ARBER, EDWARD, ed. *Transcript of the Registers of the Company of Stationers, 1554–1640*, 5 vols., London, 1875–94.

ARKWRIGHT, G. E. P., 'Elizabethan Choirboys Plays and their Music', *Proceedings of the Royal Musical Association*, XL (1913–14), 117–138.

ARMIN, ROBERT, s.v. A. B. Grosart.

— s.v. F. Ouvry.

— s.v. J. P. Collier.

ARMSTRONG, W. A., 'Elizabethan Private Theatres: Facts and Problems' (Society for Theatre Research, Pamphlet Series No. 6), London, 1958.

ASCHAM, ROGER, s.v. J. E. B. Mayor.

— s.v. W. A. Wright.

BACKUS, E. N., *Catalogue of music in the Huntington Library, printed before 1801*, San Marino (Calif.), 1949.

Bagford Ballads, s.v. J. W. Ebsworth, ed.

BALD, R. C., ed. *T. Middleton: Hengist, King of Kent . . .*, New York, 1938 [particularly p. xxxiii].

BALDWIN, T. W., 'Shakespeare's Jester', *Modern Language Notes*, XXXIX (1924), 447-55.

— *Organization and Personnel of the Shakespearean Company*, Princeton, 1927.

— *Shakspere's Small Latine and Lesse Greeke*, 2 vols., Urbana (Illinois), 1944.

Ballads and Broadsides . . . Britwell, s.v. H. L. Collmann, ed.

Ballads from Manuscripts, s.v. F. J. Furnivall, ed.

BARTLETT, JOHN, *Complete Concordance . . . Shakespeare*, London, 1894.

BASKERVILL, C. R., *The Elizabethan Jig and Related Song Drama*, Chicago, 1929.

— 'A Prompt Copy of "A Looking Glass for London and England" ', *Modern Philology*, XXX (1932-33), 29-51.

BAYLISS, S. A., 'Music for Shakespeare', *Music & Letters*, XV (1934), 61-65.

BEAUMONT and FLETCHER, s.v. A. R. Waller.

BEAUMONT, CYRIL W., tr. *Orchesography . . . by Thoinot Arbeau*, with a preface by Peter Warlock, London, 1925.

BECK, SYDNEY, 'The Case of "O Mistresse mine" ', *Renaissance News*, VI (1953), 19-23; VII (1954), 15-16 and 98-100.

— ed. *The First Book of Consort Lessons: Collected by Thomas Morley: 1599 & 1611*, New York, 1959.

BENTLEY, G. E., 'Shakespeare and the Blackfriars Theatre', *Shakespeare Survey*, I (1948), 38-50.

— *Jacobean and Caroline Stage*, 5 vols., Oxford, 1941-56.

BERNHEIMER, RICHARD, *Wild Men in the Middle Ages*, Cambridge (Mass.), 1952.

BOAS, F. S., *Shakspere and His Predecessors*, London, 1896.

— *University Drama in the Tudor Age*, Oxford, 1914.

— *Introduction to Tudor Drama . . .*, Oxford, 1933.

— *Introduction to Stuart Drama . . .*, London, 1946.

— ed. *Works of Thomas Kyd*, Oxford, 1901.

BODIN, s.v. B. Reynolds, M. J. Tooley, K. D. McRae.

BOND, R. W., ed. *Lyly: Complete Works*, 3 vols., Oxford, 1902.

BONTOUX, GERMAINE, *La Chanson en Angleterre au temps d'Elisabeth*, Oxford, 1936.

BORREN, CHARLES VAN DEN, *Sources of Keyboard Music in England*, tr. J. E. Matthew, London, [1914].

BOUGHTON, R., 'Shakespeare's Ariel, a Study of Musical Character', *Musical Quarterly*, II (1916), 538-551.

BOWDEN, W. R., *The English Dramatic Lyric, 1603-1642*, New Haven, 1951.

BOWLES, EDMUND A., 'Instruments at the Court of Burgundy', *Journal of the Galpin Society*, VI (1953), 41-51.

BOWLES, EDMUND A., 'Haut and Bas: The Grouping of Musical Instruments in the Middle Ages', *Musica Disciplina*, VIII (1954), 115–140.

— 'Musical Instruments in Mediaeval Sacred Drama', *Musical Quarterly*, XLV (1959), 67–84.

— 'Musical Instruments in Civic Processions', *Acta Musicologica*, XXIII (1961), 147–161.

BOYD, M. C., *Elizabethan Music and Musical Criticism*, Philadelphia, 1940.

BRADBROOK, M. C., *Themes and Conventions of Elizabethan Tragedy*, Cambridge, 1935; paper-back edn.: Cambridge, 1960.

BRADLEY, A. C., *Shakespearean Tragedy*, London, 1904.

— 'Feste the Jester' in *A Book of Homage to Shakespeare*, ed. I. Gollancz, London, 1916.

— *A Miscellany*, London, 1929; reprinted: London, 1931.

BREMNER, ROBERT, ed. *Thirty Scots Songs, for a Voice and Harpsichord*, 2 vols., Edinburgh, 1757.

BRENNECKE, ERNEST, *John Milton the Elder and His Music*, New York, 1938.

— 'Shakespeare's Collaboration with Morley', *Publications of the Modern Language Association*, LIV (1939), 139–149, 152.

— 'What shall he have that killed the deer?', *Musical Times*, XCIII (1952), 347–351.

— '. . . Significance of Desdemona's Willow Song', *Shakespeare Quarterly*, IV (1953), 35–38.

BRETT-SMITH, H., s.v. Stephen Gaselee.

BRIDGE, SIR JOHN FREDERICK, ed. *Songs from Shakespeare: the earliest known settings*, London, [1894].

— *Shakespearean Music in the Plays and Early Operas*, London, 1923.

BRONSON, BERTRAND H., *The Traditional Tunes of the Child Ballads*, Vol. I, Princeton, 1959.

BROOKE, C. F. T., ed. *The Shakespeare Songs*, with intr. Walter de la Mare, New York & London, 1929.

— ed. *Shakespeare Apocrypha*, 2nd ed., Oxford, 1918.

BROUGHAM, ELEANOR M., ed. *Corn from Olde Fields. An anthology of English Poems from the XIVth to XVIIth Century*, London, [pref. 1918].

BROWN, J. R., 'Riddle Song in *Merchant of Venice*', *Notes and Queries*, CCIV (1959), 235.

BULLOCK, W. L., 'English Sonnet Form', *Publications of the Modern Language Association*, XXXVIII (1923).

BURNEY, CHARLES, *A General History . . . of Music*, 4 vols., London, 1776–89; ed. F. Mercer, 2 vols., London, 1935.

BUSBY, O. M., *Development of the Fool in the Elizabethan Drama*, London, 1923.

BUSH, DOUGLAS, *English Literature in the Earlier Seventeenth Century*, Oxford, 1945, s.v. Armin, Campion, Jonson, Prynne, *et passim*; rev. edn., Oxford, 1962.

CAMPBELL, O. J., *Shakespeare's Satire*, New York, 1943.
Capt. Cox, his Ballads, s.v. F. J. Furnivall.
Caroline Lyrics, s.v. E. F. Hart.
CASE, A. E., *Bibliography of English Poetical Miscellanies*, Oxford, 1935.
CASTIGLIONE, s.v. Walter Raleigh, intr.
Catalogue of English Broadsides 1505–1897, s.v. Crawford (Earl of).
CAULFIELD, JOHN, *A Collection of the Vocal Music in Shakespeare's Plays*, 2 vols., London, 1864.
CAVALIER AND PURITAN, s.v. H. E. Rollins.
CAVALIER SONGS AND BALLADS, s.v. Charles Mackay.
CAXTON, W., s.v. Stephen Gaselee.
Century of Broadside Elegies, s.v. J. W. Draper.
CHAMBERS, E. K., *The Elizabethan Stage*, 4 vols., Oxford, 1923.
— *The Mediaeval Stage*, 2 vols., London, 1903.
— *William Shakespeare, a Study of Facts and Problems*, Oxford, 1930.
CHAPPELL, WILLIAM, ed. *R. Johnson: Crown Garland of Golden Roses* (Percy Society Publications, VI, XV), 2 vols., London, 1842 and 1845.
— ed. *Popular Music of the Olden Time*, 2 vols., London, 1855-59.
— ed. jointly with J. W. Ebsworth, *Roxburghe Ballads*, 9 vols., London, 1871–1899.
— Cf. also s.v. H. E. Wooldridge.
CHARLTON, H. B., *Shakespearean Comedy*, London, 1938.
— *The Senecan Tradition in Renaissance Tragedy*, Manchester, 1946.
— *Shakespearean Tragedy*, Cambridge, 1948.
CHILD, F. J., ed. *English and Scottish Ballads*, 8 vols., Boston, 1857–58.
— ed. *English and Scottish Popular Ballads*, 5 vols., Boston, 1882–98.
— s.v. B. Bronson.
CHILD, H. H., 'Song Books and Miscellanies', *Cambridge History of English Literature*, 15 vols., Cambridge, 1907-27, IV.109–126.
Christmas Carols Printed in the 16th Century, s.v. E. B. Reed.
CLARK, A., ed. *Shirburn Ballads*, Oxford, 1907.
CLARK, C. and M. COWDEN, *The Shakespeare Key*, London, 1879.
CLEMEN, W. H., *Development of Shakespeare's Imagery*, London, 1951.
CLIVE, H. B., 'The Calvinist Attitude to Music', *Bibliothèque d'Humanisme et Renaissance*, XIX (1957), 80–102.
COLE, ELIZABETH, 'Seven Problems of the Fitzwilliam Virginal Book', *Proceedings of the Royal Musical Association*, LXXIX (1952–53), 51–64.

COLE, ELIZABETH, 'L'Anthologie de Francis Tregian', *La Musique Instrumentale de la Renaissance*, ed. Jean Jacquot, Paris, 1955.

Coleridge's Shakespearean Criticism, ed. T. M. Raysor, 2 vols., London, 1930.

Collection of Old Ballads [anonymous], [ed. Ambrose Philips?], 3 vols., London, 1723–1725, [cf. A. E. Case, *Bibliography of English Poetical Miscellanies*, Oxford, 1935, pp. 240–243].

Collection of seventy-nine . . . ballads, s.v. J. Lilly.

Collection of Songs and Ballads, s.v. Charles Mackay.

COLLIER, JOHN PAYNE, *History of English Dramatic Poetry*, 3 vols., London, 1831.

— *Fools & Jesters; with reprint of Armin's 'Nest of Ninnies'* (Shakespeare Society Publications), London, 1842.

— *Illustrations of Old English Literature*, 3 vols., London, 1866.

— ed. *Old Ballads from Early Printed Copies* (Percy Society Publications), London, 1840.

— [ed.] *Gosson: School of Abuse* (Shakespeare Society Publications), London, 1841.

COLLMAN, H. L., ed. *Ballads and Broadsides . . . Britwell* (Roxburghe Club), London, 1912.

COOK, JOHN, 'Shakespeare and Music', *Stratford Papers on Shakespeare, 1960*, ed. B. A. W. Jackson, Toronto, 1961, pp. 21–49.

CORIN, F., 'Dirge in *Cymbeline*', *English Studies*, XL (1959), 173–9.

COWLING, G. H., *Music on the Shakespearean Stage*, Cambridge, 1913.

CRAIG, HARDIN, *Enchanted Glass*, New York, 1936; Oxford, 1950.

CRAWFORD, CHARLES, *Concordance to the works of Kyd* [with Hamlet Appendix], Louvain, 1906–10.

— *Marlowe Concordance*, Louvain, 1911–13, 1928–29, 1931–32.

CRAWFORD (EARL OF, JAMES L. LINDSAY), Bibliotheca Lindesiana: *Catalogue of a Collection of English Ballads of the Seventeenth and Eighteenth Centuries . . .*, Aberdeen, 1890.

— Bibliotheca Lindesiana: *Catalogue of English Broadsides 1505–1897*, Aberdeen, 1898.

Crown Garland, s.v. W. Chappell.

CRUM, MARGARET, 'A Manuscript of John Wilson's Songs', *The Library*, 5th Series, X (1955), 55–57.

— '. . . Music belonging to Thomas Hamond . . .', *Bodleian Library Record*, VI (1957), 373–386.

CRUTWELL, PATRICK, *The Shakespearean Moment*, New York, 1955.

CUNLIFFE, J. W., ed. *Early English Classical Tragedies*, Oxford, 1912.

CUTTS, JOHN P. Of some 30 publications which have appeared between 1952 and 1962, cf. the following:

— ed. jointly with F. Kermode, *Seventeenth Century Songs*, Reading, 1956.

— *Seventeenth Century Songs and Lyrics*, Columbia (Missouri), 1959.

— *La Musique de Scène de la Troupe de Shakespeare: The King's Men, sous le règne de Jacques I*, Paris, 1959.

Other articles have appeared in *Journal of the American Musicological Society, Music & Letters, Notes & Queries, Renaissance News, Shakespeare Quarterly, Shakespeare Survey.* Cf. particularly *Music & Letters*, 1955; *Journal of the American Musicological Society*, 1957.

DART, THURSTON. Among many publications, cf. the following: 'Morley's Consort Lessons of 1599', *Proceedings of the Royal Musical Association*, LXXIV (1947), 1–9.

— 'New Sources of Virginal Music', *Music & Letters*, XXXV (1954), 93–106.

— 'Repertory of the Royal Wind Music', *Galpin Society Journal* (1958), XI.70–77.

— ed. jointly with W. Coates, *Jacobean Consort Music* (Musica Britannica, IX), London, 1955.

— ed. *Suite . . . Brass Music . . . James I*, London, 1959.

— ed. *Byrd, Bull and Gibbons: Parthenia*, London, 1960.

DAUNEY, WILLIAM, ed. *Ancient Scottish Melodies*, Edinburgh, 1838.

DAVIS, HERBERT, ed. jointly with H. Gardner, *Elizabethan and Jacobean Studies*, Oxford, 1959.

DAY, CYRUS L., ed. jointly with Eleanore B. Murrie, *English Song Books, 1651–1702*, London, 1940.

— cf. Thomas D'Urfey, ed.

DEAN-SMITH, MARGARET, *A Guide to English Folk Song Collections, 1822–1952*, Liverpool, 1954.

— ed. *Playford: English Dancing Master, 1651*, Facsimile reprint, London, 1957.

— 'English Tunes common to Playford's *Dancing Master*, the Keyboard Books and Traditional Songs and Dances', *Proceedings of the Royal Musical Association*, LXXIX (1952–53), 1–17.

DE BANKE, CÉCILE, *Shakespearean Production Then and Now*, London, 1954: New York, 1953.

DELLA CASA, S.V. J. E. Spingarn, ed.

DELONEY, THOMAS, S.V. F. O. Mann.

DENKINGER, E. M., 'Actors' Names in the Register of St. Bodolph Aldgate', *Publications of the Modern Language Association*, XLI (1926), 91–109.

DENT, E. J., 'Musical Interpretation of Shakespeare on the Modern Stage', *Musical Quarterly*, II (1916), 523–537.

— *Foundations of English Opera*, Cambridge, 1928.

— 'Shakespeare and Music' in *A Companion to Shakespeare Studies*, edd. H. Granville-Barker and G. B. Harrison, Cambridge, 1934.

DODSLEY, ROBERT, s.v. W. C. Hazlitt, ed.

DOLMETSCH, MABEL, *Dances of England and France from 1450 to 1600*, London, 1949.

DORMER, ERNEST W., ed. *Gray of Reading*, [Ballads by William Gray, with intr. and notes], Reading, 1923.

DOUCE, FRANCIS, *Illustrations of Shakespeare*, 2 vols., 1st edn., London, 1807; 2nd edn., London, 1839.

DRAPER, J. W., ed. *Century of Broadside Elegies*, London, 1928.

DUCKLES, VINCENT, 'The curious art of John Wilson', *Journal of the American Musicological Society*, VII (1954), 93–112.

D'URFEY, THOMAS, ed. *Wit and Mirth: or Pills to Purge Melancholy*, 6 vols., London, 1719–20; intr. Cyrus L. Day [facsimile of 1876 reprint], New York, 1959.

'Early English Stage Music', *Musical Antiquary*, I (1909-10), 30–40; IV (1912–13), 112–117 [anonymous].

EBSWORTH, J. W., ed. *Bagford Ballads* (Ballad Society), 2 vols., Hertford, 1876–78.

ECCLES, MARC, 'Peerson and the Blackfriars', *Shakespeare Survey*, XI (1958), 100–106.

EDWARDS, P., ed. *Kyd: Spanish Tragedy*, London, 1959.

ELIOT, T. S., intr. *Seneca, his ten tragedies translated into English, edited by Thomas Newton, anno 1581* (Tudor Translations, 2nd Series, ed. C. Whibley), 2 vols., London, 1927.

Elizabethan and Jacobean Studies, s.v. Herbert Davis.

Elizabethan Songs . . . four stringed instruments, s.v. Peter Warlock.

ELLIS-FERMOR, UNA, 'Some Fashions of Verbal Music in Drama', *Shakespeare Jahrbuch*, XC (1954), 37–48.

— ed. with others, *New Arden Edition of Shakespeare's Works*, London, 1946.

ELSON, LOUIS C., *Shakespeare in Music*, Boston, 1901.

EMERSON, O. F., 'Shakespeare's Sonnetteering', *Studies in Philology*, XX (1923), 111–136.

EMSLEY, MACDONALD, 'Nicholas Lanier's Innovations in English Song', *Music & Letters*, XLI (1960), 13–27.

The English Ayre, s.v. Peter Warlock.

English Melodies from the 13th to the 18th Century, s.v. Vincent Jackson, ed.

English Song Books, 1651–1702, s.v. Cyrus L. Day, ed. with E. B. Murrie.

English Songs, A Selection of, s.v. J. Ritson, ed.

EVANS, THOMAS, *Old Ballads, Historical and Narrative*, with some of modern date. None of which are inserted in Dr. Percy's collection;

1st edn., 2 vols., London, 1777; 2nd edn., 4 vols., London, 1784; 3rd edn., 4 vols., rev. R. H. Evans, London, 1810.

EVANS, WILLA MCCLUNG, *Ben Jonson and Elizabethan music*, Lancaster (Penna.), 1929.

— 'Shakespeare's "Harke Harke ye Larke" ', *Publications of the Modern Language Association*, LX (1945), 95–101.

FARNHAM, W., *Shakespeare's Tragic Frontier*, Berkeley (Calif.), 1950.

FEBVRE, LUCIEN, with H.-J. Martin, *L'Apparition du Livre*, Paris, 1958.

FELLOWES, E. H. Among many publications, cf. the following:

— ed. *English Madrigal School*, 36 vols., London, 1913–24.

— ed. *English School of Lutenist Song Writers*, 32 vols., London, 1920–1932.

— ed. *English Madrigal Verse*, Oxford, 1920; 2nd edn., Oxford, 1929.

— ed. jointly with Hugh Macdonald, *Songs from the plays of Beaumont and Fletcher*, London, 1928.

— intr. *Morley: Plain and Easy Introduction to Practical Music* (Shakespeare Association Facsimiles, XIV), London, 1937.

FELVER, CHARLES S., 'Robert Armin's Fragment of a Bawdy Ballad of "Mary Ambree" ', *Notes & Queries*, New Series, VII (1960), 14–16.

— 'A proverb turned jest in *Measure for Measure*', *Shakespeare Quarterly*, XI (1960), 385–387.

— *Robert Armin, Shakespeare's Fool: A Biographical Essay* (Kent State University *Bulletin*, Research Series, V), Kent (Ohio), 1961.

FINNEY, G. L., 'Ecstasy and Music in 17th Century England', *Journal of the History of Ideas*, VIII (1947), 153–186, 273–292.

FIRTH, C. H., ed. *American Garland*, Oxford, 1915.

— ed. *Naval Songs and Ballads*, London, 1908.

— 'Ballads and Broadsides' in *Shakespeare's England*, edd. C. T. Onions and others, 2 vols., Oxford, 1916, II.511–538.

FITZGIBBON, H. MACAULEY, 'Instruments and their music . . . Elizabethan drama', *Musical Quarterly*, XVII (1931), 319–329.

— 'The Lute Books of Ballet and Dallis', *Music & Letters*, XI (1930), 71–77.

— *Story of the Flute*, London, 1914.

Fitzwilliam Virginal Book, s.v. W. Barclay Squire.

FLOOD, W. H. GRATTAN, *Early Tudor Composers*, London, 1925.

FOXWELL, A. K., *Study of . . . Wyatt's Poems*, London, 1911.

FRYE, NORTHROP, 'The Argument of Comedy' in *English Institute Essays*, New York, 1949.

— intr. and ed. *Sound and Poetry*, English Institute Essays, *1956*, New York, 1957.

FULLER-MAITLAND, J. A., s.v. W. Barclay Squire.

FULLER, THOMAS, s.v. P. A. Nuttall.

FURNESS, H. H., ed. with others, *New Variorum Edition of Shakespeare's Works*, Philadelphia, 1871 ff.

FURNIVALL, F. J., ed. with J. W. Hales, *Bishop Percy's Folio Manuscript*, 3 vols., London, 1867–68.

— ed. with W. R. Morfill, *Ballads from Manuscripts* (Ballad Society), 2 vols., London, Hertford, 1868–73.

— ed. *Captain Cox, his Ballads* (Ballad Society), London, 1871–74.

— ed. with J. Greenhill and W. A. Harrison, *All the Songs & Passages in Shakespeare which have been set to music* (New Shakespeare Society Publications), London, 1884.

GALPIN, F. W., *Old English Instruments of Music*, London, 1910; 3rd rev. edn., 1932.

— *Textbook of European Musical Instruments*, London, 1937.

GARDNER, HELEN, s.v. Herbert Davis.

— 'The Noble Moor' (Annual Shakespeare Lecture . . . British Academy), London, 1955.

GASELEE, STEPHEN, *Anthology of Mediaeval Latin*, London, 1925.

— ed. jointly with H. Brett-Smith (W. Caxton, tr.), *Ovid: Metamorphoses*, Oxford, 1924.

GIBBON, J. M., *Melody and the Lyric*, London, 1930.

Glossary of Tudor and Stuart Terms, s.v. W. W. Skeat.

GOLDSMITH, ROBERT H., *Wise Fools in Shakespeare*, New York, 1955; Liverpool, 1958.

GOMBOSI, OTTO, 'Frühgeschichte der Folia', *Acta Musicologica*, VIII (1936), 119 ff.

— *Tonarten und Stimmungen der antiken Musik*, Copenhagen, 1939.

— 'About dance and dance music in the late Middle Ages', *Musical Quarterly*, XXVII (1941), 289–305.

— 'Some musical aspects . . . English Court Masque', *Journal of the American Musicological Society*, I (1948), 3–19.

— ed. *Capirola Lute Book*, Paris, 1955.

— 'Blame not Wyatt', *Renaissance News*, VIII (1955), 12–14.

GORDON, D. J., 'Poet and Architect: the intellectual setting of the quarrel . . .', *Journal of the Warburg and Courtauld Institutes*, XII (1949), 157–178.

GORDON, PHILIP, 'The Morley-Shakespeare Myth', *Music & Letters*, XXVIII (1947), 121–125.

GOSSON, STEPHEN, s.v. [J. P. Collier, ed.].

GRAHAM, G. F., ed. *Songs of Scotland*, 3 vols., Edinburgh, 1847–49.

GRANVILLE-BARKER, H., *Prefaces to Shakespeare*, 5 vols., London, 1927–1947.

GRAY, A. K., 'Robert Armine, the foole', *Publications of the Modern Language Association*, XLII (1927), 673–685.

Gray of Reading, s.v. E. W. Dormer, ed.

GREENBERG, NOAH, ed. *An Elizabethan Song Book*, New York, 1955. (Texts edd. W. H. Auden and C. Kallman.)

GREG, W. W. Among many publications, cf. the following:

— *Bibliography of the English Printed Drama to the Restoration*, 4 vols., London, 1939–59.

— *Editorial Problem in Shakespeare*, 3rd ed., Oxford, 1954.

— *The Shakespeare First Folio*, Oxford, 1955.

— 'The Authorship of the Songs in Lyly's Plays', *Modern Language Review*, I (1905–06), 43–52.

GREW, SYDNEY, ed. 'Have you seen but a white lily grow?' (Curwen edition No. 71596), London, cop. 1923.

GROSART, A. B., ed. *Works of Robert Armin*, London, 1880.

HALLIWELL-PHILLIPPS, J. O., s.v. Phillipps.

HANDSCHIN, JACQUES, 'Mittelalterlicher Beitrag . . . Sphärenharmonie', *Zeitschrift für Musikwissenschaft*, IX (1926–27), 193–208.

HARBAGE, ALFRED, *Sir William Davenant*, Philadelphia, 1935.

— *Cavalier Drama*, New York, 1936.

— *Annals of English Drama: 975–1700*, Philadelphia, 1940.

— *Shakespeare's Audience*, New York, 1941.

— *As They Liked It: An Essay on Shakespeare and Morality*, New York, 1947.

— *Shakespeare and the Rival Traditions*, New York, 1952.

— 'The Role of the Shakespearean Producer', *Shakespeare Jahrbuch*, XCI (1955), 161–173.

HARDY, T. MASKELL, ed. *The Songs from Shakespeare's Plays*, 2 vols., London, n.d. [*ca.* 1930?].

Harleian Miscellany: A Collection . . . from the Library of Edward Harley . . ., ed. Thomas Park, 10 vols., London, 1808–13. [Various ballads: X.252–278.]

HARMAN, R. ALEC, ed. *Morley: Plain and Easy Introduction to Practical Music*, London, 1952.

HART, E. F., 'Caroline Lyrics and Contemporary Song Books', *The Library*, 5th Series, VIII (1953), 89–110.

— 'The Answer-Poem of the Early 17th Century', *Review of English Studies*, VII (1956), 19–29.

HARVEY-WOOD, H., ed. *Poems of Robert Henryson*, Edinburgh and London, 1933.

— ed. *Works of John Marston*, 3 vols., Edinburgh, 1934–39.

HAWKINS, SIR JOHN, *General History of Music*, 5 vols., London, 1776; 3 vols., London, 1875.

HAWKINS, THOMAS, *Origin of English Drama*, 3 vols., Oxford, 1773.

HAYES, G. R., *Musical Instruments . . . 1500–1750*, 2 vols., London, 1928–30.

HAZLITT, W. C., *A Manual . . . of Old English Plays*, London, 1892.

— *Handbook to the popular, poetical and dramatic literature from the invention of printing to the Restoration*, London, 1867.

— *Bibliographical collections and notes on Early English Literature . . .*, London, 1903.

— rev. *Warton: History of English Poetry*, 4 vols., London, 1871.

— ed. R. *Dodsley: Select Collection of Old Plays*, 15 vols., London, 1874–1876.

HAZLITT, WILLIAM, *Characters of Shakespeare's Plays*, London, 1817.

— *Lectures on the Dramatic Literature of the Age of Elizabeth*, London, 1821.

HEBEL, J. W., ed. jointly with H. H. Hudson, F. R. Johnson, A. W. Green, R. Hoopes, *Tudor Poetry and Prose*, New York, 1953.

HENDERSON, W. B. D., intr. *Castiglione: Cortegiano*, tr. T. Hoby, London, 1928.

HERFORD, C. H., s.v. P. Simpson.

HODGES, C. W., *Globe Restored*, London, 1953.

HOLLANDER, JOHN, 'Musica Mundana and *Twelfth Night*' in *English Institute Essays*, ed. N. Frye, New York, 1957.

— *The Untuning of the Sky*, Princeton, 1961.

HOOPES, R., s.v. J. W. Hebel.

HOSLEY, RICHARD, 'Was there a music-room in Shakespeare's Globe?', *Shakespeare Survey*, XIII (1960), 113–123.

HOTSON, LESLIE, *The First Night of 'Twelfth Night'*, London, 1954.

— *Shakespeare's Motley*, London, 1952.

HUDSON, H. H., s.v. Hebel, J. W.

HUGHES-HUGHES, A., *Catalogue of Manuscript Music in the British Museum*, 3 vols., London, 1906–09.

HUGHEY, RUTH, 'The Harington ms. at Arundel Castle and Related Documents', *The Library*, 4th Series, XV (1934–35), 388–444.

— *The Arundel Harington Manuscript of Tudor Poetry*, 2 vols., Columbus (Ohio), 1960.

HUNTER, G. K., 'Madrigal Verses from Whitney's *Choice of Emblems*', *Notes & Queries*, New Series, VII (1960), 215 f.

HUTTON, JAMES, 'Some English poems in Praise of Music', *English Miscellany*, ed. Mario Praz, II (Rome, 1951), 1–63.

ING, CATHERINE, *Elizabethan Lyrics*, London, 1951.

INGRAM, R. W., 'The Use of Music in the Plays of Marston', *Music & Letters*, XXXVI (1956), 154–164.

INGRAM, R. W., 'Words and Music', in *Elizabethan Poetry*, edd. J. R. Brown and B. Harris, London, 1960, 130–149.

ISAACS, J., *Production and Stage Management at the Blackfriars Theatre*, London, 1933.

JACKSON, VINCENT, ed. *English Melodies from the 13th to the 18th Century*, London, 1910.

JACOBSEN, MAURICE, ed. *Ophelia's Songs* (Curwen edition 71820) London, cop. 1931.

— ed. *Willow Song* (Curwen edition 71824), London, cop. 1931.

— ed. *When daffodils begin to peer* (Curwen edition 71921), London, cop. 1935.

JACQUOT, JEAN, ed. *Musique et Poésie au XVIe siècle*, Paris, 1954.

— ed. *La Musique Instrumentale de la Renaissance*, Paris, 1955.

— ed. *Fêtes de la Renaissance*, I, Paris, 1956.

— ed. *Le Luth et sa Musique*, Paris, 1958.

JOHNSON, RICHARD, s.v. W. Chappell.

Jonson, Works of Benjamin, s.v. P. Simpson.

JORGENSEN, PAUL A., *Shakespeare's Military World*, Berkeley (Calif.), 1956.

KEEL, JAMES F., ed. *Elizabethan Love Songs*, London, 1909; New York, 1913.

KERMAN, JOSEPH, 'Verdi's *Otello*', *Hudson Review*, VI, 2 (1952), 266–277.

— 'Morley and "The Triumphs of Oriana"', *Music & Letters*, XXXIV (1953), 185–191.

— 'Elizabethan Anthologies of Italian Madrigals', *Journal of the American Musicological Society*, IV (1951), 122–138.

KIEFER, CHRISTIAN, 'Music and Marston's *The Malcontent*', *Studies in Philology*, LI (1954), 163–171.

KITTREDGE, GEORGE LYMAN, ed. *Complete Works of Shakespeare*, Boston, 1936.

— ed. *Sixteen Plays of Shakespeare, with full explanatory notes*, Boston, 1946.

KNIGHT, CHARLES, ed. *Pictorial Edition of the Works of Shakespeare*, 8 vols., London, 1839–42.

KNIGHT, G. WILSON, *The Sovereign Flower*, London, 1958.

— *Wheel of Fire*, 4th edn., London, 1949.

— *The Shakespearean Tempest*, London, 1932; 3rd edn., 1953.

KÖKERITZ, HELGE, *Shakespeare's Pronunciation*, New Haven, 1953.

— *Shakespeare's Names*, New Haven, 1959.

KYD, s.v. P. Edwards.

— s.v. F. W. Boas.

LAFONTAINE, H. C. DE, *The King's Musick*, London, 1909.

LAING, DAVID, ed. *Lodge: Defence of Poetry, Music and Stage-Plays* (Shakespeare Society Publications), London, 1853.

LASCELLES, M., *Shakespeare's 'Measure for Measure'*, London, 1953.

LAW, ERNEST, 'Shakespeare's *Tempest* as originally produced at Court' (Shakespeare Association Papers, No. 5), London, [1921].

LAWRENCE, W. J., *Elizabethan Playhouse and Other Studies*, First Series, Stratford-upon-Avon, 1912. ['Music and Song in the Elizabethan Theatre', pp. 73-96; 'Who wrote the famous "Macbeth" Music?', pp. 207–224.]

— *Elizabethan Playhouse and Other Studies*, Second Series, Stratford-upon-Avon, 1913. ['Light and Darkness in the Elizabethan Theatre', pp. 1–22.]

— *Pre-Restoration Studies*, Cambridge (Mass.), 1927. ['Elizabethan Stage Jig', pp. 79–101; 'Illusion of Sounds in the Elizabethan Theatre', pp. 199-220.]

— *Physical Conditions of the Elizabethan Public Playhouse*, Cambridge (Mass.), 1927.

— *Those Nut-cracking Elizabethans*, London, 1935. ['Dumb Show in "Hamlet"', pp. 59–69; 'Bacon on Masques and Triumphs', pp. 130-143; 'Wedding of Poetry and Song', pp. 144-152.]

— 'Notes on a Collection of Masque Music', *Music & Letters*, III (1922), 49–58.

— 'Welsh Song in Elizabethan Drama', *Times Literary Supplement* (7 December 1922), p. 810.

— 'The Problem of Lyly's Songs', *Times Literary Supplement*, (20 December 1923), p. 894.

— 'Thomas Ravencroft's Theatrical Associations', *Modern Language Review*, XIX (1924), 418-423.

LAWRENCE, W. W., *Shakespeare's Problem Comedies*, New York, 1939.

LEE, SIDNEY, s.v. C. T. Onions.

LEMON, ROBERT, *Catalogue of a collection of printed broadsides . . . Society of Antiquaries*, London, 1866.

LILLY, J., ed. *Collection of seventy-nine . . . ballads*, London, 1867.

LINDSAY, J. L., s.v. Crawford (Earl of).

LINDSEY, EDWIN S., 'The Music of the Songs in Fletcher's Plays', *Studies in Philology*, XXI (1924), 325–355.

— 'The Music in Ben Jonson's Plays', *Modern Language Notes*, XLIV (1929), 86–92.

— 'The Original Music for Beaumont's Play "The Knight of the Burning Pestle"', *Studies in Philology*, XXVI (1929), 425–443.

LINLEY, WILLIAM, *Shakespeare's Dramatic Songs . . . Purcell . . . Boyce . . . Arne . . . T. Linley Junr.*, 2 vols., London, 1815–16.

LODGE, THOMAS, s.v. David Laing, ed.

LONG, JOHN H., *Shakespeare's Use of Music. A Study . . . Comedies*, Gainesville (Fla.), 1955. Cf. *Review of English Studies*, VIII (1957), 64–66.

— 'Sneak's "Noyse" Heard Again?', *Musical Quarterly*, XLIV (1958), 76–81.

LUCAS, F. L., ed. *Complete Works of John Webster*, 4 vols., London, 1928.

— *Tragedy: Serious Drama in Relation to Aristotle's Poetics*, London, 1927, rev. 1957.

LUMSDEN, DAVID, ed. *Anthology of English Lute Music*, London, 1954.

— 'English Lute Music 1540–1620—An Introduction', *Proceedings of the Royal Musical Association*, LXXXIII (1956–57).

— 'Sources of English Lute Music', *Galpin Society Journal*, VI (1953), 14–22.

LYLY, JOHN, s.v. R. W. Bond.

MCCABE, W. H., 'Music . . . on a 17th Century . . . Stage', *Musical Quarterly*, XXIV (1938), 313 ff.

MCCULLEN, J. T., 'The Functions of Songs aroused by madness in Elizabethan Drama', *Tribute to George Coffin Taylor*, Chapel Hill (No. Carolina), 1952, pp. 184–196.

MCKERROW, R. B., *A Dictionary of Printers . . . of English Books 1557–1640*, London, 1910.

— ed. *The Works of Thomas Nashe*, rev. F. P. Wilson, 5 vols., Oxford, 1958.

MACKAY, CHARLES, ed. *Collection of Songs and Ballads* (Percy Society Publications), London, 1841.

— ed. *Cavalier Songs and Ballads*, London, 1863.

MACKERNESS, E. D., 'Morley's Musical Sensibility', *Cambridge Journal*, II (1948–49), 301-308.

— 'A Speculative Dilettante' [Roger North], *Music & Letters*, XXXIV (1953), 236–242.

MCRAE, KENNETH, D., ed. *Jean Bodin: The Six Books of a Commonweale*, a facsimile reprint of the English translation of 1606, Cambridge (Mass.), 1962.

MALONE, EDMUND, ed. *Shakespeare: Plays and Poems . . . With . . . an historical account of the English stage . . .*, 10 vols., London, 1790.

— ed. jointly with J. Boswell, *Shakespeare: Plays and Poems . . . With . . . an enlarged history of the stage by the late E. Malone . . .*, 21 vols., London, 1821.

Malone Society Publications, London, 1907 ff. Cf. particularly, Collections I, Pt. I (1907), Pt. II (1908), Pt. III (1909), Pt. IV & V (1911); Collections II, Pt. I (1913), Pt. II (1923), Pt. III (1931); Collections IV (1956); Collections V (1959); Collections VI (1962).

MANIFOLD, J. S., 'Theatre Music in the 16th and 17th Centuries', *Music & Letters*, XXIX (1948), 366–397.

— *Music in English Drama: From Shakespeare to Purcell*, London, 1956.

MANN, F. O., ed. *Works of Thomas Deloney*, Oxford, 1912.

MARSTON, JOHN, s.v. H. Harvey-Wood.

MASON, DOROTHY E., *Music in Elizabethan England*, Washington (D.C.), 1958.

MAYHEW, A. L., s.v. W. W. Skeat.

MAYOR, J. E. B., ed. *Roger Ascham: The Scholemaster*, London, 1863.

Melody and the Lyric, s.v. J. M. Gibbon.

MIDDLETON, T., s.v. R. C. Bald.

MILLER, F. J., tr. *Tragedies of Seneca, translated into English verse* . . . Introduced by an essay on the influence of . . . Seneca upon early English drama by J. M. Manly, Chicago and London, 1907.

— ed. and tr. *Seneca's Tragedies, with an English translation* (Loeb Classical Library), 2 vols., London and New York, 1917.

MONCURE-SIME, A. H., *Shakespeare: His Music and Song*, London, n.d. [after 1910].

MORFILL, W. R., s.v. F. J. Furnivall.

MORLEY, THOMAS. For modern editions, cf. s.v. Fellowes, Harman, Beck.

MOORE, J. R., 'The Function of the Songs in Shakespeare's Plays', *Shakespeare Studies*, Madison (Wisconsin), 1916.

— 'The Songs in Lyly's Plays', *Proceedings of the Modern Language Association*, XLII (1927), 623–640.

— 'The Songs of the Public Theatres in the time of Shakespeare', *Journal of English and Germanic Philology*, XXVIII (1929), 166–202.

— 'Shakespeare's Collaboration with Morley', *Proceedings of the Modern Language Association*, LIV (1939), 149–152 [reply to E. Brennecke].

MOORE, ROBERT E., 'The Music to Macbeth', *Musical Quarterly*, XLVII (1961), 22–40.

MOORE-SMITH, G. C., *College Plays Performed in the University of Cambridge*, Cambridge, 1909.

MORRIS, HARRY, 'Ophelia's Bonny Sweet Robin', *Proceedings of the Modern Language Association*, LXXIII (1958), 601–603.

MUIR, KENNETH, ed. *Collected Poems of Wyatt*, London, 1949.

— *Shakespeare's Sources*, London, 1957.

MUMFORD, I. L., 'Sir Thomas Wyatt's Songs', *Music & Letters*, XXXIX (1958), 262-264.

MURRAY, J. T., *English Dramatic Companies*, 2 vols., London, 1910.

Nashe, Works of Thomas, s.v. R. B. McKerrow.

Naval Songs & Ballads, s.v. C. H. Firth.

NAYLOR, EDWARD WOODALL, *Shakespeare and Music*, 1st edn., London, 1896; 2nd edn., London, 1931.

— 'Music and Shakespeare', *Musical Antiquary*, I (1909–10), 129–148.

— *Shakespeare Music*, 1st edn., London, 1913; 2nd edn., London, 1928.

— *Poets and Music*, London, 1928.

New Shakespeare Society Publications, London, 1874–1892. Cf. also s.v. Furnivall.

New [Cambridge] *Shakespeare Edition*, s.v. J. D. Wilson.

NEWTON, RICHARD, 'In Commendation of Music', *Lute Society Journal*, No. 6 (1958), 138, 144.

New Variorum Edition of Shakespeare's Works, s.v. H. H. Furness.

NICHOL-SMITH, DAVID, *Shakespeare Criticism*, London, 1916.

NICHOLS, JOHN, *Six Old Plays*, 2 vols., London, 1779.

— *Progresses and Public Processions of Queen Elizabeth*, 3 vols., London, 1823.

— *Progresses, Processions and Magnificent Festivities of King James I*, 4 vols., London, 1828.

NICOLL, ALLARDYCE, *Stuart Masques and the Renaissance Stage*, London, 1937.

— 'Shakespeare and the Court Masque', *Shakespeare Jahrbuch*, XCIV (1958), 51–62.

NOBLE, RICHMOND, *Shakespeare's Use of Song*, London, 1923.

— 'Shakespeare's Songs and Stage', *Shakespeare Association. A Series of Papers on Shakespeare and the Theatre*, London, 1927, pp. 120–133.

NOSWORTHY, J. M., 'The Hecate Scenes in *Macbeth*', *Review of English Studies*, XXIV (1948), 138–139.

— 'Music and its Function in the Romances of Shakespeare', *Shakespeare Survey*, XI (1958), 60–69.

NUNGEZER, E., *Dictionary of Actors*, New Haven, 1929.

NUTTALL, P. A., ed. *Thomas Fuller, The Worthies of England*, 3 vols., London, 1840.

OAKESHOTT, WALTER, *The Queen and the Poet*, London, 1960.

Old Ballads, Historical and Narrative . . ., s.v. Thomas Evans.

Old Ballads from Early Printed Copies, s.v. J. P. Collier.

Old English Ballads, s.v. H. E. Rollins.

Old English Popular Music, s.v. E. H. Wooldridge.

ONIONS, C. T., ed. jointly with Sidney Lee, W. Raleigh, *Shakespeare's England*, 2 vols., Oxford, 1916 [including Onions's own 'Glossary of Musical Terms', II.32–49].

— *A Shakespeare Glossary*, Oxford, 1911; 2nd edn. 1919; rev. 1953.

OSBORN, JAMES M., 'Benedick's Song in *Much Ado*', *The Times*, 17 November 1958.

— ed. *The Autobiography of Thomas Whythorne*, Oxford, 1961.

OUVRY, FREDERIC, ed. *Quips upon Questions by John Singer* . . ., London, 1875 [actually by Robert Armin, not John Singer].

PACK OF AUTOLYCUS, s.v. H. E. Rollins.

PAFFORD, J. H. P., 'Music and the Songs in *The Winter's Tale*', *Shakespeare Quarterly*, X (1959), 161–175.

PANUM, HORTENSE, *Stringed Instruments of the Middle Ages*, tr. & ed. J. Pulver, London [1940].

Paradise of Dainty Devises, s.v. H. E. Rollins, ed.

PARK, THOMAS, ed. 'Harleian Miscellany', which see.

PARROTT, T. M., ed. *Tragedies of Chapman*, London, 1910.

PATTISON, BRUCE, *Music and Poetry of the English Renaissance*, London, 1948.

— 'Sir Philip Sidney and Music', *Music & Letters*, XV (1934), 75–81. Cf. also s.v. C. J. Sisson.

PEARN, B. R., 'Dumb-Shows in Elizabethan Drama', *Review of English Studies*, XI (1935), 385–405.

PEPSYAN GARLAND, s.v. H. E. Rollins, ed.

PERCY, THOMAS, *Reliques of Ancient English Poetry*, 3 vols., London, 1765; ed. H. B. Wheatley, 3 vols., London, 1876–77.

PERRETT, WILFRED, *Story of King Lear* (Palaestra XXXV), Berlin, 1904.

PFEIFFER, R., 'Image of the Delian Apollo and Apolline Ethics', *Journal of the Warburg and Courtauld Institutes*, XV (1952), 20–32.

PHILLIPPS, J. O. H., ed. *The Moral Play of Wit and Science and early Poetical Miscellanies* (Shakespeare Society Publications), London, 1848.

— *Works of Shakespeare*, 16 vols., London, 1853–65.

— *First Folio*, Facsimile [reduced in size], London, 1876.

— *Calendar of the Stratford Records*, London, 1863.

— *Outlines of the Life of Shakespeare*, 1st edn., Brighton, 1881; 7th edn., 2 vols., London, 1887.

PIETZSCH, GERHARD, *Klassifikation der Musik von Boethius bis Ugolino von Orvieto*, Halle, 1929.

Pills to Purge Melancholy, s.v. Thomas D'Urfey.

PLAYFORD, JOHN, s.v. Margaret Dean-Smith.

PLAYFORD, HENRY, s.v. Thomas D'Urfey.

PLUTARCH, s.v. G. Wyndham.

Political Ballads . . . Commonwealth, s.v. T. Wright.

POLLARD, A. W., ed. jointly with G. R. Redgrave, *Short Title Catalogue . . . 1475–1640*, London, 1926.

Popular Music of the Olden Time, s.v. Wm. Chappell.

POTTER, FRANK HUNTER, ed. *Reliquary of English Song*, 2 vols., New York, I, 1915; II, 1916.

POULTON, DIANA, 'The Lute Music of John Dowland', *The Consort* (June 1951), 10–15.

PRAGER, L., 'The Clown in Othello', *Shakespeare Quarterly*, XI (1960), 94–96.

PRANGE, GERDA, 'Shakespeares Äusserungen über die Tänze seiner Zeit', *Shakespeare Jahrbuch*, LXXXIX (1953), 132–161.

PRAZ, MARIO, *Studies in Seventeenth Century Imagery* (Studies of the Warburg Institute, Vol. 3), 2 vols., London, I, 'Imagery', 1939; II, Bibliography, 1947.

PRIOR, MOODY E., 'Imagery as a Test of Authorship', *Shakespeare Quarterly*, VI (1955), 381–386.

PROUTY, CHARLES T., *Sources of 'Much Ado About Nothing'*, New Haven, 1950.

— ed. *Thomas Kyd: The Spanish Tragedy*, New York, 1951.

— intr. *Mr. William Shakespeare's Comedies, Histories & Tragedies*, A facsimile edition prepared by H. Kökeritz, New Haven (Conn.), 1954.

PRUNIÈRES, HENRI, *Le Ballet de Cour*, Paris, 1914.

PULVER, JEFFREY, 'The Ancient Dance Forms', *Proceedings of the Royal Musical Association*, XXXIX (1912–13), 1–25.

— 'Dances of Shakespeare's England', Internationale Musik-Gesellschaft, *Sammelbände*, XV (1913–14), 99–102.

— *Dictionary of Old English Music and Musical Instruments*, London, 1923.

— *Biographical Dictionary of Old English Music*, London, 1927.

RALEIGH, WALTER, intr. *The Book of the Courtier, from the Italian of . . .*, *Castiglione: done into English by Sir Thomas Hoby, anno 1561* (Tudor Translations, 1st Series, ed. W. E. Henley, XXIII), London, 1900.

RAVENSCROFT, THOMAS, s.v. Peter Warlock.

REDGRAVE, G. R., s.v. Pollard.

REED, E. B., *Songs from the British Drama*, New Haven (Conn.), 1925.

— *Christmas Carols Printed in the 16th Century*, Cambridge (Mass.), 1932.

REED, ROBERT R., Jr., 'The probable origin of Ariel', *Shakespeare Quarterly*, XI (1960), 61–65.

REESE, GUSTAVE, *Music in the Renaissance*, New York, 1954; rev. edn., 1959.

REESE, M. M., *Shakespeare, His World and His Work*, London, 1953.

Reliquary of English Song, s.v. F. H. Potter, ed.

REYNOLDS, B., ed. *Bodin: Methodus as facilem historiarum cognitionem*, New York, 1945.

REYNOLDS, G. F., *Staging of Elizabethan Plays at the Red Bull Theatre 1605–1625*, New York, 1940.

RIEWALD, J. G., 'Some Later Elizabethan and Early Stuart Actors and Musicians', *English Studies*, XL (1959), 33–41.

RIMBAULT, E. F., *A Little Book of Songs and Ballads*, London, 1st edn., 1840; 2nd edn., 1851.

— *Who Was Jack Wilson?*, London, 1846.

— *Musical Illustrations of Bishop Percy's Reliques . . . Poetry*, London, 1850.

— *Rounds, Catches, Canons of England*, London, n.d. [*ca.* 1850].

RITSON, JOSEPH, *Ancient Songs and Ballads*, 1st edn., London, 1790; 2nd edn., London, 1829; 3rd edn., rev. W. C. Hazlitt, London, 1877.

— *A Selection of English Songs with their Original Airs . . .*, 3 vols., London, 1813 [2nd edn. rev. Thomas Park].

RINGLER, WM. A., ed. *John Rainolds, Oratio in laudem artis poeticae* (Princeton Studies in English, Vol. 20), Princeton (N.J.), 1940.

— *Stephen Gosson* (Princeton Studies in English, Vol. 25), Princeton (N.J.), 1942.

— 'The Praise of Musicke by John Case', *Papers of the Bibliographical Society of America*, XLIV (1960), 119–121.

ROFFE, ALFRED, *Handbook of Shakespeare music . . . from the Elizabethan age to present*, intr. A. J. Waterlow, London, 1878.

ROLLINS, H. E., *Analytical Index to the ballad entries (1557–1709) . . . in the register of stationers*, Chapel Hill (No. Carolina), 1924.

— ed. *Gorgious Gallery of Gallant Inventions* (1578), Cambridge (Mass.), 1926.

— ed. *Handefull of Pleasant Delites* (1584), Cambridge (Mass.), 1924.

— ed. *Old English Ballads, 1553–1625*, Cambridge, 1920.

— ed. *Paradyse of daynty devises* (1576–1606), Cambridge (Mass.), 1927.

— ed. *Pepys Ballads*, 8 vols., Cambridge (Mass.), 1929–32.

— ed. *Tottel's Songes and Sonnettes* (1557–87), 2 vols., Cambridge (Mass.), 1928–29.

ROSSITER, A. P., *English Drama from Early Times to the Elizabethans*, London, 1950.

Roxburghe Ballads, s.v. Wm. Chappell.

RUPPEL, K. H., 'Verdi und Shakespeare', *Shakespeare Jahrbuch*, XCII (1956), 7–18.

— 'Shakespeare und die Oper', *Shakespeare Jahrbuch*, XCV (1959), 178–192.

RYMER, THOMAS, s.v. Curt A. Zimansky.

SABOL, ANDREW, ed. *Songs and Dances for the Stuart Masque*, Providence (R.I.), 1959.

SALZMAN, L. F., 'Dildos and Fadings', *Times Literary Supplement* (7 September 1933), p. 592.

SCHAUBERT, E. V., 'Zur Geschichte der Block-Letter Broadside Ballad', *Anglia*, Neue Folge, XXXVIII (1926), 1–61.

SCHOLES, P., 'Purpose behind Shakespeare's use of music', *Proceedings of the Royal Musical Association*, XLIII (1916–17), 1–15.

— *The Puritans and Music in England and New England*, London, 1934.

SENECA, s.v. T. S. Eliot.

— s.v. F. J. Miller.

SENG, PETER J., 'The earliest known music for Desdemona's Willow Song', *Shakespeare Quarterly*, IX (1958), 419–420.

— 'An early tune for the fool's song in *Lear*', *Shakespeare Quarterly*, IX (1958), 583–585.

— 'The Forester's Song in *As You Like It*', *Shakespeare Quarterly*, X (1959), 246–249.

SHAKESPEARE SOCIETY *Publications*, 48 vols., London, 1841–53.

Shakespeare's England, s.v. C. T. Onions.

SHAKESPEARE, s.v. Alexander, Ellis-Fermor, Furness, Kittredge, C. Knight, Malone, Sisson, J. D. Wilson.

Shirburn Ballads, s.v. A. Clark, ed.

SIDNEY, PHILIP, s.v. G. Gregory Smith, ed.

SIEVEKING, A. F., 'Dancing' in *Shakespeare's England*, ed. C. T. Onions et al., II.437–450.

SIGISMUND, R., 'Die Musik in Shakespeare's Dramen', *Shakespeare Jahrbuch*, XIX (1884), 86–112.

SIMPSON, C. M., 'Tudor Popular Music: Its Social Significance', *Huntington Library Quarterly*, V (1951), 155–201.

SIMPSON, PERCY, ed. jointly with C. H. Herford, *Works of Benjamin Jonson*, 11 vols., Oxford, 1925–52.

SISSON, CHARLES J., *Lost Plays of Shakespeare's Age*, Cambridge, 1936.

— ed. *Shakespeare: Complete Works*, London, 1954. [Includes B. Pattison, 'Music and Masque', xlvii–lii.]

SKEAT, W. W., jointly with A. L. Mayhew, *Glossary of Tudor and Stuart Terms*, Oxford, 1914.

SMITH, G. GREGORY, ed. *Elizabethan Critical Essays*, 2 vols., London, 1904. [Includes Sidney's *Apology for Poetry*, I.148–207.]

SOCIETY OF ANTIQUARIES OF LONDON, s.v. Robert Lemon.

Songs and Ballads . . ., s.v. T. Wright.

SORENSEN, F., 'The Mask of the Muscovites in *Love's Labour's Lost*', *Modern Language Notes*, L (1935), 499–501.

SPENCER, ROBERT, 'The Weld Lute Book', *Lute Society Journal*, I, No. 6 (1960), 121–134.

SPINGARN, J. E., *Critical Essays of the Seventeenth Century*, 3 vols., Oxford, 1908.

— intr. *Casa: Galateo of Manners . . . Done into English by Robert Peterson* [1576] (Humanist's Library, ed. L. Einstein, VIII) London and Boston, 1914.

SQUIRE, W. BARCLAY, ed. jointly with Fuller-Maitland, *Fitzwilliam Virginal Book*, 2 vols., London and Leipzig, 1894–99.

— 'Music', in *Shakespeare's England*, ed. C. T. Onions *et al.*, II.15–32.

STEELE, M. S., *Plays and Masques at Court during the Reigns of Elizabeth, James and Charles*, New Haven (Conn.), 1926.

STEELE, R., *Earliest English Music Printing . . . to the close of 16th Century*, London, 1903.

STERNFELD, F. W., 'Dramatic and Allegorical Function of Music in Shakespeare's tragedies', *Annales Musicologiques*, III (1955), 265–282.

— '*Troilus and Cressida:* Music for the play', *English Institute Essays, 1952*, ed. A. S. Downer, New York, 1954, 107–137.

— 'Le Symbolisme Musical dans . . . Shakespeare', *Les Fêtes de la Renaissance*, I, ed. J. Jacquot, Paris, 1956, 319–333.

— 'Lasso's Music for Shakespeare's "Samingo" ', *Shakespeare Quarterly*, IX (1958), 105–115.

— 'Song in Jonson's Comedy', *Studies in the English Renaissance Drama*, ed. J. W. Bennett, New York, 1959, 310–321.

— 'Shakespeare's Use of Popular Song', *Elizabethan and Jacobean Studies*, ed. H. Davis, Oxford, 1959, 150–166.

STEVENS, DENIS, *The Mulliner Book. A Commentary*, London, 1952.

— ed. *The Mulliner Book* (*Musica Britannica*, I), 2nd rev. edn., London, 1954.

— ed. *O. Gibbons*, '*The London Cry*', London, 1956. (Novello's Part Song Book No. 1575.)

STEVENS, JOHN, *Mediaeval Carols*, London, 1st edn., 1952; 2nd edn., 1958.

— 'Elizabethan Madrigal', *Essays and Studies*, New Series, XI (1958).

— 'Music in Mediaeval Drama', *Proceedings of the Royal Music Association*, LXXXIV (1957/58), 81–95.

— *Music and Poetry in the Early Tudor Court*, London, 1961.

STOKES, E., 'Lists of the King's Musicians from the Audit Office Declared Accounts', *Musical Antiquary*, I (1909–10), 56, 119, 182, 249; II (1910–11), 51, 114, 174, 235; III (1911–12), 54, 110, 171, 229; IV (1912–13), 55, 178.

STOLL, E. E., *Othello*, Minneapolis (Minn.), 1915.

STROUP, T. B., 'Cordelia and the Fool', *Shakespeare Quarterly*, XII (1961), 127–132.

STUART, A., ed. *Music for the Tea Table Miscellany*, Edinburgh, [1725].

SULLIVAN, M., *Court Masques of James I . . .*, New York and London, 1913.

THIBAULT, GENEVIÈVE, *Chansons au luth . . .*, transcriptions: A. Mairy, commentaire: G. Thibault, Paris, 1934.
— [jointly with L. Percey], *Bibliographie . . . de Ronsard*, Paris, 1941.
— [jointly with F. Lesure], *Bibliographie . . . Le Roy et Ballard, 1551–1598*, Paris, 1955.

THOMAS, SIDNEY, 'A Note on Shakespeare's Motley', *Shakespeare Quarterly*, X (1959), p. 255.

THORNDIKE, ASHLEY H., *Influence of Beaumont and Fletcher on Shakespeare*, Worcester (Mass.), 1901.
— ed. *Minor Elizabethan Drama*, 2 vols., London, 1910; reprinted London, 1951.

TILLEY, MORRIS P., *Dictionary of Proverbs in England in the 16th and 17th Centuries*, Ann Arbor (Mich.), 1950.

TILLYARD, E. M. W., *Shakespeare's Last Plays*, London, 1938.
— *Elizabethan World Picture*, London, 1943.
— *Shakespeare's History Plays*, London, 1944.
— *Shakespeare's Problem Plays*, London, 1950.

TOOLEY, M. J., intr. & tr. *Bodin: Six Books of the Commonwealth*, abridged and translated by M. J. Tooley, Oxford, 1955.
Tudor Poetry and Prose, s.v. J. William Hebel.

VAN DEN BORREN, CHARLES, s.v. Borren.

VINCENT, CHARLES, ed. *Fifty Shakespeare Songs*, Philadelphia, 1906.

VLASTOS, JILL, 'An Elizabethan Anthology of Rounds', *Musical Quarterly*, XL (1954), 222–234.

WAITH, E. M., *Tragicomedy in Beaumont and Fletcher*, New Haven (Conn.), 1952.

WALLER, A. R., ed. jointly with A. Glover, *Works of Beaumont and Fletcher*, 10 vols., Cambridge, 1905–12.

WALDO, T. R., jointly with T. W. Herbert, 'Musical Terms in *The Taming of a Shrew*: Evidence of single Authorship', *Shakespeare Quarterly*, X (1959), 185–199.

WALKER, D. P., 'Musical Humanism in the 16th and Early 17th Centuries', *Music Review*, II (1941), 1, 111, 220, 288; III (1942), 55.
— *Spiritual and Demonic Magic from Ficino to Campanella*, London, 1958.

WARD, JOHN, 'The "Dolfull Domps" ', *Journal of the American Musicological Society*, IV (1951), 111–121.
— 'The Folia', Internationale Musik-Gesellschaft, Congress Utrecht 1952, *Kongress-Bericht*, Amsterdam, 1953, 415–422.

WARD, JOHN, 'Music for *A Handefull of Pleasant Delites*', *Journal of the American Musicological Society*, X (1957), 151–180.

— ed. *The Dublin Virginal Manuscript*, Wellesley (Mass.), 1954.

— 'The Lute Music of MS Royal Appendix 58', *Journal of the American Musicological Society*, XIII (1960), 117–125.

WARLOCK, PETER, ed. jointly with Philip Wilson, *English Ayres*, 1st edn., 4 vols., London, 1922–25; 2nd enlarged edn., 6 vols., London, 1927–31.

— ed. *Elizabethan Songs . . . for One Voice . . . and Four Stringed Instruments*, 3 vols., London, 1926.

— *The English Ayre*, London, 1927.

— ed. *Lachrymae by John Dowland*, London, 1927.

— ed. *T. Ravenscroft: Pammelia and other Rounds and Catches*, London, 1928.

— ed. *Giles Earle, his booke*, London, 1932.

WARTON, THOMAS, *History of English Poetry*, 3 vols., London, 1774–81; ed. W. C. Hazlitt, 4 vols., London, 1871.

WATKINS, RONALD, *Moonlight at the Globe*, London, 1946.

— *On Producing Shakespeare*, London, 1950.

WEAVER, ROBERT L., 'Sixteenth-Century Instrumentation', *Musical Quarterly*, XLVII (1961), 363–378.

WEBSTER, JOHN, Works of, s.v. F. L. Lucas.

WELCH, CHRISTOPHER, *Six Lectures on the Recorder and other Flutes in Relation to Literature*, London, 1911.

WELSFORD, ENID, *The Court Masque*, Cambridge, 1927.

— *The Fool: His Social and Literary History*, London, 1935.

WESTRUP, J. A., 'Domestic Music under the Stuarts', *Proceedings of the Royal Musical Association*, LXVIII (1941–42), 19–53.

WHEATLEY, H. B., ed. *Thomas Percy: Reliques of Ancient English Poetry*, 3 vols., London, 1876–77.

WHETSTONE, GEORGE, s.v. G. Smith.

WILSON, CHRISTOPHER, *Shakespeare and Music*, London, 1922.

WILSON, J. D., *Life in Shakespeare's England*, Cambridge, 1911; 2nd edn., 1913.

— ed., with others, *New* [Cambridge] *Shakespeare Edition*, Cambridge, 1921 ff.

WING, DONALD, ed. *Short Title Catalogue . . . 1641–1700*, 3 vols., New York, 1945–51.

WITHINGTON, R., *English Pageants*, Cambridge, 1918.

WOODFILL, WALTER L., *Musicians in English Society*, Princeton, 1953.

WOOLDRIDGE, H. E., ed. *Old English Popular Music by William Chappell*, a rev. edn., 2 vols., London, 1893; reprinted New York, 1961.

WRIGHT, LOUIS B., 'Extraneous Song in Elizabethan Drama after . . . Shakespeare', *Studies in Philology*, XXIV (1927), 261–274.

WRIGHT, THOMAS, ed. *Political Ballads . . . Commonwealth* (Percy Society), London, 1841.

— ed. *Songs and Ballads . . . reign of Philip and Mary* (Roxburghe Club), London, 1860.

WRIGHT, W. A., ed. *Roger Ascham: English Works*, Cambridge, 1904.

WYNDHAM, G., intr. *Plutarch's Lives of the Noble Grecians and Romans, Englished by Sir Thomas North, anno 1579* (Tudor Translations, 1st Series, ed. W. Henley), 6 vols., London, 1895–96.

YATES, FRANCES A., 'Dramatic religious processions in Paris in the late sixteenth century', *Annales Musicologiques*, II (1954), 215–270.

— *French Academies of the Sixteenth Century*, London, 1947.

— *John Florio . . .*, Cambridge, 1934.

— *A Study of Love's Labour's Lost*, Cambridge, 1936.

ZIMANSKY, CURT A., ed. *Thomas Rymer: Critical Works*, New Haven (Conn.), 1956.

Addenda to Bibliography

BAINES, ANTHONY, ed. *Musical Instruments through the Ages* (Pelican Books), Harmondsworth, 1961.

BEVINGTON, D. M., *From 'Mankind' to Marlowe . . . Popular Drama of Tudor England*, Cambridge (Mass.), 1962. [Cf. index s.v. Choristers, Instrumental music, Minstrels, Musicians, Song, etc.]

BOAS, F. S., ed. *Songs and Lyrics from the English Playbooks*, London, 1945; 2nd edn., 1947.

— ed. *Songs and Lyrics from the English Masques*, London, 1949.

BRETT, P., 'English Consort Song, 1570–1623', *Proceedings of the Royal Musical Association*, LXXXVIII (1961/62), 73–88.

CRAIK, T. W., *Tudor Interlude*, Leicester, 1958. [Cf. index s.v. Actors (adult and child), Music in plays, Songs, etc.]

CRANE, MILTON, *Shakespeare's Prose*, Chicago (Ill.), 1951. [Tragedies, pp. 128–187, *King Lear*, pp. 160–167.]

CUTTS, J. P., 'T. Heywood's "The Gentry of the King's Head" . . . and John Wilson's Setting', *Notes & Queries*, N.S., VIII (1961), 384–387.

— 'Music and *The Mad Lover*', *Studies in the Renaissance*, VIII (1961), 236–248.

— 'The Strange Fortunes of Two Excellent Princes and The Arbor of amorous Devises', *Renaissance News*, XV (1962), 2–11.

DART, T., and FELLOWES, E. H., *Morley: First Book of Airs: 1600* (English Lute Songs, Series I, xvi), rev. T. Dart, London, 1959.

DART, T., and BRETT, PH., 'Songs by . . . Byrd . . . at Harvard', *Harvard Library Bulletin*, XIV (1960), 344–365.

DART, T., intr., *Parthenia in-Violata*, foreword S. Beck, New York, 1961 [pp. 20 ff., 32 ff., *et passim*].

DAVIES, JOHN, of Hereford, s.v. Grosart, A. B.

FÄHNRICH, H., 'Die Rolle der Musik bei Shakespeare', *Musica*, XVI (1962), 243–245.

FINNEY, G. L., 'Music: a Book of Knowledge in Renaissance England', *Studies in the Renaissance*, VI (1959), 36–63.

— *Musical Backgrounds for English Literature: 1580–1650*, New Brunswick (N.J.): Rutgers University Pr., 1962.

GARTON, CHARLES, 'Poor Tom in *King Lear*', *Times Literary Supplement*, 15 December, 1961, p. 904. [Cf. also 5 January, 1962, p. 9.]

GREER, D., ' "What if a day" . . . Words and Music', *Music & Letters*, XLIII (1962), 304–319.

GROSART, A. B., ed. *John Davies of Hereford: Works* (Chertsey Worthies' Library), 2 vols., Printed for Private Circulation [Edinburgh University Press], 1878.

HENDRIE, G., and DART, T., edd. *J. Coprario: Funeral Tears, Songs of Mourning, Masque of Squires* (English Lute Songs, First Series, xvii), London, 1959.

HENDRIE, G., ed. *Orlando Gibbons: Keyboard Music* (Musica Britannica, xx), London, 1962. [Nos. 29, 30, 31, 44.]

HUNTER, G. K., *John Lyly*, London, 1962. ['Lyly and Shakespeare', pp. 298–349; 'Songs in Lyly's Plays', pp. 367–372; dumb-show pp. 371–372.]

JUMP, J. D., ed. *Marlowe: Doctor Faustus*, London, 1962.

KIMBROUGH, R., 'Origins of *Troilus* . . . Stage, Quarto, and Folio', *Publications of the Modern Language Association*, LXXVII (1962), 194–199.

LE COMTE, E. S., 'Ophelia's "Bonny Sweet Robin" ', *Publications of the Modern Language Association*, LXXV (1960), 480. [Refers to his article in *English Literary History*, XVII (1950), 87–114, particularly 93–94.]

LEWIS, ANTHONY, ed. *Shakespeare: Songs from 'The Tempest' Set by . . . R. Johnson* (Lyrebird Books), Paris, 1936.

LONG, JOHN H., *Shakespeare's Use of Music*, Vol. 2: The Final Comedies, Gainesville (Fla.), 1961.

MCMANAWAY, J. G., ed. *Joseph Quincy Adams Memorial Studies*, Washington, D.C., 1948.

MEHL, D., 'Die Funktion des "Dumbshow" im elisabethanischen Drama', Dissertation, Munich, 1960.

MEHL, D., 'Zur Entwicklung des "Play within a Play" im elisabethanischen Drama', *Shakespeare-Jahrbuch*, XCVII (1961), 134–152.

POULTON, DIANA, 'Notes on the Spanish Pavan', *Lute Society Journal* III (1961), 5–16.

RINGLER, W. A., ed. *Poems of Sidney*, Oxford, 1962 [pp. xxxv, 136, 137, 139, 151, 153, 155, 156, 566–568].

ROSS, LAWRENCE J., 'The Shakespearean *Othello*', *Dissertation Abstracts*, XX (1959), 2302. [Based on Princeton Dissertation, 1957, 3 vols., 1345 pp.]

RUBSAMEN, W. H., 'Scottish and English Music of the Renaissance in a Newly-Discovered MS', in *Festschrift Heinrich Besseler*, ed. Institut für Musikwissenschaft d. Karl-Marx-Univ., Leipzig, 1961, pp. 259–284.

SABOL, A. J., 'Two Songs with Accompaniment for an Elizabethan Choirboy Play', *Studies in the Renaissance*, V (1958), 145–159.

— 'Two Unpublished Stage Songs for the "Aery of the Children" ', *Renaissance News*, XIII (1960), 222–232.

SENG, PETER J., 'Songs, Time, and the Rejection of Falstaff', *Shakespeare Survey*, XV (1962), 31–40.

SPINK, IAN, ed. *Robert Johnson: Ayres* (English Lute Songs, Second Series, xvii), London, 1961.

STEVENS, JOHN, ed. *Music at the Court of Henry VIII* (Musica Britannica, xviii), London, 1962 [pp. 38, 105].

STRONG, R. C., 'Queen Elizabeth I as Oriana', *Studies in the Renaissance*, VI (1959), 251–260.

TUVE, R., 'Sacred "Parody" of Love Poetry, and Herbert', *Studies in the Renaissance*, VIII (1961), 249–290.

WEINER, A. B., 'Two *Hamlet* Emendations', *Notes & Queries*, N.S., IX (1962), 143–145.

WELLS, STANLEY, 'Tom O'Bedlam's Song and *King Lear*', *Shakespeare Quarterly*, XII (1961), 311–315.

WICKHAM, GLYNNE, *Early English Stages, 1300–1660*, Vol. I: 1300–1576, London, 1959. [Cf. index s.v. Choristers, Minstrels, Trumpets, etc.]

WILLIAMS, F. B., Jr., *Index of Dedications and Commendatory Verses in English Books before 1641*, London, 1962 [p. 212 s.v. Musicians, *et passim*].

WOOD, ALEXANDER, *The Physics of Music*, 1st edn., London, 1944; 6th edn., rev. J. M. Bowsher, London, 1962. [Cf. index s.v. Temperament, equal; Temperament, mean; True intonation.]

ZIMANSKY, CURT A., 'Marlowe's *Faustus*: The Date Again', *Philological Quarterly*, XLI (1962), 181–187.

I. INDEX OF LYRICS

THIS INDEX endeavours to list all of Shakespeare's lyrics, whether they occur in tragedies, comedies or histories. Some spoken poems have been included when they are likely to have been set to music before 1650, and mere allusions to lyrics and ballad tunes have also been recorded. The pages containing the music of the song are indicated in bold type. First lines are quoted as they occur in Shakespeare ('Then they for sudden joy . . .', 'When griping grief . . .') with appropriate cross references to other versions ('Some men for sudden joy . . .', 'Where griping grief . . .'). The main entry is usually by first line but when the title is better known main entry is given under the title, e.g., 'Walsingham'; or a cross-reference has been made, e.g., 'Willow Song'. In some instances, a reference to a ballad tune is unmistakeable, in others merely likely, but an attempt has been made to cover both of these categories.

The list of references, enclosed in square brackets, includes, in the case of Shakespeare's lyrics:

(a) Location in the plays by act, scene and line (the numbering follows that of the Globe edition).

(b) Location in the F text. Since the Folio has separate paging for Comedies, Histories and Tragedies, page references are preceded by the abbreviations C, H, or T. For instance, 'In youth when I did love' [Ham., V.i.67; F, T, 277] indicates Folio, Tragedies, p. 277. Since *Troilus and Cressida* follows *Henry VIII* (Histories, pp. 205–232) in the Folio, without page numbers, numbers have been supplied editorially, e.g., 'Love, love, nothing but love' [Troil., III.i.125; F, H, 246]. When a play is not printed in the Folio (*Pericles, Two Noble Kinsmen*) or when a lyric does not occur in the F text but only in Q, this is so indicated, e.g., 'Come o'er the burn, Bessy' [Lr., III.vi.27; Q].

(c) Discussion in such works as Chappell, Wooldridge, Naylor, etc. Most of these are tabulated in the List of Abbreviations. In the few cases where other authorities are cited they can be identified with the help of the Bibliography or the Addenda, e.g., Chappell, *Roxburghe*; or Addenda, Ringler, *Sidney*. Usually, the authorities listed in the index supplement those given on previous pages of this work but for the sake of convenience page numbers in Chappell and Wooldridge are always given.

A, Robin, jolly Robin, s.v. 'Hey Robin, jolly Robin'
Ad Lydiam, s.v. 'Lydia bella . . .'
Alack when I look back [William Hunnis; Brit. Mus. Add. MS 15117; Rollins, *Dainty Devices*, pp. 107, 260], 35
Alas by what mean may I make ye to know [John Heywood], 30; 47
Alas my love ye do me wrong, s.v. 'Greensleeves'
All perform their tragic play, s.v. 'Lapis Lazuli'
All that glisters is not gold [Mer.V., II.vii.65; F, C, 171]
And let me the canakin clink [Oth., II.iii.71; F, T, 319], 26; **144-146**; fitted to 'Joan Sanderson', 146, to 'Soldier's Life', 146; framed by prose, 159

And was not good King Solomon, s.v. 'Was not good King . . .'
And will he not come again [Ham., IV.v.190; F, T, 274; Chappell 237], 'Merry
Milkmaids' adapted **67** ff.; parodied in *Eastward Ho*, 67
Armin, what shall I say of thee, s.v. 'But (honest Robin) thou . . .'
Arms, and Honours, deck thy story [Webster, *Duchess of Malfi*, III.iv.9], 14
Art thou god to shepherd turn'd [AYL, IV.iii.40; F, C, 202]
As from the power of sacred lays, s.v. 'Song for St. Cecilia's Day'
As I went to Walsingham, s.v. 'Walsingham'
As ye came from the holy land, s.v. 'Walsingham'
Aspatia's song, s.v. 'Lay a garland on my hearse'
Awake ye woeful wights [Richard Edwards, *Damon and Pythias*, Malone Soc. Repr.,
line 692], 35

Be merry, be merry, my wife has all (2H4, V.iii.35; F, H, 400]
Be thy mouth or black or white [Lr., III.vi.69; F, T, 299], 175
Bell my wife, s.v. 'King Stephen . . .'
Black spirits, etc. [Mac., IV.i.43; F, T, 144], 88; 97
Blink over the burn, sweet Betty [W. Thomson, *Orpheus Caledonius*, London, 1725,
p. 15], 170
Blow, blow, thou winter wind [AYL, II.vii.174; F, C, 194], adult song 108
Bonn well Robin, title of 'Bonny sweet Robin', q.v.
Bonny sweet boy, variant of 'Bonny sweet Robin', q.v.
Bonny sweet Robin is all my joy [Ham., IV.v.187; F, T, 274; Kins., IV.i.108; Q;
Chappell 234; Wooldridge I.153], 14; 16; 57; Kins., 58; 67; **68–78**
But (honest Robin) thou with harmless mirth [John Davies of Hereford, *Works*, ed.
Grosart, II.60; first line, 'Armin, what shall I say of thee'], 113; 118
But mice and rats, s.v. 'Horse to ride . . .'
But shall I go mourn [Wint., IV.iii.15; F, C, 290]

Calen o custure me [H5, IV.iv.4; F, H, 87; Sternfeld, 'Popular Song'], 259
(Malone)
Call for the robin red-breast [Webster, *White Devil*, V.iv.89], 14
Can life be a blessing [Dryden, *Troilus and Cressida*, III.ii], 138
Canst thou not hit it, s.v. 'Thou canst not hit it'
Chevy Chase, alternative title for 'Flying Fame', q.v.
Child Roland to the dark tower came [Lr., III.iv.187; F, T, 298], 175
(The) codpiece that will house [Lr., III.ii.27; F, T, 296], 161; 174
Come away, come away, death (Tw.N., II.iv.52; F, C, 262], repetition of phrases,
89; originally intended for boy, 117; 173
Come away, come away, Hecate [Mac., III.v.33; F, T, 143; Cutts, *Musique*, p. 123;
Addenda, Spink, *Johnson*, no. xxii], 88; 97
Come drink to me [Ravenscroft, *Pammelia*, no. 68], 145
Come holy ghost, eternal God [Sternhold-Hopkins, *Psalter*], 86
Come live with me and be my love [Wiv., III.i.17; F, C, 48; Chappell 214;
Wooldridge I,123; Hart, 'Answer-Poem'; Frye, *Sound and Poetry*, p. 17]
Come my Celia, let us prove [Jonson (II.386, V.82, VIII.102, IX.719), *Volpone*,
III.vii.165; Ferrabosco, *Ayres* (Fellowes, *Lutenist Song*); Warlock, *English
Ayres*, II; Sternfeld, 'Jonson'], 35
Come, o come, my life's delight [Campion, *Third Book*, no. 23], 87
Come o'er the burn, Bessy, to me [Lr., III.vi.27; Q; Chappell 505; Wooldridge
I.121], 50; 165; 167–171; 'Come over' by Birch, 168; 'Come over' by Wager,
169; 175; **180–188**; 260 (Halliwell-Phillipps); 262 (Naylor)

Come thou father of the spring [John Wilson, *Cheerful Ayres*, 1659, cantus, p. 80], 87; 93

Come, thou monarch of the vine [Ant., II.vii.120; F, T, 351], 8; 81 f.; 86 f.; 93; contrasted with drinking song in Oth., 144; framed by verse, 158; Bacchanalian song in Plutarch, 224

Come unto these yellow sands [Tp., I.ii.375; F, C, 5], magic song, 80

Come, ye heavy states of night [Dowland, *Second Book*, no. 14], 86

Concolinel (LLL, III.i.3; F, C, 128; NS, 2nd edn., 1962, p. 149]

Constancy of Susanna, s.v. 'There dwelt a man in Babylon'

Constant Susanna, s.v. 'There dwelt a man in Babylon'

Cries of London, s.v. 'God give you good morrow . . .'

(A) cup of wine that's brisk and fine [2H4, V.iii.48; F, H, 98]

Cursed be he that stole [Marlowe, *Faustus*, III.ii.100 (ed. F. S. Boas); ix.102 (ed. J. D. Jump)], 10

Cushion dance [Chappell 153; Wooldridge I.287], adapted to 'And let me the canakin clink', 146

Damon and Pithias, s.v. 'For thou dost know, O Damon . . .'

Derry down, s.v. 'Down a-down'

Dildos and fadings [Wint., IV.iv.195; F, C, 293; Chappell 234; Naylor 81; Salzman, 'Dildos'; Jonson (V.403, X.114), *Alchemist*, V.v.42; Nashe, V.141, 153]

Do me right and dub me knight, Samingo [2H4, V.iii.79; F, H, 98; Dart, 'New Sources', p. 102; Sternfeld, 'Lasso'], 16

Do nothing but eat, and make good cheer [2H4, V.iii.18; F, H, 98]

Doleful adieu to the last Earl of Derby [Stationers' registers], 78 (source 37)

Doleful Dumps, s.v. 'When griping grief'

Done to death by slanderous tongues [Ado, V.iii.3; F, C, 120; cf. R. Greene, *Plays and Poems*, ed. J. C. Collins, II.248, 384]

Down a-down [or 'Down, down, a-down', or 'Derry down' or 'A-down, a-down; Ham., IV.v.170; F, T, 274; Kittredge SP 1008 and 1088; Chappell 350; Bronson, *Child Ballads*, no. 45; cf. also Wiv., I.iv.44; F, C, 42; Kins., III.v.140; Q], 57; 67

Embrace your bays sweetly that smile in love's sight [Thomas Howell], 31

Fading, s.v. 'Dildos and fadings'

Fair Angel of England [R. Johnson, *Golden Garland*; Chappell 319], 77 (sources 31 and 32)

Farewell, dear heart [Tw.N., II.iii.109; F, C, 261; Naylor SM 22 f.], 112

Fathers that wear rags [Lr., II.iv.48; F, T, 293], 174

Fear no more the heat o' the sun [Cym., IV.ii.258; F, T, 389; NA 223; NS 193 (line 235); Corin, 'Cymbeline']

Fie on sinful fantasy [cf. also s.v. 'Pinch him'; Wiv., V.v.97; F, C, 59], pinching song, 80

Fill the cup, and let it come [2H4, V.iii.56; F, H, 98]

(The) fire seven times tried this [Mer.V., II.ix.63; F, C, 172]

Fish, Ballad of a [Wint., IV.iv.279; F, C, 293]

Flout 'em and scout 'em [Tp., III.ii.130; F, C, 12]

Flying Fame [Chappell 198; Wooldridge I.91], 'Then they for sudden joy', 177; 'King Lear once ruled', 244

Follow me to the greenwood, title of 'Bonny sweet Robin', q.v.

Fools had ne'er less grace in a year [Lr., I.iv.181; F, T, 288], 160; 174
For bonny sweet Robin is all my joy, s.v. 'Bonny sweet . . .'
For I the ballad will repeat [All's W., I.iii.64; F, C, 233; NA 24]
For I'll cut my green coat [Kins., III.iv.19; Q; Kittredge 1410; Child, *Popular Ballads*, no. 63A]
For if the king like not the comedy [Ham., III.ii.304; F, T, 268], 129
For O, for O, the hobby-horse is forgot [Ham., III.ii.144; F, T, 267; Chappell 601; LLL, III.i.30; F, C, 128; Jonson X.212 (a) *Bartholomew Fair*, (b) *Gypsies*, (c) *Althorp*, (d) *Old Meg*; Fletcher VII.284; Kemp, *Nine Days Wonder*, sig. B.ii.^{v}; Onions 107 'quotation from a ballad'; Fellowes, *Madrigal Verse*, p. 230, no. xx], 129
For the rain it raineth every day, s.v. 'When that I was and a little tiny boy'
For thou dost know, O Damon dear [Ham., III.ii.292; F, T, 268; tune of 'Damon and Pithias'; Ward, 'Pleasant Delites', p. 167]
Fortune my foe [Wiv., III.iii.69; F, C, 50; Chappell 162; Wooldridge I.76]
(A) fox, when one has caught her [Lr., I.iv.340; F, T, 289], 174
Friars' dirge [in *Doctor Faustus*], s.v. 'Cursed be he . . .'
From the east to western Ind [AYL, III.ii.93; F, C, 195]
From the hag and hungry goblin [British Museum, Add. MS 24665; Bodleian, MS Tanner 465; Jonson VI.254 and X.251; *Le Prince d'Amour*; Wooldridge I.175], related to 'Tom's a-cold', 179 f.
Full fathom five thy father lies [Tp., I.ii.396; F, C, 5; Cutts, *Musique*, p. 131; Addenda, Spink, *Johnson*, no. x]
Full merrily the humble-bee doth sing [Troil., V.x.42; F, H, 261; NV 315]

(The) George Alow came from the south [Kins., III.v.59; Q; Child, *Popular Ballads*, no. 285]
Get you hence, for I must go [Wint., IV.iv.303; F, C, 293; Cutts, *Musique*, p. 126; Addenda, Spink, *Johnson*, no. xxiii]
Gloria tibi trinitas aequalis [plainchant], **177–178**
God give you good morrow my masters [O. Gibbons, *Cries of London*, bar 117, 'Poor naked bedlam, Tom's a-cold'], **177–180**
God Lyaeus, ever young [Fletcher (IV.89), *Valentinian*, V], boy's song, 85
(The) God of love, that sits above [Ado, V.ii.26; F, C, 120], ballad by Birch, 168
Good shepherd's sorrow, s.v. 'In sad and ashy weeds'
Greensleeves [Wiv., II.i.64 and V.v.22; F, C, 44 and 59; Chappell 227; Wooldridge I.239; Ward, 'Pleasant Delites', p. 157], 32; 69

Hanskin, s.v. 'Jog on, jog on'
Hark, hark! the lark [Cym., II.iii.21; F, T, 377; W. M. Evans, 'Harke, harke'; Cutts, *Musique*, p. 121; Addenda, Spink, *Johnson*, no. xx]
Hark, now everything is still [Webster, *Duchess of Malfi*, IV.ii.180]
Have I caught thee, my heavenly jewel [Wiv., III.iii.45; F, C, 50; Addenda, Ringler, *Sidney*, pp. 202, 480, 566]
Have more than thou showest [Lr., I.iv.131; F, T, 288], 174
Have you seen but a white lily grow [Jonson (VI.204, X.238, VIII.134, XI.49) *Devil is an Ass*, II.vi.104; ed. P. Warlock, 1929; Cutts, *Musique*, 1959, no. 26; Addenda, Spink, *Johnson*, 1961, no. xxiv], 35; 262 (Potter)
He plays the wise man then [Armin, *Quips upon Questions*, ed. Ouvry, sig. C.ii.^{v}; first line, 'True it is, he plays the fool indeed'], 109
He that has and a little tiny wit [cf. also 'When that I was and a little . . .'; Lr., III.ii.74; F, T, 296], 162; 171–173; 174; **188–192**
He that keeps nor crust nor crumb [Lr., I.iv.217; F, T, 288], 174

Heart's ease [Rom., IV.v.102; F, T, 73; Chappell 210; Wooldridge I.97], 102

(The) hedge-sparrow fed the cuckoo so long [Lr., I.iv.235; F, T, 288], 174

Hey, jolly Robin, refrain of 'In Sherwood lived . . .', q.v.

Hey non nony [cf. also refrains of 'It was a lover' and 'Sigh no more'; Ham. IV.v.165; F, T, 274; Lr., III.iv.103; F, T, 298; NA 121, line 101], Ham., 57, 67; Lr., 163 f.

Hey Robin, jolly Robin [Tw.N., IV.ii.78; F, C, 271; Naylor SM 25], 70; 113; 262 (Naylor)

Hide, o hide those hills of snow: second stanza of 'Take, o take . . .', q.v.

Hobby-horse, s.v. 'For O, for O, the hobby-horse . . .'

Hold thy peace, thou knave [Tw.N., II.iii.68; F, C, 261; Naylor SM 15], 112 (Warlock, Vlasto); 259 (Hawkins)

Honour, riches, marriage-blessing [Tp., IV.i.106; F, C, 14]

Horse to ride, and weapon to wear [Lr., III.iv.143; F, T, 298], 175

Hot sun, cool fire [Peele, *David and Bethsabe*, line 24 (ed. A. Thorndyke)], 11; 21

How can the tree but waste [Rollins, *Dainty Devices*, p. 72; Addenda, Rubsamen, 'Scottish', p. 269], 151

How should I your true love know [Ham., IV.v.23; F, T, 273; Chappell 236], 16; **58–62**; 67

Hymn in Praise of Music [Sir John Davies], 104

I am gone, Sir [Tw.N., IV.ii.130; F, C, 271], 113; music lost, 114

I call and cry to thee, o Lord [British Museum, Add. MS 15117], music by Tallis, 35

I loathe that I did love, s.v. 'In youth when I did love'

I may command where I adore [Tw.N., II.v.115; F, C, 264]

If a hart do lack a hind [AYL, III.ii.107; F, C, 195]

If it do come to pass: third stanza of 'Under the greenwood tree', q.v.

If love make me forsworn [LLL, IV.ii.109; F, C, 132]

Immortal gods, I crave no pelf [Tim., I.ii.63; F, T, 81]

Imperious Caesar, dead and turn'd to clay [Ham., V.i.236; F, T, 278], 130

In days when our King Robert rang, s.v. 'King Stephen was . . .'

In sad and ashy weeds [R. Johnson, *Crown Garland*; Chappell 202; Wooldridge I.156], 139 f.

In Sherwood lived stout Robin Hood [Robert Jones, *Fourth Book of Airs: 1609*, no. xix; refrain 'Hey, jolly Robin'], portion of last stanza quoted, 58; 71 f., **74–75**

In winter when the rain rain'd cauld, s.v. 'King Stephen was . . .'

In youth when I did love [Ham., V.i.67; F, T, 277; Chappell 217; Wooldridge I.52; cf. 'Leaping time into a crutch', Cym., IV.ii.200, NS 82 and 192; cf. 'In youth what I thought sweet', Hunnis, Rollins, *Dainty Devices*, p. 107], 8; compared with Rom. and/or Troil., 100, 132, 137; 127–131; echoed in Troil., 134; extra syllables, 145; **151–155**; scope of adult songs, 173; 267 (Warlock)

In youthful years [Richard Edwards; British Museum, Add. MS 15117; Rollins, *Dainty Devices*, pp. 10 and 185], 35

Insignis cantabitur, s.v. 'Qui me commorit . . .'

It was a lover and his lass [AYL, V.iii.17; F, C, 205; *Morley: Book of Airs: 1600*, ed. Fellowes-Dart, 1959, pp. 26–31; Chappell 205; Wooldridge I.114], refrain expanded, 36; etiquette, 56; refrain, 57

It was the friar of orders grey [Shr., IV.i.148; F, C, 221; Percy, *Reliques*, Book II, no. 18; Chappell 236]

Jephthah, judge of Israel, s.v. 'O Jephthah, judge . . .'

Joan Sanderson, s.v. 'Cushion dance'

Mellida is dead [Marston (I.132), *Antonio's Revenge*, conclusions, text not extant] 16; 18

Merry milkmaids [Chappell 295; Wooldridge I.290; Playford 29; cf. also the refrain 'Pretty milkmaids', Heywood, *Rape of Lucrece*, II.i., ed. Symonds, p. 349; ed. Pearson, V.182], **67–68**

Mounsier Mingo (Samingo) for quaffing, s.v. 'Do me right . . .'

Music to hear, why hearst thou music sadly [Sonnet No. 8], 240

My Daphne's hair is twisted gold [Lyly (ed. Bond, III.142), *Midas*, IV.i.; text of Apollo's song in edn. of 1632; edn. of 1592 has merely S.D. 'A song of Daphne to the lute'], 229

My heart is full of woe [Rom., IV.v.107; F, T, 73; Chappell 210; Wooldridge I.99], 102

My love what misliking in me do you find [*Gorgeous Gallery*; Chappell 206; Wooldridge I.107], 30

My proper Bessy [British Museum, Harley MS 2252], 169

My Robin is to the greenwood gone: title of 'Bonny sweet Robin', q.v.

My thoughts do harbour with my Silvia nightly [Gent., III.i.140; F, C, 29]

Nancy's to the greenwood gone [Allan Ramsay, *Tea Table Miscellany*], 77 (sources 33, 34)

No more dams I'll make for fish [Tp., II.ii.184; F, C, 10]

Not those young students of the heavenly book, s.v. 'Orchestra, or A Poem of Dancing'

Now farewell, good Christmas [Chappell, *Roxburghe*], 78 (source 36)

Now my charms are all o'er thrown [Tp., V., Epil., 1; F, C, 19]

O death rock me asleep [2H4, II.iv.211; F, H, 83; Chappell 238; Wooldridge I.111; Warlock, *Elizabethan Songs*, III, no. i; Hebel, *Tudor Poetry*, p. 1194; J. Stevens, *Music and Poetry*, p. 449; Nashe III.411 (line 203), V.73], by Edwards?, 35; 264 (Arkwright)

O heart, heavy heart [Troil., IV.iv.16; F, H, 252; NV 214; NS 199]

O heavenly God [British Museum Add. MS 15117; ? Kinwelmarsh; Rollins, *Dainty Devices*, 95, 251], 35

O Jephthah [Jepha], judge of Israel [Ham., II.ii.422; F, T, 263; Kittredge SP 990 and 1053; Chappell, *Roxburghe*, VI.685 and IX.593], 129

O let us howl some heavy note [Webster, *Duchess of Malfi*, IV.ii.65; Cutts, *Musique*, no. 22; Addenda, Spink, *Johnson*, no. xiv], Masque of madmen, 14

O mistress mine, where are you roaming [Tw.N., II.iii.40; F, C, 261; Chappell 209; Wooldridge I.103], 32; 112; love song, 136

O sweet Oliver [AYL, III.iii.101; F, C, 198; Wooldridge I.88], 114 f.

O' the twelfth day of December [Tw.N., II.iii.90; F, C, 261], 112

O thou Delphian God, inspire [Heywood, *Rape of Lucrece*, II.ii; ed. Symonds, p. 351; ed. Pearson, V.184], 186

(The) Old Cloak, s.v. 'King Stephen was . . .'

(An) old hare hoar [Rom., II.iv.141; F, T, 62]

On a day, alack the day [LLL, IV.iii.101; F, C, 133]

On a tree by a river a little tomtit [W. S. Gilbert], 32

On the twelfth day, s.v. 'O' the twelfth day'

Orchestra, or A Poem of Dancing [Sir John Davies; Hebel, *Tudor Poetry*, pp. 334, 1241, 1276], stanzas 66–67 (lines 456–469) on pavan and galliard, 253

Orpheus with his lute made trees [H8, III.i.3; F, H, 218; NA 90; NS 54 and 177; Day & Murrie, no. 2645; Noble 140], substitute for 'Lucius' song', 81; compared with it, 242
(The) ousel cock, so black of hue [MND, III.i.128; F, C, 152; NS 32, 123]
Over hill, over dale [MND, II.i.2; F, C, 148]

Pangs of love, s.v. 'Was not good King Solomon'
Pardon, goddess of the night [Ado, V.iii.12; F, C, 120]
Peace, ho! I bar confusion [AYL, V.iv.131; F, C, 206]
Peg-a-Ramsey [Tw.N., II.iii.81; F, C, 261; Chappell 218; Wooldridge I.248], 112
Pinch him, pinch him, black and blue [Lyly, *Endymion*, IV.iii.29 (ed. Bond, III.59, 514); Ravenscroft, *Brief Discourse*, Pollard STC 20756, no. 9; Addenda, Hunter, *Lyly*, pp. 192, 363, 372], 80
Poor naked bedlam, Tom's a-cold, s.v. 'God give you good morrow . . .'
(A) poor soul sat sighing by a gingerbread stall [Playford's *Musical Companion*], 31
(The) poor soul sat sighing by a sycamore tree [Oth., IV.iii.41; F, T, 333; Chappell 207; Wooldridge I.106; Kins., IV.i.80; Q; Brennecke, 'Willow Song'], 8; 13; **24–52**; etiquette, 55, 142; Kins., 58; compared with Ophelia, 65; interrupted, 90; no stage directions, 104; framed by verse, 158; scribe cramped for space, 184; 259 (Capell, Malone)
Poor Tom, s.v. 'Tom's a-cold'
Praise, pleasure, profit, s.v. 'Hymn in Praise of Music'
Prima nocte domum . . . [Horace, *Odes*, Book III, no. 7, lines 29–30], 228

Quem virum aut heroa [Horace, *Odes*, Book I, no. 12, lines 1–3], 229
Qui me commorit . . . insignis . . . cantabitur [Horace, *Satires*, Book II, no. 1, lines 45–46], 239
Qui passa [Chi passa per questa strada] [Kins., III.v.86; Q; Ward, 'Pleasant Delites', p. 166]

(The) raging rocks [MND, I.ii.33; F, C, 147; NS 12 and 109]
(The) rain it raineth every day, s.v. 'When that I was and a little tiny boy'
Robin, abbreviated title of 'Bonny sweet Robin', q.v.
Robin Hood, title of 'Bonny sweet Robin', q.v.
Robin Hood is to the greenwood gone, title of 'Bonny sweet Robin', q.v.
Robin Hood, Robin Hood, said little John [Chappell 397; Wooldridge I.273], 70 and 76 (source 3)
Robin Hood, Scarlet, and John [or 'Robin Hood and the Pinder of Wakefield'; Wiv., I.i.177; F, C, 40; 2H4, V.iii.107; F, H, 98; Chappell 393]
Robin is to the greenwood gone, s.v. 'Bonny sweet Robin'
Roses, their sharp spines being gone [Kins., I.i.1; Q; Noble 138–141]

Samingo, s.v. 'Do me right'
Samson, judge of Israel, s.v. 'When Samson . . .'
Schön wär ich gern, title of 'Bonny sweet Robin', q.v.
Shaking of the sheet [2H4, II.iv.243; F, H, 84; Chappell 84; Wooldridge I.228; NS 46 and 164, sv. I.222]
Sick, sick [or 'Sick tune'; Ado, III.iv.42; F, C, 113; Chappell 226; Wooldridge I.73]
Sigh no more, ladies [Ado, II.iii.64; F, C, 108], etiquette, 56; ethos, 106 f.; Ford, ed. Warlock, 107; dump, 255; 259 (Collier, Rimbault)
Sleepest or wakest thou jolly shepherd [Lr., III.vi.43; Q], 166; 175

II. INDEX OF PERSONS, PLACES, PLAYS, ETC.

Oedipus, compared with Lear, 164
Onions, C. T., 240, 250, 266
Orchésographie, s.v. T. Arbeau
Orfeo, s.v. C. W. Gluck
Orpheus, ethos, 86, 236, 241; in *Gent.*, 99; 101; 104; in Kyd, *Spanish Tragedy*, 197
Osborn, J. M., ed. *Thomas Whythorne*, 47
Oswald, James, *Caledonian Pocket Companion* . . ., 'King Stephen', 147–148, 156
Othello, general, 13, 23–24, 109, 127, 142; source of play, 90; F vs Q, 25–29; proportion of prose, 193; compared with *Ham.*, *Lr.*, *Mac.*, 65–66, 88, 144, 212; musical puns, 100, 232; 'in tune', II.i.200., 'not in tune', III.iv.123., 'out of tune', V.ii.115., 237–238; promiscuity, 24, 29, 37, 54; performance at Oxford, 24, 143; strings vs winds, 231–232; use of trumpet, II.i.180., IV.i.226., 212; songs in general, 15; 'And let me the canakin clink', II.iii.71., 145; 'King Stephen was a worthy peer', II.iii.92., 147–148, 156, 261; 'Willow Song', 25–26, 35–36, 39, 90, 158, 259, s.v. also London, Dublin, Washington, D.C.; Othello, 54, 142, 144, 213, accusation of adultery, 26, 29, 34, 37, 54, farewell to arms, III.iii.352., 229, suspicion of Cassio, 23, 237, compared with Troilus, 133; Iago, 25, 142–144, 146, songs, II.iii., 26, 54, 142, 145, played by Armin?, 142–143, 'honest' Iago, 145, 147, 159, 213, compared with Edmund, 213; Desdemona, 8, 13, 17, 21, 54, when dead, 24, characterization, 26, 66, singing, 24–35, 39, 40, 50, 53–55, 79, 142, 173, humiliation, 213, 'such a deed', IV.iii.64. and 68., 26–29; Emilia, 29, 34, 55, 158, reference to 'Willow', V.ii., 25–26, 37; Cassio, 144–147, 238, serenade, III.i., 231; Roderigo, 'gulling and bleeding', 142; Montano, 144–147; Lodovico, 213; Clown, 231; Musician, 231
Ovid, *Metamorphoses*, s.v. W. Caxton
Oxford, 24, 233; Prof. John Wilson, 108, friends and enemies of music, 114; Christ Church choristers, 115; performance of *Alchemist* and *Oth.*,

24, 143; Prof. Wm. Crotch, 'I loathe that I did love', and G. F. Nott, 151–152
Oxford University MSS, Bodleian Library, MS Mus. b.1, f. 128 (*Ant.* II.vii.118), 93; Mus. b.1, 'Take, o take', 93; MS Rawl. poet. 160 (*Troil.* III.i.125), 139; MS Don.d.58 (*Troil.* III.i.125), 139; MS Ashmole 176(*Lr.* III.vi.28), 168; MS Tanner 465 (*Lr.* III.iv.59), 180; Christ Church, Mus. 434, 'Take, o take', 93, Mus. 736, 'Sigh no more', 107, Mus. 984, 'How can the Tree', 151

Palladis Tamia: Wits Treasury, s.v. Meres
Pammelia, s.v. T. Ravenscroft
Pan, s.v. Apollo
Paradise of Dainty Devices, s.v. H. E. Rollins
Paris, Conservatoire, MS Réserve 1186 (olim 18546), 'In sad and ashy weeds', 140
Parrott, T. M., ed. *Chapman*, 20
Parsons, Robert, author of 'Willow Song'?, 35
Pattison, Bruce, *Music and Poetry* . . . *Renaissance*, 114, 155, 269; concerning Jack Wilson, 107
Paul's Children of, 1, 14–19
Peele, George, *David and Bethsabe*, 9, 11, 241; God's 'cunning tunes the music', 236; Bethsabe's song, 11, 17, 21
Pepusch, C., s.v. John Gay
Pepys Ballads, s.v. H. E. Rollins
Percy, Thomas, *Reliques* . . ., 258; 'Willow Song', 33, 59; 'King Stephen', 156
Percy Folio Manuscript, 59, 61, 156, 261
Pericles, ethos, III.ii.88., 243; use of strings, ethos, 211; 'music of the spheres', V.i.231., 245; divine intervention, 264
Pericles, s.v. G. Wilkins
Peterson, Robert, tr. della Casa, *Galateo*, strings vs winds, 227
Philip (King), etiquette, 55
Phillipps, J. O. Halliwell, 260; ed., Redford, *Wit and Science*, 30; 'Willow Song', 30; 'Come over the burn', 167, 260; cinque pas, 253

x*   323

III. INDEX OF SUBJECTS